Engineering Service Oriented Systems:

A Model Driven Approach

Bill Karakostas
City University, UK

Yannis Zorgios
CLMS Limited, UK

IGI PUBLISHING

Hershey • New York

Acquisition Editor:	Kristin Klinger
Senior Managing Editor:	Jennifer Neidig
Managing Editor:	Sara Reed
Development Editor:	Kristin Roth
Copy Editor:	Becky Shore
Typesetter:	Amanda Appicello
Cover Design:	Lisa Tosheff
Printed at:	Yurchak Printing Inc.

Published in the United States of America by
IGI Publishing (an imprint of IGI Global)
701 E. Chocolate Avenue
Hershey PA 17033
Tel: 717-533-8845
Fax: 717-533-8661
E-mail: cust@igi-global.com
Web site: http://www.igi-global.com

and in the United Kingdom by
IGI Publishing (an imprint of IGI Global)
3 Henrietta Street
Covent Garden
London WC2E 8LU
Tel: 44 20 7240 0856
Fax: 44 20 7379 0609
Web site: http://www.eurospanonline.com

Library of Congress Cataloging-in-Publication Data

Karakostas, Bill.
  Engineering service oriented systems : a model driven approach / Bill Karakostas and Yannis Zorgios.
    p. cm.
  Includes bibliographical references and index.
  Summary: "This book combines concepts from systems theory, model driven software engineering, and ontologies for software engineering into a systematic method for engineering service oriented systems"--Provided by publisher.
  ISBN 978-1-59904-968-7 (hardcover) -- ISBN 978-1-59904-969-4 (ebook)
 1. Software engineering. 2. Web services. I. Zorgios, Yannis. II. Title.
  QA76.758.K365 2008
  005.1--dc22
                         2008008469

British Cataloguing in Publication Data
A Cataloguing in Publication record for this book is available from the British Library.

All work contributed to this book is new, previously-unpublished material. The views expressed in this book are those of the authors, but not necessarily of the publisher.

Engineering Service Oriented Systems:
A Model Driven Approach

Table of Contents

Section I:
Service Concepts

Section II:
Service Languages and Standards

Chapter III

Chapter IV

Section III:
Service Engineering Concepts and Techniques

Chapter VII
A Methodology for Model-Driven Service Engineering Based on IDEF

Section IV:
Service Deployment Execution and Management

Chapter VIII
Service Deployment Execution and Management

Chapter IX
A Platform for Model-Driven Service Engineering

Foreword

Software manufacturing is such a modern industry that there is a natural assumption amongst those that come into contact with it for the first time that newness equals advanced; as has been the reality with the hardware side. Far from experiencing a Moore's Law for application software, disappointment has been a persistent experience amongst customers over decades concerning the interrelated factors of cost, flexibility, and less than optimal relations between IT and business teams.

The relatively low productivity of programming in general has had a major impact on business over the decades by driving extreme outsourcing and encouraging a wholesale shift to mass-produced, costly-to-modify products to keep the software affordable. This has lead in many cases to business processes and services having to be moulded to fit standardised software. In this way, the poor productivity of software creation and its subsequent modification has had both directly and indirectly damaging effects on business efficiency and costs.

This slowness of progress in the industry appears to arise in part from weak coalescing of thinking between the developer community, IT academia, and business/management consultancy. There has been surprisingly limited overlap or common working between them, and hence a difficultly in overcoming the huge drag created by ignorance and inertia amongst customers (risk of authorising change) and the power of vested interests, represented by the promulgation of different platforms, technology, and products with poor interoperability. There has been a gradual improvement over time, but the situation is still one of considerable confusion as to the best route forward, and all solutions proposed are partial (as the blogs and newsletters in the industry make clear).

It is surprising, but reassuring, to non-IT observers that all the components and methods necessary to build a methodology that is fully fit for purpose are in existence. This book explains how existing techniques and approaches can be combined to establish a comprehensive framework that permits developers to set down and change the specifications of business services easily and to automatically generate comprehensive application software that fully reflects the nature of the provided services, integrating legacy software as necessary.

To achieve this objective, a holistic approach to the production process is required. Neither a full top-down business view or bottom- up technology view will do the job, nor can service provision be truly liberated through software applications when any limitation imposed by platform, technology, or language remains.

The key to this vision is the treatment of the organisation as a whole through a complete systemic view of all its constituent activities, actors, mechanisms, constraints, rules, resources, and external links, together with all their interactions, and the use of semantics to describe the complete business services model that everyone can understand. The vision is completed with transformation of this business model into platform-independent computer models and then into models specific to the desired e-services technology.

This revolutionary and universal systemic methodology for the rapid creation of enterprise applications, fully tailored to each business it covers, will empower companies to react quickly to changes in their environment or strategy and become totally independent in software implementation. Meanwhile, developers can become freed of the mundane task of programming and work closely with business analysts on modelling and designing higher level business services.

The economics of application software and the agility of business-decision implementation can be transformed.

Graham Cox
Business Economist

Preface

This book is a proposal for the convolution of two—so far separate—practices, namely, business service design and electronic services (e-services) engineering. Businesses are under constant pressure to design and deliver new, innovative, and profitable services. Increasingly, such services are implemented entirely in software. The work presented in this book is based on the premise that business services need to be supported by an equally service-oriented IT infrastructure. Moreover, the book argues that the service-oriented paradigm is a gateway to the integration of the IT infrastructure with the business operational environment, across the value chain of the organization, and helps to redefine the strategic role of information systems in today's competitive environment.

The book takes a business-oriented starting point and proposes methods to engineer electronic services that leverage an organization's resources and deliver added value to shareholders, customers, and business partners. Business service models originate in the organization's strategies and synthesize its value chain (Porter, 1985). They are, in turn, transformed into operational services that are delivered through networks of coordinated Web services to consumers. Such Web services (i.e., remotely accessible software applications) need to operate within a service-oriented infrastructure that provides secure service delivery, monitoring, and continuous adaptation and enhancement.

In this respect, the book brings together Web services, a "hot" new technology that has already spawned a market for software environments, tools, and applications (Ferris & Farrell, 2003), and the service-centered organizational paradigm that is shaping the dynamic, responsive, learning and agile companies of the 21st century.

The architecture of the information infrastructure to support business services has not been treated with the same depth and rigour as that of other enterprise systems, such as, for example, enterprise resource planning (ERP). Until the arrival of Web services, no information technologies existed that could conceptually match business services. Alternative paradigms such as client server, component, and object-oriented computing do not explicitly support the principles of service orientation. The end result is information systems that do not align with the structures and processes of service-centered organizations. Subsequently, the manifestos for the strategic role of IT in business have largely been an unfulfilled vision, with management unable to leverage the full potential of the rapid technological evolution and create sustainable competitive advantage. The book is addressing this shortcoming by bringing together business and IT service design.

Target Readership

The book is a resource for IT professionals such as CIOs, IT strategists, software architects and designers, students of advanced software engineering courses, and, ultimately, for anyone responsible for implementing or managing a service-centered IT infrastructure in an organization.

The approach taken in this book is both sound, by being grounded on the latest service-oriented thinking, and pragmatic, by addressing the requirements of the modern business organizations: The book explains how to:

- Develop e-service models, namely, how to develop semantic models of the operational service environment of an organization, its structure, and its architectural requirements.
- Use a systematic, tool-supported way to decompose the business services models into networks of collaborating, computer-level e-services.
- Realize the e-services as Web service applications to support them.
- Deploy a Web services infrastructure for secure execution, monitoring, and continuous improvement of Web services.
- Understand how e-service technologies will evolve in the future and what standards and technologies will influence their evolution.

Aim of the Book

Over the past few years, the service-oriented paradigm has emerged as the software industry's latest "silver bullet," mainly due to Web-services technologies. Whilst Web services originate in computer programming as a technique to invoke a remote program function, their principles are increasingly being adopted by other software development disciplines, such as software architecture and design. Recently, the service-oriented paradigm for implementing systems started to move beyond the boundaries of programming and into the realm of enterprise IT architecture.

At the same time, services and the service-centered organization has been the subject of management theories and methods, with a new *service science* discipline gradually emerging (Spohrer, Maglio, Bailey, & Gruhl, 2007). The view of a business together with its suppliers and other partners, as a network of services creates a new framework for thinking business strategy. It enables us to identify the core competences of the organization (i.e., unique services that can not be easily copied by competitors), and to visualize the value chain (i.e., the value contributed by each service to the final outcome). This provides a practical way to realize the conceptual frameworks of strategic as well as operational management of a business, and a baseline to differentiate from the competition via the creation of new innovative services, the altering of existing ones to provide more value to the consumer, and the strengthening of customer loyalty.

Until recently, the service-centered organization lacked a suitable software technology that mirrored the business structure and the organizational processes and services. Although IT infrastructure is an essential component of an organization, its role in service provision was rather limited to basic aspects of the service delivery. Thus, organizations failed to harness IT to deliver service value to the customer. In other words, even perfectly designed and conceived services will fall short on delivery, if support from the IT infrastructure is not adequate. Furthermore, IT infrastructure may have a substantial influence on the adaptation abilities of the organization, i.e. the ability to reform its internal structure of services, in order to respond to the environment.

The rise of the service-oriented IT architectural paradigm provides new potential for eliminating the aforementioned shortcomings. Web services technologies have made it possible to integrate business services with software technology. Effectively, the business service is deployed as a number of coordinated Web services (i.e., of autonomous software applications that can be accessed remotely using Internet-oriented protocols). Subsequently, service-oriented business environments need to be supported by equally service-oriented IT infrastructures.

By using a Web-services infrastructure, companies can improve service provision in a wide spectrum of areas in order to:

- Create service level agreements based on how they want a service to be delivered to each consumer (*service customization*).
- Charge service consumers based on usage or performance.
- Select service providers based on price, performance, or reliability (*service outsourcing*).
- Prioritize access to the service based on the relative business importance of the consumer.

- Redefine the production workflow and the organizational structures (*business process reengineering*) in order to preserve high adaptation abilities to the environmental stimulus (*organizational learning*).

Motivation Behind this Book

The concept of service orientation has been the subject of scientific enquiry in fields as diverse as economics, strategic management, and information technology. The service concept is based on the premise that services are the vehicles that transfer value between various agents of the economic and business system. In that sense, the term *service* abandons traditional definitions (i.e., as an intangible good) and becomes a cross-boundary transparent concept, closely related to the survival of the organization and its ability to fulfil its mission in a network of interrelated organizations and customers.

Although service orientation per se is not a new concept in software development, it has become, for the first time, a feasible proposition, mainly due to the emergence of Web-services technologies. However, the vast majority of Web-services research is technology biased (i.e., focuses on programming standards, protocols, and software platforms for the implementation and deployment of Web services). Little attention has been paid to questions such as what new services can be discovered in a business and how they can be designed and implemented to deliver sustainable competitive advantage. As with other IT paradigms that predated Web services, it is essential to realize that Web services technology is only an enabler—the means to an end—rather than the goal itself. Web services technology, in other words, is simply the means to realize the manifestos of the service-oriented organization.

Web services on their own can not transform an organization, unless its management adopts a service-oriented view of the way it runs business processes and finds means to redesign such processes around the consumer of the service (i.e., a customer, company staff, or business partner) whose needs and expectations from the service are met and, even more, surpassed. Once integrated within such a holistic service-oriented strategy, Web services can provide a concrete technology for realizing the redesigned service-oriented organization structures and for ensuring the smooth transition to a service-management culture.

This book arrives at a time when Web service technologies have matured sufficiently to become a feasible, industrial-strength technology, with many organizations engaged in a process to become service centered. Web services can make the concept of a service-centered organization a reality. To achieve this, an organization needs to evaluate the wide range of available Web-service technologies and select those that meet its requirements. An IT infrastructure based on Web services then needs to be developed to allow the secure execution of operational services and their monitoring and continuous improvement, according to the dictations of various internal and external agents such as customers, suppliers, competitors, and so forth.

It is clear that, in order for the vision of service driven organizations to materialise, an *engineering* approach to service realization is required. Approaches such as information engineering (Martin, 1989) and IT-based business engineering (Donovan, 1994) predate the paradigm of service engineering, but whereas such approaches focused on business information and business processes respectively, service engineering targets business services. Similarly to its predecessors, service engineering advocates that an engineering approach needs to be followed in the design and realization of business software systems. All engineering disciplines rely on the construction, analysis, and manipulation of models that are underpinned by formal properties and theories. In a similar manner, the engineering of services must be based on the specification of business models and their transformation into executable software with the use of systematic and automated transformation techniques. This is, in fact, what this book aims at: to elevate the practice of realizing business services in software from a craft to an engineering discipline.

The book is organised into four sections comprising a total of XI chapters, each of them designed to bring the reader one step closer to the vision of engineering the service-centered organization with e-services.

Section I, "Service Concepts," provides the basic concepts, definitions, and standards for business services and e-services. It comprises two chapters. The introductory chapter (Chapter I) serves primarily to explain our motivations for writing this book, its targeted readership, and to provide a starting point for defining the fundamental concepts of services and service orientation. In Chapter II, we define the essential concepts that underpin services in general and, more specifically, electronically delivered and consumed services (e-services). This chapter introduces core concepts surrounding the area of services without going into technical details. This is essential to avoid confusion caused by the ever-changing and often contradicting service standards that might cause losing sight of the "big picture," that is, of the rationale and motivation behind the emergence of such standards.

Section II, "Service Languages and Standards," surveys the most important technologies available today for service realization, namely, Web services. It comprises two chapters. Chapter III reviews the technologies and standards that underpin Web services, such as the XML language and protocols for service specifications, messaging, and publishing. Web-service standards such as WSDL, SOAP, and UDDI are the subject of this chapter. Chapter IV, on the other hand, covers more advanced service standards that not only address the specification of individual services but also their "orchestration" (coordination) in the context of business processes and services of higher order and complexity.

Having established the vocabulary of concepts and standards for realizing services, the next section ("Service Engineering Concepts and Techniques") is concerned with the methodical aspects of service engineering. The section comprises 3 chapters that deal with methods for specifying, modeling, and implementing services.

An advantage of formally describing the semantics meaning of services is that it makes their automatic realization in software feasible. Thus, the computer-based descriptions of services are automatically transformed by software tools into executable Web service descriptions. This is the model-driven approach to service engineering advocated in Chapter V. Underpinning this approach are the service ontologies introduced in Chapter VI.

While Chapters III and IV consider the syntactic constructs for specifying and coordinating services, Chapter VI is concerned with the semantics of services. Web service protocols such as SOAP and WSDL cannot capture essential properties of a service such as its performance, reliability, and security and they cannot describe the service beyond a syntactical level of inputs and outputs. In Chapter VI, the concept of service ontologies is introduced. This chapter examines methods for formally ascribing *meaning* to Web services. This is essential if we want to bridge the semantic gap between the business services and their software equivalents.

Model-driven service engineering is, however, still in its infancy, as it lacks widely used practical methods and techniques. To illustrate how this paradigm for building services can be brought into mainstream practice, Chapter VII presents a model-driven service engineering method based on the system modeling approach IDEF that has been used by the authors in various commercial projects. The main benefit of this method is that it is grounded on sound theories of services, thus making service discovery, modeling, and transformation intuitive and reducing the complexities associated with the migration from business to Web services.

With Section III completing the coverage of the service engineering life cycle, Section IV tackles the issues of deploying and managing services. This section, comprising three chapters, is concerned with a diverse number of issues such as architectures and environments, security, and life-cycle management of e-services.

No matter how sound and efficient a service realization method is, its value will be diminished without underpinning from an enterprise-wide e-services infrastructure for developing, executing, and managing services. Without such infrastructure, realized business services are stand-alone areas of automation that fail to have the desired impact on the organization. In Chapter VIII, an architectural framework for introducing services to the organization in a disciplined manner is proposed. This framework has been coined "service-oriented architecture" (SOA). The chapter also discusses technologies and standards for service execution, security, monitoring, and management.

In line with the overall theme of the book, Chapter IX presents a case study of a service development execution and management platform that provides model-driven, service design, generation, and deployment. Through presentation of this platform, the chapter highlights the general desirable features and capabilities of service management environments.

Chapter X validates the application of the concepts methods techniques and technologies covered in all previous chapters, through a real-life case study. Going beyond the simple sketching of a solution, this chapter addresses the whole systematic process of identifying modeling, and realizing business services in software. The business area used in this case study, accounts payable and receivables, was chosen because it is common across all types of organizations. This avoids the pitfalls of demonstrating the proposed solutions using either "toy" examples or narrow business subjects that may require specialist knowledge.

Chapter XI revisits the topics discussed in the previous chapters and sketches a possible future for service-oriented organizations, by drawing on progress in areas such as the Semantic Web, software agents and intelligent services. Attempting to forecast where such rapidly evolving technologies are heading is always a formidable task. Chapter XI extrapolates a vision of a future, in which e-services play a central part in architecting and implementing all types of enterprise information systems. We expect future generations of Web services to possess capabilities that are at the moment the preserve of artificial intelligence and Semantic Web systems. Such services will be far closer to their business counterparts. In fact, the next generation of semantic Web services will be created and driven directly by models of the business, rather than manually crafted. In turn, this will allow services to be deployed in many more commercial situations and, therefore, offer the opportunity for new types of business services to be developed.

Final Thoughts

The business world is evolving at an increasingly rapid pace. Information technology has traditionally assisted in accelerating this change by altering the economic environment, and by offering the means to companies to operate more effectively. We are now at the threshold of an era where businesses are becoming increasingly electronically conducted (i.e., are becoming *e-businesses*), and increasingly service-oriented (Janssen & Gordijn, 2005).

Service has become the central concept for visualizing an organization's value chain, formulating the corporate strategy, and managing the value-creation process. Service is the main business vehicle for delivering value to the customers of an enterprise, by satisfying their individual customized expectations and wishes. Service thinking goes beyond the traditional approach of activity and process orientation, by putting emphasis on the core competencies of an organization. As such, service must be at the core of companies' supporting IT infrastructures.

The challenge for IT is to provide a breakthrough to support the service-oriented e-business of the 21st century. Existing paradigms and technologies for building software such as client server, components, and Web technologies fall short in meeting these challenges. The demand is now for IT systems that mirror the service-oriented structure of the organization and underpin the business services. This requires a new discipline for implementing services: *service engineering.* In this book, we propose a methodical approach to the discovery, modeling, and realization of business services. We argue that by following this approach, organizations can be confident that their IT systems will never fall out of sync with the business. Moreover, this approach greatly reduces the eternal weaknesses of IT (obsolescence and system upgrading) by showing how business and IT services can coexist and coevolve in total synergy.

We hope that the readers will find the concepts and methods presented in this book of genuine value, and bring them into fruition in the design and delivery of innovative and profitable, IT-enabled business services.

References

Donovan, J. J. (1994). *Business re-engineering with information technology.* Upper Saddle River, NJ: Prentice Hall.

Ferris, C., & Farrell, J. (2003). What are Web services? *Communications of the ACM, 56*(6), 31.

Janssen, M., & Gordijn, J. (2005). Editorial preface: E-services special issue. *International Journal of E-Business Research, 1*(3), i-iii

Martin, J. (1989). *Information engineering* (Vols. 1-3). Upper Saddle River, NJ: Prentice Hall.

Porter, M. (1985). *Competitive advantage.* New York: Free Press.

Spohrer, J., Maglio, P. P., Bailey, J., & Gruhl, D. (2007). Steps toward a science of service systems. *IEEE Computer, 40*(1), 71-77.

Acknowledgment

The authors would like to acknowledge the help of all involved in the collation and review process of the book, without whose support the project could not have been satisfactorily completed.

In particular, we would like to thank all the members of the CLMS team in Athens that assisted us with the preparation of Chapters V, VII, and the case study of Chapter IX.

The three anonymous reviewers of the book, for their invaluable comments and suggestions during the preparation of the draft manuscripts.

Finally, in no particular order, the authors would like to acknowledge organizations and committees such as the World Wide Web Consortium (W3C), Object Management Group Inc (OMG), Organization for the Advancement of Structured Information Standards (OASIS), IBM Alphaworks, European Semantic Systems Initiative (ESSI), and many others, for their excellent Web resources on the standards and technologies investigated by the book.

Last but not least, our thanks go to the publishing team of IGI Global, whose contributions throughout the whole process, from inception of the original idea to final publication have been excellent and most helpful.

Bill Karakostas and Yannis Zorgios
January 2008

Section I

Service Concepts

Chapter I

Introduction to Services

Introduction

Over the past few decades, organizations have witnessed dramatic changes in their environment. The globalisation of the economy with the emergence of Asia's new economic powerhouses, the rise of the knowledge economy, the rapid growth and sometimes equally rapid decline of disruptive technologies and business models are some examples of the modern economic environment, within which organizations must survive. At the same time, requirements from shareholders have become increasingly pressing. Stock markets demand high returns on investments, while strong competition narrows the profit margins. On the other hand, consumers continue to evolve in a process that began in the 1980s, to become more health and image conscious, eclectic in their purchasing choices, and not conforming to one-size-fits-all solutions, preferring individuality and customization, even of commodity products.

Suddenly, companies from every sector are offering services or total solutions and customer care rather than simply products. The reason for that is that most, if not all, mainstream consumer products have become commodities. Where competition is no longer possible in other ways apart from cost, it is impossible to improve profit margins. One way to achieve that is by selling services associated with the main offered product (Vandermerwe & Rada, 1988).

For example, many car manufacturers today sell services together with vehicles (mainly conventional services such as car servicing, but also, more profitably for them, financial services). Evidence suggests that combined servicing and financing can be a lot more profitable to the car manufacturer than the selling of the car itself. It is not uncommon these days for the product to be sold as an add-on to the service, rather than the other way around. Telecom operators sell telephones and other communications devices at a nominal cost, or even give them free to buyers of their telephone services. The same applies to, for example, media broadcasters, who supply the electronic equipment free or at a below cost to subscribers.

For organizations such as banks, services have always been a more integral and fundamental part of their business. The financial organizations core business is the management (borrowing, lending, and investing) of financial assets. One source for borrowing money is individual investors (i.e., people holding savings and investment accounts with the banks). As in many other industries, banks find it difficult to compete on a cost basis alone, therefore they need to adopt a *service differentiation strategy* in order to differentiate from the competition and to attract investors. Such services typically include investment advice, but they can also be totally independent from the mainstream banking to include, for example, travel-related services.

Finally, there is the case of so-called pure service organizations. A solicitor's firm or management consultancy, for example, does not sell physical products, such as cars (or even virtual ones) like investment accounts; it offers professional services. In this case, the service *is* the product.

It can be argued that service is an integral part of today's organizations value chains, them being manufacturing, financial or professional services sectors. Even if the core product of the organization is not services, the latter can become an integral part of the product package and, if appropriately delivered, yield competitive advantage.

Despite the central role of service in contemporary organizations, existing strategic frameworks emphasize instead the concept of *process* as the core part of their business value chain. In this context, derived value is perceived as the end result of a chain of value adding business processes, which, in turn, can be viewed as transformations of materials to products delivered to customers (i.e., inbound logistics, production, outbound logistics). The concept of activity has become central to business management and has inspired a number of popular activity-based management tools and techniques, such as *activity based costing and management* (Cooper & Kaplan, 1992). However, activity-oriented thinking is not suitable for service-centered organizations.

Service-centered thinking implies that a network of services, rather than a chain of processes, creates value. The term *value grid* has been coined to highlight the fact that competition in the value chain has been shifting away from the strict linear view assumed by the traditional value chain model, towards grid-like collaborations (Pil & Holweg, 2006). Services provide capabilities to various internal or external agents, regardless of the organizational boundaries and the traditional operational environments. They formulate a network, in the sense that the provided capabilities are delivered via electronic means and, as such, services are separated from the material dimension of the operational environment. The electronic nature of the capabilities enhances organizational flexibility to develop different ways for delivering value and to differentiate from the competitors. For instance, a traditional publishing company utilizes resources such as printers to produce physical copies of books to sell to its customers. In this manner, the publisher's resources are mobilised to add value for the consumers (readers) by delivering a product (i.e., a book). These days, most publishing companies have added the Internet to their traditional product delivery channels. Using the Internet as a distribution channel, allows consumers to use widely available Web browsers and search engines to search online databases of e-books and articles, and to create electronic profiles to receive targeted information such as about new publications in topics of their interests. Thus, Internet-based services (e-services) give the consumers the capability to use the publishing company's resources in different ways (i.e., by customizing the consumed service to their needs).

Service-centered organizations, therefore, depend on the rapid growth of informational technologies and their potentiality to migrate traditional services to an electronic environment, namely to provide electronic services (e-services). However, this requires a abandoning the traditional view of the business environment as a flow of resources across activities, where information technology only plays a supporting role. Indeed, today, despite the fact that e-service is a concept of ever-growing significance, there is a prominent lack of:

- A view of e-service that conveys both its business and software dimensions.
- A standardized methodology for identifying and describing e-services within the organizational value chain.
- An automated method to derive realizable (executable) services from business service models.

In the following sections, we will attempt to address the first of the aforementioned shortcomings, by providing rigorous definitions of fundamental service concepts. Solutions for overcoming the other shortcomings will be proposed in following chapters.

The "Service" Concept

We propose an all encompassing view of service, that is, as the act and result of making available some resources belonging to an entity called the *service provider,* to an entity called the *consumer,* who, as a result, acquires a *capability*. *Service* is, therefore, a set of capabilities provided by a *service provider*, which is an entity (e.g., an organization) that either owns the resource or controls its supply, or coordinates its delivery, to deliver capabilities. In particular, the service has a specific utility for the consumer, which determines its value

Service-oriented thinking requires that each available resource in the organization is treated as a potential service, in the sense that each resource can be utilized and transformed, by some process, to become a realizable capability. Subsequently, a service focuses on providing such capability and is distinct from the means by which it is delivered (i.e., the process). In turn, process is the mobilization, coordination and control of people and other business resources (including IT ones) by a service provider, that is geared towards offering some defined benefit/capability to a service consumer.

This definition makes possible to distinguish services from other forms of resource ownership transfer, because in service provision the consumer never owns the resource utilized/consumed. In fact, a consumer receives capabilities without owning specific resources. These capabilities synthesize a service, from which consumers obtain value.

The aforementioned definition encompasses both *core business services* and *support services*. Core business services are those that constitute the essence of the providing organization (e.g., a business consultancy or medical service), whereas support services are add-on services that relate to a core business service or product.

Figure 1. The service aspect of resources

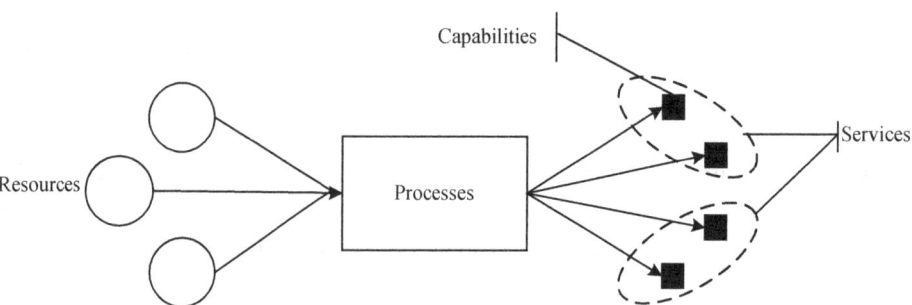

Finally, the concept of service must be separated from the means used to deliver the service to the consumer. The latter is the framework through which consumers experience services and, therefore, affects the utility delivered to the consumers, regardless of the potential capabilities that a service may offer. This framework is usually perceived in the *context* of a service interface, which is described in the following section.

The Service Interface

A service cannot always be defined in tangible and quantifiable terms; the reason being that each consumer has a set of experiences and subjective interpretations for perceiving and experiencing the capabilities that a service offers. Furthermore, a capability offers different utility to different consumers who as a result, formulate different expectations about the potential benefits of acquiring the capability.

It is important to identify factors that are often soft, rather than hard/quantifiable, that affect the consumer's experience of the service. Once such factors are understood, they must be related to the components or parts of the process that delivers the service. Such components/parts are the people and other resources, such as machinery, that contribute towards the delivery and consumption of the service. Obviously, not all of such components are visible to the service consumer. Even more, the way a specific service is delivered is not always relevant for the consumer.

Equally, it is unreasonable to expect that, in general, a service provider has explicit knowledge of each consumer's requirements. Thus, the service provider needs a

Figure 2. Service and interface

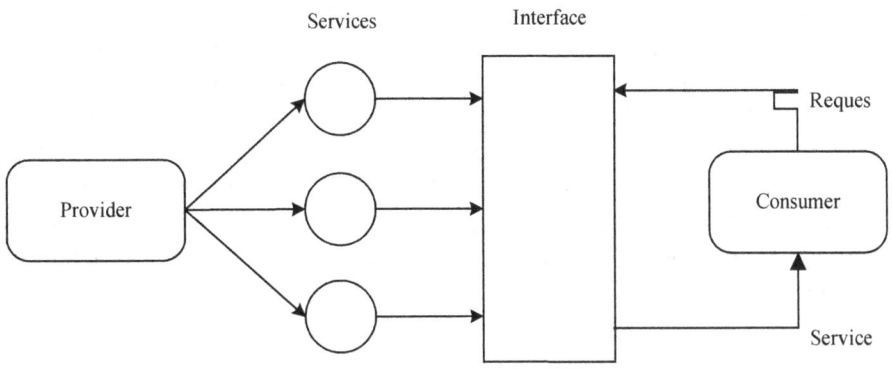

mechanism that provides consumers with the ability to express service requirements in a standardized way, to enable it to adjust the provided service.

Consumers need to communicate their requirements from a service, and to experience the actual service through an *interface*. This is the visible part of the service. An interface can consist of humans such as the customer facing personnel in a company, or machines such as a touch screen of an information kiosk. The interface is only the channel for interaction between the consumer and the service. What actually takes place behind the interface is a *process*, which coordinates resources to deliver the service to the consumer. Since such process is transparent to the consumer, it does not matter how it is implemented, as long as the end result (the service) is satisfactory and meets the consumer's specific criteria.

E-Services

Consumers therefore experience service through interfaces. For many types of services this interface has to be physical, as the consumer needs to be physically present at the point where the service is being delivered. In other cases, however, the service can be provided and consumed from a distance, by using a communication channel such as the telephone or the Internet. When the service involves interaction over a digital channel, it is called *electronic service* or, in short, *e-service*.

Increasingly, a large number of services are delivered electronically (i.e., as e-services). Even if some services cannot easily be offered in an electronic manner, it is possible for supporting or add-on services to be delivered in such manner. For example, an airline flight service is primarily physical, as the passengers need to bring themselves on board a plane in order to consume the service. Yet, several associated (added-on) to flight services are e-services. Such services are concerned with information exchanged between the parties about the primary service, for example flight time information or passenger seating arrangements and meal preferences. Clearly, added-on services are distinct from the core business services offered to the consumer. Airline customers, for example, do not purchase flight information—they purchase airline seats. However, it is often the support services that determine whether a consumer will go ahead with the consumption of the core service or not. For many consumers, the ability to prebook specific seats and meals on the plane can provide sufficient reason to prefer one airline over its competitors that do not offer such services. As companies in many sectors find it hard to compete on a product quality or price basis, it is often support services that enable them to provide more value to their consumers, to differentiate from their competitors, and to gain competitive advantage.

Deriving E-Services

The aforementioned definition of e-service adopts a broad perspective, which, in turn, may require a paradigm shift. For many, service-oriented thinking is difficult due to reasons such as the following:

1.   Service concepts such as service provider, consumer, and capabilities have no standard agreed meanings.
2.   Services are about the dynamic interaction of business processes rather than static associations.
3.   Many individuals have a more traditional perspective of services that does not include the electronic service possibilities.

To address these difficulties, a systematic and rigorous service-oriented methodology needs to be formulated with a precise understanding of what e-services are. A precise definition of e-services is also important in the specification phase during the development of the e-services infrastructure.

The proposed service engineering methodology defines the state-of-affairs within the organization and extracts the e-services by identifying service consumers, providers and capabilities. The stages of the methodology are presented in Figure 3.

First, the operational environment is described in terms of processes. Processes utilize resources and information and transform inputs to outputs. As such, processes constitute important elements of the organizational value chain. However, from the complex system of business process, we isolate those processes important for the value chain and the operational environment. This is achieved by identifying the

Figure 3. The methodological approach for delivering e-services

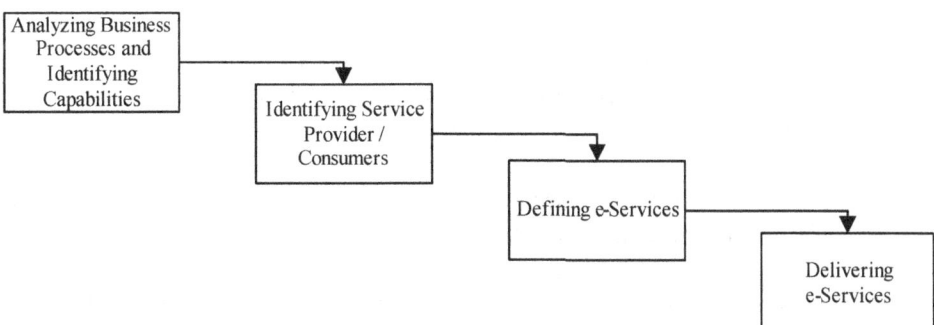

capabilities that a process provides with respect to the consumed resources, and evaluating their relative importance in the value chain. At the end of this stage, we have defined the core business processes and the delivered capabilities.

Second, having identified and established the capabilities allocated within the organizational value chain, we can identify service consumers and providers. Capabilities are provided to serve the requirements of specific entities or processes at task performance. Subsequently, each recorded capability can be associated with:

- *Service consumers*, namely actors that use capabilities to enhance their performance.
- *Service providers* of such capabilities.

The third stage, involves the definition of the e-services. As stated earlier, an e-service is a set of capabilities. However, capabilities are grouped under the broader concept of the e-service, by clarifying the scope of the service. The primary purpose of a service is to satisfy the requirements and the restrictions posed by the service consumers and, thus, to contribute at the achievement of the business goals. As such, capabilities within the same scope may be classified as a service.

The final stage is to define how the service will be delivered to a consumer via electronic means. This is achieved by modeling e-service through an appropriate computer oriented framework, and by employing software technologies. Modeling e-services is essential for depicting the dynamic nature of the service and its interaction with the environment. The dynamic nature of e-service though, must be supported by an equally dynamic software technology.

It is obvious that the last stage of the aforementioned methodology is critical for the successful implementation of the e-services. For this reason, the next section presents a modeling framework and architectural perspective of technologies for enabling e-services.

Enabling Infrastructure for E-Services

To develop IS infrastructures for e-services, a set of technologies is required. First, e-services must be modeled using a standardized *semantic framework*. The modeling framework must be semantic to facilitate shared understanding amongst all stakeholders. It, also, must be standardized to avoid communication problems caused by inconsistent or ambiguous descriptions. Another major implication of developing a standardized semantic modeling framework for e-services, is the establishment of a *service-oriented architecture* (SOA). SOA is a dynamic and flexible architecture platform since it relies on the concept of the service layer. A service-layer-based approach enables to define in real-time services, their providers and consumers, according to the continuous evolving business environment. This is achieved by using development tools based on Web service technologies. SOA is discussed more extensively in Chapter VIII of this book.

Modeling E-Services

Modeling services requires a theoretical baseline and an analytical tool, which together allow the delivery of a metamodel framework for describing explicitly (1) the inputs to the service, (2) the scope of the service, (3) the mechanisms employed to deliver the service, and (4) the outcome of the service.

The theoretical baseline is *general systems theory* (Checkland, 1981). General systems theory emphasizes that real systems are open to, and interact with, their environments. Rather than reducing a system (e.g., an organization) to the properties of its parts or elements (e.g., departments or processes), systems theory focuses on the arrangement of and relations between the parts, which connect them into a whole (cf. holism). Thus, the same concepts and principles of organization underlie different scientific disciplines (physics, biology, technology, sociology, etc.), providing a basis for their unification. Systems concepts include: system-environment boundary, input, output, process, state, hierarchy, goal directedness, and information. These concepts are used to reduce the dynamic complexity of an organization and to focus on its critical elements. However, the application of General Systems Theory to the problem of modeling services requires an analytical model that allows the standardization of the modeling process.

In this book, the analytical framework employed for this purpose is based on an adapted version of the *integration definition for function modeling 0* analysis method (IEEE, 1998). Integration definition for function modeling 0 (IDEF0) will be discussed extensively in Chapter VII. IDEF0 provides semantics descriptions of the operational environment, developed around the basic graphical notation of function box (Figure 4). Function box represents the basic organizational subprocess or unit of analysis (e.g., department, activity). Each side of the function box has a standard meaning in terms of box/arrow relationships. The side of the box with which an arrow interfaces reflects the arrow's role. Arrows entering the left side of the box are inputs. Inputs are transformed or consumed by the function to produce outputs. Arrows entering the box on the top are controls. Controls specify the conditions required for the function to produce correct outputs (usually interpreted as "information"). Arrows leaving a box on the right side are outputs. Outputs are the data or objects produced by the function. Finally, arrows connected to the bottom side of the box represent mechanisms, namely, the means that support the execution of the function.

Figure 4. IDEF0 semantics

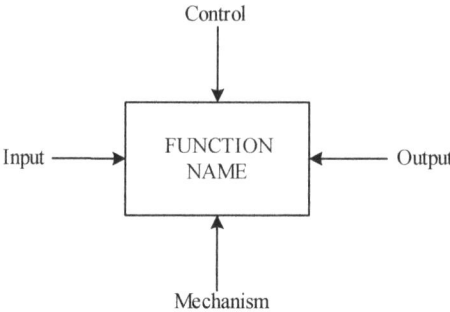

Figure 5. IDEF0 model for services

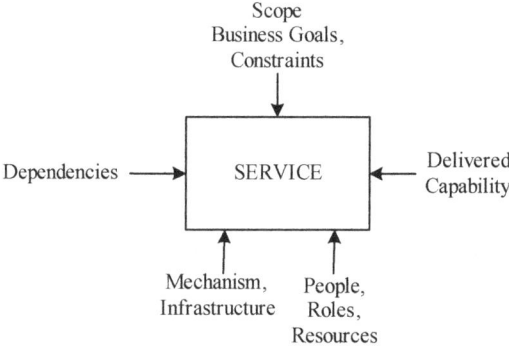

In adapting IDEF0 for service modeling purposes, the function box corresponds to the service. The service has inputs, which are the conditions or prerequisites for delivering the service; outputs, which are the delivered capabilities; and mechanisms, which are the people, IT infrastructure, and other systems that deliver the service. Finally, the service has a perspective (scope), which is defined by the business context of the service, such as the business goals or consumer requirements the service supports (Figure 5). Note that IDEF0 provides the ability to expand the aforementioned analysis. For instance, multiple inputs/outputs may be defined for the same service, and also a service may be considered as a part of a wider network of services.

Service-Oriented Architecture

In the context of e-services, where the interface between the service and its consumer is of point-and-click type (e.g., a Web-delivered service) the service mechanisms should be transparent to its consumers. Even in cases where the service provided by the organization is rented, aggregated, or brokered from others, this should be hidden from the consumer who should experience the business service in a seamless manner. To make this possible, a service-oriented architecture (SOA) is required to unify processes, systems and other resources of the organization, under the service paradigm (Pallos, 2001).

SOA introduces the concept of service layer, in order to separate the roles of service provider and consumer (Papazoglou & Georgakopoulos, 2003). A service layer is an interface that ensures the virtual transparent representation of services without reference to a specific implementation/system or provider. Subsequently, a consumer's request is not directed to a specific provider but to the service layer, which, in turn, coordinates distributed providers in order to satisfy the request. Furthermore, a service layer enables each service provider (1) to effectively manage and operate the underlying technologies without affecting the consumers and (2) to be specialized at a specific type of service increasing its efficiency.

This approach is extremely powerful, as it enables each request to be managed, monitored, routed, and prioritised according to previously configured business objectives. This makes possible the built of a real-time view of requests being made and fulfilled, and to understand which processes or business partners are consuming which services. Should a service-level agreement exist that promises to deliver a service to a particular requester within a particular period of time, it is possible to change the priority of the service, to ensure that the service-level agreements are not missed. Similarly, if a service provider suffers unexpected downtime and is no longer available, the service layer may route requests to an alternative provider that may be available. SOA enables the understanding of how the organizational value is created and the relevant contribution of each service provider to the value chain of the organizational network. It also allows tracing the cost of each service and therefore allows a more accurate perception of the relationship between cost and value created. Because of this, organizations have started to realize that using services helps to produce return of investment (ROI) cases, by showing the costs involved in making the service available, and comparing that with the lines of business that the service supports. This ROI case may also be continually updated by monitoring how the service is consumed and for which business purpose. This can lead to an accurate assessment of the value of particular services, and whether the development costs and ongoing maintenance of the service makes it worthwhile.

Web Services

Until recently, the implementation of e-services infrastructures based on the SOA paradigm was hampered by the fact that there was no cheap and standard electronic infrastructure to allow any service provider to offer services to any consumer. This problem was largely overcome by the widespread usage of the Internet, which is a ubiquitous technology for digital communications. The other major obstacle was that the lack of standard methods the providers could use to advertise electronically what type of services they are offering, allowing consumers to search and locate such services. This was overcome with the use of online information places, similar to telephone directories ("yellow pages"). The last obstacle remaining today is how to find a way for the service to be precisely described in order to be understood by nonhuman consumers. As long as the consumer of the service remained human, Web sites and Web pages written in HTML largely avoided this problem. Provided that the Web page is in a language the user can read, it is possible to use Web pages for interacting, exchanging information, and navigating through a Web site. However, since not all service consumers are humans, the service provision model that relies upon displaying HTML pages starts to break down. This is the point where Web services leap into action.

The World Wide Web Consortium (W3C) defines Web services as a software system designed to support interoperable machine-to-machine interaction over a network (W3C, 2004). A Web service has an interface described in a machine processable format (called *WSDL,* and discussed extensively in Chapter III). Other systems interact with the Web service in a manner prescribed by its description, using SOAP messages that are typically conveyed using HTTP with XML serialization, in conjunction with other Web-related standards (that will also be covered in Chapter III). Web services are inherently application neutral and provide the important advantages of standardization, neutrality and implementation independence, that can be applied to an infinite number of possibilities. This book assumes Web services as the building block for realizing e-services. While e-services can be implemented using older Web technologies (e.g, HTML and scripting languages such as CGI and Java applets), Web services offer the closest proximity to the concept of e-service. A Web service provides mechanisms for describing the offered service in an unambiguous way and for accessing it in an automated way. Humans, but also nonhuman consumers (such as software programs) can access an e-service implemented as a Web service. More importantly, everything the consumer needs to know about the offered service is described in its interface.

This is not to say that the Web services are not without their weaknesses and limitations. Whilst the consumer can find out about the service by looking at its interface, the service is in no position of knowing about its consumers and their actual preferences and requirements. This might ensure that the service is not tied down to a particular consumer or consumers and it is open to as many consumers as desired, but, on the other hand, it makes the service less flexible. Also, when the provider changes the interface of the service, it becomes difficult or impossible to inform all existing consumers about it. Finally, there are many features of the service that cannot be described using its WSDL specification (i.e., things like its performance, reliability, and so on). Chapter VI will discuss ways to overcome this limitation of current Web service standards.

Web services, therefore, suffer currently from limited customization ability and from limited two-way interaction between the service and the consumer. Also, the current languages used for describing Web services such as WSDL are rather too low level to allow the description of more business-oriented types of services. In this book, we show how the core Web service standards can be augmented to allow the description of the meaning of services (see Chapter VI). Also, service implementation is still at best a semiautomatic process, and there is a significant development gap between the business service and its Web service equivalent. This gap is bridged at present by manual writing of specifications and designs that translate business service descriptions into computer executable Web service definitions. We argue that this process is inefficient and hampers the businesses effort to realize their services in software. In this book we propose that, to bridge the gap between business and executable services, *a model driven transformation* approach is needed. Under this approach, business oriented definitions of services are transformed to executable service implementations. This approach is described extensively in Chapters V and VII.

The Book's Vision of Service Engineering

The book's vision of service engineering is summarized in Figure 6. The book argues that service engineering must be a model driven, business focused approach that automates activities of model generation and transformation across business and computing domains to derive executable e-services. At the top layer of the diagram of Figure 6 is a value chain model that drives the identification and modeling of business services. The business oriented/technology neutral modeling language IDEF0, is used for modeling activities in this layer. Business services are large granularity entities that need to be mapped to *atomic* services of finer granularity. Such atomic services are found in *ontological* models that capture the services' functional/behavioral semantics and organize them in hierarchies/taxonomies that correspond to business areas or even to whole business industries. As it will be explained in Chapter 6, service ontologies are platform independent, computer oriented descriptions of services that have standard and formal semantics. This allows services to be discovered, composed into higher order services and ultimately reused. Thus,

Figure 6. The book's view of service engineering

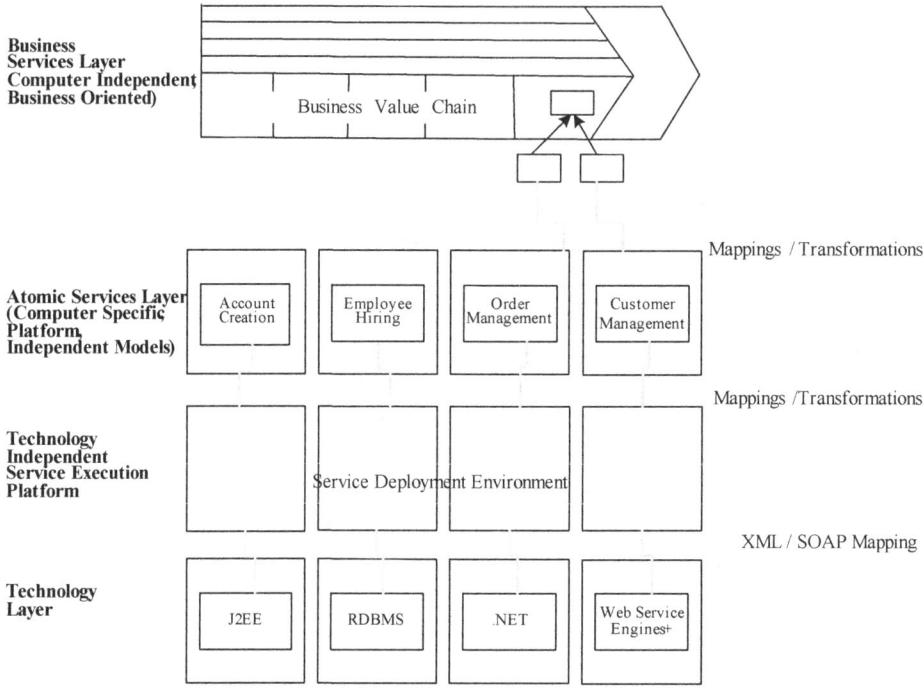

the atomic services layer becomes an important tool of service engineering during service identification, design and reuse.

A *platform-independent service model* consists of a network of atomic services and can be executed after it has been transformed to a *platform-specific model*. A platform-independent solution allows the organization's intellectual assets (i.e., the knowledge it has accumulated about how to create and provide services) to be protected from changes in technology. Web services are currently the dominant technology for implementing services; however, in the future it may be superceded by a better alternative. Thus, platform-independent models need to be transformed to one or several platform-specific models depending on the technology infrastructure(s) that an organization intends to use. A company can, for example, use purpose specific or proprietory technologies for internal system integration, together with more standardized Web services technologies for integration projects with its partners.

Therefore, the vision of Figure 6 cannot become a reality without the ability to automatically map, transform, and generate executable services from higher level, business-oriented service descriptions. Also, identifying, selecting and composing services can quickly become tedious and inefficient without the use of automated tools and environments. This book therefore argues that to realize such visions of service engineering, paradigms such as ontology and model driven software engineering need to be introduced. Thus, the book devotes considerable effort in reviewing the state of the art in emerging approaches to software development and suggesting how they could eventually become mainstream practices of services engineering.

Book Organization

This book therefore presents a roadmap for realizing the service-centered organization in software by:

- Identifying value adding services in an organization,
- Modeling and specifying them,
- Automatically translating business services into executable services, and
- Deploying and managing them.

Service engineering must handle the complete service life cycle (Chapter II) covering both the provider and consumer perspectives, addressing issues of service management and support for architectural frameworks (Chapter VIII). Service engineering is impractical without the existence of sound and methodical practices for service identification, modeling design, and implementation. Thus, the book is centred on the proposal of a system-oriented method for service modeling (Chapter VII) that is augmented with concepts and technologies from the areas of Semantic Web ontologies (Chapter VI) and model-driven software development (Chapter V). The book therefore shows how employing technologies, languages, and practices of the Semantic Web, ontologies, and model-driven development can provide the core for a sound service engineering method.

To add substance to the proposed methods and techniques, examples of service engineering in various domains (airlines, health care, financial services), are proposed throughout this book. The book demonstrates the use of automated environments for service engineering by presenting such an environment in Chapter IX and then, in Chapter X, applies it to a complete case study of realizing services in the domain of financial accounting.

Progress in Web services has been made possible due to the existence of standards that all major software players have adhered to. The book therefore makes extensive reference to the various standards that underpin service technologies, as proposed, for example, by international organizations such as W3C (http://w3c.org) and OASIS (http://oasis-open.org). However, since many of these standards are still evolving, the book can only speculate on their actual contributions to the goals of service engineering. As many of such standards and proposals have not been tested in practice, the book cannot guarantee their correctness and accuracy in what they propose to achieve. Although excerpts from specifications and examples based on such standards and proposals, are used throughout the book, it should not be implied that the book endorses any of them, nor that such specifications and examples are always complete and/or accurate. Core Web service standards are by now stable, but other standards are still in a state of flux. It is advisable that the readers of this book visit regularly the Web sites describing the various Web services standards to obtain the most up to date versions. The book, therefore, while being up-to-date with standards for service engineering, tries to keep as much as possible standards and technology independent. Instead, the book lays the foundations of services engineering on more fundamental concepts and principles derived from systems

Figure 7. Organization of the book

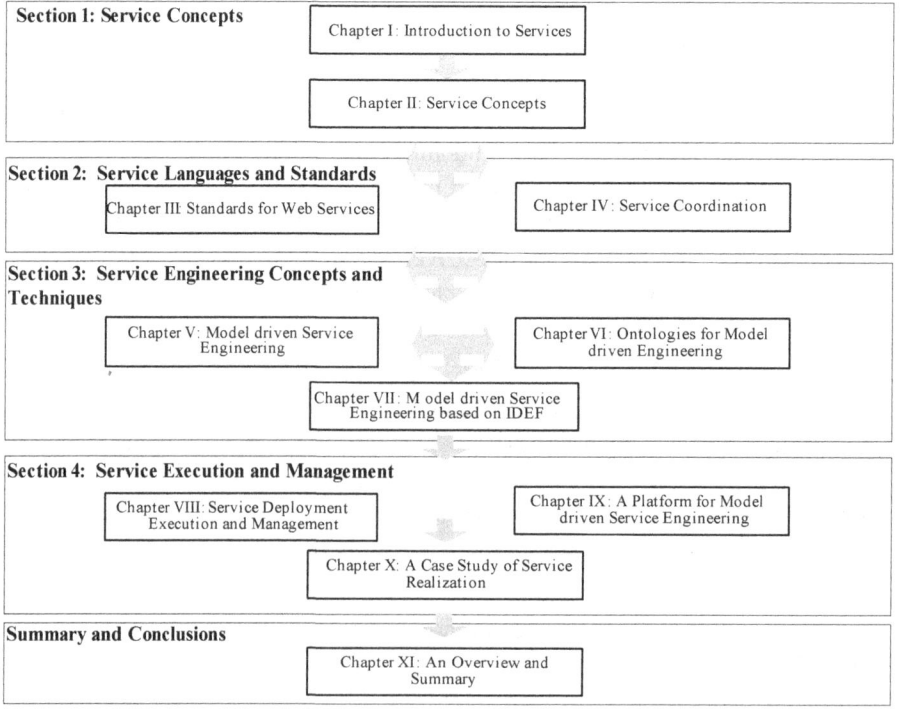

theory. At the same time, the book makes a prediction as to how current standards and technologies for e-services are going to evolve in the future (Chapter XI).

Whenever the book needs to demonstrate specific methods for service engineering, it does so in a pragmatic manner, by adopting established system modeling techniques such as IDEF. It is not our aim to add more service-oriented notations and formalisms to the many existing ones. However, as the IDEF notation is grounded in systems theory, we believe it is more suitable for service identification and design, compared with methods based on process-oriented concepts. Thus, the book presents a service engineering methodology based on the fundamental principles and concepts of IDEF family of languages, suitably extended and adapted to suit the needs of service modeling.

Figure 7 shows the logical organization of the book using a roadmap view.

References

Cooper, R., & Kaplan, R. S. (1992). Activity-based systems: Measuring the Costs of Resource Usage. *Accounting Horizons, 6*(3), 1-13.

IEEE. (1998). *IEEE Standard for functional modeling language—Syntax and semantics for IDEF0* [IEEE Std 1320.1-1998]. Software Engineering Standards Committee of the IEEE Computer Society.

OMG. (2007). *Unified modeling language.* Retrieved March 15, 2007, from http://www.uml.org

Pallos, M. S. (2001, December). Service-oriented architecture: A primer. *EAI Journal,* 32-35.

Papazoglou, M. P., & Georgakopoulos, D. (2003). Service-oriented computing. *Communications of the ACM, 46*(10), 25-28.

Pil, F. K., & Holweg, M. (2006). Evolving from value chain to value grid. *MIT Sloan Management Review, 47*(4), 72-80.

Stafford, T. S. (2003). E-services. *Communications of the ACM, 46*(6), 26-28.

Stafford, T. F., & Saunders, C. (2003). Moving towards chapter three. *E-Service Journal, 3*(1), 3-5.

Vandermerwe, S., & Rada, J. (1988). Servitization of business: Adding value by adding services. *European Management Journal, 6*(4), 314-324.

W3C. (2004). *Web services architecture.* Retrieved March 15, 2007, from http://www.w3.org/TR/ws-arch/

Chapter II

Service Concepts

Introduction

Services are something we routinely experience in everyday life as consumers. Also, depending on our profession, we may deal with services as providers. School teachers, hairdressers, and airline pilots are three examples of professions that offer services to consumers. The typical domestic dwelling is connected to several services such as services for drainage, electricity, and water supply. Architects and house builders take into account the local availability of external services and arrange the house's drainage, heating and plumbing accordingly. Gas heating, for example, requires the availability of a gas supply service. If such service is not available, the house's heating system must be based on an alternative fuel such as oil. This will, in turn, impact other decisions about the design of the house, such as, for example, the provision of space for an oil storage tank.

External services are provided according to some exact specifications and standards set by their providers. The electricity company, for example, will ensure that the frequency of the supplied electricity will be either 50Hz or 60Hz, within a given tolerance range, and that its service will be available continuously. If the company fails to meet such service standards (e.g., due to power failures that last for longer than a specified period), an electricity company will usually offer compensation to its customers.

Provision of consumer services such as electricity is pretty much standardized today. This in turn allows standard equipment such as cabling, sockets, and so on to be used for wiring a house without knowing (or caring) in advance who the actual electricity supplier is going to be. Consumers, if they choose to, can even switch to a different supplier that offers lower rates (cheaper electricity) or a better service. That, of course, could have never been an option if, every time the electricity supplier changed, the whole house had to be rewired to match the service of the new supplier. Furthermore, consumers, in general, do not know, nor care, how the company that supplies them with electricity acquires it in the first place (i.e., whether it generates it in its own power stations or buys it from some other supplier). Neither they are interested in whether the company owns the power transmission lines or uses someone else's transmission network.

For consumers, therefore, services such as gas and electricity operate in a transparent manner. Electrical appliances, for example, must be connected to the electricity service (i.e., to the building's electrical network) by using a standard plug and socket. Services such as electricity and gas have standardized interfaces. In the case of domestic electric power supply, the company stipulates the exact type of cable, amperage, and voltage that it can provide to connect to the consumer unit; this is the interface of the service and is specified to very exact standards.

Standard utility services such as water, electricity, and telephony are now commodities because of the maturity and standardization of the technologies used by the respective industries. In other types of services, though, there is significant less standardization, and thus the opportunity for the consumer to choose between different services that differ significantly from each other in their characteristics as well as in the required interface to the actual service. Interior designers will normally provide you with a total customized service, one that is based on the size and location of the rooms in your house, the type of furniture etc. It is extremely unlikely that two clients will receive exactly the same advice from an interior designer. We call these *customizable* services. In contrast, the services offered by the water or electricity supply company are *standardized*.

During the construction of a house, a number of services from architects, interior designers, electricians, and so forth are typically employed. Such services are essentially independent from each other, but somehow, they need to be integrated under a common architecture (a *framework*) that is controlled by the person or company who have commissioned the building of the house, and/or the architect responsible for its overall shape and design.

Figure 1. Service supply for a typical house

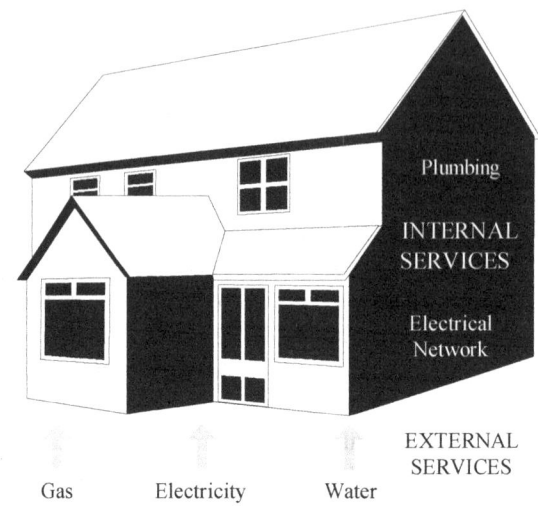

In other words, the role of someone like the house architect is to coordinate all services supplied by other parties under a common framework.

At this point, the reader might start to question the purpose of discussing building services in a book that is supposed to be concerned with electronic (software) services. However, such discussion does serve a purpose, namely to illustrate how ubiquitous services are and how they transcend all areas of human activity, including the construction of houses as well as computing. Computer-based services might, at first, appear to be quite unrelated to services such as gas supply and house design. However, viewed from an abstract enough point, they have, in fact, many similarities. Concepts such as consumer, provider, interface, internal, external, coordinated services are ubiquitous and universal. It is often helpful to cross-apply ideas and concepts from other service areas to computer e-services. E-services are a relatively new area, and certainly a lot less standardized than more conventional types of services and therefore can benefit from reuse of existing ideas and practices. One of the aims of this book is to introduce an approach for evolving the engineering and supply of e-services in a way that parallels the evolution of other utility services such as electricity and water supply. To achieve that, the discipline of service engineering needs to agree on concepts and terminology for e-services (Jones, 2005). This is the purpose of this chapter: to propose a core set of e-service concepts, or, in other terms, a *service reference model* (OASIS, 2006).

Service Concepts

In this chapter, we are concerned with the concept of service as provided by businesses such as hospitals, schools, banks, and airlines. We argue that all types of services are essentially about the provision of a *capability* to a consumer. The difference between offering a service and selling a product is that, unlike the selling of tangible products, in services there is no transfer of ownership from the provider to the consumer. In service provision, some resources of the provider are being made available to the consumer in order for the latter to acquire a capability, something that he/she values. Typically, when receiving a service, the consumer uses the resources of the provider for a specified period (e.g., for the duration of a flight or for the duration of a training course). Sometimes the providers resources are allocated exclusively to one consumer (e.g., a seat on an airplane can be allocated to only one passenger), and sometimes they are shared amongst many consumers (i.e., many students may share the services of an instructor in a training course). This principle applies equally to conventional services as well as to e-services. While in a conventional service such as a flight service, the consumer is granted access to a physical resource (e.g., an airplane seat), in an e-service, the consumer is granted access to information resources (data) and computational capabilities of the provider. One thing that makes conventional and e-services different from one another is the *interface*—the mechanism through which the service is offered to the consumer and is made accessible by. To access physical resources, the consumer needs to use tangible interfaces. An airline service requires airports with departure lounges where the customer needs to be physically present in order to consume the service. Similarly, a real (as opposed to a virtual) classroom requires the student to be physically present in it in order to receive the tuition. The classroom, the interaction between student and tutor and other means and aids of tuition can be considered to be the interface to the service. On the other hand, an informational service about flight departures does not require the physical access of resources thus it can be a purely electronically accessed via a medium such as the Internet. We discuss in more depth the concept of the interface later on in this chapter.

To recap, services that involve access to physical resources cannot be consumed through an electronic interface. The buyer of a flight ticket needs to physically occupy the seat in order to consume the flight service. However, there are additional services that can be offered by a provider that help the consumer identify, select, possibly customize, and ultimately consume the service. As these services are information based, it is possible to deliver them (and access them) over an electronic medium.

The ultimate purpose of this book is to show how such business services (i.e., services that can be digitized) can be engineered in software. However, to achieve that, we need first to understand the relationship between a physical business service and its electronic counterpart, the e-service.

The purpose of this chapter, therefore, is to discuss the fundamental constituting parts of a service. Understanding and agreeing upon the definition of a service and of its constituting parts, is the first prerequisite for service engineering. The service language and vocabulary must describe services in a way that is understood by business users, who are not necessarily software experts. We simply cannot expect business users to make sense of technical terms used in Web services such as WSDL, SOAP, XML (discussed in Chapter III), and the like. Because e-services have been evolving in a bottom-up fashion (i.e., from the computer programming area), technical jargon is largely used to describe them. There is a large gap between the terminology used for service programming and the business terminology for services that is more diverse and less standardized. In this chapter, therefore, we use mainly informal concepts to explain services, while in the next chapter we map such concepts to the more standardized terminology used for e-services and Web services.

Core Service Concepts

Service supply these days constitutes the largest part of the economic activity. Services companies are now the driving force in most developed countries, surpassing manufacturing ones in economic output. Of course, even companies that offer primarily physical/discrete products, such as car manufacturers, in practice offer not just the physical product but a complete package that includes services such as maintenance, insurance, and other types of after sales care and support. Many companies today pride themselves on not simply selling products, but offering a "complete service."

Although free services do exist, most services involve some financial exchange between the consumer and the supplier, where the former pays the latter for the provision of the service. Before the two parties enter in the service provision, some kind of contract needs to be established. In simple services that involve persons, this contract is often implicit: A consumer agrees to receive the service from the supplier and typically pays the supplier after the service has been provided. This type of situation applies to services offered, for example, by hairdressers or dentists (the customer pays after he receives a haircut or a dental treatment). For more complex service offerings, though, a formal contract that has a legal validity is almost always established.

Therefore, in order for a service provision to take place there has to be a *provider* and a *consumer,* and a *contract* has to be established between them. The service is then consumed/accessed through some sort of *interface* (see Figure 2).

Figure 2. Four fundamental service concepts

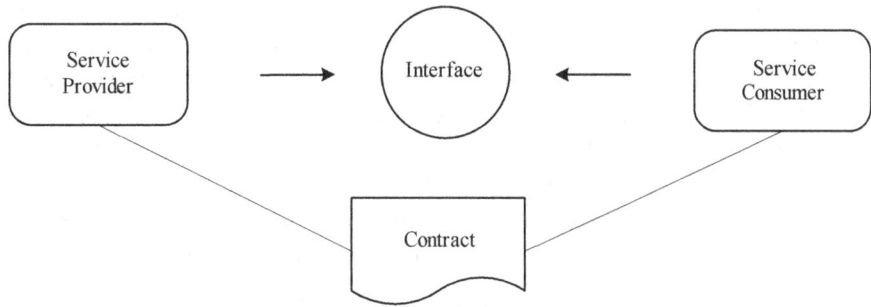

The promise of the service is access to some resources or capabilities, subject to certain conditions (or agreements) between the parties. To fulfill the service promise, the service provider needs to mobilize resources such as people, machinery information, and know-how/skills.

To make things slightly more formal, we define service as a capability offered by an entity called a provider to an entity called a consumer. We use the term *entity* to refer to different types of providers and consumers, such as organizations, individuals, and computer programs. The term *capability* means that the consumer has access (exclusive or shared) to some resources, usually for a limited period of time. The consumption/access of the resource then gives to the consumer the desired capability. Occupying, for example, a seat on a plane that is flying from location A to location B gives the passenger the capability to move from A to B. Attendance of a training course entails that, through access to instructors and training material, upon (successful) completion of the course, the trainee obtains certain knowledge or skills/capabilities.

Offering a service, as opposed to selling a capability, means that the resource is never actually owned by the consumer. This contrasts with the sale of a product where, upon completion, is owned by the consumer. For example, to get a seat on an airplane, means that the seat (resource) is made available to the passenger for a specific period (i.e., for the duration of a flight). Airlines refer to that as selling a seat, although, of course, they do not sell the physical seat—they make it available (exclusively) to a passenger for the duration of a flight.

Because of the lack of a concrete product whose ownership changes, in a service situation, services are intangible entities and thus harder to pinpoint and grasp. Service-oriented organizations do not offer tangible products that are bought and owned by customers; they provide services (i.e., access to resources and capabilities that they own and let customers use for a limited period) on a shared or exclusivity basis and, usually, for a fee. Thus, the primary business of a courier service is the capability of moving physical goods from one location to another within a specified timeframe. To be able to provide this service, a courier company owns resources such as a fleet of vehicles, drivers, warehouses and depots, as well as more staff and systems to coordinate the logistics of the operations. Additionally, the company has capabilities like the ability to coordinate the movement of such resources. The company's resources and capabilities are offered to customers on a shared and varied basis (e.g., with different promises of delivery such as next-day delivery, economy delivery, and so on). We call such services *core business services*. A core service is essentially the reason that service companies such as couriers exist.

Today, more and more companies that do not belong to the services sector, such as manufacturers, are adding services to their core offerings. Car manufacturers, for example, regularly add finance services and after sales support packages to the sale of cars. Such services are not core business services; they are additional services that add value to their customers by offering information about their vehicles, financing their purchase, and providing after sales support. We call the services that an organization builds around its core business services *support services*. In some types of industries, such as the financial one, both the core business service and the support services can be delivered/accessed electronically (i.e., without the need for any physical proximity between the resource and its consumer). Support services are not the primary business services, and they would not exist without the primary services. However, they are equally important, because they help customers acquire information about the core service (or product), evaluate it, receive it, and obtain a satisfying after-sales experience. In many industry sectors, support services matter almost as much as the primary services or products. Car manufacturers with inefficient dealership networks and inadequate after sales support will see their sales falling, as many customers tend to value such services as much as the quality of the vehicles themselves.

Figure 3. The spectrum of business services

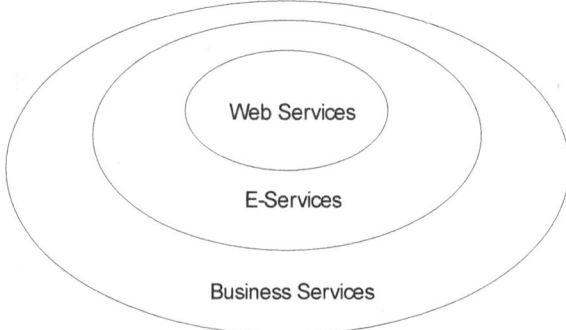

In the example of domestic services we used in the beginning of this chapter, we mentioned services such as electricity, gas, and water: Such services allow other, perhaps more complex ones, to be built on top of them.

We call such services *infrastructure services*. Without the availability of gas, water, and electricity services, it becomes very difficult to build a habitable dwelling. Infrastructure services therefore facilitate the development and provision of other services.

As we mentioned earlier, few core business services are totally virtual (i.e., do not require the manipulation of some physical resources). However, supporting services can be entirely virtual, as they often convey information about the primary services. Such services communicate information about the resource to the consumer and/or about the consumer's intention with regard to the service back to the resource owner. Because electronic data (conveying information) can travel much faster than physical entities, information services can connect the consumer and the service provider, assuming, of course, the existence of a communications link between them. Figure 3 shows the spectrum of business services, where e-services support core business services and Web services provide the infrastructure for e-services.

Resources

Resources are the capabilities of the service provider that must be in place in order to be able to provide a service. By capabilities, we mean tangible entities such as machinery as well as intangible ones (information and knowledge know-how). We said previously that service provision is usually the availability (on a limited time basis, exclusively or shared) to the consumer of a resource belonging to the provider. Such resources are physical (as an airplane seat) or intangible (as the services of a financial consultant). However, to allow the consumer to locate and access the service additional resources are needed. These are usually communications channels (e.g., an airline's Web site) or brokers (a travel agent through which the airline sells seats). Sometimes, offering a service mainly involves combining the supplier's own resources with those of third parties. The example of an airline selling flights via a travel agent is one such an example. Overall, we can say that a resource is a very generic and ubiquitous concept that includes tangible as well as intangible things. The way resources are utilized in the context of the service depends on both the type of the resource and of the service. Tangible resources are not shareable normally; they may be used by one consumer at a time. Thus, for example, a (human) travel advisor resource can only deal with one customer at a time. Intangible resources such as information on the other hand are highly *shareable* and flexible as they can be replicated infinitely and utilized in different service settings. In the following chapters, we will see how information resources can participate in the establishment and delivery of flexible electronic services (i.e., services that can be customized for individual consumers).

Service Interface

Services are accessible via interfaces. An interface is the connection between the consumer of the service and the service and defines the possible way(s) the consumer can access and consume the service. Interfaces are essential elements of a service. An interface is capable of fully and completely defining the type of service the provider is offering. An interface is also the only way a consumer can access (and therefore consume) the service. Interfaces to physical services have to be physical themselves. Everything that the passenger has to interact with in order to get to his seat on the airplane (check-in desk, waiting lounge, departure gate) is part of the interface. Accessing the service through the interface, involves a sequence of interactions between the consumer and provider of the service, that typically have to be performed in some predefined order. At a minimum, these include a *request* from the consumer and a *response* from the provider of the service. To board a flight, for example, the passenger must physically present herself to some check-in point and then follow a number of steps that comprise the check-in and boarding procedure, which will ultimately allow her to physically occupy a seat on the airplane. Some of these steps involve acts of communication between the consumer and the service interface, and some of these are via *message exchanges*. A message is a communication between the provider and consumer that is written, spoken, or involves some other kind of signaling. The message in service provision is the basic unit of communication, and involves a sender and one or more recipients. A message can be a *request* that requires a response, or a *notification* (that does not require a response). A message is sent from the consumer to the provider or vice versa, via the service interface, and usually invokes some action on the party that receives the message. As with everyday conversational acts, the participants in message-based conversations must agree on the language, vocabulary and grammar they use. Vocabulary determines the possible words used in a specific conversation, while grammar describes the allowed combinations of such words. In the context of service-based messages, the interface must specify what types of messages the service can accept and what types of responses it can generate in response to such messages.

Service Interfaces as Contracts

As mentioned earlier on, a contract (even an implicit one) is always established when a service is offered by a provider and, subsequently, accepted by a consumer.

Table 1. Service pre- and postconditions

Service consumer (passenger)	Service provider (airline)
Precondition: Passenger Check-in at least 2 hours before scheduled departure time. Bring only acceptable baggage. Pay ticket price.	**Precondition**: Refuse to carry passenger who is late, has unacceptable baggage, or has not paid ticket price
Postcondition: Fly to the wanted destination	**Postcondition**: Must ensure that passenger reaches his desired destination

Each party expects some benefits from the contract, and accepts some obligations in return. The service provider expects some kind of reward (typically a financial reward from the provider), while the consumer expects a capability as a result of the service. Usually, what one of the parties sees as an obligation is a benefit for the other. The aim of the contract document is to spell out these benefits and obligations. A contract document protects both the consumer, by specifying what to expect from the service, and the provider, by stating that the provider is not liable for failing to carry out tasks outside of the specified scope. Depending on the complexity of the service, a contract can be a multipage legal document. Many service providers issue a "terms and conditions of service" document for prospective customers. It is assumed that, by agreeing to receive the service, the customer agrees to the terms and conditions stated in the contract. A tabular form, such as the one in Table 1 (illustrating a contract between an airline and a customer), is often convenient for expressing the terms of such a contract:

Table 1 shows that a service contracts has two sides: the consumer side and the provider side, with each side having two parts: a *precondition* and a *postcondition*. The precondition states what the corresponding party must do before entering the service agreement. The postcondition states what is the outcome of the service. For the service consumer the outcome is a new capability or a change of state (e.g., the passenger is now at a new location).

Abstract, Concrete, and Aggregate Services

Because services are not tangible, they can be defined at various levels of abstraction/ detail. An abstract service refers to consumers, providers, contracts and interfaces, without providing concrete examples or details of these concepts. An airline, in the provision of a flight service, does not usually stipulate the exact aircraft that is going to be used. This allows the airline to decide which airplane to use for the service at the time of providing it, based, for example, on what happens to be available at the time. Passengers also, are usually willing to accept the service based on its abstract definition. A concrete service, on the other hand, is a *realization* or *instantiation* of an abstract service. Passengers of the airline receive concrete, not abstract services. However, all steps and interactions between consumer and provider (agreements, contracts), are based on the description of an abstract service.

Aggregate or *composite* services are services created from the combination of other services. Thus, a composite service depends on the availability of other services for its provision. In contrast, *atomic* services do not depend on any other services. A composite service for example is a holiday package services that consist of a flight, car hire, and accommodation services. Consumers may experience the composite service through a single interface, but they are aware of the service's constituting components. Often, consumers are allowed to configure a composite service, for example, by selecting the accommodation type in a holiday package. Composite and atomic services will be revisited in Chapters IV and VIII.

Service Dependencies

In addition to composition, services may also be related to each other in different ways. Collaborating organizations cooperate to provide value added services. Although services may be simple, they may also be aggregated from different sources, again reflecting real world business activities. To provide a flight service, an airline requires the services from many other providers such as the airport services (airport space, fuel and catering services, baggage handling services, insurance companies to underwrite the airline), and so on. In service dependencies, a service usually coordinates other services. In contrast to the composite service example, the consumer may not be aware of all the other services the main service depends upon. For example, flight passengers are not usually aware of or do not interact with the aircraft refueling services. In general, we say that a service X depends on another service if the availability of service X depends on the availability of service Y.

Provider vs. Consumer Service Viewpoints

Because services are intangible and often quite complex, it is useful to describe then from different perspectives or *viewpoints*. We have already define *provider* as the entity (human, organization, computer, etc.) that is responsible for providing making available the service to the consumers. A *consumer* is the entity (human, organization, computer, etc.) that uses the service for its own purposes (i.e., in order to acquire some capabilities). It is an obvious thing to point out that it makes no sense to have a service without a consumer, or consumers, for it. The consumer together with the provider and the service (which implies the existence of a contract between them), is the trinity of service-oriented thinking; you cannot have service provision without all three concepts being present. This leads to the obvious question of which of these three concepts is the most important or dominant in a service model.

Providers and consumers are two orthogonal/independent concepts in the service model. Even when both consumers and suppliers of the service belong to the same organization, it is important to consider them separately, as each of them has a distinct role in the service context that needs to be understood and described in a service model. Modeling then needs to take place from both the consumer and the provider's *viewpoints*. One of the benefits from modeling both viewpoints independently from one another is *flexibility*.

Even in circumstances where the provision and consumption of a service is under the control of the provider, it can be a mistake to manage both sides of the service collectively, because their clear separation and independence may be compromised. Service consumers may change their requirements regarding the actual functionality of the service or the terms of its usage (the service contract). Providers may alter the service also in terms of functionality or non-functional issues (e.g., performance). If the two sides are not modeled independently, the flexibility to adapt, upgrade, or substitute either side independently of the other, may be lost or compromised.

In the following we discuss the steps and actions taking in a typical service offering, both from the consumer and provider perspectives.

Services from the Consumer's Perspective

The steps below correspond to what a typical consumer would have to do to obtain a service from a provider. The steps aim to be as generic as possible. In many situations, one or more of these steps will be omitted, for example, if there is only one service provider, if the service agreement is not negotiable, and so on.

- Specify the requirements for the type of service wanted.
- Identify providers offering this service and obtain information about them and the service they provide.
- Evaluate alternative services based on the requirements and service information.
- Select the service provider that best meets the requirements.
- Obtain information about the service execution preconditions, such as the resources required for the consumption of the selected service.

- If the terms of service provision are negotiable, negotiate an agreement with the service provider about the use of the service and, if both parties come to an agreement, establish a service usage contract.

- If the service is not free, pay for the service according to the agreed payment model (one-off, per usage, etc.).

- During the delivery of the service, monitor the progress of the provided service.

- Possibly renegotiate and modify the service contract (e.g., cancel the service) during its delivery.

- When the contract expires, the service delivery is terminated.

To be possible to carry out the above steps, certain capabilities of the consumer, provider, or from a third party must be in place. The capability to compare different services (from different providers), for example, may not be offered by the provider itself but by some kind of intermediary (broker). This implies the existence of information similar to the telephone directory that lists service providers and their respective services. Below we outline the activities that take place inside each step.

Specifying the Service

To specify a service, the consumer must describe the capabilities expected to be provided by the service. Since capabilities can be a fairly abstract and/or vague concept, the consumer may decide to use terms from a universally agreed list of capabilities. "Fly as a commercial passenger" is an easily understood capability. Other capabilities may be more complicated or technical and require a more precise/formal description. To describe capabilities in a manner understood by computer programs, formal computer interpretable languages must be employed. This might be the only way that all involved parties (consumer, intermediary, provider) agree on the exact meaning of services. Such languages will be discussed in Chapters III and VI.

Identify Providers Offering this Service and Obtain Information about Them and the Service they Provide

This is essentially concerned with the issue of bringing the provider and consumer together. In the older days, this was achieved through established physical locations such as the high street of the market town, which consumers would visit to access the providers' services. Printed media, radio and television, allowed the advertisement of the service provider's location and contact information. In recent years, this has been supplemented by the Web and Internet's ability to publish information that is instantly accessible from anywhere. Although this could, in theory, provide a fee paying service, it is typically a free one, with the service provider (or another third party) paying for the cost of advertising for the service. We will revisit electronic market places and business e-directories in Chapter III.

Select a Service Provider out of many Similar ones

In these days of proliferation of service offerings and intense competition, where many companies compete for the same market segment, it is important for the consumer to be able to choose from amongst similar service offerings. Assistance in choosing a service will be typically provided by such organizations as brokers, consumer associations and other *info-mediaries*.

Obtain Information about the Service Execution Preconditions such as Resources Required for the Consumption of the Service

The consumer needs to ensure that she is capable of fulfilling the service contract from her side. A prospective passenger, for example, must ensure that she will be able to make it to the specified departure airport at least 2 hours prior to departure. Such information should be part of the service interface.

Negotiate an Agreement with the Service Provider and Establish a Service Usage Contract

In business services, there will be typically a negotiation process where both parties negotiate the terms and conditions (pre- and postconditions) of the service delivery. This negotiation includes financial and legal aspects. Other services are nonnegotiable; consumers must simply accept the provider's terms and conditions.

Monitor the Progress of the Provided Service

It is important that the consumer (or someone else on the consumer's behalf) monitor the service during its delivery to ensure that it is provided according to the agreed contract.

Possibly Renegotiate and Modify the Service Delivery (e.g., Cancel) While it is Being Delivered

It may be possible to renegotiate the terms and conditions of the service while it is being delivered. For example, airlines are often allowed to change the travel conditions by putting the passenger on a different flight or changing the departure time. Similarly, the passenger may decide to upgrade his ticket, if this is permitted.

Pay for the Service According to the Agreed Payment Model (One-Off, Per Usage and So On)

There are many different ways to pay for a service:

- No payment if the service is provided on a for free basis.
- After the service has been delivered. This is the typical scenario for consumer services such as dental, hairdressing and restaurants.
- Upfront: The service is paid for upfront. An airline will typically require the passenger fare to be paid prior to departure.
- One-off payment: An one-off payment will guarantee the consumer access to the service repeatedly (usually over a specified period of time). A membership fee for a health club will guarantee access to its facilities for a specified period (e.g., a year).
- Pay per use: This type of payment assumes that the consumer has continuous access to a service and pays for it every time he decides to use it. Some health clubs, for example, allow members to use their services by paying a fee each time they visit them.

Figure 4 shows a diagram of the service life cycle from a consumer perspective.

Services from the Provider's Perspective

The last section looked at services from the perspective of the consumer. Looking at them from the orthogonal perspective of the provider yields a rather different dimension. As we already said, primary business services are the reason that the provider of services is in business. Typically, a supplier will offer a core of primary business services accompanied by many support services. Support services are not necessarily owned or controlled by the provider (i.e., they can be subcontracted to third parties).

Figure 4. Service lifecycle (consumer perspective)

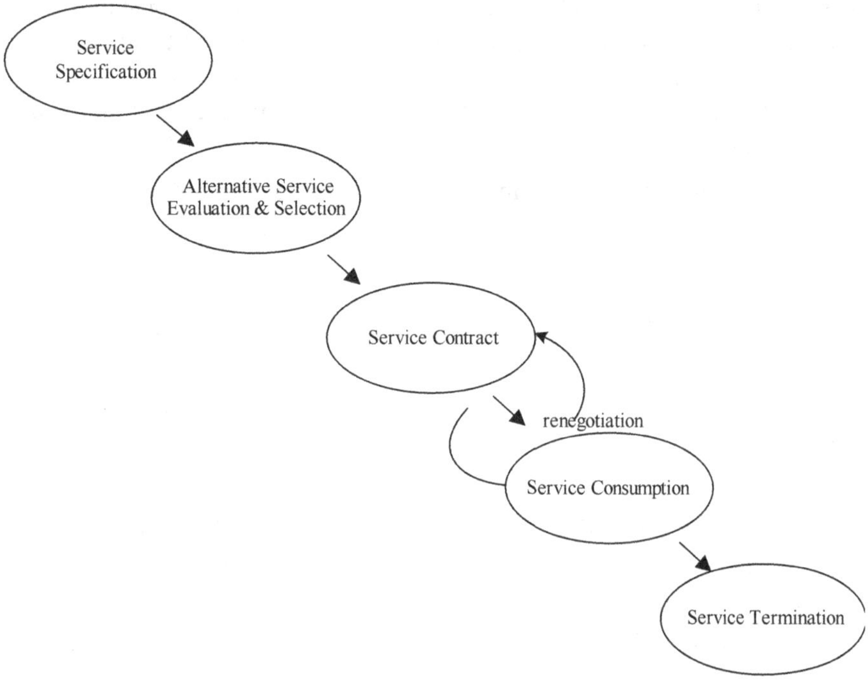

The service provider has probably managed to stay in business by selling its services, despite the competition, in a profitable way. To be able to offer the service(s) the provider must have in place a network of processes and resources, some of them owned by itself and some by its business partners. To be able to offer services, an airline company runs several processes such as crew training, flight operations, catering, and aircraft maintenance. Typically, airlines will *outsource* some of these processes (such as catering) to third parties (business partners). Outsourcing though may have various implications for the performance of the service. To be able to offer services, it is important that the airline must coordinate its own *services* with those of its partners. In order to operate a particular flight, the airline needs to co-ordinate crew re-sourcing, plane servicing and inspection, airport services, ground services, fuel and catering services. Not only such services must be operational, they must also be *synchronized*. Flight crew must be available at a specified time, the passengers must be onboard and the plane inspected and refueled before it can take off. Coordination and control of the delivery of such resources as crew, plane, supplies, and fuel is essential for the delivery of the service.

To recap, to offer a service the provider needs to mobilize a network of resources, which may include the use of services from third parties. In many cases, it is how well such coordination is done that determines the quality of the service, i.e., the things the customer values about the service. Airlines for example, subcontract many of their services that are critical for quality from the consumer perspective to third parties. One of them is catering: airlines can receive damaging criticism when their onboard catering is not up to passenger expectations. The quality of a service therefore inevitably depends on the quality of its constituting parts (other services), as well as on how well everything is coordinated.

Below are some typical steps in the life cycle of service provision, from the perspective of a provider.

Life Cycle of a Service (From a Provider Perspective)

The life cycle of a service can be seen as the sequence of the following activities/steps:

- **Service identification:** Identify what services can be provided to customers in a profitable way (this will be discussed in more detail in Chapter VII).

- **Service design:** Design the service taking into account customer expectations (quality issues) the company's strengths (e.g., unique resources, know-how, partner network resources, and so forth. This may involve combining own services with services of partners (Chapter IV).

- **Service realization:** Realize the service in a way that it is supported by the company's software systems (discussed in more detail in Chapters V and VII).

- **Service operation:** Deploy the service (discussed in Chapters VIII and IX).

- *Service monitoring and adaptation*: Monitor the service delivery and adapt it if necessary (i.e., when deviating from the agreed contract. See Chapter VIII).

- **Service retirement:** Withdraw the service. Possibly substitute it with another service.

The diagram of Figure 5 shows the service life cycle from a provider's perspective in a schematic way.

Summary of Service Concepts

Table 2 summarizes the main service concepts discussed so far, and provides short definitions and examples for each of them.

Figure 5. Service lifecycle (provider perspective)

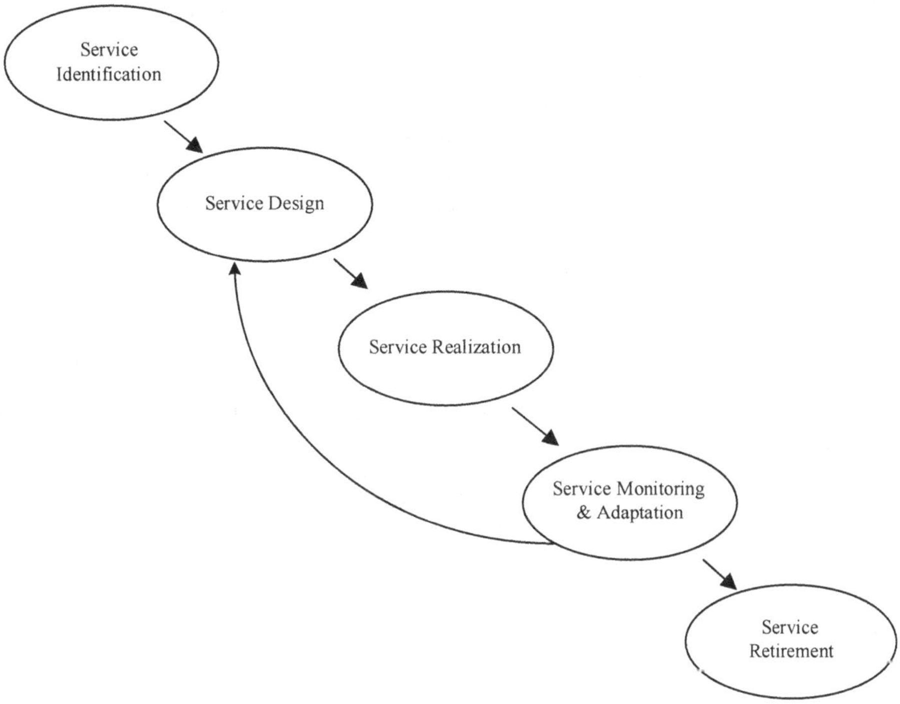

Modeling the Service-Oriented Organization

Previous sections of this chapter covered the fundamental concepts of a service such as consumer, provider, and service contract. In contrast, this section is concerned with how to apply such concepts to model a service-oriented organization. In this section we will limit the discussion to concepts and principles of service modeling (i.e., without employing specific modeling methods and languages, which is the task of Chapter VII).

A model of a service-oriented organization depicts the organization in terms of a network of coordinated services and the resources they utilize. There are several reasons why we need to model services. Service modeling is a type of *business (organization)* modeling. In general, business (organization) modeling is used in many different disciplines such as management, economics, and software development. Businesses are modeled with the purpose of improvement and optimization

Table 2. Main service concepts

SERVICE CONCEPT	SHORT DEFINITION	EXAMPLE
Service	Provision of access to a resource without ownership of it; acquisition of a capability	Fee paying passenger flights
Service supplier	An entity that supplies a service	Airline
Service consumer	An entity that consumes a service	Passenger
Service interface	A mechanism through which the service can be consumed	Airline ticket office, Airline Web booking site
Resource	A tangible (e.g., human, machinery) or intangible (process, information, or another service) entity used as part of the service	Crew, airplane, ticket reservation system
Service contract	A contract between the consumer and supplier stating the terms, conditions and obligations for entering the service for both parties	Terms and conditions of service for commercial airlines passengers (usually issued with the ticket)
Core business service	The service which coincides with the primary/core business activity of the entity that provides it	Commercial-passenger services, cargo services
Support service	A service offered in conjunction with one or more core business services.	In-flight catering service, customer loyalty services (rewards regular customers)

of the business processes, analysis and simulation using financial models, and for automation using Information Technologies (software applications, databases) Many notations and techniques for modeling business systems are in use today, most notably SADT, IDEF, UML, and others. The majority of such notations and techniques have origins in the modeling of simple production processes and/or software programs. They view organizations as functions that act upon inputs (e.g., raw materials or data) to produce outputs (i.e., finished products or other data). Such approaches to business modeling, adopt a production line approach to work which is a legacy of the manufacturing era. The production line approach, perceives a business as a production line where raw materials are gradually being transformed to finished products. This, of course, is an oversimplification for even the simplest of manufacturing organizations. A typical manufacturing process includes parallel streams of activities, synchronization amongst them, feedback, and other such concepts. However, due to the production-line way of thinking that has dominated manufacturing economies, even service industries such as finance and health are often modeled around business processes. Process models of organizations are constructed on the same principles and assumptions (i.e., that work activities are linear, synchronous, and function based). This notion (i.e., that organization processes or activities transform inputs to outputs) does not reflect accurately what happens in a service organization (i.e., how the company actually makes its money). An airline's business model is not about converting customer booking enquiries into reservations. What makes the customer choose the company over its competitor in the first place is how the airline's services are combined to create an attractive package for the customer. This can be a combination of price, choice, flexibility, quality of the in-flight service, and so on. This effective combination of tangible and intangible factors is what makes a *repeat* customer—a customer who has been satisfied by the service provision and is happy to use the same service over and over again. Thus, airlines make their money by selling services to their customers. By focusing on the modeling of an airline's processes such as check-in, flight management, and aircraft maintenance, we are not gaining any insight into what makes the airline successful (or otherwise). In other words, the passengers do not choose the airline on the basis of how it does things (processes) but rather on the basis of the capabilities and value-added benefits it offers to them. Only by modeling its services is it therefore possible to understand the basis upon which the airline competes and makes profits. Thus, services must be modeled in their own right, as first-class citizens. In this chapter, we approach service modeling in an informal way. This may be sufficient for describing services at a strategic business level; however, once we start delving into the internals of services, we need a more formal and systematic approach. Such an approach will be introduced gradually over the following chapters.

Principles of Service Modeling

A process-oriented model is one that shows coordination of activities that transform inputs to outputs. In a process oriented architecture, cohesion of the activities is a prerequisite. There must not be any slack, delays in information, on so forth as this will ultimately affect the quality of the end result which is the delivery of a product to the customer. *Quality* is what the customer values; this can be an attribute of the product or the processes associated with the product life cycle (Berry, Parasuraman, & Zeithaml, 1988). Quality attribute is something that can be objectively measured (such as the speed of delivery or the aftercare support response) or something embedded in the product itself (e.g., its design, aesthetics, etc.), that cannot be described in a quantitative manner.

A process-oriented architecture therefore integrates people, tasks, and other resources (including information) to deliver products that meet or surpass the customer expectations. The service-oriented architecture starts with a different premise: It identifies the services that can be offered to and valued by the customer, and then designs the network of resources that deliver such services, taking into consideration the company's unique strengths and those of its partners. Such services (core business services) need to be described at a level of abstraction that corresponds to real-world activities, resources, and recognizable business functions. *Service models,* therefore, allow business users to understand service descriptions and policies. We need business oriented service models because we cannot expect business users to make sense of technical jargon such as WSDL, SOAP, XML (standards reviewed in Chapter III) and the rest.

When modeling a service-oriented organization, several principles/guidelines have been proposed (i.e., CBDI Forum, 2005; Erl, 2005).

Services Often Depend on Other Services and can be Combined with each Other in Several Possible Ways

A business service can be a combination (aggregation/composition) of other services that interact with each other and with the consumer. When modeling the business service, it is important to verify that the behavior of the composite service satisfies the consumer requirements. At any time, we should be able to substitute parts of the service—that is, substitute a human delivered service for an automated one—in order to improve the overall behavior of the system (e.g., security or performance) without affecting the remaining services.

Service Identification and Selection

The capabilities and resources/assets of an organization can be combined into services in many possible ways. This aims to make efficient use of the company's resources while, at the same time, maximize the profit making potential of the services. Another goal is to maximize *the reuse* of capabilities/assets (i.e., to allow them to operate in as many different service contexts as possible).

Level of Abstraction and Granularity

One of the key design issues for service modeling is to determine the *level of abstraction* and *granularity* of each service. Services must be modeled in a way that hides complexity and makes them manageable, flexible, and reusable as possible. Modeling should consider carefully what level of abstraction is required at each stage, and choose the appropriate granularity accordingly. In other words, business people require service models of different granularity than computer experts.

Service Modeling that is Independent from its Realization

Service modeling should be carried out, initially, without reference to implementation technologies, in order to determine their correct purpose and granularity. Ultimately, some of these business level services will either be realized as new e-services, become based on the functionality of existing systems, or acquired from third party service providers. What is important is to maintain traceability between the (logical) business services and their realization (e-services). The principles of service traceability are discussed in more detail in Chapters V and VII.

Service Specification via its Interface Description

A core principle of service-oriented modeling is that the service interface should be the only thing visible to the consumer. In software engineering, this principle is called *interface-based design* or *design by contract* (Meyer, 1986). The interfaces of services described at a business level of abstraction are going to be business interfaces rather than technical ones (i.e., software component interfaces). However, by following this principle, we are capable of tracing business interfaces through to Web-service (software) interfaces, as we will demonstrate in Chapter VII.

Service Contracts

As we previously argued, a contract is a key concept in service-oriented thinking. The formal contract is the instrument that allows us to select remote services and trust their provision according to the *service level agreements* (SLAs) specified in the contract. Contracts are also important for both sides of the service: Consumers can change providers that offer the same contract, based on issues such as pricing. Providers can internally modify and improve the service while maintaining a consistent contract with the consumers.

Understanding Services from Both Provider and Consumer Viewpoints

Providers and consumers of services have different requirements and viewpoints (van Eck & Wieringa, 2003). From the provider viewpoint, services must be designed with a view of minimizing the risk from third party services. If the service provider is dependent upon a few key third parties, this can represent a potential risk. We can reduce such dependencies by making the design of the service dependencies more flexible; this, however, may lead to the contradicting goals of making a very general interface design, versus making an optimized efficient one.

Model Services at a Granularity that Matches Customer Requirements

Business services should be immediately recognized as such by consumers. The right level of abstraction to expose as a service is, therefore, the level of functionality that is recognizable by, and useful to, the consumer of the service. There is no point in publishing, for example, technical flight data for passengers who simply want an estimated arrival time. If the right level of abstraction has been identified, there is a good chance that the service level agreements (contract) can be formally published and used (i.e., monitored and enforced).

Service Implementation must be Hidden from the Consumer

Although there are situations where the service realization details need to be known by the consumer (e.g., for issues of trust or when provider and consumer are the same entity), it makes good design practice to hide the implementation knowledge from the consumer. The service consumer should not make any other assumptions about the service availability and usage, apart from what is stated in the service interface and contract. As we argued above, this offers benefits both to the consumer (who is given the flexibility to switch to different services) and to the provider (who can modify the service implementation without changing its interface).

Formalized Service Functionality Description

Publishing is a significant issue for the service provider. Publishing the technical service contract will be the concern of Chapter III, where protocols such as WSDL and UDDI will be introduced; however, there is potentially much more to service publishing. The specification of a service needs to define not just the interface, but also the service behavior that is not necessarily exposed by the interface. In addition, there is the question of dependencies, both functional and nonfunctional, and the issue of trust. Also, preconditions must be in place prior to execution, and then the services must certify the post conditional state(s), perhaps prior to committing the changes. Much of this information must be captured in the specification of the service. Chapter VI discusses methods for formally describing such information.

Service-Oriented Business Architecture

Business architecture is the internal organization of a company's units and departments, resources (people, buildings, machinery, etc.) and ways of doing things (activities, processes). Few businesses have been designed according to some prespecified architecture/blueprint; most have evolved to their current form through both systematic and random changes caused by a combination of internal and external causes.

A service-oriented architecture is one where the company is not organized around functions, departments or processes but around services. Such architecture should be the ideal business organization of services companies. Service organizations have no physical product to manufacture, store, or distribute. In such organizations, the core business model is no longer based on the conversion of raw materials into finished goods. Instead, the company buys in services and sells services, and the core value proposition is the conversion of input services into output services. This calls for a very different kind of business architecture model that allows services to combine and interact to make other services.

A service-based business architecture is organized around the principle of giving the customer a capability, being that a desired state of himself, or of a product, or the ability to do things. It is very common for an enterprise to buy in services of one kind, and sell services of a different kind. For example, an airport authority buys in a range of responsibility-based maintenance services and sells landing slots to airlines. A rail network operator may subcontract track maintenance to engineering firms and sell network capacity to train operators.

One of the challenges facing such enterprises is that the mapping between the input services and the output services is often very complex. If you want to deliver a given quality of service to your customers, you need to convert this service level agreement into a series of separate service levels, which are then negotiated with your subcontractors (Sprott, 2004).

Service-Modeling Notation

To visualize a service-oriented architecture at a strategic business level, it is useful to devise a simple and informal diagrammatic notation that depicts a service, its main components and the service interactions. We propose modeling constructs for each of the following service concepts, as in Table 3.

The model of Figure 6 shows a flight business service and its supporting network of services. We use this model as a logical architectural model (i.e., to describe the core business services, their interfaces and their dependencies) without revealing

Table 3. Service modeling notation

The service itself: We use a rectangle to show a service with the name of the service appearing inside the rectangle.	Service name
The service interface. We use a circle to model a service interface. Services can have multiple interfaces. A straight line connects a service to its interface. The name of the interface is shown inside the circle.	Interface name
The dependency relationship between two services or between a service and the resources it uses. We use a dotted arrow to show service dependency	·············▶
Messages exchanged between services and consumers are shown using an arrow connecting them. Usually, the name of the message appears above the arrow	Message name —▶
The packaging of services. We use a dotted rectangle in which we include the services we want to package. The name of the package (aggregate service) is also shown as label	Package name
The service consumer. We use a rectangle to represent the service consumer with the word <<consumer>> and the type/role of the consumer as labels	<<consumer>>
The resources the service consumes. As the type of such resources can vary, we use as label the type of resource enclosed in '<<>>'	<<resource>>

any implementation details. The service consumer (the passenger) interacts with the service through its "check-in" and "board flight" interface. In Figure 6, the flight service is shown as having two more interfaces ("book flight" and "board flight"). All these are business-level interfaces rather than software ones. The "book flight" interface can be realized by the booking desk of a travel agent company, the airline's office at the airport, or a Web page in a Web site. A "book flight" interface is instantly recognized by both customers and business staff of the airline, as this is the contact point for customers wishing to book a flight. Similarly, a "get flight" information interface can be realized by a notice board, a telephone-based service, or a Web-based one.

As shown in Figure 6, the "flight" service is supported by a network of other services ("airplane inspection", "refueling" and so on). Although not shown in the diagram, some of these services are provided by third parties (i.e., business partners of the airline). If we used the aforementioned model for other purposes, for example, to identify outsource or in-source opportunities, it would have been worthwhile to include the names of the service providers in the diagram.

As one might argue, the flight service is rather too abstract as it encompasses lots of different types of consumers and possible types of interaction with the airline. However, what is considered to be the "right" level of the service is relative, as it depends on the purpose of the model. The above service model is a strategic one,

Figure 6. Services model for an airline

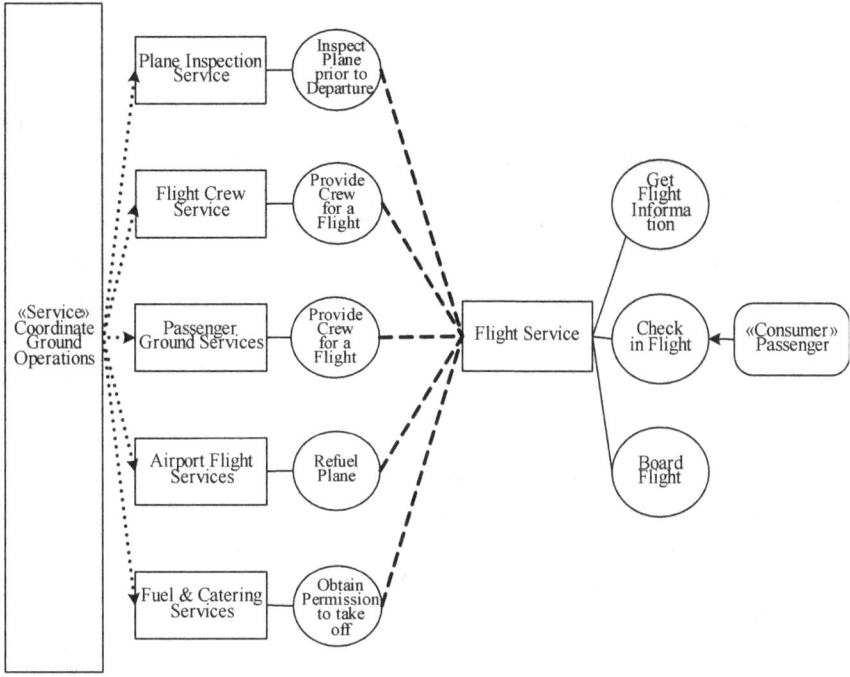

Figure7. A composite service

because it provides an overview of the flight service together with the network of supporting services and other resources. The flight service could indeed by seen as a package of related ("support") services such as "check in services," "airport passenger services," and "departure services." Check in services assist the customer to check in for a flight, perhaps by employing alternative methods such telephone or the company's Web site. To model the service components (constituting services), we use the service package notation as shown in Figure 7.

Chapter Summary

This chapter has discussed the ubiquitous concept of a *service*, one that encompasses the myriad business service types we encounter in everyday life. Although covering a diverse ground of businesses and activities, services share some fundamental common characteristics. We discussed concepts such as service consumer, service provider, contract, and interface before we moved to the subject of service modeling. A very important principle in service modeling is the separation of the consumer and provider viewpoints. Modeling the service from the consumer perspective allows us to improve the service to meet the consumers' quality expectations. Modeling the service from the providers' perspective, on the other hand, allows us to improve the service (e.g., by making it more cost effective to offer) whilst maintaining a consistent interface to the consumer. Services are accessible through interfaces that act as contracts between the service provider and consumer. Ideally, everything the consumers need to know about the service should be documented in the interface—all service implementation should be transparent to them. In this chapter we also discussed the issue of service-oriented organizations. Service-oriented modeling abandons the old production-line view of organizations and shows them as networks of interacting services, processes, and resources. The informal graphical service models we used in this chapter served to illustrate service-oriented organizations at a strategic level. We are going to revisit service-oriented modeling in Chapter VII using more formally defined modeling notations. In the meantime, the next chapter is concerned with the building blocks for service realization, Web services.

References

Berry, L. L., Parasuraman, A., & Zeithaml, V. A. (1988). The service quality puzzle. *Business Horizons, 31*(5), 35-43.

CBDI Forum. (2005). *Basic service concepts.* Retrieved March 15, 2007, from http://www.cbdiforum.com/public/events/workshops/downloads/Communicating_SOA_files/frame.htm

Erl, T. (2005). *Core principles for service-oriented architectures.* Retrieved March 15, 2007, from http://www.looselycoupled.com/opinion/2005/erl-core-infr0815.html

Gordijn, J., & Janssen, M. (2003). *Introduction to the First International E-Services Workshop.* Paper presented at the First International E-Services Workshop (ICEC 03), Pittsburgh, PA.

Jones, S. (2005). Toward an acceptable definition of service. *IEEE Software, 22*(3) 87-93.

Meyer, B. (1986). *Design by contract* (Tech. Rep. TR-EI-12/CO). Interactive Software Engineering.

OASIS. (2006). *Reference model for service-oriented architecture 1.0.* Retrieved March 17, 2007, from http://www.oasis-open.org/committees/tc_home. php?wg_abbrev=soa-rm

Sprott, D. (2004). *Service oriented architecture: An introduction for managers* (CBDI report). Retrieved September 3, 2007, from ftp://ftp.software.ibm. com/software/websphere/pdf/cbdireport_soa_july2004.pdf

Van Eck, P., & Wieringa, R. (2003). Requirements engineering for serviceoriented computing: A position paper. Paper presented at the first International E-Services Workshop (ICEC 03), Pittsburgh, PA.

W3C. (2004). *Web services architecture.* Retrieved March 15, 2007, from http:// www.w3.org/TR/ws-arch/

Section II

Service Languages and Standards

Chapter III

Standards for Web Services

Introduction

Chapter II presented the main concepts underlying business services. Ultimately, as this book proposes, business services need to be decomposed into networks of executable Web services. Web services are the primary software technology available today that closely matches the characteristics of business services. To understand the mapping from business to Web services, we need to understand the fundamental characteristics of the latter. This chapter therefore will introduce the main Web services concepts and standards. It does not intend to be a comprehensive description of all standards applicable to Web services, as many of them are still in a state of flux. It focuses instead on the more important and stable standards. All such standards are fully and precisely defined and maintained by the organizations that have defined and endorsed them, such as the World Wide Web Consortium (http://w3c.org), the OASIS organization (http://www.oasis-open.org) and others. We advise readers to visit periodically the Web sites describing the various standards to obtain the up to date versions.

Table 1. Mapping e-services to Web services standards

E-SERVICE CONCEPT/FEATURE	CORRESPONDING WEB SERVICE CONCEPTS AND STANDARDS
Language for e-service specification	XML, XML Schema
Formal service description/contract	WSDL
Channels through which the service can be consumed	Port types, ports
Advertisement of the service	UDDI, ebXML repositories
Interaction with the service	SOAP

Table 1 sets the context of this chapter by mapping major concepts and features of e-services to Web service technologies and standards. Although, as shown in Table 1, Web services provide all the basic *ingredients* (standards/concepts) for implementing and delivering e-services, it does not mean that such standards and technologies are yet fully mature/useable or sufficient. Their limitations will be discussed in the remaining of this chapter.

Web Services Definitions

According to the World Wide Web Consortium (W3C), a Web service is a software system designed to support interoperable machine-to-machine interaction over a network (W3C, 2004). A Web service has an interface that is described in a machine-processable format such as the XML-based WSDL (described later in this chapter).

A simplified definition of Web services is as a collection of functions that are packaged as a single unit and exposed, or made available, over a network for use by other software programs (Cayron, 2002).

As seen from the above definition, a Web service has many of the elements required to realize e-services such as an interface and message-based interaction over a network between provider and consumer. Therefore using Web services to deliver e-services has several advantages, namely:

- Web services are a new emerging standard that has been created by the W3C Consortium which is also responsible for other Web standards such as HTML and HTTP. Being a universal standard, means that services delivered as Web services have more chances of reaching as many consumers as possible. This would have not been possible to the same extent if services use a proprietary technology known and available to only a few.

- Research and development in Web services has resulted in several technologies that can be used to realize provider and consumer requirements for service delivery such as privacy, security, two way interactions during service delivery, and so on.

- Web services can be even used as *wrappers* to other service delivery methods and channels. So for example if a company has implemented a service delivery method using telephony, it can *wrap* Web services around this method and effectively reuse it. In this way the company can leverage its existing investments

However, there are limits to the potential applicability of Web services as a service delivery technology. As explained earlier on, Web services are originally and primarily a technique for invoking remotely the functionality of a software application. This method is not suited for all possible types of e-service delivery; this creates a potential limitation of Web services as an enabler of e-services.

The XML Language

Web services standards cannot be effectively understood or explained without reference to their underpinnings, the extensible markup language (XML). XML (W3C, 2006) is a simple, very flexible text format derived from another earlier data definition language, SGML. Originally designed to meet the challenges of large-scale electronic publishing, XML is also playing an increasingly important role in the exchange of a wide variety of data on the Web and elsewhere. XML describes a class of data objects called *XML documents* and partially describes the behavior of computer programs that process them.

XML documents are made up of storage units called *entities*, which contain either parsed or unparsed data. Parsed data is made up of *characters*, some of which form *character data* and some of which form *markup data*. Markup encodes a description of the document's storage layout and logical structure. XML provides a mechanism to impose constraints on the storage layout and logical structure.

The main differences between XML and Web's main language the *hypertext markup language* (HTML) are:

- XML is not a replacement for HTML.

- XML and HTML were designed with different goals (i.e., XML was designed to describe data and to focus on what data is; HTML was designed to display data and to focus on how data looks).

Listing 1. XML document containing the profile of customer John Smith

```
<Customer>
        <Name> John Smith </Name>
        <Age>30</Age>
        <MaritalStatus> Married</MaritialStatus>
        < NumberOfChildenNumber>0</ NumberOfChildren>
        < Job_Title>Programmer</ Job_Title>
</Customer>
```

- HTML is about displaying information, XML is about describing information.
- XML allows new elements to be defined by the programmer.
- XML separates presentation from data.
- HTML is for Web browsers; XML is for data transfer.

An example of an XML document containing information about a customer with name John Smith is illustrated in Listing 1.

This document contains data (*profile*) of a *customer*, perhaps a customer of an e-service. Words enclosed between "<" and ">" are called *tags*. They represent the types of data this XML file contains. Words contained between tags are the actual data. Therefore <Age> and </Age> are the tags used for the *age* data type, and *30* is the actual age data, which in this particular example represents the age of customer John Smith. The XML document of Listing 1 is formatted according to an *XML schema*. The concept of XML schemas is discussed in the following section.

XML Schema Languages

XML schemas express shared vocabularies and allow rules constraining the structure and data contents to be specified. They provide a means for defining the structure, content and semantics of XML documents. There are currently a number of different schema language representations. In this section, a description of the two most known schema languages, DTD, and XSD will be given.

Document Type Definition (DTD)

The *document type definition* (W3C, 2007) specifies the structure of an XML document to allow XML parsers to understand and interpret the document's contents. The DTD contains the list of tags, which are allowed within the XML document along with their types and attributes.

More specifically, the DTD defines how elements relate to one another within the document's tree structure and specifies which attributes may be used with which elements. Therefore, the DTD constrains the element types that can be incorporated in the document and determines its conformance. An XML document, which conforms to its DTD, is said to be *valid*.

Although DTDs appeared before XSD (described in the next section), they have now lost popularity in comparison to XSDs.

An XML language is defined in a DTD. The DTD is either contained in a *"<!DOC-TYPE>"* tag, contained in an external file and referenced from a *"<!DOCTYPE>"* tag, or both.

XML provides an application independent way of sharing data. With a DTD, independent groups of people can agree to use a common DTD for interchanging data. An application can use a standard DTD to verify that the data sent or received from the outside world is valid.

The DTD of Listing 2 states that a customer comprises a customer name and customer address. In turn, address comprises a street, city, state and zip elements.

XML Schema Definition Language (W3C, 2004)

An *XML schema definition* (XSD) consists of components such as type definitions and element declarations. These can be used to assess the validity of well-formed

Listing 2. A DTD for customer profiles

```
<!ELEMENT Customer (Name, Address+)>
<!ELEMENT Name  (#PCDATA)>
<!ELEMENT Address (Street+,City,State)>
<!ELEMENT Street (#PCDATA)>
<!ELEMENT City (#PCDATA)>
<!ELEMENT State (#PCDATA)>
<!ELEMENT Zip (#PCDATA)>
```

element and attribute information items, and furthermore may specify augmentations to those items and their descendants. This augmentation makes explicit information which may have been implicit in the original document, such as normalized and/or default values for attributes and elements and the types of element and attribute information items

Schema-validity assessment has two aspects:

- Determining local schema validity—that is, whether an element or attribute information item satisfies the constraints embodied in the relevant components of an XML schema.

- Synthesizing an overall validation outcome for the item, combining local schema validity with the results of schema-validity assessments of its descendants, if any.

Listing 3 shows the XML schema for the customer entity.

Benefits of the XML Schema Language

XML schema is therefore a more advanced version of DTD. DTD has several disadvantages from schema, such as lack of support for strong data typing, syntax that is not XML based, and lack of expandability. Schema was introduced to overcome those drawbacks. The most important advantages of XML schema are:

- Syntax is very similar to XML. This means that the schema can be edited by using any XML editor.

Listing 3. Sample XML schema for customer profiles

```
<?xml version="1.0" ?>
- <Schema name="CustomerProfile.xsd" xmlns="urn:schemas-microsoft-com:xml-data" xmlns:
dt="urn:schemas-microsoft-com:datatypes">
  <ElementType dt:type="string" name="Name" content="textOnly" model="closed" />
  <ElementType dt:type="string" name="Address" content="textOnly" model="closed" />
  <ElementType dt:type="int" name="Age" content="textOnly" model="closed" />
  <ElementType dt:type="string" name="Marital_Status" content="textOnly" model="closed" />
  <ElementType dt:type="int" name="NChildren" content="textOnly" model="closed" />
  <ElementType dt:type="string" name="Employed" content="textOnly" model="closed" />
```

- Data types are not limited to string, integer, long, float; it also supports custom data types.

- XSDs are more robust and flexible than DTDs. Schemas are XML documents, unlike DTDs, which contain non-XML syntax. Schemas also support namespaces, which are required to avoid naming conflicts, and offer more extensive data type and inheritance support.

- XML schema provides content-based validation (the order in which the child elements are nested) and also provides data type validations. Its functionality and validation checks are supported for simple and complex data types.

- XML schema is easily extendible to incorporate more features in the future.

XML provides a simple way of representing data, but it says nothing about the standard set of data types available and how to extend that set (e.g., whether an integer is a 16, 32, or 64 bit). Such details are important to enable interoperability. The XML schema (XSD) specifies some built-in types and language to define additional types. Web services platforms use XSD as their type system. When a Web service is build, the data types that are used must be translated to XSD types to conform to the Web services standards.

XPath

XPath (Kay, 2005) is a W3C standard that consists of a syntax for defining parts of an XML document. It uses path expressions to navigate through XML documents. XPath is a major element in XSLT. Without XPath knowledge it is not possible to create XSLT documents.

XPath uses path expressions to select nodes or node-sets in an XML document. These path expressions look similar to the structures used to organize directories and files in a computer system. XPath includes over 100 built-in functions for string values, numeric values, date and time comparison, node and name manipulation, sequence manipulation, boolean values, and so on.

In XPath, there are seven kinds of nodes: *element, attribute, text, namespace, processing-instruction, comment, and document (root) nodes*. XML documents are treated as trees of nodes. The root of the tree is called the document node (or root node).

The XML document of Listing 4 records information about a customer. More specifically, it consists of two sections, one containing the personal details of the customer and one containing information about all the purchases that he or she has made from the company. This consists of information about the type of purchase (book, CD, etc.) as well as the value and date of the purchase.

Example of nodes in the XML document in Listing 4 are:

<customer> (document node)

<age>30</age> (element node)

Atomic values are nodes with no children or parent (e.g., *John Smith* and *30*).

Items are atomic values or nodes. Each element and attribute has one parent. In the previous example; the personal element is the parent of the name, age, and dateof-birth elements. Element nodes may have zero, one, or more children. In Listing 4, the purchasetype, purchasedate, purchasevaule elements are all children of the purchase element.

Siblings are nodes that have the same parent. In the previous example; the name, age, and date of birth elements are all siblings. Ancestors are a node's parent, parent's parent, and so on. In the customer XML schema example; the ancestors of the age element are the customer personal data element and the customer element. Descendants are a node's children, children's children, etc.

XPath uses path expressions to select nodes in an XML document. The node is selected by following a path or steps. The most common path expressions are shown in Listing 5.

Listing 4. An XML document storing customer information

```
<?xml version="1.0" encoding="ISO-8859-1"?>
<customer>
 <personal data>
  <name>John Smith</name>
  <dateofbirth> < 1 December 1977> </dateofbirth>
  <age>30</age>
 </personal data>
 <purchases>
  <purchase>
   <purchasetype> book> ></purchasetype>
    <purchasedate> 10 March 2007 </purchasedate>
    <purchasevalue> 30 </purchasevalue>
  </purchase>
  <purchase>
   <purchasetype> cd </purchasetype>
    <purchasedate> 20 May  2007 </purchasedate>
     <purchasevalue> 20 </purchasevalue>
  </purchase>
 </purchases>
</customer>
```

Listing 5. Common path expressions

Expression	Description
nodename	Selects all child nodes of the node
/	Selects from the root node
//	Selects nodes in the document from the current node that match the selection, no matter where they are
.	Selects the current node
..	Selects the parent of the current node

Listing 6. Path expressions

Path Expression	Result
customer	Selects all the child nodes of the customer element
/customer	Selects the root element customer **Note:** If the path starts with a slash (/) it always represents an absolute path to an element!
personal/	Selects all elements that are children of personal
//personal	Selects all personal elements no matter where they are in the document
customer//personal	Selects all personal elements that are descendant of the customer element, no matter where they are under the customer element

Listing 7. Path expressions with predicates

Path Expression	Result
/purchases/purchase[1]	Selects the first purchase element that is the child of the purchases element
/purchases/purchase[last()]	Selects the last purchase element that is the child of the purchases element
/purchases/purchase[last()-1]	Selects the last but one purchase element that is the child of the purchases element
/purchases/purchase[position()<3]	Selects the first two purchase elements that are children of the purchases element
/purchases/purchase[price>20]	Selects all the elements of the element that have a purchase value element with a value greater than 20
/purchases/purchase[price>25]/ purchasetype	Selects all the purchase type elements of the purchase elements of the purchases element that have a purchase value element with a value greater than 25

Listing 6 shows some path expressions that apply to the previous customer schema.

Predicates are used to find a specific node or a node that contains a specific value. They are always embedded in square brackets. Listing 7 contains some path expressions with predicates as well as the result of the expressions:

For selecting unknown nodes, XPath uses wildcards, as in Listing 8.

Listing 9 shows some path expressions and the result of the expressions:

By using the | operator in an XPath expression, several paths can be selected. Listing 10 contains some path expressions and the result of the expressions.

An XPath axis defines a node-set relative to the current node.

A location path can be absolute or relative. An absolute location path starts with a slash (/) and a relative location path does not. In both cases the location path consists of one or more steps, each separated by a slash. For example, an absolute location path looks like:

Listing 8. XPath wildcards

Wildcard	Description
*	Matches any element node
@*	Matches any attribute node
node()	Matches any node of any kind

Listing 9. Path expressions

Path Expression	Result
/purchase/*	Selects all the child nodes of the purchases element
//*	Selects all elements in the document
//title[@*]	Selects all title elements which have any attribute

Listing 10. Path expressions results

Path Expression	Result
//purchase/purchasedate	//purchase/ purchasevalue	Selects all the purchasedate and purchasevalue elements of all purchase elements
//purchasedate	//purchasevalue	Selects all the purchasedate and purchasevalue elements in the document

/step/step/...

A relative location path looks like:

step/step/...

Each step is evaluated against the nodes in the current node-set. A step consists of:

- An axis (defines the tree-relationship between the selected nodes and the current node)
- A node-test (identifies a node within an axis)
- Zero or more predicates (to further refine the selected node-set)

The syntax for a location step is: *axisname::nodetest[predicate]*

Listing 11. Xpath axis

AxisName	Result
Ancestor	Selects all ancestors (parent, grandparent, etc.) of the current node
ancestor-or-self	Selects all ancestors (parent, grandparent, etc.) of the current node and the current node itself
Attribute	Selects all attributes of the current node
Child	Selects all children of the current node
Descendant	Selects all descendants (children, grandchildren, etc.) of the current node
Descendant-or-self	Selects all descendants (children, grandchildren, etc.) of the current node and the current node itself
Following	Selects everything in the document after the closing tag of the current node
Following-sibling	Selects all siblings after the current node
Namespace	Selects all namespace nodes of the current node
Parent	Selects the parent of the current node
Preceding	Selects everything in the document that is before the start tag of the current node
Preceding-sibling	Selects all siblings before the current node
Self	Selects the current node

Examples

The following expression selects all the purchase nodes under the purchases element:

xmlDoc.selectNodes("/purchases/purchase")

The following expression selects only the first purchase node under the purchases element:

xmlDoc.selectNodes("/purchases/purchase[0]")

The following expressions selects the text from all the purchasedate nodes:

xmlDoc.selectNodes("/customer/purchases/purchase/purchasedate/text()")

XSLT

XSLT (Kay, 2005) is a language used to transform XML document into other XML document, or another type of document in Web languages, such as HTML or XHTML. XSLT, which stands for *extensible style sheet language transformations*, is part of XSL (*extensible style sheet language*). XSL consist of three parts:

Listing 12. Axis examples

Example	Result
child::purchase	Selects all purchase nodes that are children of the current node
child::*	Selects all children of the current node
attribute::*	Selects all attributes of the current node
child::text()	Selects all text child nodes of the current node
child::node()	Selects all child nodes of the current node
descendant::purchase	Selects all purchase descendants of the current node
ancestor::purchase	Selects all purchase ancestors of the current node
ancestor-or-self::purchase	Selects all purchase ancestors of the current node—and the current as well if it is a purchase node
child::*/child::purchasevalue	Selects all purchasevalue grandchildren of the current node

- XSLT
- XPath which is also a language for defining parts of a XML document
- XSL-FO, a language for formatting XML documents

The main functionality of XSLT is the transformation of one XML document to another, and also the addition or removal of new elements into the output file. It can sort or rearrange the XML file elements and make decisions, based on conditions, about which elements to display. XSLT uses XPath in order to define matching patterns for the purpose of transformation. XPath, introduced in the previous section, is used to navigate through elements and attributes in XML documents. In the transformation process, XSLT uses XPath to define parts of the source document that should match one or more predefined templates. When a match is found, XSLT will transform the matching part of the source document into the result document.

XSLT became a Web standard by a W3C recommendation on November 16, 1999. Therefore, according to W3C, a transformation expressed in XSLT describes rules for transforming a source tree into a result tree. The transformation is achieved by associating patterns with templates. A pattern is matched against elements in the source tree. A template is instantiated to create part of the result tree. The result tree is separate from the source tree. The structure of the result tree can be completely different from the structure of the source tree. In constructing the result tree, elements from the source tree can be filtered and reordered, and arbitrary structure can be added.

Style-Sheet Declaration

The root element that declares the document to be an XSL style sheet is <xsl:stylesheet> or <xsl:transform>. The way to declare an XSL style sheet according to the W3C XSLT Recommendation is:

```
<xsl:stylesheet version="1.0"
xmlns:xsl="http://www.w3.org/1999/XSL/Transform">
```

or

```
<xsl:transform version="1.0"
xmlns:xsl="http://www.w3.org/1999/XSL/Transform">
```

To get access to the XSLT elements, attributes and features the XSLT namespace must be displayed at the top of the document.

The xmlns:xsl="http://www.w3.org/1999/XSL/Transform" points to the official W3C XSLT namespace. The following example shows how the XML document ("customer.xml") of Listing 13, is transformed into XHTML file that contains a list of all purchases made by that particular client including their type and value.

First an XSL Style Sheet ("customer.xsl") nust be created using the following transformation template (Listing 14).

The XSL style sheet must then be referenced inside the XML document ("customer. xml").

The <xsl:template> element is used for building templates. The **match** attribute is used to associate a template with an XML element. The match attribute can also be used to define a template for the entire XML document. The value of the match attribute is an XPath expression (see Listing 16).

The **<xsl:template>** element defines a template. The **match="/"** attribute associates the template with the root of the XML source document. The content inside the <xsl:template> element defines some HTML to write to the output. The last two lines define the end of the template and the end of the style sheet. The <xsl: value-of> element can be used to extract the value of an XML element and add it

Listing 13. Customer schema

```
<?xml version="1.0" encoding="ISO-8859-1"?>
<customer>
 <personal data>
  <name>John Smith</name>
  <dateofbirth> < 1 December 1977> </dateofbirth>
   <age>30</age>
 </personal data>
 <purchases>
  <purchase>
   <purchasetype>  book> ></purchasetype>
    <purchasedate>  10 March 2007 </purchasedate>
    <purchasevalue> 30 </purchasevalue>
   </purchase>
  <purchase>
   <purchasetype>  cd </purchasetype>
    <purchasedate>  20 May  2007 </purchasedate>
     <purchasevalue> 20 </purchasevalue>
   </purchase>
  </purchases>
</customer>
```

to the output stream of the transformation (see Listing 17).

The result of the transformation above will look like this:

Summary of purchases

Purchase type	Value
book	30

In this example only one line of data was copied from the XML document to the output.

However, by using the **<xsl:for-each>** element we can loop through the XML elements, and display all of the records. The XSL <xsl:for-each> element can be used to select every XML element of a specified node-set (see Listing 18).

The result of the transformation above will look like the following table:

Listing 14. Customer transformation template

```
<?xml version="1.0" encoding="ISO-8859-1"?>
<xsl:stylesheet version-"1.0"
xmlns:xsl="http://www.w3.org/1999/XSL/Transform">
<xsl:template match="/">
 <html>
 <body>
  <h2>Purchases</h2>
  <table border="1">
  <tr bgcolor="#9acd32">
   <th align="left">purchasetype</th>
   <th align="left">purchasevalue</th>
  </tr>
  <xsl:for-each select="customer/purchases/purchase">
  <tr>
   <td><xsl:value-of select="purchasetype"/></td>
   <td><xsl:value-of select="purchasevalue"/></td>
  </tr>
  </xsl:for-each>
  </table>
 </body>
 </html>
</xsl:template>
</xsl:stylesheet>
```

Listing 15. Customer XSL stylesheet

Listing 16. XPath expressions

```
<?xml version="1.0" encoding="ISO-
8859-1"?>
<?xml-stylesheet type="text/xsl"
href="customer.xsl"?>
<?xml version="1.0" encoding="ISO-
8859-1"?>
<customer>
 <personal data>
  <name>John Smith</name>
  <dateofbirth> < 1 December 1977>
</dateofbirth>
   <age>30</age>
 </personal data>
 <purchases>
  <purchase>
   <purchasetype> book> ></
purchasetype>
   <purchasedate> 10 March 2007
</purchasedate>
   <purchasevalue> 30 </
purchasevalue>
   </purchase>
  <purchase>
   <purchasetype> cd </purchasetype>
   <purchasedate> 20 May 2007
</purchasedate>
    <purchasevalue> 20 </
purchasevalue>
   </purchase>
 </purchases>
</customer>
```

```
<?xml version="1.0" encoding="ISO-
8859-1"?>
<xsl:stylesheet version="1.0"
xmlns:xsl="http://www.w3.org/1999/XSL/
Transform">
<xsl:template match="/">
 <html>
 <body>
  <h2>Summary of customer
purchases</h2>
   <table border="1">
    <tr bgcolor="#9acd32">
     <th>purchasetype</th>
     <th>purchasevalue</th>
    </tr>
    <tr>
     <td>.</td>
     <td>.</td>
    </tr>
   </table>
 </body>
 </html>
</xsl:template>
</xsl:stylesheet>
```

Summary of purchases

Purchase type	Value
book	30
cd	20

We can also filter the output from the XML file by adding a criterion to the select attribute in the <xsl:for-each> element. Valid filter operators are:

Listing 17. Customer.xsl "value-of" example

```
<?xml version="1.0" encoding="ISO-8859-1"?>
<xsl:stylesheet version="1.0"
xmlns:xsl="http://www.w3.org/1999/XSL/Transform">
<xsl:template match="/">
 <html>
 <body>
  <h2>Summary of purchases</h2>
  <table border="1">
   <tr bgcolor="#9acd32">
    <th>Purchase type</th>
    <th>Value</th>
   </tr>
   <tr>
    <td><xsl:value-of select="customer/purchases/purchase/purchasetype"/></td>
    <td><xsl:value-of select=" customer/purchases/purchase/purchasetype "/></td>
   </tr>
  </table>
 </body>
 </html>
</xsl:template>
</xsl:stylesheet>
```

- • = (equal)
- • != (not equal)
- • < less than
- • > greater than

In Listing 19, the XSLT selects only purchases that were cds and outputs also the date the purchase was made.

The result of the previous transformation will look like this:

Summary of CD purchases

Date	Value
20 may 2007	20

Other XSLT constructs for manipulating XML documents include:

Listing 18. Customer.xsl "for-each" example

```
<?xml version="1.0" encoding="ISO-8859-1"?>
<xsl:stylesheet version="1.0"
xmlns:xsl="http://www.w3.org/1999/XSL/Transform">
<xsl:template match="/">
  <html>
  <body>
   <h2> Summary of purchases</h2>
   <table border="1">
    <tr bgcolor="#9acd32">
     <th>Purchase type</th>
     <th>value</th>
    </tr>
    <xsl:for-each select="/purchases/purchase/">
    <tr>
     <td><xsl:value-of select="purchasetype "/></td>
     <td><xsl:value-of select="purchasevalue"/></td>
    </tr>
    </xsl:for-each>
   </table>
  </body>
  </html>
</xsl:template>
</xsl:stylesheet>
```

The <xsl:if> Element

This is used to put a conditional *if* test against the content of the XML file, using the following Syntax. To add a conditional test, the <xsl:if> element is added inside the <xsl:for-each> element in the XSL file:

```
<xsl:if test="expression">
  ...
  ...some output if the expression is true...
  ...
</xsl:if>
```

The <xsl:choose> Element

The <xsl:choose> element is used in conjunction with <xsl:when> and <xsl:other-wise> to express multiple conditional tests. Its syntax is as follows:

Listing 19. Customer.xsl value of select example

```
<?xml version="1.0" encoding="ISO-8859-1"?>
<xsl:stylesheet version="1.0"
xmlns:xsl="http://www.w3.org/1999/XSL/Transform">
<xsl:template match="/">
 <html>
  <body>
  <h2>Summary of CD purchases</h2>
  <table border="1">
   <tr bgcolor="#9acd32">
     <th>Date</th>
     <th>Value</th>
   </tr>
   <xsl:for-each select="customer/puchases/purchase[purchasetype="cd"]">
   <tr>
     <td><xsl:value-of select="purchasedate"/></td>
     <td><xsl:value-of select="purchasevaluet"/></td>
   </tr>
   </xsl:for-each>
  </table>
 </body>
 </html>
</xsl:template>
</xsl:stylesheet>
```

```
<xsl:choose>
 <xsl:when test="expression">
  ... some output ...
 </xsl:when>
 <xsl:otherwise>
  ... some output ....
 </xsl:otherwise>
</xsl:choose>
```

For inserting a multiple conditional test against the XML file, the <xsl:choose>, <xsl:when>, and <xsl:otherwise> elements can be added to the XSL file:

The <xsl:apply-templates> Element

The <xsl:apply-templates> element applies a template to the current element or to the current element's child nodes. The <xsl:apply-templates> element applies a template to the current element or to the current element's child nodes. If we add a select attribute to the <xsl:apply-templates> element it will process only the child element that matches the value of the attribute. We can use the select attribute to specify the order in which the child nodes are processed.

Web Services Standards

Web services standards are essentially a set of specifications for Web service technologies proposed and maintained by organizations such as W3C and OASIS. The specifications are deliberately modular, and as a result there is no one document that contains them all. There are a few *core* specifications that are supplemented by others which are still evolving. The most common are:

- SOAP, which is an XML-based, extensible message format, with *bindings* to underlying protocols (e.g., HTTP, SMTP, and XMPP).
- WSDL, which is an XML format that allows service interfaces to be described, along with the details of their bindings to specific protocols.
- UDDI, which is a protocol for publishing and discovering metadata about Web services, to enable applications to find Web services.
- WS-Security, which defines how to use XML Encryption and XML Signature in SOAP to secure message exchanges. These standards will be discussed in Chapter VIII.
- WS-Reliable Messaging which is protocol for reliable messaging between two Web services.
- WS-Reliability, which is an OASIS standard for reliable messaging between two Web services.

The rest of this chapter will concentrate on the older and more stable protocols of WSDL, SOAP, and UDDI. Other Web service protocols will be reviewed in Chapters IV and VIII.

Web Services Description Language (WSDL)

Web services description language (WSDL) is an XML-based language used to define Web services and describe how to access them (Christensen, Curbera, Meredith, & Weerawarana, 2001). Being XML-based, WSDL is both machine and human readable, which is an important advantage. Some modern development tools can generate a WSDL document describing any Web service as well as consume a WSDL document and generate the necessary code to invoke the Web service.

WSDL is the keystone of the *universal description, discovery, and integration* (UDDI) initiative spearheaded by major software companies. UDDI is an XML-based registry for businesses worldwide, which enables businesses to advertise themselves and their services on the Internet. WSDL is the language used to do this. It is discussed in the next section.

Figure 1 shows an example of a Web service and a client invoking it in two different ways: either by using SOAP or HTTP GET. Each invocation consists of a request and a response message.

Figure 2 shows the same example with WSDL terminology pointing out the various elements that WSDL describes.

In order to illustrate WSDL, an example is shown in Listing 20 describing a service called "*Flight Information Service.*"

The <*definitions*> element is the root element of the WSDL document. In this section the WSDL namespace is declared as the default namespace for the document so all elements belong to this namespace unless they have another namespace prefix. All other namespace declarations are omitted from this example to keep it clear.

Each service is defined using a service element. Inside the service element, the different ports can be specified on which this service is accessible. A port specifies the service address (e.g., http://localhost/demos/wsdl/flightservice.asp).

Each port has a unique name and a binding attribute. When using SOAP, the port element contains a "<*soap:address/*>" element with the actual service address. In this example the soap namespace prefix refers to the namespace (http://schemas.xmlsoap.org/wsdl/soap/).

This namespace is used for SOAP-specific elements within WSDL. Such elements are also known as WSDL SOAP extension elements.

A Web service does not have to be exposed using SOAP. For example, if the Web service is exposed via HTTP GET, the port element would contain an "<*http:address/*>" element similar to the following script:

```
<http:address location="http://localhost/demos/wsdl/devxpert/departuretimeGET.asp"/>
```

A Web service therefore, can be accessible on many ports such as SOAP and HTTP GET and possibly even via SMTP. For a Web service, all three ports can be made available, each one with a different name.

Figure 1. A client invoking a Web service

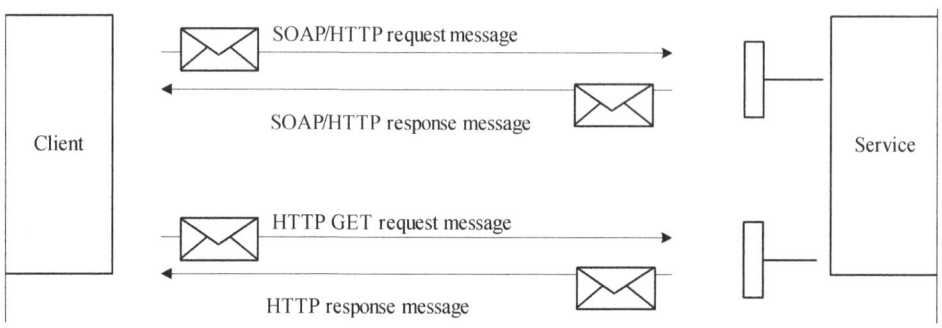

Figure 2. WSDL terminology describing Web services architecture

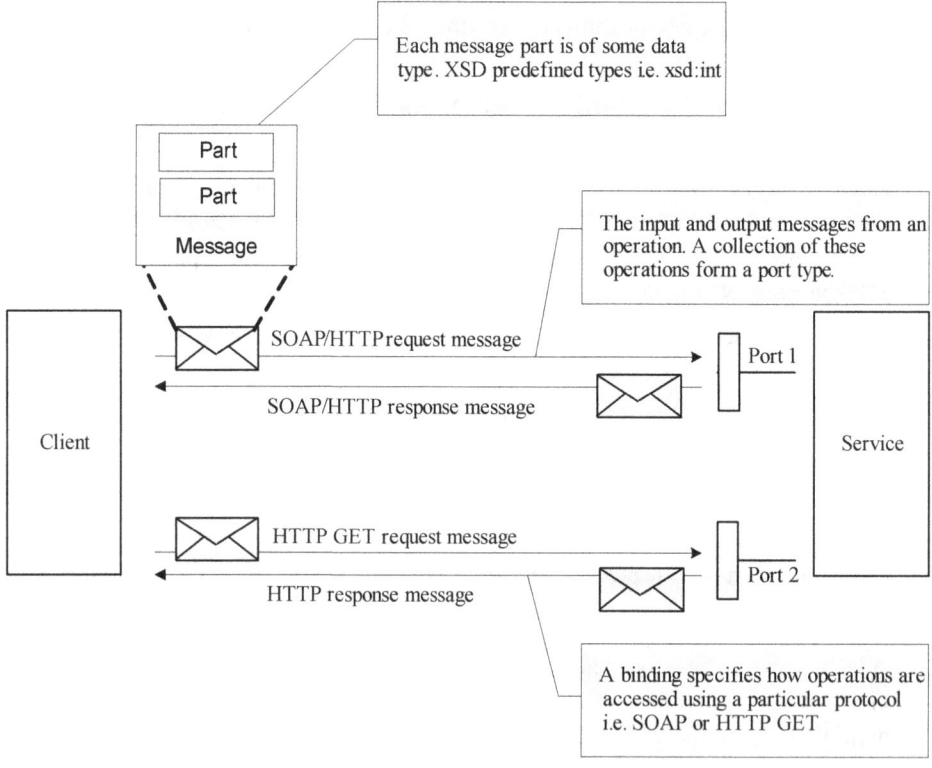

Messages and Simple Object Access Protocol (SOAP)

In the Web services approach, services are accessed and consumed by using messages. Also all interactions between a service's resources and also between services are done through messages. When we use the term *message* in this context, will basically mean that all of the following apply:

- A message has an originator and one or more recipients.
- A message will be transmitted to its recipients though some network(s) which is a direct or indirect link between sender and recipient. We make no assumptions that it will necessarily be delivered to them.

Listing 20. WSDL for a flight information service

```
<?xml version="1.0" encoding="UTF-8"?>
<definitions name="Flight Information Service"
  targetNamespace="http://FlightInformation.wsdl/FlightInformationService/"
  xmlns="http://schemas.xmlsoap.org/wsdl/"
  xmlns:tns="http://FlightInformation.wsdl/FlightInformationService/"
  xmlns:xsd="http://www.w3.org/2001/XMLSchema" xmlns:xsd1="http://FlightInformation/">
  <import location="anyElement.xsd" namespace="http://FlightInformation/"/>
  <import location="FlightInformationService.xsd" namespace="http://FlightInformation/"/>
  <message name="getDepartureDetailsRequest">
    <part name="flightNum" type="xsd:int"/>
  </message>
  <message name="getDepartureDetailsResponse">
    <part name="result" type="xsd1:anyElement"/>
  </message>
  <message name="getUKAirportsRequest"/>
  <message name="getUKAirportsResponse">
    <part name="result" type="xsd1:ArrayOfString"/>
  </message>
  <message name="getFlightNumberRequest">
    <part name="FlightInformation" type="xsd:string"/>
    <part name="departureAirport" type="xsd:string"/>
```

continued on following page

Listing 20. continued

```
    <part name="destinationAirport" type="xsd:string"/>
    <part name="departureDate" type="xsd:string"/>
    <part name="departureTime" type="xsd:string"/>
    <part name="depGate" type="xsd:int"/>
  </message>
  <message name="getFlightNumberResponse">
    <part name="result" type="xsd:int"/>
  </message>
  <message name="getFlightAvailabilityRequest">
    <part name="travelClass" type="xsd:string"/>
    <part name="depAirport" type="xsd:string"/>
    <part name="depDate" type="xsd:string"/>
    <part name="destAirport" type="xsd:string"/>
    <part name="noPassengers" type="xsd:int"/>
  </message>
  <message name="getFlightAvailabilityResponse">
    <part name="result" type="xsd1:anyElement"/>
  </message>
  <message name="getDestinationAirportsRequest"/>
  <message name="getDestinationAirportsResponse">
    <part name="result" type="xsd1:ArrayOfString"/>
  </message>
  <message name="getFlightPriceRequest">
    <part name="flightNum" type="xsd:int"/>
    <part name="flightClass" type="xsd:string"/>
  </message>
  <message name="getFlightPriceResponse">
    <part name="result" type="xsd1:anyElement"/>
  </message>
  <message name="getAllFlightInformationTimetableRequest"/>
  <message name="getAllFlightInformationTimetableResponse">
    <part name="result" type="xsd1:anyElement"/>
  </message>
```

continued on following page

Listing 20. continued

```
<message name="getArrivalDetailsRequest">
  <part name="flightNum" type="xsd:string"/>
</message>
<message name="getArrivalDetailsResponse">
  <part name="result" type="xsd1:anyElement"/>
</message>
<portType name="FlightInformationService">
  <operation name="getDepartureDetails" parameterOrder="flightNum">
      <input message="tns:getDepartureDetailsRequest" name="getDepartureDetailsReq
uest"/>
      <output message="tns:getDepartureDetailsResponse" name="getDepartureDetailsR
esponse"/>
  </operation>
  <operation name="getUKAirports">
    <input message="tns:getUKAirportsRequest" name="getUKAirportsRequest"/>
    <output message="tns:getUKAirportsResponse" name="getUKAirportsResponse"/>
  </operation>
  <operation name="getFlightNumber" parameterOrder="FlightInformation departureAirport
destinationAirport departureDate departureTime depGate">
      <input message="tns:getFlightNumberRequest" name="getFlightNumberRequest"/>
      <output message="tns:getFlightNumberResponse" name="getFlightNumberRespon
se"/>
  </operation>
  <operation name="getFlightAvailability" parameterOrder="travelClass depAirport depDate
destAirport noPassengers">
      <input message="tns:getFlightAvailabilityRequest" name="getFlightAvailabilityRequ
est"/>
      <output message="tns:getFlightAvailabilityResponse" name="getFlightAvailabilityRe
sponse"/>
  </operation>
  <operation name="getDestinationAirports">
      <input message="tns:getDestinationAirportsRequest" name="getDestinationAirports
Request"/>
      <output message="tns:getDestinationAirportsResponse" name="getDestinationAirpo
rtsResponse"/>
```

continued on following page

Listing 20. continued

```
        </operation>
        <operation name="getFlightPrice" parameterOrder="flightNum flightClass">
          <input message="tns:getFlightPriceRequest" name="getFlightPriceRequest"/>
          <output message="tns:getFlightPriceResponse" name="getFlightPriceResponse"/>
        </operation>
        <operation name="getAllFlightInformationTimetable">
          <input message="tns:getAllFlightInformationTimetableRequest" name="getAllFlightIn
formationTimetableRequest"/>
          <output message="tns:getAllFlightInformationTimetableResponse" name="getAllFligh
tInformationTimetableResponse"/>
        </operation>
        <operation name="getArrivalDetails" parameterOrder="flightNum">
          <input message="tns:getArrivalDetailsRequest" name="getArrivalDetailsRequest"/>
          <output message="tns:getArrivalDetailsResponse" name="getArrivalDetailsRespon
se"/>
        </operation>
      </portType>
</definitions>
```

- A message may be synchronous or asynchronous. In synchronous messages the sender halts all activities until some response is received associated with that message. In asynchronous messages the sender continues with other activities after he sends the message.
- A message must be understood (at least in part) by the recipients
- A message may or may not require a reaction from the recipient. A message may result in a response from the recipient which may be in terms of one or more messages.

Interaction using messages can be in one of the following ways:

- **One-way:** The recipient receives a message.
- **Request-response:** The recipient receives a message, and sends a correlated message to the sender.

- **Solicit-response:** The recipient sends a message, and receives a correlated message.
- **Notification:** The recipient sends a message.

Although messages are only one possible type of human communication, they are sufficient as the only mechanism necessary for coordinating resources to be used for the delivery of services. Messages are also used in the communication between the consumer and the service provider. The assumption here is that the consumer and the service are in separate locations. Message-based communications allow the consumer to find out about the service and for some types of services totally access them (consume them). However, in many cases a sequence of messages between the consumer and the service will be required. This sequence forms a dialogue.

SOAP stands for *simple object access protocol* and provides the standard mechanism used for invoking Web services (W3C, 2003). SOAP implies that the underlying Web service representation is an object when in fact it does not have to be. The Web service can be written as a series of functions in any programming language and still be invoked by using SOAP. The SOAP specification provides standards for the format of a SOAP message and how SOAP should be used over HTTP. SOAP also builds on XML and XML schema definition (XSD) language to provide standard rules for encoding data as XML.

Like UDDI, SOAP is XML based. Moreover, SOAP is a generally accepted standard for Web services and the reason for SOAP's widespread adoption is its simplicity. SOAP is "lightweight"—that is, it involves a relatively small amount of code, and it is fairly easy to understand. The basic item of transmission in SOAP is the SOAP *message*, which consists of a mandatory SOAP *envelope*, an optional SOAP *header*, and a mandatory SOAP *body*.

Listing 21 shows a SOAP message, designed to retrieve the time of a flight. Specifically, the SOAP message makes a request to "*GetFlightTime,*" passing it a symbol called DEF. "*GetFlightTime*" is an operation performed by a Web service, and DEF is the symbol for a specific flight. Clearly, for the request to be satisfied, "*GetFlightTime*" needs to be described, and its description needs to specify that the operation takes a flight symbol as input and returns a flight time as output. This is not done in SOAP. Instead it's done through the Web services description language (WSDL) that was described in the previous section.

For the purposes of this example, it is assumed that a WSDL document exists for a Web Service and in that document, the "*GetFlightTime*" operation is appropriately defined.

The SOAP message therefore consists of the following items:

Listing 21. SOAP message

```
<SOAP-ENV: Envelope
 xmlns:SOAP-ENV=
  "http://schemas.xmlsoap.org/soap/envelope/"
 SOAP-ENV:
  encodingStyle=
   "http://schemas.xmlsoap.org/soap/encoding/">
    <SOAP-ENV:Header>
     <t:Transaction xmlns:t="some-URI">
       SOAP-ENV:mustUnderstand="1">5
     </t:Transaction>
    </SOAP-ENV:Header>
    <SOAP-ENV:Body>
            <m:GetFlightTime xmlns:m="some-URI">
      <symbol>DEF</Symbol>
     </m: GetFlightTime>
    </SOAP-ENV:Body>
</SOAP-Envelope>
```

- **Envelope:** The Envelope element is the top element of the envelope. In Listing 21, the Envelope element specifies two parameters: an XML namespace and an encoding style. An XML namespace is a collection of names that can be used in XML element types and attribute names, in other words an XML schema. The example points to the *uniform resource identifiers* (URI) *http://schemas.xmlsoap.org/soap/envelope*. This URI defines the XML schema for SOAP messages.

  The *encodingStyle* attribute identifies the encoding style. An encoding style identifies the data types recognized by SOAP messages and specifies rules for how these data types are serialized, that is transformed into a stream of bytes, for transport across the Web. The example points to the URI *http://schemas.xmlsoap.org/soap/encoding/*. This URI specifies the encoding style for "Section 5" encodings, the ones described in Section 5 of the SOAP specification.

- **Header:** As mentioned earlier, the header is optional. However, if it is included in a SOAP message, it must be the first child of the Envelope element. The Header element, through attributes, extends the SOAP message in a modular way. A SOAP message travels from an originator (provider) to a final destination (consumer), potentially passing through a set of intermediate nodes along the message path. Each node is an application that can receive and forward SOAP messages. The SOAP header can be used to indicate some additional processing at a node independent of the processing done at the final destination. In the example in Listing 21, the Header element indicates that this is a transaction (a URI specifies the namespace for the transaction). The header

Listing 22. An example of the body of a SOAP Response

```
<SOAP-ENV:Body>
    <m:GetFlightTimeOutput xmlns:m="some-URI">
        <FlightTime>19:30</FlightTime>
    </m: GetFlightTimeOutput>
</SOAP-ENV:Body>
```

could just as easily have specified attributes for another type of process, such as authorization checking. The attribute value *mustUnderstand=1* means that the initial node in the SOAP message path must process the header. The value 5 is passed to the initial node as input.

- **Body:** The SOAP body contains the main part of the SOAP message. In particular, the Body element contains information for the final recipient of the SOAP message. In the above example, the Body element contains two items of information: *GetFlightTime* (with its namespace) and the symbol DEF. This information is passed to the final destination. The application at that destination needs to understand the request and take the appropriate action. As mentioned earlier, for the purposes of this example, it is assumed that a WSDL document exists for a Web service, and in that document, the *GetFlightTime* operation is appropriately defined. Based on the information in the WSDL document, it is assumed that the application calls the *GetFlightTime* operation, passing it the DEF symbol as input. The WSDL document also indicates that the output returned by the *GetFlightTime* operation is a time. The returned time information is also passed in a SOAP message. The body of the response is illustrated in Listing 22.

Messages in ebXML

The ebXML initiative (http://www.ebxml.org) has also defined a *message service protocol* (ebMS) that enables the secure and reliable exchange of messages between two parties (OASIS ebXML Messaging Services Technical Committee, 2002).

Because ebMS was designed as a complete solution, it includes a well-defined set of extensions that directly use SOAP's extensibility mechanism. For example, ebMS defines SOAP header elements for carrying sender identification information, business-collaboration context information, and so on. ebMS also identifies and adopts specific security technologies for countering commonly perceived security risks related to B2B transactions (further discussed in Chapter VIII).

EbMS defines a rich set of context information, which can be adapted easily to the SOAP extensibility model. Listing 23 shows an example of how ebMS can carry

Listing 23. SOAP extensibility in ebMS

```
<SOAP:Header>
     <eb:MessageHeader SOAP:mustUnderstand="1" eb:version="2.0">
   <eb:From>
         <eb:PartyId>urn:duns:123456789</eb:PartyId>

<eb:Role>http://rosettanet.org/roles/Buyer</eb:Role>
   </eb:From>
   <eb:To>
       <eb:PartyId>urn:duns:912345678</eb:PartyId>
       <eb:Role>http://rosettanet.org/roles/Seller</eb:Role>
   </eb:To>
   <eb:CPAId>20001209-133003-28572</eb:CPAId>
   <eb:ConversationId>20001209-133003-28572</eb:ConversationId>
   <eb:Service>urn:services:SupplierOrderProcessing</eb:Service>
   <eb:Action>NewOrder</eb:Action>
   <eb:MessageData>
       <eb:MessageId>20001209-133003-28572@example.com</eb:MessageId>
       <eb:Timestamp>2001-02-15T11:12:12</eb:Timestamp>
   </eb:MessageData>
   <eb:DuplicateElimination/>
   </eb:MessageHeader>
</SOAP:Header>
```

context information via SOAP extensions. In this business scenario, an organization with a *data universal numbering system identifier* (DUNS) such as 123456789 wants to reliably send a purchase order to the seller organization identified by DUNS 912345678. To automate this business process, the two organizations would typically comply with roles defined by a standards body, such as RosettaNet (http://www.rosettanet.org). Such definitions outline the participants' roles in the business process in terms of obligations and expectations.

EbXML uses SOAP header extensions for many context information categories:

- *From and To.* These elements identify the message's sender and intended recipient using either logical ID or the parties' physical address. The PartyID subelement of the From and To elements contains the identification information, and its attribute type indicates the identifier strings' domain. The optional role subelement indicates the From or To party's authorized role. Its value should match the one specified in the agreement between the two parties (for example, that Party A is a seller and Party B is a buyer).

- *CPAId.* Prior to transactions, the parties can use an electronic agreement form, which includes the values of various parameters governing their message exchange. For the message receiver, CPAId is valuable in that it identifies the sender's exact set of parameter values.

- *ConversationId.* This element uniquely identifies the messages exchanged between parties while executing the CPAId agreement. In simple terms, for long-running business processes in which multiple messages are being exchanged, each side must maintain the process state. When a party receives a particular request, it can use the request's state identifier to figure out, for example, which stopped process must be resumed and so on.

- *Service.* This element identifies the service that acts on the incoming message.

- *Action.* A service can take several different actions on an incoming message; the Action element uniquely identifies the particular action an incoming message requests.

- *MessageData.* This is a complex structure that includes four subelements. First, to guarantee that the message is delivered once and only once, each message must carry a unique MessageId. Second, the message must have a Timestamp showing when it was produced. Third, acknowledgment and exception messages must carry a *RefToMessageId*, which identifies the related message. Finally, while reliable messaging systems guarantee message delivery once and only once, network and node failures can cause unacceptable delays. The messages must therefore carry expiration information in the TimeToLive subelement, which indicates whether recipients should consider the message live and useful, or stale and discardable.

- *DuplicateElimination.* Business-critical applications are easier to design if the messaging layer can guarantee that duplicate messages are suppressed. To that end, the DuplicateElimination element prescribes the message delivery behavior of at-most-once or best-effort style messages. Combined with the optional SequenceNumber header, this element ensures reliability in message delivery.

- *Description.* A human-readable description of the message's purpose or intent.

- *Manifest.* Often, one or more business documents must be sent and processed together. This element contains a list of documents, their media type, references that can validate the document's structure, and so on.

Universal Description, Discovery, and Integration (UDDI)

Universal description, discovery and integration (UDDI) is a platform-independent framework for describing services, discovering businesses, and integrating business services by using the Internet (OASIS, 2004). More specifically, UDDI is a directory for storing information about Web services, which they communicate via the SOAP standard. This directory consists of Web services interfaces described by the WSDL language.

UDDI is a cross-industry effort driven by all major platform and software vendors, as well as a large community of marketplace operators, and e-business leaders.

A UDDI registry provides simple information about the Web service provider namely:

- **Who it is:** A registration includes the name of the Web service provider and can include additional identifiers such as a *North American industry classification system* (NAICS) code, or a *Dun & Bradstreet* D-U-N-S number. D&B D-U-N-S number is a unique nine-digit identification sequence, which provides unique identifiers of single business entities.

- **What it is:** A registration includes the name of a Web Service and, typically, a brief description.

- **Where it is:** A registration contains *binding templates* that point to an address where the service can be accessed.

- **How to request it:** A registration contains the ways that describe the interface for the Web Service.

Each registry that conforms to UDDI is operated at its own site and hence the UDDI specifications refer to this as the *operator* site. The operator site contains the master copy of its registry. However, the collection of UDDI registries is replicated. If a business searches for a Web service in a registry at one operator site, the search is done across the information in the master copy, including the information replicated from the other UDDI registries.

The UDDI specifications define how to publish and discover information about Web services in an UDDI-conforming registry. More specifically, the specifications define a UDDI schema and a UDDI API. The schema identifies the types of XML data structures that comprise an entry in the registry for a Web Service. The API describes the SOAP messages that are used to publish an entry in a registry, or discover an entry in a registry. The UDDI schema and the UDDI API are described in detail in the following sections.

UDDI Schema

The UDDI schema identifies the types of XML data structures that comprise an entry in the registry for a Web Service. Figure 3 illustrates the schema. It shows the five types of XML data structures that comprise a registration.

Figure 3. UDDI schema elements

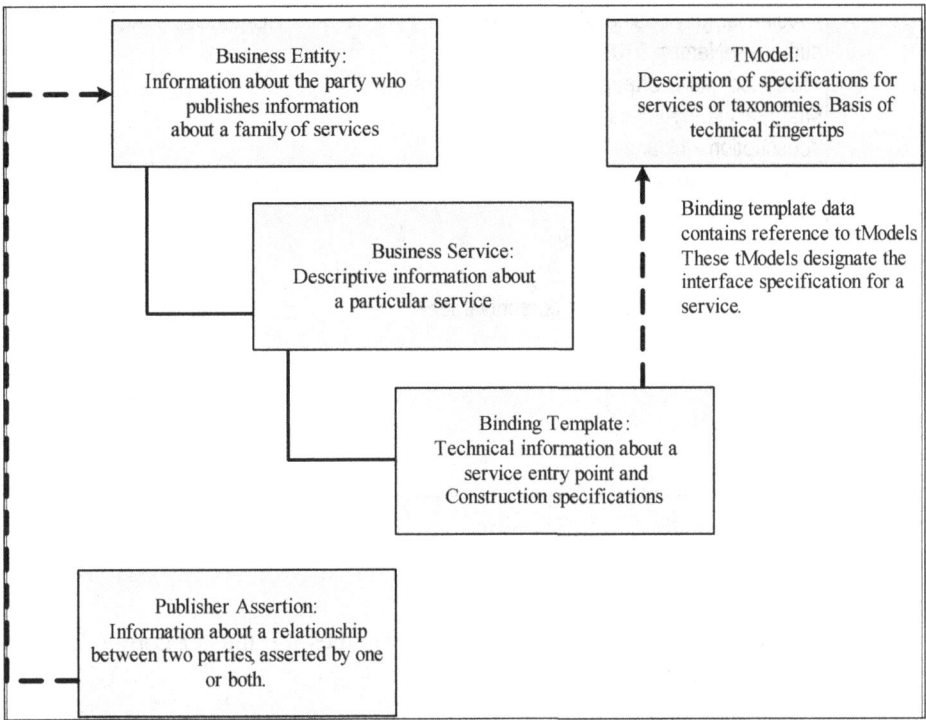

The five types of XML data structures that comprise the UDDI schema are explained as follows:

Business Entity

This structure represents all known information about a business or entity and the services that it offers. From an XML standpoint, a business Entity is the top-level data structure that holds descriptive information about a business or entity.

A business Entity element contains attributes that:

- Uniquely identify the business Entity with a *businessKey*. The key is a Universal Unique Identifier (UUID) that is generated by the registry. The mechanism that produces UUIDs guarantees uniqueness through a combination of hardware addresses, timestamps and random numbers.
- Name the individual who published the business Entity data (*authorizedName*).

Listing 24. Part business entity structure for UDDI schema

```
<businessEntity businessKey="35AF7F00-1419-11D6-A0DC-000C0E00ACDD"
authorizedName="0100002CAL"
  operator="www.CheapAirlines.com/services/uddi">
<name>Cheap Airlines Ltd</name>
<description xml:lang="en">
  The source for all products
</description>
<contacts>
<contact>
<personName>Bob Smith</personName>
<phone>
  (0800)1111111
</phone>
</contact>
</contacts>
```

- Specify the UDDI registry site that manages the master copy of the businessEntity data (*operator*).

- Other elements within the structure identify the name recorded for the business or entity (*name*), and optionally specify additional information about the business or entity.

Listing 24 shows part of a complete Business Entity structure for a company named Cheap Airlines Ltd. The company provides various Web services, including an online ticket buying service.

Business Service

This structure identifies a service provided by the business or entity that is represented by the parent Business Entity. A business or entity can provide multiple services, so there can be multiple business Service elements within a business Entity. The set (or *family*) of business Service elements are specified in a business Services structure.

Listing 25 shows part of a complete business Service structure for an online product ordering service offered by Cheap Airlines Ltd. Notice especially the *categoryBag* element, which is used to specify a classification scheme (a *taxonomy*). In this example, the taxonomy is the *North American industry classification system* (NAICS).

Listing 25. Part business service structure for UDDI

```
<businessServices>
<businessService serviceKey="
  2AB346C0-2282-43B0-756B-0003CC35CC1D">
<name>Online Ticket Purchasing</name>
<description xml:lang="en">
  Buying tickets online
</description>
<categoryBag>
  ntis-gov:naic
<categoryBag>
```

Binding Template and tModel

A binding Template along with a tModel provides two important pieces of information about a Web Service: its technical specification and its *accessPoint*. A technical specification (also called a *technical fingerprint*) typically provides details about things such as protocols and interchange formats used in communicating with the service. The *accessPoint* is an address, such as a uniform resource locator (URL) or e-mail address, at which the service can be called. Contained within a binding Template structure is a *tModelInstanceInfo* element that references a tModel by its key. The referenced tModel provides the technical specification. There can be multiple binding Template elements for the family of services identified in a business Services structure. The multiple binding Template elements are specified in a binding Templates structure.

Listing 26 illustrates part of a complete binding Template structure for the online ticket buying service offered by Cheap Airlines Ltd. Notice the reference to the tModelKey in the *"tModelInstanceInfo"* element.

Publisher Assertion

This structure is used as a way of asserting a relationship between one business Entity and another. For example, the structure can be used to show that two businesses are subsidiaries of the same company. To assert the relationship, each of the two businesses Entity structures specify its own publish Assertion structure. However, the information in each structure needs to be exactly the same.

Listing 26. Part binding template structure for UDDI schema

```
<bindingTemplates>
<bindingTemplate bindingKey="
 4BC7C340-2398-12E6-887C-0005AC33CC2D"
<description>
 JAXRPC (SOAP/HTTP )-based binding
</description>
<accessPoint>
 http://www.CheapAirlines.com:8080/tickets/
</accessPoint>
<tModelInstanceDetails>
<tModelInstanceInfo tModelKey="UUID:
 36E13526-4553-3265-B5F7-C4B522E75A05" />
</tModelInstanceDetails>
```

UDDI API

The UDDI API describes the simple object access protocol (SOAP) messages that are used to publish an entry in a registry (the *Publish* API), and those that are used to discover an entry in a registry (the *Inquiry* API).

Publish API. There are a variety of messages defined in the Publish API. What they have in common is that they perform some action related to one of the types of structures that comprise the UDDI schema. For example, the Publish API message *save_business* is used to save or update one or more complete business Entity structures in a registry.

Listing 27 shows an example of a message that saves the business Service structure (named *Online Ticket buying*). The *authinfo* element is used to specify an authentication token. This is a value that is a standard part of UDDI's authentication mechanism and needs to be specified in all Publisher API calls. The authentication token is obtained by issuing a call to *get_authToken*.

Inquiry API. The Inquiry API contains two types of messages: *find* messages, which search UDDI registries for entries that meet specified search criteria; and *get* messages, which retrieve detailed information about a specified registration. For example, the Inquiry API message *find_business* is used to search for all registered business entities that meet search criteria specified in the call. Listing 28 shows the *find_business* message that searches for all business entities whose registered name begins with the characters Flight Tickets.

The call returns a *businessList* structure that contains information about each matching business, and summaries of the *businessService* elements exposed by those businesses.

Listing 27. Part binding template structure for UDDI schema

```
<save_service generic="2.0" xmlns=um:uddi-org:api-v2">
<authinfo>authentication token goes here ...</authinfo>
<businessServices>
<businessService serviceKey="
 2AB346C0-2282-43B0-756B-0003CC35CC1D">
<name>Online Ticket buying</name>
<description xml:lang="en">
 Use this service to purchase tickets over the Web
</description>
```

Listing 28. Part structure of an inquiry API for UDDI API

```
<find_business generic="2.0" xmlns=um:uddi-org:api-v2">
<name>Flight Tickets%</name>
</find_business>
```

The *get* messages include those that return detailed information about one or more business entities (i.e., *get_businessDetail* or *get_businessDetailExt*).

Alternatives to UDDI

While UDDI has enjoyed some acceptance in the commercial world, some other competing or complimentary standards for Web services directories have also been proposed. EbXML registry is one of them (OASIS, 2006). The *electronic business XML working group* (ebXML; http://www.ebxml.org) initiated by the United Nations body for Trade Facilitation and Electronic Business and the Organization for the Advancement of Structured Information Standards (Oasis; http://www.oasis-open.org) focuses on standardizing XML business specifications. An ebXML registry provides services for sharing information on conducting electronic business and provides publishing and discovery of that information. The registry allows organizations to locate business process information and other artifacts needed for electronic business. Key features and functions of an ebXML registry include registration of any type of object, associations between any two objects, links to external content, life-cycle management of objects, flexible query options, security functions, inter-registry cooperation, and event archiving for a complete audit trail.

Chapter Summary

This chapter presented the technologies and standards underpinning Web services. The key technology on which Web services are built is the XML language. The main benefits of using XML-based Web services standards are as follows:

- **Standardization:** Standardization in information representation and transfer is crucial to e-services. XML is a platform and application independent, vendor-neutral notation. XML relies on other technologies, in particular, SGML for syntax, URIs for name identifiers, *extended backus naur form (EBNF) for grammar* and unicode for character encoding, which are all standards.

- **Longevity:** Proprietary electronic data formats can and often do become *legacy formats. XML on the* other hand, cannot possibly become a legacy data format as everything about XML is open. Future versions of XML will always be *backwards compatible. XML data w*ill never need to be rekeyed. Even if a system that uses XML becomes obsolete, the XML data will remain accessible in the long term.

- **Manageability:** XML is programmable—there are several programming models such as DOM that allow to programmatically traverse an XML document. This is one of its major attractions when processing high-volume documents such as those produced in an e-service context (orders, invoices, confirmations, etc.). In contrast, other document formats are notoriously difficult to process in an automated fashion. The benefits of the high-level of automation that can be achieved with XML really become apparent as the volume of information increases. Moreover, mistakes due to human editing are often an inevitable consequence of manual document manipulation. The amount of human effort involved in manually processing documents is enormous and would make the efficient provision of e-services simply too costly.

- **Neutrality:** In addition to being simple to create and parse, XML is neither platform nor vendor specific. In the context of e-services, technologies that are neutral is often more important than being technically superior. As service needs to be delivered to myriads of possibly not known in advance customers it is important to assume a neutral standard than to cater for every possible technology used by customers or even worse force customers (and partners) to adopt a own proprietary technology.

- **Coordinatin with partners:** As it has been already said, providing e-services often requires coordination with services of other companies XML-based standards simplifies service coordination, for the following reasons:
  - The only thing that is to be mutually agreed upon is the XML vocabulary (schema) that will be used to represent data.

- ° Neither company has to know how the other's back-end systems are organized, which does not put any extra technical burden whilst maintaining privacy requirements. All that is required is that each company develops the *mappings* to transform XML documents into the internal format used by the back-end systems.
- ° XML-based solutions are scalable. If a new partner is added in an e-services value chain, there is no need by the host partner to interact with the systems of the new partner. All that is required is that the new partner follows the protocol established by the hosting partner.

The next chapter will present languages and methods for composing and coordinating Web services.

References

Cayron, S. (2002). *ACORD emerge XML framework.* Retrieved March 15, 2007, from www.acordconference.org/2002/downLoads/Monday/XML%20framework%20standard.pdf

Christensen, E., Curbera, F., Meredith, G., & Weerawarana, S. (2001). *Web services description language* (WSDL, 1.1). Retrieved March 15, 2007, from http://www.w3.org/TR/wsdl

Clark, J., & DeRose, S. (Eds.).(1999, November 16). *XML path language (XPath)* (Version 1.0). Retrieved March 15, 2007, from http://www.w3.org/TR/xpath

Ferris, C., & Farrell, J. (2003). What are Web services? *Communications of the ACM, 56*(6), 31.

Kay, M. (Ed.). (2005). *XSL transformations* (XSLT, Version 2.0). Retrieved March 15, 2007, from http://www.w3.org/TR/xslt20/

OASIS. (2004). *UDDI Version 3.0.2: UDDI spec technical committee draft, dated 20041019.* Retrieved March 15, 2007, from http://uddi.org/pubs/uddi_v3.htm

OASIS.(2006). *OASIS ebXML registry TC.* Retrieved March 15, 2007, from http://www.oasis-open.org/committees/tc_home.php?wg_abbrev=regrep#technical

OASIS ebXML Messaging Services Technical Committee. (2002, April 1). *Message service specification* (Version 2.0). , Retrieved March 15, 2007, from http://www.oasis-open.org/committees/ebxml-msg/documents/ebMS_v2_0.pdf

Roy, J. & Ramanujan, A. (2001). Understanding Web services. *IT Pro.* 69-73.

W3C. (2004, October 28). *XML schema part 0: Primer* (2nd ed.). Retrieved March 16, 2007, from http://www.w3.org/TR/xmlschema-0/

W3C. (2006). *Extensible mark-up language* (XML, 1.0). Retrieved March 15, 2007, from http://www.w3.org/TR/REC-xml

W3C. (2007). *DTD tutorial.* Retrieved March 16, 2007, from http://www.w3schools.com/dtd/default.asp

Chapter IV

Service Coordination

Introduction

Chapter III introduced standards for Web service specification, such as WSDL and SOAP. With the use of such standards, Web service designers can model the functionality of a service in terms of inputs and outputs, thus allowing the consumers of the service to understand what to expect (and what not to expect) from the service, before actually using it. As we have said already, a Web service offers some well defined functionality to its consumers, which, however, due to the very essence of the Web service, has a rather focused and narrow scope. The reason is that, in general, we aim to develop Web services that are as much useful as possible for a wide range of consumers. Thus, the Web service becomes a reusable *building block* for something more complex such as a business service. It is unlikely that a business level service can be provided by a single Web service. Instead, a complex business service has to be layered on top of several Web services that *coordinate* with each other to deliver the business service. The capability for coordination however, is not unique to Web services. Business resources (people, activities, equipment, etc.)

must be coordinated to deliver processes (Dayal, Hsu, & Ladin, 2001). Business processes themselves must be coordinated within a single company or even across several companies, in order to deliver higher level business results such as the fulfillment of a supply chain.

Web services were conceived originally as stand-alone computing entities, thus the service standards discussed in Chapter III do not consider the aspect of coordinating collaborating services. However, these standards were soon augmented with new proposals about how Web services can coordinate with each to deliver complex functionality. Thus, this chapter aims to explain the following things:

- What is business process coordination and why it is needed?
- What is coordination at the Web services level and its different flavors such as *orchestration* and *choreography?*
- What languages and standards exist for Web services coordination?
- Present in more detail the most significant of these standards, namely the Business Process Execution Language for Web services (BPEL4WS, or BPEL for short).

Business Process Automation

Business process automation can be defined as the use of information technologies (more specifically business process management, workflow management, and enterprise integration software) to partially or fully automate the execution and management of business processes. Organizations strive to integrate and automate their business processes such as order processing, procurement, claims processing, inventory management, and administration in order to improve efficiency and speed to market (Ghalimi & McGoveran, 2004). The basis of business process automation is event/trigger-based synchronisation of business activities. When an activity starts, terminates, or ends abruptly due to an error/exception, an event needs to be generated to notify other activities that are potentially affected by the change of state in this activity. For example, the successful completion of a sales activity where a product has been sold to a customer needs to generate an event that will trigger a manufacturing activity/process to manufacture the sold product. The system(s) that coordinate such activities are the basis for business process automation and management. Increasingly, such systems are implemented using the technologies of Web services, as we shall see in the rest of this chapter.

Automation therefore enables companies to realize the following benefits:

1. *Integration and interaction* of applications that run on different and potentially incompatible software platforms.

2. *Automatic control of business processes,* wherein workflows can be automatically controlled by business interactions, depending on certain triggers, without the need for human interaction.

3. *Reuse* of business activities, which enables composition of higher level services from existing activities.

4. *Simplification* of process, wherein with automation, manual steps can become redundant and processes become simplified. In particular, the interfaces between processes where one process "hands over" to another one can become simpler.

5. *Flexibility,* wherein processes are built as a network of coordinating activities, which can be easily rearranged if necessary.

6. *Extensibility,* wherein the modular organization of business processes allows the addition of new partners, customers, and suppliers and customization of the details to meet evolving business requirements.

7. *Process monitoring and management,* wherein the monitoring of the reliability of each individual activity allows corrective actions to be made (e.g., compensation for failed activities).

8. *Improved customer service,* which is facilitated by customer data integration providing a consistent view of the customer, no matter what the interaction channel (i.e., Portal, call center, etc.) is.

9. *Cost-savings,* which are achieved by elimination of non-value-adding activities, the reuse of activities, and reduced costs of process interoperation.

However, automation has drawbacks too, namely:

1. Complex management structures for monitoring and control of processes. The management of processes is becoming more complicated as it now involves not only the company but also its partners.

2. Need to redesign (sometimes quite drastically) the existing business process. The cost of redesigning (also called *reengineering*) of the existing process can be prohibitively large and have, sometimes, unforeseen consequences.

Business Process Management (BPM)

A business process is a sequence of activities triggered by a business event such as an invoice, request for proposal, or a request for funds transfer. The process is driven by business rules that invoke activities and subprocesses. Activities and subprocesses are assigned to resources, which are organizational units that are capable and authorized to play specific roles in the processes (Endl & Knolmayer, 1998). The definitions of the rules, activities, subprocesses, and resource policies constitute a *process description*. An execution of a business process consists of invoking existing business services. A process manager system manages the state of a business process and routes requests among participating applications. Most business process management systems allow branch logic to determine the next step in a process, after a step completes, so that different sequences of steps can be followed according to the outcome of the branch logic. Often a graphical tool is used to model the path, the decision points, and the branch logic. The branch logic is usually called *rules*. Instead of representing a process as a flow diagram, some systems simply use a collection of rules to represent the process without explicitly delineating the paths (Dayal et al., 2001). Such systems are generally more flexible in capturing the dynamic behavior of processes. During execution time, an event triggers the process management system to create an instance of the process; the process management system then coordinates the step execution and monitors and records the history. However, not all business processes are suited for handling by process management systems. A process can be highly structured (the business rules and sequences that the tasks follow are predetermined and pre-scripted), semistructured (parts of the rules are pre-scripted, parts of the rules may be modified or scripted on the fly—often referred to as an ad hoc process), and unstructured (there do not exist repeatable patterns of rules or sequences among the tasks, and participants often need to meet at the same time to perform work). One of the challenges in business process management has been to provide end-to-end support for business processes that span from highly structured to highly unstructured.

Business Process Management Technologies and Standards

Different forms of *middleware* have been suggested to enable integration and automation of business processes, both within and across organizations. Middleware is a generic term to describe systems that facilitate the communication between two or more software applications. These include *message brokers, transactional queue managers,* and *publish/subscribe mechanisms* (Myerson, 2002).

- A message broker is a type of middleware that ensure that messages exchanged between applications are delivered in a secure and reliable way.

- Transaction queue managers are middleware systems that ensure that distributed activities are executed using the principles of transactions such as atomicity, consistency, integrity, and durability.

- Publish subscribe middleware is based on the principle of event producers and consumers. Applications publish events to which other applications subscribe. Once an event is generated, applications that have published their interest to this category of event are notified by the middleware.

A business process management system (or *business process manager*) is therefore a middleware system that provides a central point of control for defining business processes and orchestrating their execution. The process manager records the execution state of the process and routes requests to process component applications or human participants to execute tasks. Business process managers deal with both human and automated tasks. Such systems typically provide transactional support and recovery of business processes. The process definition is based on a commonly agreed business interaction protocol, such as the protocol for online purchase or auction. The process execution is not performed by a centralized workflow engine (discussed in the next section) but by multiple engines collaboratively.

To summarize, BPM is a collective term for technologies such as workflow; enterprise application integration; event processing; and business process reengineering, automation, and integration (Ghalimi & McGoveran, 2004). Related to BPM are the following terms and concepts:

- *Workflow* (discussed in the next section), which is the movement of documents and/or tasks through a work process. *Enterprise application integration* (EAI), which refers to the use of software and computer systems' architectural principles to integrate a set of enterprise computer applications.

- *Business-to-business (B2B) integration,* which is the mechanism for linking automated processes between trading partners.

- *Business process automation,* which is the use of software applications to map and simulate the requirements of a business process in BPM.

- *Business process integration,* which is the structured coordination of logically related business process.

Workflow Management

As previously defined, workflow management system is the set of software program(s) that will either completely or partially support the processing of work item(s) in order to accomplish the objective of a workflow process activity instance or instances (Fischer, 2001). Workflow software technologies, like business process management technologies, in general, have evolved from diverse origins. While some offerings have been developed as pure workflow software technologies, many have evolved from image management systems, document management systems, relational or object database systems, and electronic mail systems (Schmidt, 1999). Workflow technologies have been applied for many years successfully in business processes management and more recently in Web service-based processes. However, most workflow management systems implement proprietary process models that hamper interoperability between different systems and applications. To address that problem, the Workflow Management Coalition (WfMC, 1998) has proposed a metamodel for workflow systems interoperability. WfMC identifies the result of the workflow design-time phase (i.e., the process definition) as one of the potential areas of standardization to enable the interchange of process definition data between different build-time tools and run-time products. In its proposal for a workflow process definition language, WfMC attempts to unify the different modeling approaches of the workflow management systems and more general business process management tools.

The core concepts of the WfMC metamodel are:

- **Tasks:** Each task is an action or a set of actions handled as a unit. They require a set of resources, and when these resources include humans they usually play a role for each task.

- **People (users):** The tasks are performed in a defined order by specific human resources (or agents playing the human roles) based on rules or business constraints.

- **Roles:** Each role defines a set of potential competencies that exist in the organization. They are defined independently of the people to whom the roles will be assigned.

- **Routing:** Each routing defines the sequences of steps that the documents (or data) must follow within the workflow system.

- **Transitions:** Transitions are logical rules that determine the flow of the document within the system. They express what action is going to be executed depending on the value of logical expressions. The rules can have varying complexity with multiple options, variations, and exceptions.

- **Data:** Data are the documents, files, images, registers in the database and other type of information used to perform the work.

Rationale for Business Process Coordination

To understand the rationale behind the emergence of technologies and standards for Web service collaboration, we need to consider the business requirements for process collaboration and coordination. One of the ongoing business objectives is to make processes more efficient via automation. Automated business processes are easier to coordinate, as the labor intensive and costly aspects of manual coordination, are replaced by computer based automation and coordination. Web services provide a suitable vehicle for coordinating processes via automation.

In general, *business process collaboration* refers to the joint effort involved in the execution of a business process by a number of business partners (Dayal et al., 2001). Business process collaborations tend to have the following characteristics:

- Internal processes of partner companies consisting of a sequence of internal activities, each manipulating some data and having one or more logical start and end points.
- Intermediate or end points of a process that needs to be synchronized with an external process belonging to a different partner.
- Interoperability relationships between the two processes in terms of synchronization signals, data conversions, security protocols, and so on.

Framework for Collaborative Processes

The starting point of the collaborative process framework is the common definitions of collaborative business processes. There are at least three prerequisites for effective use of common business process definitions:

- A common business process metamodel and its associated schema language, so that business processes can be codified in a standard way.
- A mechanism for common process descriptions, including business documents associated with these processes, to be easily reused as building blocks for more complex processes, or customized for the special needs of vertical industries or geographical segments.

- A mechanism for enterprises to publish their ability to participate in specific roles of common business processes as process flow enabled Web services, so that potential partners can automatically discover each other and engage in the process execution.

Thus, the interoperability aspect is the most crucial characteristic of business process collaboration. Interoperability is described in terms of operations required to facilitate data and control exchanges between processes belonging to different partners. Such operations are

1. Instantiate/initiate: a process
2. Invoke a process which must follow an instantiate or initiate operation.
3. Change the state of the process to one of the following:
   - Waiting
   - Suspended
   - Terminated
   - Disconnected
   - Continued

Concepts of Choreography and Orchestration

Since coordination of business processes is a prerequisite for collaboration of business partners, it is important that the rules and patterns of such coordination must be formally described and agree. The terms *choreography* and *orchestration* share the same origin although they have slightly different meanings. Both concepts refer to how different processes may work together, like musicians in an orchestra do, by following the commands of a conductor, which in this case is a process coordinator.

The problem of combining existing workflow processes seamlessly into a particular collaboration and coordination cannot be resolved without business process choreography. A *choreography* describes the behavior of the process from a client's point of view. Choreography shows how a process interacts with its users who might be humans or automated systems, including those of other processes. In a business process, choreography tracks the sequence of messages exchanged between customers, suppliers, and other business partners. A choreography description defines precisely the sequence of interactions between a set of cooperating processes in order to promote a common understanding between partners. Multiple choreographies can be defined for a process and hence multiple modes of interactions may exist for the same process. To be able to define this interaction we need to be able to refer to the state of the process which, as stated previously, can be one of active, waiting, suspended, and so on. We also need to be able to express the allowed change of state using rules. A specific state is described by a set of explicitly defined attributes and values of a process. State transition rules have the form:

if *condition* **then** *updates*

where *condition* is expressed in terms of properties of the process' inputs, attributes and outputs and updates express the changes of the latter's attribute values or class membership.

Orchestration in contrast defines how a process may invoke other processes in order to achieve the required functionality. Orchestration is defined in terms of sequences and conditions in which one process invokes other processes in order to realize a user goal. An orchestration is therefore the pattern of interactions between processes that must be followed in order to achieve a goal.

Similarly to choreography, *orchestration* is state-based and uses rules to define transitions between states. The difference with respect to choreography is that in orchestration the rules are extended to link the orchestration to other goals or processes. Business process choreography therefore represents interoperability patterns between business processes, while orchestration provides the rules about how different processes may act together, and in what sequence.

The Importance of Choreography for Coordination and Collaboration of Business Processes

Today's companies rarely operate in a self-sufficient manner; they are parts of long and often complex supply chains. For supply chains to be effective, companies need to consider their business processes in terms of all of the companies or processes involved in the chain. The management of the information flow among trading partners can make or break the trading partners and the business in the long run. The idea of business process choreography today encompasses the coordination and collaboration of the traditional business partners enhanced with the capabilities of new technologies such as Web services (Gortmaker, Janssen, & Wagenaar, 2004).

In turn, this makes possible

1.   The promotion of a common understanding between partners;

2.   The automatic validate conformance of individual processes; and

3.   The assurance of interoperability and robustness.

Therefore, the purpose of the choreography model is to illustrate and elements of the business process that are relevant to its interaction with other processes. This may aid in understanding the present processes and may reveal interoperability issues requiring adjustment.

Web Services Orchestration

Coordinating resources to deliver services is essentially an issue of information management. Information about the state of a resource (i.e., characteristics such as capacity, availability, location, etc.) must be made available to other resources when and as needed. When such information is made available in a digital format, it can be transmitted through an electronic network such as the Internet. The digital delivery of such information means that the recipients of such information can be not only humans, but also computer applications that can process such information on behalf of humans.

Coordinating resources requires the description of coordination patterns and rules. If resources are viewed as active rather than passive entities, coordination can be done through direct interaction with the resource. Although the concept of an active resource is more intuitive for some types of resources (like humans) than others (like airplane seats) there are advantages in treating all resources as active. In their digital equivalent, even passive resources such as airplane seats can be made active (i.e., as programs that can execute and interact with other programs). In resource coordination, we are interested in finding out information about a resource such as its status, capacity, and availability. As we said in Chapter II, some resources are shareable while others are not. It is a good design principle to keep information about the resource's status *within* the resource.

In the context of Web services, coordination of multiple Web services in an *orchestration* may be required to ensure the correct result of a series of operations comprising a single business transaction. Whenever coordination occurs, the propagation of additional information (the coordination *context*) to coordinated participants is required. The coordination context contains information such as a unique identifier that allows a series of operations to share a common outcome. The outcome is typically defined in terms of coordinated state persistence operations. For example, in a Web services-based architecture, a SOAP header block might contain context information that is propagated when interacting with a coordinator, or when multiple participants exchange SOAP messages in order to create a larger interaction such as a process flow or other aggregation of services. A Web services coordinator maintains a list of participants and ensures that each participant receives the result of the coordinated interaction. A coordinator can also be a participant, creating a tree of subcoordinators or peer-coordinators that cooperate to further propagate the result. For example, when one of the participants generates a fault, the coordinator ensures that all other participants are notified. A Web services coordinator sends and receives SOAP encoded messages for interoperability with any type of participant, regardless of operating system, programming language, or platform. The important point is that this information in such messages is specific to the type of coordination being performed: to identify the coordinator(s), the other participants, recovery information in the event of a failure, and so on. The type of coordination protocol that is used may vary depending upon the circumstances. What is needed, therefore, is a standardization on a coordination framework (coordination service) that allows users and services to register with it and customize it on a per-service or per-application basis.

None of the core Web service specifications (SOAP, WSDL, UDDI, etc.) we discussed in Chapter II were designed to provide mechanisms by themselves for describing how individual Web services can be interconnected to create reliable and dependable business solutions with the appropriate level of complexity. The technology industry has not yet produced a single standardized Web services view of how to define and implement business processes so that such connections can be described. To address the concerns and needs of their customers, several major software vendors have developed and proposed languages and standards for coordinating Web services. Some of those standards are presented next, and the most important of them, BPEL, is more extensively discussed in the final section of this chapter.

Requirements for Web Services Orchestration

From the aforementioned definition of orchestration, it can be concluded that for an effective orchestration, Web services should:

1. Have the ability to invoke other Web services in an asynchronous way to achieve reliability, scalability, and adaptability. This enables a business process to invoke Web services concurrently rather than sequentially in order to enhance performance.

2. Be able to manage exceptions and transactional integrity for long-running processes (i.e., processes that may run for several hours or even days). The

exception management includes error handling and transactional integrity is managed through *compensation* techniques.

3. Be dynamic, flexible, and adaptable to meet the changing needs of a business. The orchestration engine enables flexibility by providing a clear separation between the logic of the business process logic and the Web services that realize it. An orchestration also handles the overall process flow by calling the appropriate Web services and determines the next steps to be completed.

4. Enable reusability by exposing Web service interfaces for processes to have access to it. Reusability is particularly helpful when there is a need to compose higher level processes from existing orchestrated processes.

Differences Between Web Services Orchestration and Choreography

So, although terms *Web services orchestration* and *choreography* are sometimes used interchangeably, they are different. Choreography provides the necessary information to enable communication with the Web service from the client point of view, while orchestration describes how the Web service makes use of other Web services in order to achieve its capability. Therefore, Web services orchestration will be used to describe the creation of business processes, either executable or collaborative, that utilize Web services.

Web services may be combined into larger scale conversations by means of choreographies. A choreography is the documentation of the combination of Web services, omitting the details of the actual messages involved in each service invocation, and focusing on the dependencies between the services.

• A Web service choreography decomposes a business capability (business service) in terms of interaction with the Web service, while

• A Web service orchestration decomposes a business service in terms of functionality required from other Web services.

Therefore, the distinction between choreography and orchestration reflects the difference between communication and cooperation. The choreography defines how to communicate with the Web service in order to consume its functionality. The orchestration defines how the overall functionality is achieved by the cooperation of more elementary Web service providers.

Web Services Choreography and Orchestration Standards

Web services orchestration standards specify how Web services can be connected together to create higher level business processes. These include standards such as BPEL, WSCI, and BPML. Web services orchestration standards have emerged as the automation of business processes over the Internet, is increasingly implemented as Web services. The automation of business processes is facilitated by *orchestration servers* (i.e., systems that execute the specifications of orchestrations).

Several specifications for conceptual and syntactic models for Web service coordination have been proposed (Snell, 2002); for example:

1. Business process execution language for Web services (BPEL4WS).
2. Web services transaction (WS-Transaction). This will be discussed in Chapter VIII.
3. Web services coordination (WS-Coordination). This will be discussed in Chapter VIII.

Other standards aim to reduce the complexity of choreographing Web services. They are reviewed briefly below while BPEL4WS is more extensively discussed in the next section.

WS-CDL

WS-CDL (Box et al., 2004) is an XML-based language that describes peer-to-peer collaborations of Web services. WS-CDL defines, from a global viewpoint, the observable behavior of the Web services, and the order of message exchanges required to accomplishing a common business goal. WS-CDL contains rules that describe how different services may act together, and in what sequence. In this way, it complements orchestration languages such as BPEL, which describe one side of the interaction rather than the full system.

Web Services Conversation Language (WSCL)

This is an XML-based specification layered on top of WSDL that is proposed by Hewlett-Packard (W3C, 2002). The Web services conversation language (WSCL), is defining conversations between service providers and consumers. WSCL can be used in conjunction with other service description languages such as WSDL, to provide binding information for abstract service interfaces, or to specify what abstract interfaces supported by a concrete service.

XLANG

This is another specification for XML descriptions layered on top of WSDL, proposed by Microsoft (2001). XLANG provides the means to describe the service interface of a process. Its major features include:

- Constructs for sequential and parallel control flow
- Long-running transactions with compensation
- Custom correlation of messages
- Flexible internal and external exceptions handling
- Modular behavior description
- Dynamic service referral
- Multi-role contracts

Web Services Flow Language (WSFL)

This is IBM's XML based proposal for ordering activity execution and data exchanges in a process (IBM, 2001). It is also layered on top of WSDL, and describes the Web services interfaces and their protocol bindings. It defines both the execution sequence and the mapping of each step in the flow to two specific operations, such as a *flow model,* for representing a series of activities in the process, and a *global model* for binding each activity to a Web service instance. WSFL supports exception handling but no direct support for transactions.

Business Process Modeling Language (BPML)

The Business Process Management Initiative has developed the XML-based BPML (BPMI, 2001). BPML is a metalanguage for modeling executable private business processes. BPML is complementary to public collaborative process description languages, such as BPSS (OASIS, 2001).

The BPEL Specification

BPEL (*business process execution language*) or *business process execution language for web services* (BPEL4WS) is a business process orchestration language that was created from the merging of IBM's WSFL and Microsoft's XLANG (Andrews et al., 2003). BPEL was proposed in 2002 as a standard approach to connecting Web services. BPEL is an XML-based workflow definition language that allows businesses to describe complex business processes that can both consume and provide Web services.

BPEL is a layer on top of WSDL that used to specify the actions that should take place in a business process and their sequence. However, while WSDL is stateless, BPEL records the states for processes in order to determine what should be done and to enable long-lived business transactions. The BPEL specification models the behavior of both *executable* and *abstract* processes composed of Web services. An executable process specifies the partners involved in the process, the messages exchanged between the partners, the execution order of the activities that constitute the process, and the fault and exception handling that specifies the process.

The BPEL standard defines:

1. A model and a grammar for describing the behavior of a business process based on interactions between the process services and the services of its partners.

2. The way the interactions of multiple Web services with these partners are coordinated to achieve a business goal as well as the logic necessary for this coordination.

3. Systematic mechanisms for dealing with business exceptions and processing faults.

4. The way individual or composite activities within a process are to be compensated in cases where exceptions occur or a partner requests a reversal.

BPEL is therefore an orchestration and not a choreography language. The most significant benefit of using BPEL lies in unlocking the potential of Web services to increase the level of automation and thus lower the cost in establishing cross-enterprise automated business processes.

BPEL depends on the Web services standards discussed in Chapter 3. More specifically, BPEL depends on:

1. XML specifications including;
   - WSDL 1.1: WSDL messages provide the data model used by BPEL processes.

- XML Schema 1.0: XML Schema type definitions also provide the data model used by BPEL processes.

- XPath 1.0: which provides support for data manipulation.

2. WS-Addressing used by BPEL for Web service endpoint references (Box et al., 2004).

In BPEL all external resources and partners are represented as WSDL services. BPEL is extensible in order to accommodate future versions of these standards, specifically the XPath and related XML standards. Like ebXML discussed in Chapter 2, BPEL manages distributed processes in terms of their creation, execution, and control. BPEL supports the following elements:

- *Partners,* which are either Web services that a process invokes or Web services that invoke a process. Partners must provide *port types* and the process invokes an operation of that port type. The process may also provide another port type that the partner can invoke. *Partner link types* show that there is a partnership relationship between two parties.

- *Variables,* which define the messages that are exchanged during a process and the data that determine the business logic of the process.

- *Simple activities,* which are the steps involved in the process that have no structure. Simple activities include *receive, reply, invoke, assign, wait, throw, compensate, terminate* and *empty.*

- *Structured activities,* which combine simple activities using sequence, switch, pick, while, flow, and scope control structures similar to those of programming languages.

- *Compensation* and *fault handlers,* which enable a process to undo certain activities and to explicitly catch execution errors.

Abstract processes in BPEL are sometimes referred to as business protocols, because they specify mutually visible message exchange behavior for each party involved in the protocol without revealing its internal implementation. Abstract processes use all the concepts of BPEL but approach data handling in a way that reflects the level of abstraction required to describe public aspects of the business protocol. Specifically, abstract processes handle only protocol-relevant data.

Executable processes are sometimes referred to as interaction protocols, because the logic and state of the process determines the nature and sequence of the Web service interactions conducted by each business partner.

End-point references is the mechanism for dynamic selection and assignment of services or communication of port-specific data for services. It enables the selection of a provider for a particular type of service and for invocation their operations.

Message properties are means of naming and representing distinct data elements within a message. These are divided into Application-visible data: (e.g., for correlating service instances with messages and message context protocol relevant data; for security, transaction, and reliable messaging).

Process elements and properties are the activities and links that make up the business process, where activities are the operations in a business process and links connect a source activity to a target activity.

Correlation set is a named group of properties shared by all messages in the correlated group. To create correlation sets, partners must have a stable business relationship and should be statically configured to send documents related to the interaction to the URLs associated with the relevant WSDL service ports. The exact location and type of the token in the relevant messages is fixed and instance independent.

Only the value of the token is instance dependent. Therefore, the structure and position of the correlation tokens in each message can be expressed declaratively in the business process description. Correlation sets can be either global or local.

Event handlers are the facilitators of message and alarm events during the normal behavior of a scope.

Message events ensure that the specified event waits for a particular message to arrive.

The Message attributes include:

- The partnerLink attribute defines the partner link on which the request is expected to arrive.

- The portType and partner specify the location of the event.

- The variable attribute identifies the variable containing the message received from the partner.

- The operation attribute identifies the appropriate port type and operation that is invoked by the enablement of each onMessage event handler.

- The correlation attribute is interpreted and used in the same way a receive activity applies correlation.

Alarm events are used for signifying timeout conditions.

The Alarm attributes include:

- The partnerLink for the partner link on which the request is expected to arrive.

- The duration after which the event will be executed.
- The exact time the alarm will be fired.

Fault handlers determine the activities that must be performed in response to faults resulting from the invocation of a service.

Sources of faults can be:

- Reponses to invoke activity based on fault definition in a WSDL operation,
- A programmatic throw activity with a specified name and data.
- Faults from an external scope.
- Platform-specific ones such as communication failures that can occur in a business process instance

Fault handling occurs when there is a switch from the normal processing pattern in a scope of a business process. Therefore, a business process that involved successful fault handling at any stage is considered to be abnormal.

Compensation handlers on the other hand allow the scope to delineate a part of the behavior that is meant to be reversible. A compensation handler is a binding for the compensation activities in the following way:

- It must receive data about the current state of the process and return data regarding the results of the compensation.
- It must be explicitly specified because the compensation behavior is a part of the business logic and protocol in business transactions.
- If a scope being compensated by name was nested in a loop, the instances of the compensation handlers in the successive iterations are invoked in reverse order.

Data handling in BPEL consists of received and sent messages. Features of data handling include:

- The present value of data.
- **Process-level attributes:** Used for queries and expressions (e.g., for the selection of nodes in assignment, property definition, and others).
- **Expression language:** Specifies the expression language used in the process.

- **Variable:** The container that enables the maintenance of a state by holding messages/data that constitutes the state of a process.

Variables are specified as input or output messages for receive, invoke, and reply activities. They are defined as WSDL message types, XML simple types, or XML schema. Variables are declared in and belong to a particular scope namely: global and local. Finally, variables can be hidden in an outer scope by declaring a variable with an identical name in an inner scope. Variables can be initialized by property assignment or message reception.

Expressions are the combination of message selections, properties, or literal constants to produce a new value for a variable property or selection. Examples of expressions include

- *Boolean-valued expressions*: transition, join and while conditions, as well as switch cases.
- *Deadline-valued expressions*: "until" attribute of onAlarm and wait.
- *Duration-valued expressions*: "for" attribute of onAlarm and wait
- *General expressions:* such as Assignment which is the data referred to by the "from" and "to" specifications and must be of compatible types for validity.

BPEL Activities

Activities in BEPL are classified *as basic, structured, event handling and, error handling.*

Basic activities; make up the basic BPEL model and they include;

- *Receive,* which involves getting the data as an input from a client or a call back from a partner Web service to instantiate a business process. Receive allows execution blocking until a matching message arrives.
- *Reply,* which returns the output message in response to the one input message received via the receive activity. It is applicable to synchronous operations only and has two official responses namely: *normal* and *fault.*
- *Invoke,* which executes a Web service through synchronous or asynchronous operations on a port type offered on a partner. Synchronous invocation is also known as a *request-response* operation requires both an input and an output message, while asynchronous invocation is known as a *one-way* operation because it only requires the input message.

- *Wait,* which allows a specified period of time or allocates a deadline for the execution or invocation of an operation.

Structured activities. These describe how a business process is composed by structures of basic activities using patterns for control, data flow, handling of faults and external events, and coordination of message exchanges between process instances.

Control structures include:

- *Sequence,* which defines the order of execution of activities.
- *Flow,* which is a structured activity that processes the input data from the receive element by executing activities in parallel. It enables concurrency and synchronization using links to express synchronisation dependencies.
- *Switch,* which enables conditional behavior by selection of branches in a business process.
- *While,* which enables repetition of an activity until a certain condition is true.
- *Wait,* which allows waiting for a specified period of time or allocates a deadline for the execution or invocation of an operation.
- *Pick,* which is a set of activity/event branches that will be selected based on the activity associated with it.

Event handling activities, which include:

- *Scope,* which defines a nested activity and its behavior context by determining variables, fault handlers, and compensation handlers.
- *Assign,* which assigns or updates the value of a variable. It can be used to construct and insert new data using expressions to copy:
- data from one variable to another
- endpoint references to and from partner links
- message properties to and from variables
- simple computations on properties and variables (e.g., add to quantity)
- literal value as a source value to a destination.

Error handling activities, which include:

- *Throw,* which relates a fault from inside a business process. It provides a unique fault name and optionally provides a fault variable.

- *Terminate,* which discontinues active executable processes.

- *Empty,* which enables the insertion of a *no-op* instruction to enable concurrency, synchronisation of activities, or catching and suppression of faults in a business operation.

- *Compensate,* which invokes compensation on an inner scope that has already been completed normally. It is a major part of the error-handling framework and can only be used in a fault handler of the scope that immediately encloses the scope for which compensation is to be performed, or in a compensation handler of the scope that immediately encloses the scope for which compensation is to be performed.

A BPEL Example

To illustrate the function and benefits of the BPEL, we will show its application to a real-world business process about online ticket purchasing involving multiple airlines. An excerpt from the BPEL process definition is shown in Listing 1.

Listing 1 shows the partial definition of a BPEL process for online ticket purchasing. The process defines the types for messages (i.e., interfaces for sending itineraries, for invoicing, etc.), the ports, or services, supported (e.g., for invoicing, ticket delivering, etc.) as well as the partner links (i.e., between the invoice requester and the invoice sender, between the shipper of the ticket and its recipient, etc.). For each ports fault messages are also defined for situations where, for example, an itinerary cannot be fulfilled by the airlines.

Listing 1. Example onlin- ticket-buying process in BPEL4WS

```
<process xmlns=http://schemas.xmlsoap.org/ws/2003/03/business-process/
name=OnlineTicketPurchasingProceess"
<import namespace="http://airlines.org/xsd/purchaseticketsonline"
    location="http://airlines.org/xsd/purchaseticketsonline.xsd"/>

<message name=" Itinerary Message">
  <part name="customerInfo" type="sns:customerInfo"/>
  <part name="purchaseOrder" type="sns: Itinerary "/>
```

continued on following page

Listing 1. continued

```
</message>
<message name="InvMessage">
  <part name="IVC" type="sns:Invoice"/>
</message>
<message name=" Itinerary FaultType">
  <part name="problemInfo" type="xsd:string"/>
</message>
<message name= Itinerary Message>
  <part name="schedule" type="sns:scheduleInfo"/>
</message>

<!-- portTypes supported by the purchase ticket online process -->

<portType name="purchaseticketPT">
  <operation name="sendItinerary">
    <input message="pos:ItMessage"/>
    <output message="pos:InvMessage"/>
    <fault name="cannotComplete Itinerary "
        message="pos:orderFaultType"/>
  </operation>
</portType>
<portType name="invoiceCallbackPT">
<operation name="sendInvoice">
    <input message="pos:InvMessage"/>
  </operation>
</portType>
<portType name="shippingCallbackPT">
  <operation name="sendSchedule">
    <input message="pos:scheduleMessage"/>
  </operation>
</portType>
```

continued on following page

Listing 1.continued

```
<!-- portType supported by the invoice services -->

<portType name="computeTicketPricePT">
  <operation name="initiatePriceCalculation">
    <input message="pos:POMessage"/>
  </operation>
  <operation name="sendTickePrice">
    <input message="pos:TicketPriceInfoMessage"/>
  </operation>
</portType>


<!-- portType supported by the shipping service -->

<portType name="shippingPT">
  <operation name="requestShipping">
    <input message="pos:shippingRequestMessage"/>
    <output message="pos:shippingInfoMessage"/>
    <fault name="cannotCompleteOrder"
        message="pos:orderFaultType"/>
  </operation>
</portType>


<plnk:partnerLinkType name="purchasingLT">
  <plnk:role name="FlightbookingService">
    <plnk:portType name="lt: PT"/>
  </plnk:role>
</plnk:partnerLinkType>


<plnk:partnerLinkType name="invoicingLT">
  <plnk:role name="invoiceService">
    <plnk:portType name="pos:computePricePT"/>
```

continued on following page

Listing 1.continued

```
  </plnk:role>
  <plnk:role name="invoiceRequester">
    <plnk:portType name="pos:invoiceCallbackPT"/>
  </plnk:role>
</plnk:partnerLinkType>


</definitions>
```

Technologies and Standards for Automating Business Processes Choreographies

The automation of business processes choreographies is a prerequisite for business to business (B2B) integration. Defining and managing business processes choreographies is a more complex problem than defining and managing Web services. In order to do e-commerce and B2B commerce, we must be able to specify both business processes and choreographies. The specific messages that are exchanged as part of a choreography to trigger business processes within the trading partners' own systems. The trading partners might be different companies or might be different administrative domains of the same company; thus, both business process definition and interaction pattern definitions are important in this technology.

There exists a mix of concrete technologies for describing these things, including ebXML's *business process specification schema* (a proposal for a standard business process metamodel) and RosettaNet's *partner interface processes* (PIPs). PIPs is a specialized system-to-system XML-based dialog that defines business processes between trading partners. Each PIP specification includes a business document with the vocabulary, and a business process with the choreography of the message dialog (RosettaNet, 2007).

What are important here are the processes and interactions, rather than these specific technologies. We can use UML activity and interaction models to define processes and choreographies in a technology-independent fashion. We can also define mappings to the various implementation technologies.

Figure 1 is an example of a UML activity model, which is similar in some respects to a traditional flowchart. This activity model describes a business process in which a company examines a customer enquiry. If it comes from a new customer, it creates a new customer (instance); otherwise, it tries to locate the customer information (e.g., in a database). This type of activity model can drive a generator that produces code and XML for some specific implementation technology.

Figure 1. UML activity model

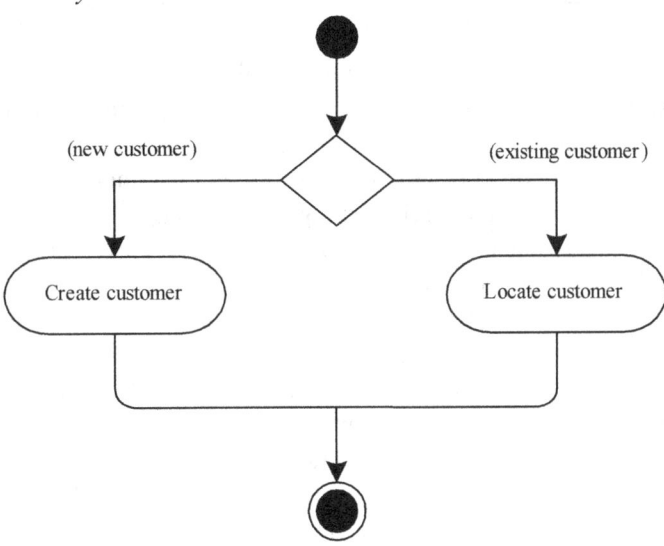

Figure 2. Partner interaction model in UML

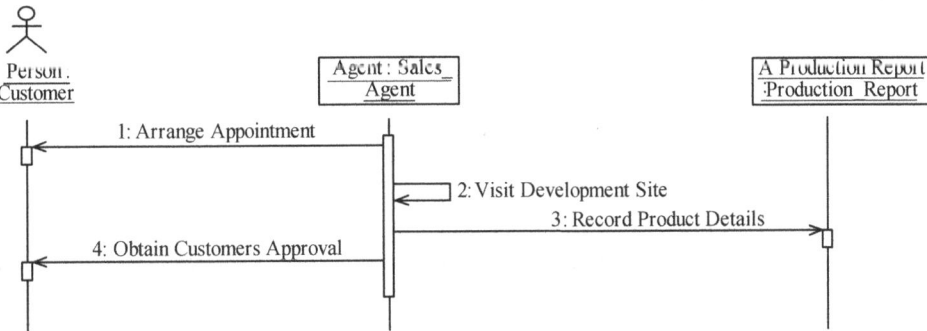

Figure 2 is a UML interaction model. It specifies a choreography of messages among various parties in support of a business activity. This kind of interaction pattern is crucial for business to business (B2B) commerce. Such interaction models can provide additional input to generators of Web service choreographies for BPEL and other languages. OMG, ebXML, and RosettaNet are laying a foundation of standards for business process and choreography definition. They are also developing standard mappings that specify how to map these definitions to various implementation technologies. Such a standards-based edifice is required if B2B commerce is to succeed on a large scale.

Chapter Summary

This chapter had an in depth look into the issues surrounding business process and service coordination. In an ever-increasing, open, competitive environment companies need to engage in multiple partnerships, which are often temporary and dynamic, to deliver complex services to their customers. By coordinating their internal Web services and orchestrating them with the Web services of their partners, companies are able to deploy complex e-services. However, the task of composing Web services into complex orchestrations and choreographies becomes increasingly challenging as the number of the Web services increases and their interactions become more complex in typical business scenarios. Thus BPEL descriptions of such orchestrations can quickly become long and unwieldy. There is also the problem of actually ensuring that the different Web services are compatible, especially as they may belong to different partners. As we shall see in Chapter VI, WSDL is not, on its own, sufficient to guarantee that. The problem of coordination therefore requires a more advanced solution than the one offered by standards such as SOAP and WSDL. Thus, Chapter VI will present a new approach to describing Web services that goes beyond SOAP and WSDL, by providing additional semantic information about the Web service, that is, effectively about the real-world meaning of the Web service and its constituting parts.

References

Andrews, T., Curbera, F., Dholakia, H., Goland, Y., Klein, J., Leymann, F., et al. (2003). *Business process execution language for Web services* (Version 1.1). Retrieved March 16, 2007, from http://xml.coverpages.org/BPELv11-May-052003Final.pdf

Banerji, A., Bartolini, C., Beringer, D., Chopella, V., Govindarajan, Karp, A., et al. (2002). *Web services conversation language* (WSCL, 1.0). Retrieved March 15, 2007, from http://www.w3.org/TR/wscl10/

Box, D., Christensen, E., Curbera, F., Ferguson, D., Frey, J., Hadley, M., et al. (2004, August 10). *Web services addressing (WS-Addressing) W3C member submission.* Retrieved March 17, 2007, from http://www.w3.org/Submission/ws-addressing/

BPMI. (2001). *Business process modeling language (BPML).* Retrieved March 15, 2007, from http://www.bpmi.org/bpml-spec.htm

BPMI. (2007). *Business process modeling notation (BPMN).* Retrieved March 15, 2007 from http://www.bpmn.org/

Dayal U., Hsu, M., & Ladin, R. (2001). Business process coordination: State of the art, trends and open issues. *The VLDB Journal*. Retrieved July 13, 2006, from http://www.dia.uniroma3.it/~vldbproc/001_003.pdf

Endl, R., & Knolmayer, G. (1998). *Modeling processes and workflows by business rules*. Bern, Germany: University of Bern, Institute of Information Systems.

Fischer, L. (2001). Workflow: An introduction. In *Workflow handbook 2001*, Workflow Management Coalition.

Ghalimi, I., & McGoveran, D. (2004, April). Standards and BPM. *Business Integration Journal*.

Gortmaker, J., Janssen, M., & Wagenaar, R. W. (2004). The advantages of Web service orchestration in perspective. In M., Janssen, H. G., Sol, & R. W. Wagenaar (Eds.), *Proceedings of the Sixth International Conference on Electronic Commerce (ICEC'04)*.

IBM. (2001). *Web services flow language (WSFL)*. Retrieved March 15, 2007 from http://www4.ibm.com/software/solutions/Web services/pdf/WSFL.pdf

Kavantzas, N., et al. (Eds.). (2004, December 17). Web services choreography description language (Version 1.0.) W3C Working Draft.

Medjahed, B., Bouguettaya, A., & Elmagarmid, A. K. (2003). Composing Web services on the Semantic Web. *The VLDB Journal, 12,* 333-351.

Microsoft. (2001). *XLANG*. Retrieved March 15, 2007 from http://www.gotdotnet.com/team/xml_wsspecs/xlang-c/default.htm

Myerson, J. M. (2002). *The complete book of middleware*. CRC Press.

OASIS. (1999). *Electronic business using extensible markup language (ebXML)*. OASIS, United Nations/ECE Agency CEFACT.

OASIS. (2001, May 11). ebXML business process specification schema (Version 1.01). Retrieved March 16, 2007 from www.ebxml.org/specs/ebBPSS.pdf

RosettaNet. (2007). *RosettaNet partner interface processes (PIPs)*. Retrieved March 16, 2007, from http://portal.rosettanet.org/cms/sites/RosettaNet/Standards/RStandards/pip/index.html

Schmidt, M. T. (1999). The evolution of workflow standards. *IEEE Concurrency*, 44-52.

Snell, J. (2002). *Automating business processes and transactions in Web services, an introduction to BPELWS, WS-Coordination and WS-transaction. IBM emerging technologies.* Retrieved March 15, 2007, from http://www-128.ibm.com/developerworks/Web services/library/ws-autobp/

WfMC. (1998, August). Workflow Management Coalition, Process Definition Interchange (Version 1.0 Beta). [WfMC Document WfMC-TC-1016-P].

Section III

Service Engineering
Concepts and Techniques

Chapter V

Model-Driven Service Engineering

Introduction

This chapter argues that modeling is at the core of every service engineering method. Modeling not only allows us to understand business services but, what is equally important, to transform them into software-realized services.

In general, models provide abstractions of a physical system that allow engineers to reason about that system while ignoring irrelevant details and focusing on relevant ones (Brown, 2004). All forms of engineering and science rely on models to understand complex, real-world systems. Models are used to predict system properties, reason about how changes in some parts of it will affect the rest of a system, and communicate key system characteristics to various stakeholders. The models may be developed as a mock-up or blueprint prior to implementing the physical system, or they may be derived from an existing system or a system in development, as an aid to understanding its behavior.

Models are therefore artifacts that represent real-world objects at some abstract level, giving the engineers the opportunity to modify, test, and preview certain properties of the actual object, in a cost- and effort-effective manner. Model construction also allows engineers to receive feedback from the stakeholders and validate their requirements early in the process.

In the electronics industry, models of circuits are utilized by computer-controlled machinery in order to produce the physical hardware circuits without human intervention. This idea of automating production of hardware has influenced recent thinking about how software should be developed. This premise of deriving software programs directly from software models, in the same way that hardware is manufactured from designs, is the essence of *model-driven development* (MDD) that is discussed in this chapter. MDD promises increased productivity by speeding up delivery times. To deliver such benefit, MDD is based on the concept of highly automated software environments for model management (Atkinson & Kühne, 2003).

Since the objective of service engineering is to realize business services as software programs (e.g., Web services), the principles of MDD apply to service engineering, too. Thus, the chapter examines MDD in the context of concrete service realization from abstract service models. The infrastructure for MDD is currently growing constantly with the introduction and evolution of standards; however, there are still a number of issues to resolve. As a result, although MDD is recognized to be a promising proposal for the future, it currently lacks general acceptance and applicability in the software industry.

Nevertheless, as we argue in this chapter, the future of service engineering is inextricably linked with progress in model-driven software development.

The Use of Modeling in Software Development

Today, the majority of software developers still produce exclusively code; that is, they do not produce any other software artifacts at all. Instead, they rely almost entirely on the code they write, and they express their model of the system they are building directly in a programming language such as Java, C++, or C# within an integrated development environment (IDE), such as IBM Web Sphere Studio, Eclipse, or Microsoft Visual Studio. Of course, code produced in this manner implicitly contains more abstract models that, however, are hidden inside programming language constructs such as modules, packages, libraries, and so forth.

Any separate modeling of software designs is informal and intuitive, and only exists on paper drawings, or in the programmers' heads. This approach, while adequate for small projects, fails to scale up to larger ones where properties of the system under development, such as its internal construction (architecture), needs to communicated to a larger group of stakeholders, some of whom will be responsible to continue to maintain the system even after the original development team has gone.

Informal vs. Formal Software Models

Because software models and model-driven software development are at the heart of the MDD approach, to better understand MDD, it is appropriate to first look at how application developers use modeling.

In the software development world, modeling has a rich tradition, dating back to the early days of programming and even to other engineering disciplines such as electronics and mechanical engineering. The most recent innovations have focused on notations and tools that allow users to express system perspectives of value to software architects and developers, in ways that are readily mapped into the programming language code that can be compiled for a particular operating system platform (Brown, 2004). The current state of this practice employs the *unified modeling language* (UML) as the primary modeling notation. UML allows development teams to capture a variety of important characteristics of a system in a number of models. Transformations among these models are primarily manual. UML modeling provides guidance on how to maintain synchronized models as part of a large-scale development effort.

One useful way to characterize current practice is to look at the different ways in which the models are synchronized with the source code they help describe. This is illustrated in Figure 1 that shows the spectrum of modeling approaches in use by software practitioners today. Each category identifies a particular use of models in assisting software practitioners to create executable applications (code) and the relationship between the models and the code.

To date, much of the use of UML has been for informal modeling, in which UML is employed to sketch out the basic concepts of a system. For informal modeling, UML has significant advantages over other informal diagrams that usually are constructed using boxes connected with arrows. This is because the UML notation constructs have very specific meanings. In contrast, the meaning of the boxes and lines in a

Figure 1. The modeling spectrum

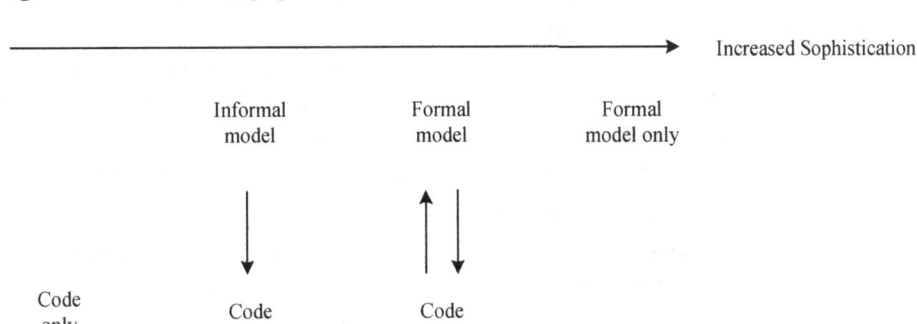

typical "system diagram" is subject to the interpretation of the reader. However, informal UML models are not amenable to automated processing to transform to executable code. A similar situation exists with text; an informal textual description of the functions of a program cannot be compiled and executed the way corresponding source code can be.

In contrast to informal UML models, formal UML models are precise and sufficiently detailed (i.e., *computationally complete*). In a formal UML model, the visible elements must be precise enough to drive code generation. A formal UML model must also be syntactically complete. In an informal UML model, it is common, and accepted, to leave out certain properties such as the cardinalities for some of the associations in a class diagram or the declaration of types for the objects attributes. In contrast, in a formal UML model, this kind of informality is not acceptable, as syntactical incompleteness makes it impossible for a code generator to process the model. However, at the same time, formal UML models need to be technology independent to allow business experts to validate them and to implement the business logic they describe. If, for example, business rules have been captured only in code, it becomes very difficult to trace them back to the original requirements of the business users. This is a serious problem in enterprise software development, where it is critical to maintain the traceability of requirements. If the requirement that a piece of code addresses are not known, it becomes difficult to maintain that code if the requirement changes. Thus, it becomes evident that not only software models must be formal and complete but cater for both the business experts and the developers alike. In the sequel, we see notations and standards for creating such models or more accurately speaking, *metamodels* using UML.

UML Metamodeling Standards

As explained in the previous section, models that describe software can be classified as structured or unstructured, according to the strictness of the rules they comply to. Unstructured models are merely informal expressions of ideas that do not conform to rules, giving designers the opportunity to express their views of the system with unlimited freedom. Examples of unstructured models include descriptions in natural language, whiteboard diagrams, or computer drawings using a graphics tool. On the other hand, structured models have a well-defined set of structural elements and rules that they must obey. Those rules can be provided either informally (e.g., with natural language statements) or in a structured artifact that is called a *metamodel* (also referred to as *domain-specific language* or *modeling language*).

A further classification of structured models can be made, based on their formality. Formal models have precise and unambiguous semantics, based on well-understood and accepted mathematical concepts, while semiformal models define some of their semantics with informal notations such as natural language, to allow different interpretations in different contexts, thus providing greater flexibility. Examples of formal models are those expressed in notations such as Z and B, while semiformal modeling technologies include among others MOF, EMF, and the newly proposed Microsoft Domain-specific Languages Framework, discussed below. Therefore, however useful, unstructured models are difficult to parse and interpret in an automated manner.

UML Profiles

As was already mentioned, UML is a diagrammatic notation used for modeling object-oriented systems that was initially designed as a sketching language. However, when UML started to became popular, tools emerged that could generate code out of UML diagrams. Today, there are plenty of tools that use extensions of UML called *UML profiles* (OMG, 2007), in order to design and generate full working systems for domains such as Web applications and Web services.

A UML profile is a UML dialect defined via UML's built-in extension mechanisms. The UML specification explains how to define a profile by selecting a subset of UML and then using the UML extension facilities to extend that subset. For example, the object class "Flight Information," shown in Figure 2, uses a stereotype <<Business Entity>> to indicate that certain classes represent business information entities (the double angle brackets denote a stereotype). This has effectively extended the notion of a UML class to create a new type of class that represents business information entities. Stereotypes can be used to extend not only the UML class construct but also to extend any of the other UML modeling constructs such as attribute, operation, association, and so on.

Similarly, the class "Flight Information Service", of Figure 2, uses a <<Service>> stereotype to indicate that the class represents a business service. A code generator can be written, to recognize that a <<Service>> is not the same as a <<Business Entity>> and to treat it differently.

Figure 2. UML stereotypes

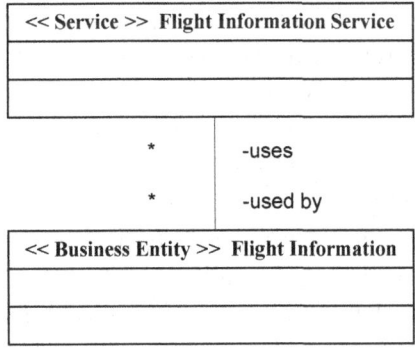

Another useful UML extension mechanism is the tagged value. Tagged values let you define modeling properties that UML does not support "out of the box." For example, when you define an association in UML, it does not allow you to state whether or not the reference at each end should be implemented as an XML HREF (hypertext reference) or, alternately, by an IDREF (attribute value).

The previous examples illustrate the two fundamental usages of UML profiles. One is to model a particular domain, such as business information and business services. There are also UML profiles for other domains, such as real-time systems and telecommunications. In the context of Web services, one profile can be used to model the technology-independent aspects of a service and others for parameterizing the mappings to specific service-realization technologies. A good UML tool makes it easy to remove and restore all of the elements of a model that stem from one particular profile. This makes it easy to (1) maintain a purely abstract version of the model, which would not include, for example, the XML aspects of the system, and (2) superimpose technology dependent aspects.

However, UML's profiling mechanisms impose fairly strict limits on defining new modeling constructs. A standard related to UML, called the *meta object facility* (MOF), proposed by OMG (2006) provides much more freedom to define new modeling constructs that extend or supplement UML. MOF will be discussed in later sections, in the context of model-driven architectures.

Serialising UML to XML

There are several different approaches for mapping formal UML models to implementation technologies. One approach is embodied in an OMG standard, called *XML metadata interchange* (XMI) (OMG, 2005). This standard defines mapping rules that specify how to generate an *XML document type definition* (DTD) or schema (both of which were explained in Chapter III), from a class model. The generated DTD or schema, defines a format for representing instances of the classes in XML documents (XMI).

Listing 1 shows the results of running the class model shown in Figure 3 through an XMI generating tool. The result is an XSD, and the last portion of Listing 1 shows a fragment of that generated XSD which corresponds to the Employee class. It shows XML definitions for the three attributes of Employee, namely Name, Position, and Salary. Although it is not evident from the small fragment of the generated XSD shown here, the various semantic elements of the model, such as the properties of associations, affect how the XSD is generated.

As was previously mentioned, the idea of generating concrete software artifacts from abstract models is viable only if it allows engineers who understand the concrete technologies to fine-tune the generation rules. XMI gives the engineer a number

Figure 3. UML class "Employee"

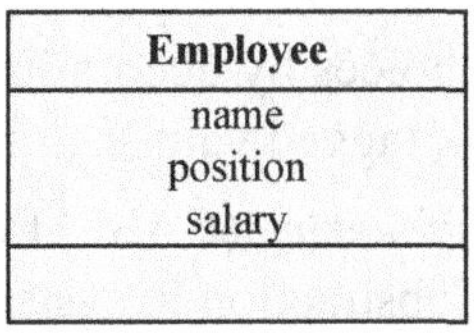

Employee
name position salary

Listing 1. XMI example

```
<?xml version="1.0"?>
<XMI xmi.version="1.2" xmlns:UML="org.omg/UML/1.4">
<XMI.header>
 <XMI.documentation>
  <XMI.exporter>xmiorg.org stylesheet</XMI.exporter>
 </XMI.documentation>
 <XMI.metamodel xmi.name="UML" xmi.version="1.4"/>
</XMI.header>
<XMI.content>
<UML:Model xmi.id="M.1" name="employee" visibility="public"
        isSpecification="false" isRoot="false"
        isLeaf="false" isAbstract="false">
 <UML:Namespace.ownedElement>
  <UML:Class xmi.id="C.1" name="employee" visibility="public"
        isSpecification="false" namespace="M.1" isRoot="true"
        isLeaf="true" isAbstract="false" isActive="false">
  <UML:Classifier.feature>
   <UML:Attribute xmi.id="A.1" name="name" visibility="private"
          isSpecification="false" ownerScope="instance"/>
   <UML:Attribute xmi.id="A.2" name="position" visibility="private"
          isSpecification="false" ownerScope="instance"/>
   <UML:Attribute xmi.id="A.3" name="salary" visibility="private"
          isSpecification="false" ownerScope="instance"/>
  </UML:Classifier.feature>
  </UML:Class>
  </UML:Namespace.ownedElement>
 </UML:Model>
</XMI.content>
</XMI>
```

Copyright © 2008, IGI Global. Copying or distributing in print or electronic forms without written permission of IGI Global is prohibited.

of choices governing XML production. Each of these choices is expressed as a parameter. A mapping that provides such choices is called a *parameterized mapping*. The engineer indicates her choices by decorating the model with actual values of those parameters, using UML tagged values.

Computer aided software engineering (CASE) tools are an example of previous attempts at raising the level of abstraction in system development. CASE tools have not been widely successful, and a significant factor in this lack of success was that they do not provide engineers with the level of control that parameterized mappings offer (Guelfi, Ries, & Sterges, 2003).

Metamodeling Frameworks

Today, there are a number of object-oriented modeling technologies that are used in practice for model-driven development. Those discussed in this section are either standards, open source, or have a published architecture and a substantial user base.

Meta-Object Facility (MOF)

The meta-object facility (MOF) is an OMG standard that provides a metadata management framework and a set of services to enable the development and interoperability of model and metadata systems. With MOF, developers can define the abstract syntax of modeling languages, validate models against metamodels, and serialize them into XML metadata interchange (XMI), described previously. MOF is also complemented by the *object constraint language* (OCL) (OMG, 2002), an expression language tailored for defining complex validity constraints that MOF itself cannot capture. The most well-known metamodel defined in MOF and OCL is the UML metamodel (OMG, 2007), that defines the structural rules and semantics of the *unified modeling language*. UML is the industry standard and de facto modeling language for object-oriented systems.

Eclipse Modeling Framework (EMF)

The Eclipse Foundation (http://www.eclipse.org) is an organization formed by major software vendors whose main purpose is to provide a platform for development tools interoperability. The Eclipse Modeling Framework (EMF) is a modeling framework built on top of the Eclipse platform, in an effort to provide a practical approach to modeling and model management for Java developers. EMF provides an integrated graphical editor for ECore metamodels and a framework (EMF.Edit) for generating graphical editors for new modeling languages from their ECore metamodel. Moreover, EMF provides tools for extracting models from Java annotated source files, and XML schema documents. While EMF started as an independent modeling framework, in its latest versions it is aligned with the MOF 2.0, featuring model validation with OCL and storage capabilities using XMI.

Microsoft Domain-Specific Languages Framework

At the time of writing this book, the Microsoft Domain-Specific Languages Framework is under development and, periodically, beta releases are made available to the public. Therefore, although it is anticipated that this framework will play an important role in the further development of MDD, it is still early to discuss technical details of this approach. In general, the framework introduces a new language for defining metamodels. Metamodel-based tools exist that can generate extensible model editors as plug-ins for the Visual Studio development environment. The serialization format of both models and metamodels is, as with the previous two approaches, based on a dialect of XML.

Other Metamodeling Technologies

- MetaEdit+ (http://www.metacase.com) is a commercial modeling environment that facilitates visual definition of domain-specific languages and models, model validation, and code generation.
- XMF-Mosaic is a framework that extends OMG standards such as MOF and OCL, with more powerful mechanisms such as XCore and XOCL to facilitate the design and management of modeling languages (http://albini.xactium.com/Web /index.php?option=com_content&task=blogcategory&id=27&Itemid=46).
- The Generic Modeling Environment (http://www.isis.vanderbilt.edu/proj-ects/gme/) is an open source framework for defining modeling languages and designing models using advanced graphical editors.

All the frameworks discussed follow a common pattern: Each one introduces a metamodeling language that is used to define new modeling languages (metamodels). Metamodels are used to validate models and to drive or generate language-specific model editors to enable designing models in a graphical manner. Finally, both metamodels and models are *serializable* (i.e., translatable to XML) using either a dialect of XML (e.g., MOF, EMF, MSDSL, XMF, GME) or a proprietary representation (e.g., MetaEdit+).

Introduction to Model-Driven Engineering

Advances in languages and platforms during the past 2 decades have raised the level of software abstractions available to developers, thereby alleviating one major problem with earlier efforts known as *computer-aided software engineering* (CASE). CASE focused on developing software methods and tools that enabled developers to express their designs in terms of general graphical programming representations, but suffered from the inability to scale to complex, production-scale systems in a broad range of application domains. Thanks to the maturation of third-generation languages such as Java and C++, and with the introduction of better development environments, software developers are now better equipped to shield themselves from complexities associated with creating applications using earlier technologies.

Despite these advances, though, several problems remain. At the heart of these problems is the growth of platform complexity, which has evolved faster than the ability of general-purpose languages to mask it (Schmidt, 2006). Moreover, since these platforms often evolve rapidly and new platforms appear regularly, developers spend considerable effort manually porting application code to different platforms or newer versions of the same platform. Another costly problem with today's software development is that most application and platform code is still written and maintained manually, which incurs excessive time and effort. There are also limits to the interoperability that can be achieved by creating a single set of standard programming interfaces.

Model-driven engineering (MDE) is a promising approach to address platform complexity and the inability of general-purpose languages to alleviate this complexity and express domain concepts effectively (Schmidt, 2006). MDE refers to the systematic use of models as primary engineering artifacts throughout the engineering life cycle. MDE can be applied to software, system and data engineering. MDE is also referred to as model-driven development (*MDD)*. The variant of the MDD philosophy defined by the Object Management Group (OMG) is called *model-driven architecture* (MDA). MDA, the OMG's flavor of the MDD philosophy is the focus of the following sections. OMG's MDA framework separates business-oriented decisions from platform decisions, to allow greater flexibility when architecting and evolving systems. Application architects use the MDA framework as a blueprint for expressing their enterprise architectures, and employ the open standards inherent in MDA as their *futureproofing* against vendor lock-in and technology evolution (OMG, 2002).

The MDA Concept

Model-driven architecture is an initiative of the software industry to raise the level of abstraction in how systems are been developed. This follows a history of similar attempts to raise the level of abstraction using compilers, high-level languages, computer-aided software design environments, and so on.

The OMG organization was formed to help reduce complexity, lower costs, and hasten the introduction of new software applications. OMG is accomplishing this goal through the introduction of the MDA architectural framework with supporting detailed specifications. These specifications, OMG believes, will lead the industry towards interoperability, reusable, portable software components and data models.

OMG defines MDA as an approach to system development that utilizes the power of models in that work. It is model driven because it provides a means for using models to direct the course of understanding, design, construction, deployment, operation, maintenance, and modification. However, MDA is not merely an approach to system development using models; it is also a software-systems development philosophy that separates the specification of system functionality from the specification of the implementation of the functionality on a specific technology platform. To this end, the MDA defines an architecture for models and a set of guidelines for structuring specifications expressed as models.

MDA is an open, vendor-neutral approach to system interoperability, relying on standards such as the unified modeling language (UML), meta object facility (MOF) and XML metadata interchange (XMI). Enterprise solutions can be built using these modeling platforms, including CORBA, J2EE, .NET, and Web-based platforms.

OMG is now promoting MDA as a way to develop systems that more accurately satisfy customers' needs, and that offer more flexibility in system evolution. The MDA approach builds on earlier system specification standards work, and provides a comprehensive interoperability framework for defining interconnected systems.

Summary of the MDA Theory

Following a long tradition of using models to represent key ideas in software development, MDA provides a conceptual framework for using models and applying transformations between them as part of a controlled, efficient software development process. The basic assumptions and parameters governing MDA usage are:

- Models help developers understand and communicate complex ideas.
- Many different kinds of elements can be modeled, depending on the context, offering different views of the problem domain that must ultimately be reconciled.
- There are commonalities at all levels of these models—in both the problems being analyzed and the proposed solutions.

- Applying the ideas of different kinds of models and transforming them between representations enables the identification and reuse of common approaches.

- In what it calls *model-driven architecture*, OMG has provided a conceptual framework and a set of standards to express models, model relationships, and model-to-model transformations.

- Tools and technologies can help to realize this approach, and make it practical and efficient to apply.

MDA, therefore, is an emerging set of standards and technologies focused on a particular style of software development—one that prescribes certain kinds of models to be used, how these models may be prepared, and the relationships among the different kinds of models. MDA provides an approach for:

- Specifying a system independently of the platform that supports it.
- Specifying platforms that support the future system.
- Choosing a particular platform for the system being developed.
- Transforming the system specification into one for a particular platform.

Modeling has had a major impact on software engineering, and it is critical to the success of every scaleable solution. However, there is great variety in what the models represent and how they are used, and not a general consensus as to what is MDA practice. There is a general agreement though, that MDA is more closely associated with approaches in which code is (semi-) automatically generated from more abstract models, and that employ standard specification languages for describing those models. We will explore this concept in the next section.

Principles of MDA

In MDA, transformations can be applied to abstract descriptions of aspects of a system to add detail, make the description more concrete, or convert between representations. Distinguishing among different kinds of models, allows us to think of software and system development as a series of refinements between different model representations. These models and their refinements are a critical part of the development methodology for situations that include refinements between models representing different aspects of the system, addition of further details to a model, or conversion between different kinds of models.

Three ideas are important here with regard to the abstract nature of a model and the detailed implementation it represents:

- **Model classification:** We can classify software and system models in terms of how explicitly they represent aspects of the platforms being targeted. In all software and system development, there are important constraints implied by the choice of languages, hardware, network topology, communications protocols and infrastructure, and so on. Each of these can be considered elements of a solution "platform". An MDA approach helps us to focus on what is essential to the business aspects of a solution being designed, separate from the details of that "platform"

- **Platform independence:** The notion of a platform is rather complex and highly context dependent. For example, in some situations, the platform may be the operating system and associated utilities, while in other situations it may be a technology infrastructure such as J2EE or .NET; or even a particular configuration of a hardware-system architecture. In any case, it is more important to think in terms of what models at different levels of abstraction are used for what different purposes, rather than to be distracted with defining the *platform* (Brown, 2004).

- **Model transformation and refinement:** By thinking of software and system development as a set of model refinements, the transformations between models become first class elements of the development process. This is important because a great deal of work takes places in defining these transformations, often requiring specialized knowledge of the business domain, the technologies being used for implementation, or both. We can improve the efficiency and quality of systems, by capturing these transformations explicitly and reusing them consistently across solutions. If the different abstract models are well-defined, we can use standard transformations. For example, between design models expressed in UML and implementations in J2EE, in many cases, we can use well-understood UML-to-J2EE transformation patterns that can be consistently applied, validated, and automated.

Underlying these model representations, and supporting the transformations, is a set of metamodels. The ability to analyze, automate, and transform models, requires a clear, unambiguous way to describe the semantics of the models. Hence, the models intrinsic to a modeling approach must themselves be described in a model, which we call a *metamodel*. For example, the standard semantics and notation of the UML are described in metamodels that tool vendors use for implementing the UML in a standard way. The UML metamodel describes in precise detail the meaning of a class, an attribute, and the relationships between these two concepts.

Because many aspects of a system might be of interest, various modeling concepts and notations can be employed to highlight one or more particular perspectives, or views, of that system, depending on what is relevant at any point in time. Furthermore, in some instances you can augment the models with hints, or rules that assist in transforming them from one representation to another. It is often necessary to convert to different views of the system at an equivalent level of abstraction (e.g., from a structural view to a behavioral view), and a *model transformation* facilitates this. In other cases, a transformation converts models offering a particular perspective from one level of abstraction to another, usually from a more abstract to less abstract view, by adding more detail supplied by the transformation rules.

Four principles underlie the OMG's view of MDA (OMG, 2002):

• Models expressed in a well-defined notation are a cornerstone to understanding systems for enterprise-scale solutions.

• The building of systems can be organized around a set of models by imposing a series of transformations between models, organized into an architectural framework of layers and transformations.

• A formal underpinning for describing models in a set of metamodels facilitates meaningful integration and transformation among models, and is the basis for automation through tools.

• Acceptance and broad adoption of this model-based approach requires industry standards to provide openness to consumers, and foster competition among vendors.

To support these principles, the OMG has defined a specific set of layers and transformations that provide a conceptual framework and vocabulary for MDA. An alternative term for these layers is *viewpoints,* which are abstractions that use selected set of architectural concepts and structuring rules, in order to focus on particular concerns within that system. More specifically, OMG identifies four types of viewpoints: *computation independent model* (CIM), *platform-independent model* (PIM), *platform-specific model* (PSM) described by a platform model (PM), and an *implementation-specific model* (ISM). These are explained below:

• **Computation independent viewpoint:** The computation independent viewpoint focuses on the environment and the requirements for the system. The details of the structure and processing of the system are hidden or are, as yet, undetermined.

• **Platform-independent viewpoint:** The platform-independent viewpoint focuses on the operation of a system while hiding the details necessary for a particular platform. A platform-independent viewpoint shows the part of the complete specification that does not change from one platform to another. A platform-independent view may use a general-purpose modeling language, or a language specific to the area in which the system will be used.

- **Platform-specific viewpoint:** The platform-specific viewpoint combines the platform-independent viewpoint with an additional focus on the detail of the use of a specific platform by a system.

MDA separates certain key models of a system, and brings a consistent structure to these models. Models of different systems are structured explicitly into PIMs and PSMs. How the functionality specified in a PIM is realized, is specified in a platform-specific way in the PSM, which is derived from the PIM via some transformations. The following section further clarifies the meaning and usage of CIM, PIM, and PSM models.

Business Modeling: Computation Independent Business Model (CIBM)

In all software development projects there are important constraints implied by the choice of languages, hardware, network topology, communications protocols, infrastructure, and so on. Each of these can be considered elements of a solution platform. A CIBM approach helps focus on what is essential to the business aspects of a solution being designed, separate from the details of that platform

OMG specifies a CIBM as a view of a system from the computation-independent viewpoint (OMG, 2002). A CIBM does not show details of the structure of systems. The CIBM plays an important role in bridging the gap between the domain experts about the domain and its requirements on the one hand, and those that are experts of the design and construction of the artifacts that together satisfy the domain requirements, on the other. CIBM is also referred to as the *business domain model*. The business domain model describes knowledge about the business domains, independent of specific software or business processes that might be used.

Platform-Independent Models (PIM)

The PIM is a view of a system from the platform-independent viewpoint. The PIM exhibits a specified degree of platform-independence, so as to be suitable for use with a number of different platforms of similar type. PIM can be seen therefore as a specification of the functionality of system that is independent of the technology that will be used to implement the functionality. Furthermore, PIMs provide a formal specification of the structure and function of the system, and are independent of any computing platform. Drawing from these views, one can say that the CIBM is a component of the PIM since the platform-independent component view describes computational components and their interactions in a platform-independent manner. These components and interfaces, in turn, are a way of realizing some more abstract information system or application, which itself helps realize a CIBM.

Platform-Specific Model (PSM)

PSM describes how specific technology can be utilized to implement the functionality described in a PIM. PSM is tailored to a system, in terms of the implementation constructs that are available in one specific implementation technology. PSMs contain components that apply to the target platform and architecture. A PIM is transformed into one or more PSMs. For each specific technology platform, a separate PSM is generated.

According to OMG (2002), a PSM is a view of a system from the platform-specific viewpoint. A PSM combines the specifications in the PIM with the details that specify how that system uses a particular type of platform.

For a given system, there are cross-model refinement correspondences between business models, platform-independent components, and platform-specific components. Similarly, interactions between two systems may be specified at the platform-specific, platform-independent, and even the business-model levels of abstraction.

For MDA, a platform is meaningful only relative to a particular point of view—in other words, one person's PIM is another person's PSM (Brown, 2004). For example, a service model may be a PIM with respect to choice of service implementation architecture, if that model does not prescribe a particular choice of service realization technology. However, when a decision is made to use particular service technology, such as Web services, the model is transformed to a Web service-specific PSM. The new model may still be a PIM with respect to choice of service execution technology (e.g., J2EE and .NET), certainly with respect to target operating system and hardware. This is illustrated in Figure 4.

As a result, an MDA tool may support transforming a model in several steps, from initial analysis model to executable code. Alternatively, a tool may transform a model from UML to executable code in a single step.

Figure 4. An example of PIM to PSM transformations

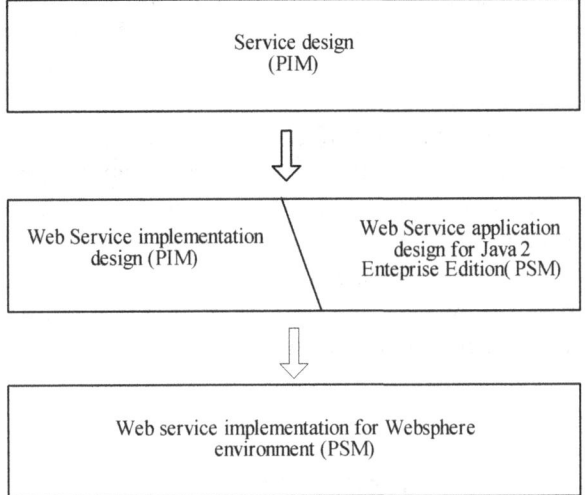

Figure 5. A simplified example of PIM to PSM transformation

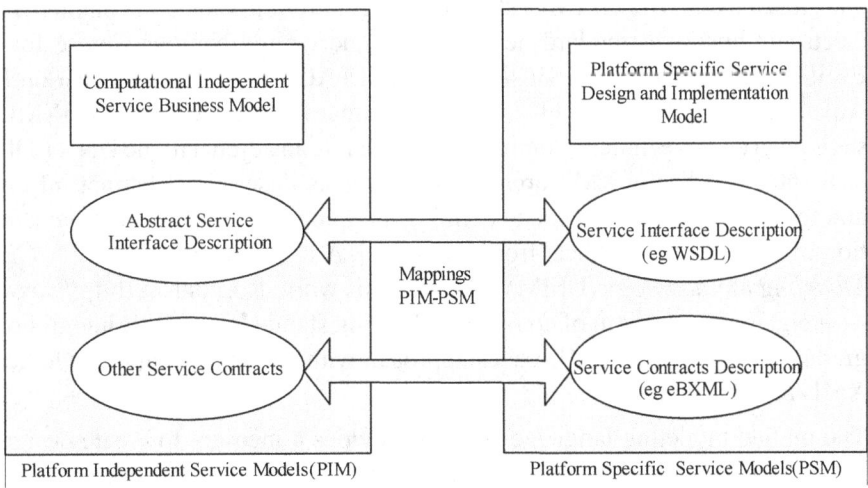

Another PIM to PSM Transformation Example

Figure 5 shows a simplified example of a platform-independent model (PIM) and its transformation into three different platform-specific models (PSM).

The simple PIM in Figure 5 represents the description of an abstract service in terms of interface and other contracts it needs to provide. At this level of abstraction, the model describes important characteristics of the domain in terms of classes and their attributes but does not describe any platform-specific choices about which technologies will be used to represent them. Figure 5 illustrates three specific mappings, or transformations, defined to create the PSMs, together with the standards used to express these mappings. For example, one approach is to export the PSM expressed in UML into XML (WSDL) format, using standard definitions expressed as either XML schema definitions (XSD) or document type definitions (DTD). This can then be used as input to a code generation tool (discussed later on in this Chapter) that produces interface definitions in Java for each of the classes defined in the UML. Usually, a set of rules is built into the code generation tool to perform the transformation. However, the code generation tool often allows those rules to be specifically defined as templates in a scripting language.

Standards for MDA

MDA is therefore a strategic architecture for the OMG. In addition, the model-driven approach is being adopted by other industry standards organizations, notably ebXML and RosettaNet. The ebXML, standard, originally introduced in Chapter III, is an electronic business standard developed by the United Nations Centre for Trade Facilitation and Electronic Business (UN/CEFACT) and the Organization for the Advancement of Structured Information Standards (OASIS; OASIS ebXML Messaging Services Technical Committee, 2002). It is an adjunct to the UN's EDIFACT EDI standard. The ebXML architecture involves describing abstract information and service models in UML, and defining mappings that support automatic generation of XML-based artifacts from the model. A UML profile called *UN/CEFACT Modeling Methodology* (UMM) is driving this work. RosettaNet (http://www.rosettanet.org) is a consortium of companies defining standards for B2B integration. It is gradually moving to a UML-based approach with automatic mappings to generate XML-based artifacts.

The unified modeling language (UML) provides a medium to create designs that are precise enough to drive code generators, and yet abstract enough to remain independent of technology. UML is used for capturing and expressing the essence of information and services, and is thus the basis for OMG's model-driven architecture (MDA).

The OMG's MDA concept provides an open, vendor-neutral approach to system interoperability via OMG's established modeling standards: unified modeling language (UML), meta object facility (MOF), XML metadata interchange (XMI), and common warehouse metamodel (CWM). Descriptions of enterprise solutions can be built using these modeling standards, and transformed into a major open or proprietary platform, including CORBA, J2EE, .NET, and Web-based platforms.

The MDA Process

The MDA development process starts with the well-known and long established idea of separating the specifications of the operations of a system from the details of the way the system uses the capabilities of its platform.

The MDA paradigm development process consists of the following steps (Miller & Mukerji, 2003):

1. Identify business requirements for an application.

2. Develop UML diagrams for the domain model, independent of any particular technology (J2EE, Microsoft .NET, CORBA, etc.). This UML model represents the core business services and components. As explained previously, this UML model is called platform-independent model (PIM) because it is completely technology-independent, that is, the same regardless of whether you use J2EE or .NET. This model is built using UML modeling capabilities of an MDA-specific modeling tool.

3. Build UML diagrams for the application, specific to a particular technology (e.g., Java 2 Enterprise Edition). This UML model will follow design patterns specific to the targeted technology. As explained above, this UML model is called *platform-specific model* (PSM). This model can be built manually, or partially generated using an MDA tool and fine-tuned manually in areas that require customisation.

4. Finally, from the platform-specific model generate the application code using an MDA tool.

To develop an application using MDA, it is necessary to first build a PIM of the application, then transform this, using a standardized mapping into a PSM, and, finally, map the latter into the application code.

Whatever the ultimate target platform may be, therefore, the first step when constructing an MDA-based application is to create a platform-independent model expressed via UML. This general model can then be transformed into one or more specific platforms, such as EJB (Java), .NET, Web services, and so on.

A complex system may consist of many interrelated models, organized along well defined layers of abstraction, with mappings defined from one set of models into another. Within this global set of models, *horizontal* transformations may occur inside a single layer of abstraction, in addition to the typical *vertical* transformations across layers. Applying a consistent architectural style across viewpoints of the system is one illustration of such a horizontal transformation. Other examples include:

- Within a CIM, create a target model containing all of the business rules defined in the core business model.
- Within a PIM, create a target model containing only the data elements defined in the conceptual model.
- Within a PSM, create a target test model from a class model.

Note also that a PSM at one layer of abstraction may assume the role of a PIM with regard to a further transformation down into another layer. This pattern can be repeatedly applied to successive models, each one playing the role of either a PIM or a PSM.

Transformation Mappings

OMG defines model transformation as a process of converting one model to another model of the same system. The PIM and other information are combined by the transformation to produce a PSM.

An MDA mapping provides specifications for how to transform a PIM into a particular PSM. The target platform model determines the nature of the mapping. While part of the transformation can result from a manual exercise, the intent is to automate as much of the process as allowed by the MDA tool/environment in use.

Transformation rules between models can be expressed:

- At the type level, from types specified in the PIM language to types expressed using the PSM language. In UML, examples of such types referred to here include class, attribute and operation.
- In accordance to patterns of type usages in the PIM.
- At the metamodel (MOF) level, for transformations that need to bridge model languages.

Where generic mappings or patterns are shared across multiple applications, it may be possible to automatically transform a PIM, perhaps after annotating it with some platform information, to different target PSMs, fully or partially, from a single shared PIM. Figure 6 applies regardless of whether the mapping is automated or manual.

A mapping, therefore, is a set of rules and techniques used to modify one model in order to get another model. Mappings are used for transforming:

1. **PIM to PIM:** This transformation is used when models are enhanced, filtered or specialized during the development life cycle, without needing any platform

Figure 6. Shared patterns of PIM<-> PSM mappings

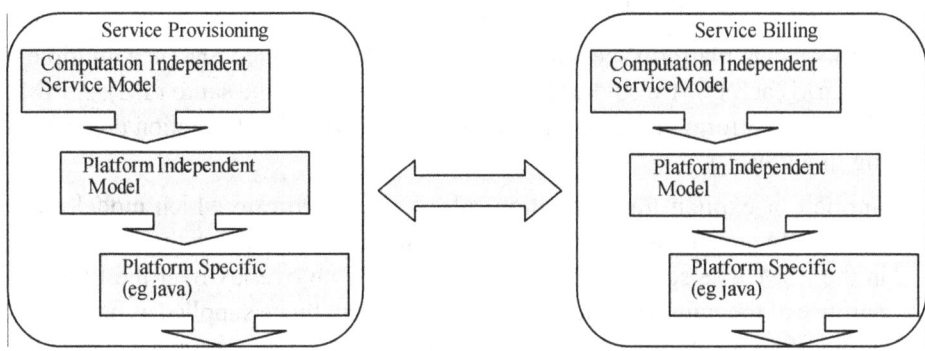

dependent information. One of the most obvious mappings is the analysis to design models transformation. PIM to PIM mappings, are generally associated with model refinement.

2. **PIM to PSM:** This transformation is used when the PIM is sufficiently refined to be specified in terms of the execution infrastructure. The projection is based on the platform characteristics. Describing these characteristics should be done using UML description. Going from a logical component model to a physical existing component model is an example of PIM to PSM mapping.

3. **PSM to PSM:** This transformation is needed for component realization and deployment. PSM to PSM mapping are generally associated with platform dependent model refinement.

4. **PSM to PIM:** This transformation is required for abstracting models of existing implementations in a particular technology, into a platform-independent model. This procedure often is hard to automate fully. It can be supported by tools, though. Ideally, the result of this mapping will match the corresponding PIM to PSM mapping.

Transformations can use different mixtures of manual and automated transformation with a range of tool support for model transformation.

Marking Models

Type mappings are generally insufficient to specify a complete transformation: additional rules are required to specify that certain types in the PIM must be annotated (marked) a specific way in order to produce the desired output in the PSM. This extra information cannot be determined from the PIM itself. A mark represents a concept in the PSM which is applied to an element of the PIM in order to indicate how that element is to be transformed.

Marks, being platform specific, are considered part of the PSM (in a multiple PSM scenario each PSM would use different marks against the same PIM). A PIM plus all of the platform marks constitutes the input to the transformation process resulting in a PSM.

Implicit or explicit transformation rules exist to indicate which model elements in the PIM are suitable for certain marks, in order to generate the desired element in the PSM. The set of marks can be viewed as an overlay over the PIM, for the purpose of the transformation. This set can optionally be supplied as part of a UML profile. Another option is to associate a set of marks with a template containing the rules according to which instances in a model are to be transformed. These rules can specify which values in the source model can be used to fill the parameters of the template.

Mapping Languages

A model transformation mapping must be specified using some language, be it a natural language, an action language, or a dedicated mapping language. The OMG is currently in the process of adopting the MOF Query/View/Transformation (QVT) specification as a portable mapping language.

Recording the Transformations

A record of the transformation should include a chart indicating which PIM elements were mapped to which PSM elements, and include the mapping rules used for each part of the transformation. Another way to organize transformation mappings is via an *inheritance hierarchy*. For example, a mapping to create a database information model could be specialized for specific database vendors.

Generating Code and Other Artifacts

The final step in a transformation process is to generate the implementation code as well as perhaps other kinds of supporting artifacts such as configuration files, component descriptor files, deployment files, build scripts, and so on. The more completely the application semantics and run-time behavior is captured in the PSM, the more complete the generated artifacts can be. Depending on the maturity and quality of the MDA toolset, code generation varies from significant to substantial or, in some cases, even complete. However, even minimal automation simplifies the development work and represents a significant gain because of the use of a consistent architecture for managing the platform-independent and platform-specific aspects of applications. Model-driven code generation is discussed in subsequent sections of this chapter.

Benefits of the MDA Approach

The main benefits from the adoption of MDA therefore, are (Kontio, 2005):

- **Productivity:** As with all code-generation approaches, the fact that artifacts are generated automatically increases the overall productivity.

- **Consistency:** MDA requires the PIMs to be synchronized with the PSMs and the PSMs to be synchronized with the code. This enhances consistency between the artifacts of the process and allows navigation between different levels of abstraction.

- **Portability:** Since the most effort is consumed on the definition of PIMs, those PIMs can be automatically transformed to different PSMs for different software platforms.

- **Faster development time.** By generating code rather than hand-writing each file, the effort required to write the same files over and over again is avoided. For example, in the J2EE approach, you sometimes need to write six or more files to create just one EJB component. Most of this can be automated with an intelligent code-generation tool. Moreover, MDA can result in increased long-term productivity by reducing the rate at which primary artifacts become obsolete. This happens because models are expressed using concepts much less bound to the underlying implementation technology and more closely related to the problem domain.

- **Architectural advantage.** With MDA, a system is described using higher level modeling languages such as UML, not just by modeling programming level classes, This procedure forces the developers to actually think about the architecture and model behind the system, rather than simply diving into coding, which many developers still do.

- **Improved code maintainability.** Most organizations have problems keeping their application architectures and application code consistent in their projects. Some developers will use well-accepted design patterns, while others will not. By using an MDA tool to generate your code, rather than writing it by hand, you give all developers the ability to use the same underlying design patterns, since the code is generated in the same way each time. This is a significant advantage from the maintenance perspective.

- **Increased portability across middleware vendors.** If you need to switch between middleware platforms (e.g., switching between J2EE and .NET), the platform-independent UML model (PIM) is reusable. From the PIM, one should be able to regenerate the code for the new target platform. While not all of the code can be regenerated automatically, the ability to regenerate a large proportion of one application certainly would save time over having to rewrite it all from scratch.

Limitations of MDA

Model-driven architecture is a model-oriented approach as it is based on creating, mapping and transforming various models of the system. Then, as mentioned above, the engineers attempt to transform the models into working code, using transformations. Although MDA is supposed to be a platform-independent approach to development, in practice the vast majority of MDA-compliant tools rely on UML. Therefore, in order to model a system of a specific domain (e.g. J2EE) the modelers have to design an extension of UML (UML Profile) that represents the concepts of the domain. Moreover, engineers have to develop the transformations that will turn those models into working code. Of course, this requires a significant level of metamodeling and meta-programming expertise, which the average engineer or modeler is not likely to have. Therefore, MDA compliant vendors ship their products with ready to use UML Profiles and transformations for commonly addressed domains such as J2EE or relational databases. Although this removes the burdens of metamodeling and template composition, the following points should be considered:

- Although there is an effort to define a standard transformation mechanism for UML (queries-views-transformations), this mechanism is currently supported only by experimental software. Therefore, each MDA-compliant tool uses a proprietary mechanism in order to define the transformations.
- Moreover, although UML models can be exchanged between tools using the XML metadata interchange format (XMI), vendors have developed their own extensions, making the exchange of models (especially of complex ones), between tools of different vendors, a tedious process.
- Finally, modifying existing UML profiles and transformations in order to fit the preferences of the engineer, requires complete understanding of the structure of the profiles and knowledge of the transformation language used by the tool.

The use of proprietary mechanisms for transformations and the difficulty of interchanging models between tools of different vendors, lead users to a lock-in situation.

Moreover, taking into consideration the level of experience required to perform changes to the existing UML profiles and transformations, explains why a substantial amount of people in the software development community consider MDA tools as a new type of CASE tools (France, Ghosh, Dinh-Trong, & Solberg, 2006).

Generating Code from Models

Computer research has been continually working to raise the abstraction level at which software engineers write programs. From binary code to assembly, and from there to procedural and object-oriented languages, the aim has always been to develop more expressive mechanisms that allow the programmer to develop more robust, extensible, portable and well-organized code with less effort. Code generation is essentially about building (and using) software that generates code and relevant artifacts like documentation and diagrams (Herrington, 2003).

In a *model-centric* approach, the system models have sufficient detail to enable the generation of a full system implementation from the models themselves. To achieve this, the models may include, for example, representations of the data, business logic, and user interface elements. If there is any integration with legacy data and services, the interfaces to those elements may also need to be modeled. The code generation process may then apply a series of patterns to transform the models to code, frequently allowing the developer some choice in the patterns that are applied. This approach often makes use of standard or proprietary application frameworks and runtime services that constrain the types of applications that can be generated. Hence, tools using this approach typically specialize in the generation of particular styles of applications However, in all cases the models are the primary artifact created and manipulated by developers.

A *model-only* development approach is one where developers use models purely as aids to understanding the business or solution domain, or for analyzing the architecture of a proposed solution. Models are frequently used as the basis for discussion, communication, and analysis among teams within a single organization or across multiorganizational projects. These models frequently appear in proposals for new work, or decorate the walls of offices and cubes in software labs as a way to promote understanding of some complex domain of interest and to establish a shared vocabulary and set of concepts among disparate teams (Marekj, 2007). In practice, the implementation of a system, whether from scratch or as an update to an existing solution, may be disconnected from the models. An interesting example of this is the growing number of organizations that outsource implementation and maintenance of their systems, while maintaining control of the overall enterprise architecture.

Model-Driven Code Generators

The size and scope of code generators varies from short custom-made scripts or programs that run in console mode with minimal input providing predefined output to visual enterprise tools that can generate entire systems from complex model definitions. Code generators such as inline expanders have been proven to be of great use in everyday tasks and are therefore popular with many developers. Nevertheless, they have a limited scope. Such tools, are usually designed and therefore limited to interacting with source code of only one programming language and their behavior (and output) is usually predefined by the vendor and it is hard (if not impossible) for the programmer to modify them according to his needs.

A more generic solution to the need for automatic generation of code is provided by the so-called *model-driven template based code generators*. A typical high-level architecture of a template based–model-driven code generation system is outlined in Figure 7. The code generator takes as input models and templates and, by using the information provided in the models, it transforms the templates to programs. For the purpose of better understanding, a simple example follows in Figure 8.

Figure 7. Architecture of a typical model driven template based code generator

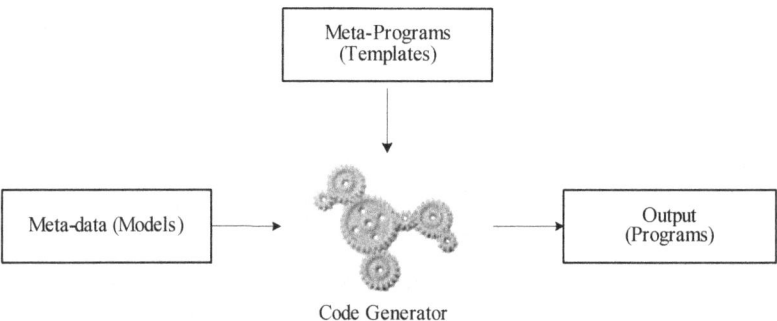

Figure 8. SIMPLE model driven code generator

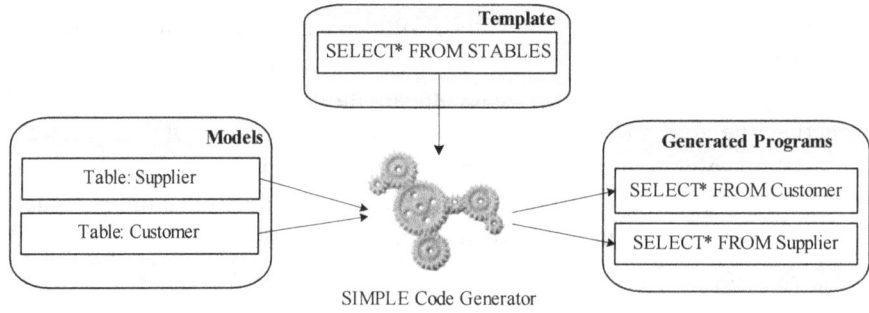

The SIMPLE code generator reads the model files, the template and for each model, it replaces the variable TABLE in the template with the value specified in the model (Customer and Supplier, respectively), to produce the two SQL Statements shown in the right side of the above diagram.

The advantage of model-driven template-based code generators, compared to the other forms of code generation, is that the user can specify both the contents and the format of the code produced. This broadens the domain of this category of generators and makes them suitable for a wider range of tasks in the development process. Today, there is a range of model-driven code generators available either as commercial products or as open-source projects. They offer code-production automation, generation, and maintenance of complete working systems based on models which range from database schemas to complex UML models, using a variety of languages to express the template directives.

The core elements that characterize a template-based model-driven code generator are the type of models it consumes in order to generate code, the type of language it uses to express the directives in the templates, and the life cycle of the generated code. In this section, the most popular approaches to those aspects are discussed.

The following types of code generators provide strong support for MDA:

- Tools that offer a high degree of automation in model definitions and transformations, typically targeted to specific application domains for which complex transformation rules appropriate to that domain can be predefined.
- Tools designed for a more general purpose, but which can be configured to support MDA via end-user and third-party tool vendor extensions and customizations, typically targeted to a broader range of application domains.

Templates

The language in which the templates are written is a very important characteristic of the code generator. A language suitable for composition of templates should be brief, powerful, and close to the domain that the code generator targets. Since a language cannot support all those features to the maximum extent at the same time, a balanced approach is taken. In this section, different types of languages are presented and their advantages and disadvantages are discussed.

Domain-Specific Languages

In this approach, the templates that the code generator uses are written in a simple language that applies to the domain only (e.g., databases). Such languages usually contain features only for iteration and output and do not provide advanced features like calculations, definition of functions, macros, and so on. The advantage of these languages is that they are relatively easy for the developers to learn, since they usually include only a small number of concepts and expressions relative to the domain. Moreover, because of their simplicity, the probability of logical errors in the templates is reduced. The most important drawback of such approaches is the lack of extensibility, inherent in such languages.

General-Purpose Languages

The other approach is to use general-purpose languages for the definition of the templates. Use of such languages gives the developer unlimited computational features, but it also involves the risk of introduction of logical errors in the templates, since their syntax is more complex. There are two categories in this category of languages:

Strongly Typed Languages

In this approach, the language used to define the functionality of the template is a strongly typed language like Java or C#. Use of a strongly typed language, allows the developers to identify and resolve more logical errors using static analysis. Nevertheless, the syntax of such languages involves a lot of typecasting, variable declaration, and so on, which increase the size of the templates and makes them more time-consuming to write and maintain.

Loosely Typed (Scripting) Languages

On the other hand, scripting languages like the velocity template language (VTL), JavaScript or VBScript relieve the developer of the overhead of declarations and typecasting and produce smaller, easier to write templates. Of course, the use of such languages makes the appearance of run-time errors in the templates more probable as only syntactical errors can be caught during compilation, while other errors will be identified only in run-time.

The benefits of strongly over loosely typed languages, for the purpose of textual content generation, have been extensively debated over the last years, in the area of server side languages. Experience has shown that strongly typed languages are quite an overhead for that purpose, and therefore scripting languages (PHP, Perl, etc.), or loosely typed variations of strongly typed languages (VBScript.NET for VB, Velocity, and Web Macro for Java and JavaScript for C#) are preferable.

Source Models for Code Generators

Any piece of structured information that is accessible to the generator and can lead to production of code is considered to be a model, in the context of model-driven code generation. Although such information can be obtained from a large number of sources (source code files, configuration files, proprietary descriptors), database schemas are commonly used for the purpose of code generation.

For data-oriented systems, it is a common tactic to design the structure of the database first and then to develop the code. Database-driven code generators parse the schema of a database, build an object model, and make it available to the engineer to manipulate through the templates in order to produce the data-access code, classes, documentation, and so on. Database schema-driven code generators have been proven to effectively generate the data access tier of many applications. Nevertheless, their scope is limited to data-oriented systems, and even there, the information the database schema carries by itself is not capable of leading to the effective generation of the upper tiers of the system (e.g., user interface or Web application).

Advantages of Model-Driven Code Generation

From both a qualitative and a quantitative perspective, the main advantages of using code generation techniques vs. hand coding are not much different than those of writing programs in a third-generation language (like Java) compared to writing the same programs by coding in assembly. In general, it is recognized that model-driven code generation enhances the produced software from (at least) the following perspectives:

Quality

Writing repeated blocks of code is not the most interesting activity for developers, and it may in fact increase the probability of making errors. Moreover, in case of absence of other code generation tools, developers tend to make use of the most widely known code generation technique (i.e., copy-paste) from similar code blocks. When developers copy-paste code, they tend to fit the operational parts only and forget to alter the comments, thus leading to inconsistent comments. Moreover, the possibility of errors in the original file being copied-pasted in more source-code files across the system is implied. In the case that the error is identified, the erroneous code will have to be corrected manually in all the files, which is a tedious task. Since a code generator can be configured to generate the repeated parts of the code, the developer is relieved of this task and can be utilized for more interesting parts of the software process. Moreover, assuming that its implementation and configuration are error-free, a code generator is far more reliable in the production of redundant code than a human being, since it follows well-defined and deterministic rules seamlessly and does not loose focus.

Consistency

Development of software is a process during which the developers acquire experience both in the domain, the programming language, and the code libraries used. Therefore, assuming that the developers are not at their peak of experience when the process starts, it is most likely that during the development process they will discover better ways of utilizing the capabilities of the development environment and, therefore, producing higher quality code. Nevertheless, because of time constraints, it is not always the case that the improvements identified and applied in the code written during the latest stages of development will be propagated to the code written in the early phases of development. In such cases, the code becomes inconsistent in the sense that almost identical functionality is implemented with different rationale and style across the code base. Furthermore, as developers gain experience in the domain and the architecture, they tend to abandon discipline and to invent shortcuts, by removing elements of the architecture that they do not consider important, in order to speed up the development process. Introduction of model-driven code generation enhances the consistency of the code base greatly. When an improvement is identified and tested, the changes can be propagated to previously written code, by changing the templates and regenerating the code. Moreover, as the code generator is a piece of software, it follows precisely rules thus producing code that is always compatible and consistent to the architecture of the system.

Agility

There are many reasons why the structure or the functionality of the code has to be modified (sometimes even radically), in the middle of the development process. Those reasons might include changes in the requirements, or the adoption of a new more efficient overall architecture. In these situations, it is important to have an agile process that embraces change. Hand writing of code, is by far a process inherently hostile to change. This happens because each piece of code is unique, and the only way to perform a change is to modify manually all the parts of the system that need to be changed. In contrast, the advantage of model-driven template-based code generators is that the information (or a big part of it) concerning the functionality and structure of the code exists in the models and the templates respectively.

Therefore, in order to embrace a change, the engineer has to modify the templates and/or the models and regenerate the code to fit the new requirements. Of course, no one can claim that the transition could be fully automated, but, in conjunction with a good overall design, code generation could save many man-hours, thus making the change more welcome.

Portability

A higher level of abstraction always enhances portability, as it relieves the developer or designer from dealing with lower level aspects of the system. Using a model-driven template-based code generator means that the designer using the same metadata can generate code that supports different software and hardware platforms by modifying the templates. Therefore, the concept of portability in this context refers to the potential of building different systems that run on different platforms, rather than building systems that run on many platforms which is what portability usually means.

Separation of Concerns

Another major benefit from the introduction of model-driven code generating techniques in the development process is that the nontechnical users can help in the refinement of models that are closer to their domain of understanding than code. Moreover, the engineers responsible for the authoring of templates are guaranteed to be the only ones to affect the overall design, while developers are given a more guided work plan and more specific responsibilities.

Speed of Development

Generating code instead of manually writing it can enhance the overall speed of the development process, thus contributing to shorter release cycles. Case studies have demonstrated that the introduction of model-driven code generation to the software process has increased the overall speed by a factor of 3 to 10.

Increased Time Allocated to Preliminary Phases

Since the majority of the code is generated, the designers and the architects of the system have more time to refine the design. At the same time, the developers can experiment and investigate the target language, the components and the external systems that will be used in more detail. This will allow them to enhance their knowledge of the technological environment, and to make informed decisions about which techniques should be followed, as such decisions are not dictated by the amount of code to be written.

Risks from Adopting Code Generation

Adopting code generation techniques in the context of the development process may not always lead to the desirable results. In contrary, it may lead to delay of the overall process and low-quality code. Some of the reasons that can make code generation fail are presented below:

Software not Suitable for Code Generation

Adoption of code generation imposes the need for an effort in the early stages of the process in order to choose and configure (or implement) the code-generation framework. This effort consumes resources and, in order for the overall process to be successful, it has to pay off in the later stages. In order to do so, the code should contain a large number of repeatable blocks. If this is not the case, the software might not be suitable for code generation, and the initial effort will probably be wasted.

Poor Quality of Code Generation Software

Configuration of the generator involves authoring and testing of templates, composition of models, and tests on the quality of the produced code. As with any development process, poor quality of the tools that support it lead to extended development schedules and dissatisfaction among the developers. Moreover, in the context of code generation, there is always the danger of a dead end. There might be cases when the engineer will wish to do more than the implemented features of the code generator can offer. However, if the generator is not extensible, there is a danger that the engineer will either have to compromise with a vendor-supported solution or abandon the generator altogether, thus wasting all the time he has invested on configuring it so far.

Poor System Design

Code generation cannot, and should not, substitute a good design. Just because the generator can produce redundant code quickly, it does not mean that the importance of abstraction and reusability should be underestimated. Especially in situations where the generated code is altered by the developers, (and therefore cannot be overwritten by the code generator), generating lots of poorly designed code will possibly lead to a maintenance nightmare.

Lack of Communication

When the code generator is introduced to the developers, one of the most important issues is to ensure that everybody has a clear understanding of its scope. In the context of a system that involves code generation, three types of files exist:

- Files that are edited exclusively by the code generator.
- Files that are edited both by the developers and the code generator.
- Files that are edited exclusively by the developers.

If developers modify files (or regions) that they are not supposed to, the code generator will overwrite their modifications in a future generation step, thus bringing them to the unpleasant position of losing the hand written code. Therefore, the first two types of files should be clearly identified and communicated to the developers. Moreover, for the files that are edited both by the developers and the generator, the rules for successful coexistence of handwritten and generated code must be made clear.

Rejection of Code Generation

Code generators produce in seconds what usually takes hours or days to be written by hand. This is a reason why it is common for developers to regard code generators as competitors believing that code generators will eventually replace them. Moreover, some developers consider code generators as CASE tools and therefore are reluctant to use them. In the past decades, many CASE tools appeared that claimed to be able to create whole applications with minimal programming. The result was nonreadable and therefore nonmodifiable source code that could only be understood by the tool that had created it. In order to convince the developers about the usefulness of code generation, a smooth integration process must be followed. In the beginning, secondary pieces of code can be generated. Then, the developers should be allowed to discover themselves the benefits of using a generator and identify new pieces of code that could be generated as well.

XML and Code Generation

With regard to code generation, XML is used in conjunction with XSLT (see Chapter III) to transform XML documents into other text based artifacts (e.g., code, documentation). Nevertheless, since XSLT was initially designed for transformations between different forms of XML documents, it does not scale up for production of non-XML textual artifacts.

MDD and Service Engineering

Developing enterprise-scale services requires an approach to software architecture that helps architects evolve the service models in flexible ways. This approach should permit reuse of existing services, in the context of new capabilities that implement business functionality in a timely fashion, even as the target infrastructure itself is evolving. One important concept, considered central to addressing this challenge *service-oriented architectures* (SOA). Enterprise solutions can be viewed as federations of services, connected via well-specified contracts that define their service interfaces. The resulting system designs are frequently called *service-oriented architectures* (SOAs). Flexibility can be enhanced in a system's architecture, by organizing a system as a collection of encapsulated services making calls on operations defined through their service interfaces.

Service Integration with MDD

The fundamental principle in applying MDD to services integration is raising the level of abstraction that we view services at (Frankel & Parodi, 2002). The MDD approach offers similar productivity gains for service development as for other types of enterprise applications. In raising the level of abstraction, it also lessens or avoids disruptions to the system in the face of changes to services. MDD can therefore be applied to services in order to increase the resilience of the implementations as Web services technologies evolve.

The first generation of Web services has resulted in software tools that utilize object and component technologies in implementing Web services. Such tools generate the required WSDL, SOAP, and other XML files and generate code (e.g., Java or .NET components) that binds the Web services to the systems and databases. These tools relieve the programmers from intensive hand coding of technology-specific artifacts. However, services are much coarser grained than existing programming objects and components. The business services we need to expose to customers, generally contain much more application logic than is present in any single existing programming language, object, or component. Services therefore, are compositions of much finer grained software artifacts. New model-driven service engineering environments must facilitate the integration of services, whose design is driven by business requirements, with other software artifacts used in the business. Simplistic approaches that exposes as Web services software that is already in use by the enterprise, will not succeed because those individual software artifacts are not likely to provide the level of functionality needed. Once a specific service has been identified according to these criteria, designers need to answer the following questions:

- What are the information resources that need to be manipulated by the services?
- What is the functionality that must be provided by the service?

If these questions can be answered using formal models, then the artifacts that implement the services using some set of technologies (such as Web services) can be automatically constructed.

Another important benefit from composing business services from lower level, finer grained business functions and information entities is that service logic is separated from service interface. That is, the same business service might be offered via a Web service, a Web page, an application screen, or as a message to a wireless hand-held device. Because we want to reuse these composed business services in these different contexts, we need to isolate the core service logic from other functionality. This core logic must therefore be independent of the implementation technologies used to expose the service, such as WSDL, HTML and so on. Regardless of which technology we use, we would like to use the same platform and technology independent models of business services. By describing these services in a manner that is independent of the technical mechanisms we use to expose them, we make it possible to reuse them in any number of contexts. This separation of the executable service functionality from the technologies used to access them, matches the requirement to formally capture the essence of a service in a fashion that is independent of WSDL, SOAP, and so forth. As was already stated in Chapter III, technologies for Web services are in flux, and also, there are several different ways of combining these technologies. Having Web services developers program directly to these technologies can create rapid obsolescence and is far too labor intensive.

MDD, on the other hand, allows us to design services at a more abstract level than that of technology-specific implementations. Services systems built using MDD, exhibit more flexibility and agility in the face of technological change, as well as a higher level of quality and robustness, due to the more formal and accurate capturing of business requirements and knowledge.

We must step back from the technology, in order to understand that it is the added value that the service offers to the consumer that is of primary importance, not the technology that delivers it. The importance of Web services lies in the fact that information can be exposed and accessed programmatically over the Internet. However, the MDD paradigm and indeed the message conveyed by this book is that environments for realizing business services should be independent of particular technologies as possible This approach promotes the ability to generate technology-specific Web service implementations automatically or semiautomatically rather than forcing programmers to construct them entirely by hand.

Chapter Summary

This chapter has described how the principles of model-driven development and the Object Management Group's model-driven architecture (MDA), can be used to develop services in a way that improves programmer productivity and avoids obsolescence of the services implementations.

MDA is essentially about using modeling languages as programming languages to program systems at a higher level of abstraction than is possible using languages such as Java and C++, thus improving development productivity. MDA uses the unified modeling language (UML), a widely accepted standard managed by the OMG, to capture and express the essence of information and services, which is thus the basis for MDA. Using UML profiles or metamodeling approaches such as MOF, modeling constructs appropriate to a specific domain can be defined. Generators can then be created that can transform a system specification into a partial or full implementation of the system. When we specify systems at a higher level of abstraction, we also increase their longevity, because the specifications are less tied to underlying computing environments that are always in flux.

Profiles for abstract business information and business service specification, along with XMI's profile for selecting XML production options, exemplify our MDD influenced approach to service realization that will be presented in Chapter VII. Generators based on mappings of these languages to XML, WSDL, and other implementation technologies, form the other crucial piece of our MDD framework for Web services. From the perspective of Web services, an MDD approach would use computer independent models to specify services precisely and in a technology-independent manner. MDD allows Web services to be derived from traceable business requirements. It also sets the stage for automatic generation of at least part of the XML and code, such as Java code, that implements the services. Finally, it makes it easier to retarget the services to use different Web services implementation technologies when required.

MDD principles and MDD-based standards will contribute to the emergence of a new paradigm for service realization. Companies can prepare for the advent of this technology by becoming familiar with defining Web services in a technology-independent fashion. The purpose of such an approach is to protect the investment in Web services as the underlying technologies change. The design and implementation of Web services should be approached within the context of a multitiered modeling architecture that supports service realization across multiple access channels to the services. B2B business document exchange, rich clients, Web browsers, and wireless devices can be the most common access channels. The automation of business processes and "choreographies" of business-to-business interactions (see Chapter IV) is another goal for MDD. Defining and generating such cooperative processes, is much more difficult than simply defining and generating Web services, but progress is being made on this front.

In developing services, technology is secondary to the information and the services that use and create the information. Our goal should be to provide an environment in which those who produce individual Web services can do so in a way that is as independent of specific Web service implementation technologies as possible.

To summarize, MDD is, in simple terms, the philosophy of constructing a succession of software models of varying specificity/detail using the technique of transformation or mapping. MDD is still work in progress with even the fundamental concepts of MDA still evolving. As we have seen, the benefits of MDD are numerous and relate to the speed and quality of developing software systems. In the context of this book, MDD is seen as a promising approach for specifying and realizing business services. This, however, raises the question of where the different service models originate from. Here, ontologies that will be extensively discussed in the next chapter have a role to play. A service ontology will provide an "off the shelf" model of the service that can be, with the application of MDD, translated to an operational service model (i.e., to one that is executed in software). Ontologies, therefore, provide general-purpose capabilities that allow organizations to construct customized, model-driven approaches for their own business.

Like MDD, service engineering is still in its infancy and more of a craft than a truly engineering practice. However, as automating services requires implementing business models in software, it becomes evident that the future of service engineering lies in its ability to model services at various levels of abstraction and, most important, to integrate the flow of information through these models. This approach allows the different service stakeholders to contribute to a project, through the types of models that best match the kinds of information and decisions they make.

In summary, MDD is still in its early stages. There are significant benefits for service engineering to be gained from MDD now, but its full potential will be probably be reached only after a number of years of evolution.

References

Atkinson, C., & Kühne, T. (2003). Model-driven development: A meta-modeling foundation. *IEEE Software, 20*(5), 36-41.

Brown, A. (2004). *An introduction to model driven architecture. Part I: MDA and today's systems.* Retrieved August 22, 2007, from http://www.ibm.com/developerworks/rational/library/3100.html

France, R. B., Ghosh, S., Dinh-Trong, T., & Solberg, A. (2006). Model-driven development using UML 2.0: Promises and pitfalls. *IEEE Computer, 39*(2), 59-66.

Frankel, D., & Parodi, J. (2002). *Using MDA to develop Web services.* Retrieved March 15, 2007, from http://www.iona.com/archWeb service/WSMDA.pdf

Guelfi, N., Ries, B., & Sterges, P. (2003). MEDAL: A CASE Tool Extension for model-driven software engineering. In *Proceedings of the IEEE International Conference on Software: Science, Technology & Engineering* (p. 33).

Herrington, J. (2003). *Code generation in action.* Manning.

Kontio, M. (2005). *Architectural manifesto: The MDA adoption manual.* Retrieved March 16, 2007, from http://www-128.ibm.com/developerworks/wireless/library/wi-arch17.html

Marekj, (2007). *Archive for the 'uncategorized' category.* Retrieved August 22, 2007, from http://www.marekj.com/category/uncategorized/

Miller, J., & Mukerji, J. (Eds.). (2003). *MDA guide* (Version 1.0.1.) Retrieved March 15, 2007, from http://www.omg.org/docs/omg/03-06-01.pdf

OASIS ebXML Messaging Services Technical Committee. (2002). *Message service specification* (Version 2.0). Retrieved March, 15, 2007, from http://www.oasis-open.org/committees/ebxml-msg/documents/ebMS_v2_0.pdf

OMG. (2002). *Model driven architecture.* Retrieved March 15, 2007, from http://www.omg.org/mda/

OMG. (2005). *MOF 2.0/XMI mapping specification* (Version 2.1). Retrieved March 16, 2007, from http://www.omg.org/cgi-bin/apps/doc?formal/05-09-01.pdf

OMG. (2006). *Meta object facility core specification* (Version 2.0). Retrieved March 16, 2007, from http://www.omg.org/technology/documents/formal/MOF_Core.htm

OMG. (2007). *Unified modeling language* (Version 2.0). Retrieved March 15, 2007, from http://www.omg.org/technology/documents/formal/uml.htm

Poole, J. D. (2001). *Model-driven architecture: Vision, standards and emerging technologies.* Paper presented at ECOOP 2001 Workshop on Meta-Modeling and Adaptive Object Models.

Schmidt, D. C. (2006). Model-driven engineering. *IEEE Computer, 39*(2), 25-31.

Ying Huang, Y., Kumaran, S., & Chung, J-Y. (2005). A model-driven framework for enterprise service management. *Information Systems and E-Business Management, 3,* 201-217.

Chapter VI

Ontologies for Model-Driven Service Engineering

Introduction

In Chapter II we discussed the fundamental properties and concepts of a service. Concepts like interface, contract, service provider and service consumer are universal (i.e., they apply to all types of services). However, in as much as they are intuitive and universal, service concepts such as the aforementioned lack widely agreed upon semantics. The term *semantics* is used by disciplines such as philosophy, mathematics, and computer science to refer to "the meaning of things." Meaning is usually attributed to a concept via its association with other concepts. In everyday speech, defining, for example, a "car" to be a kind of a "vehicle" is an attempt to attribute meaning to "car" by associating it with another, more abstract concept called "vehicle." If the recipient of this definition already understands the concept of a vehicle, then he/she can also understand the concept of car via its association with the more abstract/generic concept vehicle.

Ultimately, attributing semantics to concepts requires two things: the use of linguistic constructs such as "is a kind of" or "is similar to" to describe their associations to other concepts, and a dictionary that contains concepts of various degrees of abstraction/specificity. Such dictionary must contain some primitive concepts that are not defined in terms of any other concepts in the vocabulary. If, for example, we know that our audience does not know the meaning of *vehicle,* we can define a vehicle to be "a kind of machinery used for transportation" and define terms such as *machinery* and *transportation* using other concepts, if necessary. Naturally, this cannot continue ad infinitum, as our vocabulary must contain a finite number of such concepts.

Semantics are therefore used to achieve common understanding and consensus on the meaning of various abstract or concrete concepts. In turn, common understanding is needed when information and knowledge regarding such concepts need to be communicated. When a car salesperson needs to communicate information about cars to his or her potential customers, he or she will use written or verbal words to convey information about the cars. Standard terms used in the course of everyday life are assumed to be shared by the car salesman and his or her clients. More technical terms, however (e.g., those describing technical details about the car's engine) might have to be defined. Assuming that they are relatively free from too much technical jargon, car brochures manage to get information across to the intended buyers because they contain information described in common language terms. The semantics of such terms are built in the human language used to describe them, and the majority of people share a common vocabulary of that language.

So far we have assumed that the recipients of such communication of semantics are humans. Thanks to the inherent flexibility of natural ("human") languages such as English, French, and so on, semantics can be captured and transmitted fairly easily, by using linguistic constructs. This is how humans acquire knowledge about new concepts. When, however, one or more of the parties involved in such communication are software programs, human languages become unsuitable for conveying semantics. One of the main problems is that one cannot always assume that the receiving and transmitting software programs will share the same vocabulary of concepts. To be able to teach a software program the concept of a car by associating it with a vehicle, we need to know whether the program already understands (i.e., has some kind of internal representation) of the concept of a vehicle. We also need to ensure that the program understands the meaning of the semantic association "is a kind of" in order to infer the properties of the new concept car via its association to the more generic concept vehicle. Unfortunately, this is not always the case. Different programs usually make different assumptions about how to internally represent and use knowledge. If, for example, one such program models internally a car as an "automobile", any attempt to communicate with such program knowledge about cars would be futile.

Let's return now to the main topic of this book, services, and imagine a situation where a car salesman tries to advertise a car selling service to potential customers who happen to be software agents (acting on behalf of human buyers). It would be impossible for the car salesperson to convey semantics of the service to the buyers without sharing with them some concepts about cars. If the buyer and seller know each other in advance, it is possible for them to agree on the set of concepts they want to exchange information about. However, if your potential buyer is unknown, as, for example, when selling on the Internet to potentially anyone, this is not possible. Therefore, the service providers need to ensure that they describe their services in a way that is comprehensible by all potential buyers, who can be humans or software programs. The only way to achieve that, is by defining in advance sets of concepts and semantics that everyone agrees upon, and by using only such concepts and their interrelationships to convey semantic information. The semantics of these concepts have to be machine processable (i.e., described in a language that allows software programs to process definitions and compute inferences) in order to establish an understanding about the information that is conveyed. One approach to achieve that is called "ontologies" and represents the main discussion topic of this chapter.

More specifically, this chapter discusses the role of ontologies in service engineering. It will demonstrate how ontologies, combined with the model-driven development (MDD) paradigm introduced in the previous chapter, can be used in the specification, development, and execution of e-services. Ontologies represent the attempt to attach machine-processable semantics to the volumes of information available on the Web. This effort was coined the *Semantic Web* by the World Wide Web inventor, Tim Berners-Lee (i.e., the next generation Web that contains knowledge as opposed to merely data). Although the goals of the Semantic Web go beyond business and Web services, they benefit equally well them too. The ability to offer e-services requires a common understanding/consensus between providers and consumers of such services, regarding aspects such as the service content, contract, and other properties as these were discussed in Chapter I. As, increasingly, service exchanges are carried out between software programs rather than humans, such consensus can be achieved using shared ontologies. This will allow programs to automatically interact (i.e., negotiate, buy, sell, etc.) with services, without the need for human intervention. What are service ontologies, and how they are used, will be the topic of the following sections of this chapter. We will discuss the computer languages that exist today to define such ontologies, and will give examples of their usage in service discovery, composition, provision, and consumption scenarios.

In Chapter VII we will see how service ontologies support the automatic derivation of services (i.e., designing, developing, and adapting/customizing services). This capability of ontologies is also hugely important in today's e-business environment, where the ability to rapidly design, deploy, and configure e-services is paramount. Ultimately, Chapter VII will combine the concepts of MDD and ontologies to demonstrate a business knowledge-driven approach to service engineering.

What are Ontologies

As we said about, the concept of ontologies is rooted in disciplines such as philosophy, mathematical logic, and computer science. Essentially, ontologies are an attempt to provide formal meaning to a domain (Gruber, 2007). The term *domain* (also called "universe of discourse") has philosophical connotations and means an area of knowledge pertaining to some part of the physical or conceptual world. Domains do not exist independently; they are the results of human initiative to organise and classify the diverse universes of intellectual and physical activities that they are occupied with. A domain, therefore, is, for the purpose of this book, a set of concepts together with their interrelationships that share some common aspects. Since domains are not crisply bounded, what does and what does not belong to a particular domain can be an issue of debate and, ultimately, a matter of consensus amongst the people that define that domain. Also, domains can be parts of other domains, or themselves comprising other subdomains.

The reason ontologies are defined in terms of domains has to do with the practical need to bound the rather huge, and therefore difficult to manage, number of concepts produced by human intellectual activity. Thus, even so-called universal ontologies do not cover every possible concept used by humans but rather target a small set of generic concepts (i.e., concepts that are used across many different and diverse domains). As our approach to ontologies is not philosophical but practical, we are interested in ontologies that relate to the domain of business (e-)services and to technologies used for e-service engineering, such as Web services. Thus, the concepts that will populate our ontology are e-service specific; however, the languages that we will use to describe such concepts are general-purpose ontology languages. This is analogous to the use of natural language to describe domain concepts (e.g., English language vocabulary and grammar can be used to describe any possible concept in any possible domain). Ultimately though, everything is based upon the syntactic and semantic structures of the language used. In fact, although ontologies have their foundations in artificial intelligence languages (which in turn are based on some kind of mathematical logic), ontologies for the Semantic Web are XML based. (XML was introduced in Chapter III.) The main reason for that is the universal recognition of XML as a language for describing data on the Web and its inherent flexibility in building complex data structures out of simpler ones. Additionally, many automated software tools exist to manipulate XML data and schemas, making XML-encoded data easier to process automatically.

Several XML-based ontology languages are in use today, due to the fact that they target specific domains. So, for example, RDF, described later on in this chapter, is an early attempt to ascribe formal semantics to Web resources. OWL-S, also discussed here, builds, on RDF-S (RDF schema) in order to express ontologies in the domain of service engineering. Therefore, an ontology language uses language constructs based on XML, and defines in a metamodel how these can be combined together to construct ontologies.

As a matter of fact, when describing an ontology, we need to refer to the following four separate concerns that the ontology deals with:

- The domain it targets.
- The language it uses.
- The metamodel employed by that language.
- The mathematical foundation the ontology language is based on.

The Relation of Ontologies to Service Engineering

Ontologies assist service engineering in the following ways (Farrell & Lausen, 2006):

- They help to reuse service models. This is important, as businesses can, for example, reuse service best practices rather than develop services from scratch.
- They model, not only static relationships between service concepts, but dynamic behavior, too. This is necessary, in order to describe how services interact with the consumers at runtime.
- Information can be added to ontology elements, to show quality of service. Again this is required, in order to obtain a complete picture of the service (i.e., both its functional and nonfunctional properties).

The aforementioned properties of ontologies will be revisited in the last section of this chapter.

Ontologies for Business Services

The ontology shown in Figure 1 is a high-level model of service concepts that uses the UML notation for object class diagrams. This ontology effectively identifies the key concepts in a service context and models their interrelationships. To instantiate this ontology, one would have to specialise these concepts for a specific business

Figure 1. A service ontology in UML

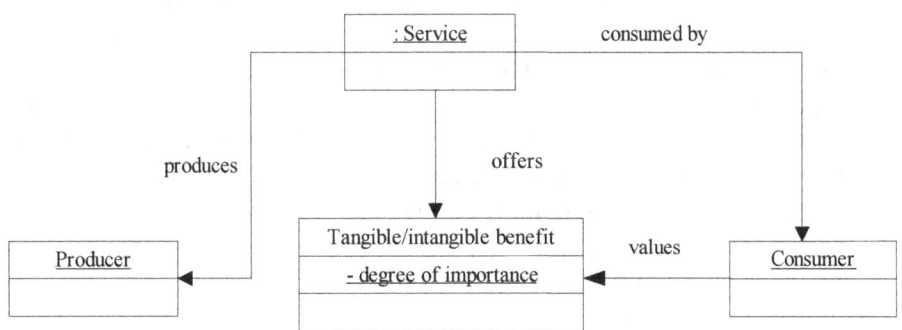

domain. For example, in the domain of e-banking, the Service object class would have to be instantiated to the different e-banking services (such as online account balance checking, online payment, etc.). Similarly, Consumer class would have to be instantiated to the different types of consumers of this e-service (such as, e.g., individual-customer, or corporate-customer). Tangible and intangible benefits would be two object classes that model the service quality attributes valued by the consumers/customers. That would include tangible benefits (e.g., free overdraft), and intangible ones (benefits such as security, convenience, etc. would be potential candidates).

The disadvantage of ontologies such as the aforementioned is that they contain essentially static descriptions of service elements and, thus they are not much more than glorified databases. They do not, for example, tell us how consumers use the service, or in what steps of their interaction with the service consumers can experience the benefits of the service. Also, although UML object class models can be serialised to XML which is a machine language, they do not have a way to capture additional information such as rules and constraints that add more semantics to the service model. This is the reason why some special purpose ontology languages have been proposed. The most significant of them will be reviewed in the following sections, paying particular importance to languages specifically targeting the semantic description of Web services.

Using Ontologies to Describe Web Services

The World Wide Web Consortium Web services architecture (W3C, 2004) defines two aspects of a Web service. The first is the syntactic functional description as represented by WSDL (discussed in Chapter III). The second is described as the semantics of the service and is not covered by a WSDL specification. In practice, the semantic description is either missing or informally documented. This means, however, that by simply examining the WSDL description of a service, we cannot unambiguously determine what the service does. Although we can see the syntax of its inputs and outputs, we do not know what these mean. Indeed, two services can have the same syntactic definition but perform significantly different functions. For example, two services that take a parameter of type "string" and return a "float" can perform completely different functions. One could be a *getProductPrice()* service, that takes the name of a product (string) as input and returns product price (float), while the other could be a *productAvailabilityCheck()* service, that takes an XML document as a string consisting of many parameters such as product, date, quantity. and so on and returns the quantity (float) that is available for the requested date and item. Similarly, two syntactically dissimilar services can perform the same function. For example, two services both of which provide item availability check interfaces can have syntactically different looking interfaces. One service, called *CalculateOrderCost()*, could take an XML document as a string and return the total cost of an order as float, while another service, by the name *OrderCostCalculator()*, could expose the individual parameters separately, instead of packaging them in an XML document. Syntactically, these two services look very different but perform the same function of calculating the total cost of an order.

Semantic annotation of Web services has been proposed as an approach to address the aforementioned issues, by initiatives, projects, and languages, such as WSMO, OWL-S, and SWSA/SWSL. Some of these will be discussed more extensively in the following sections of this chapter.

Languages for Describing Ontologies

RDF

RDF (W3C, 1999), which stands for resource description framework, is a relatively simple ontology language for describing resources on the Web. Because of the simplicity of its basic concepts, RDF has provided the basis for defining more powerful ontology languages such as OWL-S that is described in subsequent sections of this chapter. RDF assumes that each resource is described by properties that have values. So, each resource is described by triples of the type (S, P, O), where S is the resource (called the *subject*), P is the property (called *predicate,* in RDF terminology), and O is the value (which RDF calls the *object*).

Resource can mean anything of value to someone, so when applied to information resources on the Web, RDF can be used to ascribe semantics to such information. We can use, for example, RDF to describe the semantics of data about companies (bookstores) that sell books online. To do that, we need to define concepts such as bookstore, book, and the relationship between the two, called supply book. We can then create triples (S, P, O), where S is a bookshop, P is the property supply book, and O is the unique identifier of a book (such as its ISBN number). To be able to define unique identifiers for resources, RDF uses URIs—Unique Resource Identifiers, which are similar to Web addresses (i.e., have a format like http://www...). URIs can be expressed as full URIs (e.g., http://www.wsmo.org/2004/d2/) or as qualified names that are resolved using namespace declarations.

For example, to uniquely define the relationship "supply book," we can use the following URI: http://www.bookstoreconcepts.org/BookStoreConcepts#supplyBook

To be more precise, as it can be seen from the previous example, RDF uses URIRefs to identify resources. A URIRef consists of a URI and an optional Fragment attached to the URI with the hash symbol (#). In the previous example, the fragment is called *supplyBook*. Therefore, to indicate that a bookstore with id *BooksOnlines* supplies a book with ISBN 12345XXX, and title *A Web Services Primer,* we can create the RDF graph of Figure 2. A set of URIRefs constitute a *vocabulary*.

As RDF is a graphical language, in order to be understood by computers, RDF definitions must be serialised (translated) to XML. Listing 1 shows the RDF graph of Figure 2 translated to XML.

RDF Schema

RDF schema (RDF-S) semantically extends RDF to enable us to talk about classes of resources, and the properties that will be used with them. It does this, by giving special meaning to certain RDF properties and resources. RDF schema provides the means to describe application specific RDF vocabularies.

OWL and OWL-S

OWL (W3C, 2004), is built on top of RDF. OWL semantically extends RDF-S and is based on an earlier language, DAML+OIL. OWL has a rich set of modeling constructs such as individuals, properties and classes. OWL-S is a language based on OWL for creating service ontologies and publishing them on the semantic Web, so that the searching for a service can be performed based on its semantics, not only on keywords (Martin et al., 2007). The aim of OWL-S is to allow service consumers to locate, select, consume, compose, and monitor Web services automatically.

Figure 2. An RDF example

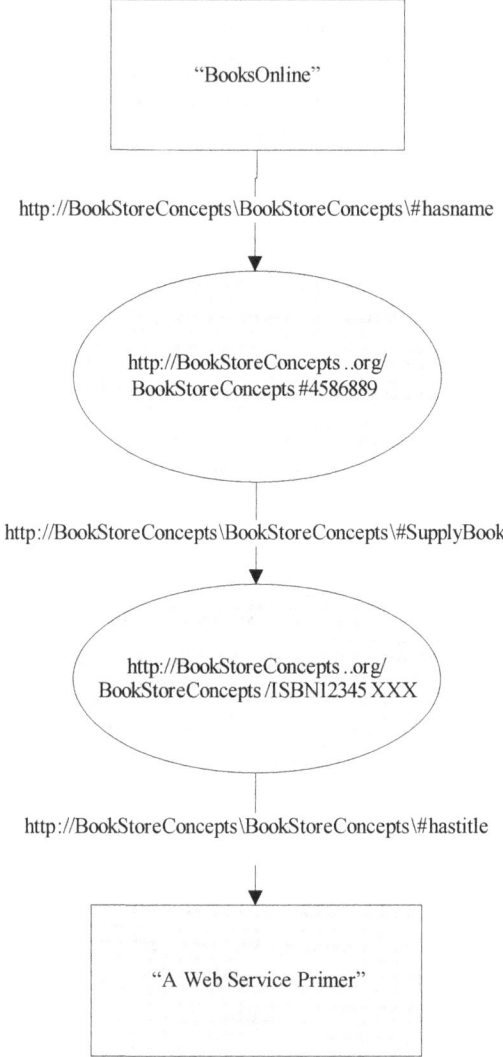

OWL-S is a language that is still evolving, however, its service modeling capabilities indicate the shape that e-services semantics are likely to form. Therefore, the next sections discuss the key features of OWL-S as a representative example of the type of e-service concepts we need to model and reason about using ontologies.

OWL-S considers both primitive, or "atomic" services, and complex, or "composite" services. Atomic services are ones where a single Web-accessible program, is invoked by a request message, performs a function, and perhaps produces a single response to the service consumer. In Chapter II we called these simple *information services,*

Listing 1. RDF example

```
<?xml version="1.0"?>
<rdf:RDF xmlns:rdf="http://www.w3.org/1999/02/22-rdf-syntax-ns#"
xmlns:rdfs="http://www.w3.org/2000/01/rdf-schema#"
xmlns:BookStore="http://www.bookstoreconcepts.org/BookStoreConcepts#"
xml:base="http://www.bookstoreconcepts.org/BookStoreConcepts">
<rdf:Description rdf:ID="4586899">
<BookStore:hasHomepage rdf:resource="http://www.booksonline.com "/>
<BookStore:hasName>BooksOnline</BookStore:hasName>
<BookStore:supplyBook rdf:resource= #="ISBN12345"/>
</rdf:Description>


<rdf:Description rdf:ID="ISBN12345">
<Bookstoreconcepts:hasTitle>A Web services Primer</BookStoreConcepts:
hasTitle>
</rdf:Description>
</rdf:RDF>
```

because they typically return some information about the state of a resource to the consumer, such as, for example, the time of a particular flight. In contrast, what we called *composite* services in Chapter II are composed of many primitive services, and may involve several steps in the interaction between the service consumer and the service(s). An example service, would be an airline passenger contacting an e-service to book a ticket.

OWL-S aims to support the following service capabilities:

Automatic Web Service Discovery

According to the OWL Service Coalition, OWL-S allows the description of a service capabilities in a way that allows other software programs (called "software agents"), that act on behalf of a service consumer to locate it and decide whether it suits the requirements of the consumer or not. In the flight-booking example, a ticket-booking service would not only advertise its main functionality (i.e., to allow passengers to book tickets for a flight), but also other associated information, such as constraints as to how that booking should be made. A service, for example, might require that the booking can be made only by using a valid credit card (which is a constraint on the use of the service). Thus, a software agent would check such constraints to decide if the service is suitable for the consumer whose behalf it acts upon.

Automatic Web Service Invocation

According to the OWL Service Coalition, Automatic Web service invocation, allows a software agent to execute a remote Web service by examining its interface and deciding on the order, meaning, and other properties of its input parameters and outputs, including any error messages the service might produce. All these should be made possible without having to reprogram or reconfigure the agent beforehand (i.e., an agent should be able to invoke any service it encounters for the first time, without requiring any kind of modification). In the airline service example, an agent should be able to invoke the found service by understanding the order and meaning of its input parameters, perhaps by referring to some ontologies about flight bookings. The agent, for example, needs to know that the input parameter *credit card number* refers, according to an ontology for credit cards, to a unique and valid number that must be submitted to the ticket booking service. The agent, also, must be able to understand that the *booking reference number* is a confirmation that the booking has been made successfully, and must be used when referring to this booking.

Automatic Web Service Composition and Interoperation

According to the OWL Service Coalition, this involves the automatic selection, composition, and interoperation of Web services to perform some complex task, given a high-level description of a goal. For example, the user may want to make all the travel arrangements for a holiday (the "goal"). Currently, the user must select the Web services, specify the composition manually, and make sure that any software needed for the interoperation of services that must share information is written. With OWL-S, the information necessary to select and compose services is encoded in the service Web site. Software can be written to manipulate these representations, together with a specification of the goal, in order to realize that goal automatically. To support this, OWL-S provides descriptions of the prerequisites and consequences of invoking individual services, and a language for describing service compositions and data flow interactions.

The structuring, therefore, of OWL-S service ontologies is motivated by the need to deal with the following questions when considering a service:

- What does the service provide to prospective consumers? The answer to this question is given in the "profile" which is used to advertise the service.

- How is the service used? The answer to this question is given in the "process model."

- How does one interact with the service? The answer to this question is given in the "grounding" of a service. A grounding provides the needed details about protocols for interacting with the service.

In summary, the service profile provides the information needed for an agent to discover a service, while the service model and service grounding, together, provide enough information for an agent to make use of a service, once found. Service profiles, process models and service groundings, are discussed in the following sections.

Service Profiles

As explained in Chapter I, an environment for service provision and consumption involves at least the following three parties: the service consumer, the service provider, and infrastructure components such as registries. The role of the registries is to match the request with the offers of service providers to identify which of them is the best match. Web service registries such as UDDi were discussed in Chapter III. According to the authors of OWL-S (Martin et al., 2007), the service profile provides a way to describe the services offered by the providers, and the services needed by the requesters. An OWL-S Profile describes a service as a function of three basic types of information: the organization providing the service, the function the service performs, and a host of features that specify characteristics of the service. These three pieces of information are discussed next.

The provider information consists of contact information about the organization that provides the service. For instance, contact information may refer to the maintenance operator that is responsible for running the service, or to someone that may provide additional information about the service.

The functional description of the service is expressed in terms of the transformation produced by the service. Specifically, it specifies the inputs required by the service and the outputs generated. Also, the profile describes the preconditions required by the service and the expected effects that result from the execution of the service.

Finally, the profile allows the description of nonfunctional properties of the service. This includes things such as the category of a given service and the quality rating of the service, for example, how responsive, reliable etc the service is, an estimate of the service's maximum response time, and its geographic availability. (Service quality and other nonfunctional properties will be reviewed in Chapter VIII.) Before using a service, a consumer may wish to check what kind of service it is dealing with, therefore, a service may want to publish its rating. It is up to the service consumer to use this information, to verify that it is indeed correct, and to decide what to do with it.

The Relation of Profile to Process Model

While the profile of a service provides a detailed description of the service, the process model controls the consumer's interaction with the service, accoring to the OWL Service Coalition. Although the Profile and the process model play different roles during the interaction with a Web service, they are two different representations of the same service. Both profile and process model specify the input, output, precondition, and results of a service; however, the latter might do so in a more detailed manner than the former. This is similar to an airline advertising itself in some kind of yellow pages directory (service profile), but providing the detailed terms and conditions (process model) only to customers who book a flight with it. The designers of the service profile can decide to what detail they want to advertise the service capabilities in a registry. This will determine whether the service will be included in the results of a search carried out by a consumer, or not. A very generic service profile may result in the service being ignored by some specific searches that seek particular characteristics in a service. In Chapter II, we suggested that services should be modeled at different levels according to the intended audience (e.g., business users or software experts).

Modeling Services as Processes Using Ontologies

The OWL Service Coalition proposes that the detailed perspective on how a consumer can interact with a service is modeled as a *process*. An *atomic* process is a description of a service that expects one (possibly complex) message and returns one (possibly complex) message in response. A *composite* process is one that maintains some state; messages the consumer sends may change the state of the process. A process has zero or more inputs that represent the information that must be specified for the service to produce a particular kind of result. Services can have any number of outputs, which is the information that the process provide back to the consumer. There can also be any number of preconditions. All preconditions must hold, in order for the process to be successfully invoked. Finally, the process can have any number of effects. Outputs and effects can depend on conditions that hold true at the time the process is performed.

Atomic processes are directly invoked (by passing them the appropriate messages). They have no subprocesses and execute in a single step, as far as the service consumer is concerned. For each atomic process, a grounding that enables a service consumer to construct messages to send to the process, and to deconstruct the service's replies, must exist.

Simple processes are not invocable and are not associated with a grounding, but, like atomic processes, they *have* single-step executions.

Composite processes in contrast, are decomposable into other (noncomposite or composite) processes; their decomposition can be specified by using control constructs such as *Sequence* and *If-Then-Else*. A composite process is, therefore, a behavior (or set of behaviors) the consumer can perform by sending and receiving a series of messages. If the composite process has an overall effect, then the client must perform the entire process in order to achieve that effect. A process can often

Listing 2. OWL-S example

```
<?xml version="1.0" encoding="iso-8859-1"?>
<definitions name="FlightTicket"
targetNamespace="http://www.someURL/FlightTicketBooking.wsdl"
xmlns="http://www.w3.org/2004/08/wsdl"
xmlns:tns="http://someURL/ FlightTicketBooking.wsdl"
xmlns:xs="http://www.w3.org/2001/XMLSchema"
xmlns:xsd1="http://someURL/ FlightTicketBooking.wsdl"
xmlns:wssem="http://someURL/ FlightTicketBooking.wsdl"
xmlns:BookFlightTicketOntology="http://www.someURL.FlightTicketBooking.owl"
      <xs:complexType name="ProcessBookFlightTicket">
       <xs:all>
        <xs:element name="billingInfo" type="xsd1:Billing"/>
        <xs:element name="flightticket" type="xsd1:FlightTicket"/>
       </xs:all>
      </xs:complexType>
          <xs:element name="ProcessBookFlightTicket" type="xs:string"
          wssem:modelReference="BookFlightTicketOntology #BookingConfirmation"/>
     </xs:schema>
    </types>
    <interface name="FlightTicketBooking">
        <operation name=" ProcessBookFlightTicket " pattern="wsdl:in-out"
            wssem:modelReference=" BookFlightTicketOntology " >
        <input messageLabel ="BookFlightTicketRequest"
        element="tns: ProcessBookFlightTicket "/>
        <output messageLabel ="processBookFlightTicketResponse"
        element="processBookFlightTicketResponse"/>
            <wssem:precondition name="SeatsAreAvailable"
        wssem:modelReference=" BookFlightTicketOntology #SeatsAreAvailable"/>
        <wssem:effect name="TicketBookedEffect"
        wssem:modelReference=" BookFlightTicketOntology #TicketBooked"/>
        </operation>
    </interface>
</definitions>
```

be viewed at different levels of granularity, either as a primitive, undecomposable process or as a composite process. These are sometimes referred to as "black box" and "glass box" views, respectively.

An OWL-S Ontology Example

In the example of Listing 2, we present the partial definition of a Web service for the booking of a flight ticket. The semantic concepts and their relationships are modeled in an OWL ontology—BookFlightTicket.owl The inputs, outputs and operations of the BookFlightTicket service are annotated with semantics which are based on an ontology called FlightTicketBooking.

Grounding an OWL-s Service to a Concrete Realization

In general, the *grounding* of a service specifies the details of how to access the service in terms mainly of protocol and message formats, serialization, transport, and addressing. A grounding can be thought of as a *mapping* from an abstract to a concrete specification of those service description elements that are required for interacting with the service. In OWL-S, both the *ServiceProfile* and the *ServiceModel* are thought of as abstract representations; only the *ServiceGrounding* deals with the concrete level of specification.

According to the OWL Service Coalition, OWL-S does not include an *abstract* construct for explicitly describing messages. Rather, the abstract content of a message is specified, implicitly, by the input or output properties of some atomic process. Thus, atomic processes, in addition to specifying the basic actions from which larger processes are composed, can also be thought to be the communication primitives of an abstract process specification.

Concrete messages, however, *are* specified explicitly in a grounding. The central function of an OWL-S grounding is to show how the abstract inputs and outputs of an atomic process are to be realized concretely as messages. One possible grounding for OWL-S is to the Web Services Description Language WSDL (see Chapter III). This grounding approach can also be used with other specification protocols.

As described in Chapter III, WSDL is an XML format for describing network services as a set of endpoints operating on messages containing either document-oriented or procedure-oriented information. The operations and messages are described abstractly, and then bound to a concrete network protocol and message format, to define an endpoint. Related concrete endpoints are combined into abstract endpoints (services). WSDL is extensible to allow description of endpoints and their messages, regardless of what message formats or network protocols are used to communicate. OWL-S approach to grounding is generally consistent with WSDL's concept of *binding.* Indeed, by using the extensibility elements already provided by WSDL, along with one new extensibility element proposed by OWL-S, it is easy to ground an OWL-S atomic process.

This approach allows a service developer, who is going to provide service descriptions for use by potential clients, to take advantage of the complementary strengths of OWL-S and WSDL. From the abstract perspective of a service specification, the developer benefits by making use of OWL-S' process model, and the more expressive OWL's class typing mechanisms, relative to XML schema definition (XSD). From the perspective of the concrete service, the developer benefits from the opportunity to reuse the extensive work done in WSDL (and related languages such as SOAP), and software support for message exchanges based on these declarations, as defined to date for various protocols and transport mechanisms.

According to the DAML-S Coalition, an OWL-S/WSDL grounding involves a complementary use of the two languages, in the sense that both languages are required for the full specification of a grounding and because the two languages do not cover the same conceptual space. As indicated by Figure 3, the two languages *do* overlap in specifying what WSDL calls "abstract types,', which in turn are used to characterize the inputs and outputs of services. WSDL, by default, specifies abstract types using XML Schema, whereas OWL-S allows for the definition of abstract types as OWL classes. However, WSDL/XSD cannot express the semantics of an OWL class. On the other hand, OWL-S has no means to express the binding information that WSDL captures. Thus, an OWL-S/WSDL grounding uses OWL classes as the abstract types of message parts declared in WSDL, and relies on WSDL binding constructs to specify the formatting of the messages. An OWL-S/WSDL grounding is based upon the following three correspondences between OWL-S and WSDL.

An OWL-S atomic process corresponds to a WSDL *operation.* Different types of operations are related to OWL-S processes as follows:

- An atomic process with both inputs and outputs corresponds to a WSDL *request-response* operation.

Figure 3. Mapping between OWL-S and WSDL

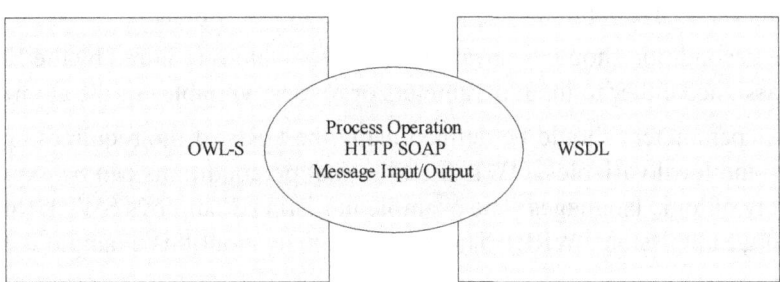

- An atomic process with inputs, but no outputs, corresponds to a WSDL *one-way* operation.

- An atomic process with outputs, but no inputs, corresponds to a WSDL *notification* operation.

- A composite process with both outputs and inputs, and with the sending of outputs specified as coming before the reception of inputs, corresponds to WSDL's *solicit-response* operation.

To accommodate the WSDL-supported practice of providing multiple definitions (within different port types) of the same operation, OWL-S allows for a one-to-many correspondence between an atomic process and multiple WSDL operations. The set of inputs and the set of outputs of an OWL-S atomic process each correspond to WSDL's concept of *message*. More precisely, OWL-S inputs correspond to the parts of an input message of a WSDL operation, and OWL-S outputs correspond to the parts of an output message of a WSDL operation. The types (OWL classes) of the inputs and outputs of an OWL-S atomic process, correspond to WSDL's extensible notion of *abstract type* (and, as such, may be used in WSDL specifications of message parts).

To construct an OWL-S/WSDL, the messages must be defined in WSDL, and the operations by which an atomic process may be accessed, and then specify correspondences (1)-(3). Because OWL-S is an XML-based language and its atomic process declarations and input and output types already correspond to WSDL types, it is easy to extend existing WSDL bindings for use with OWL-S, such as the SOAP binding.

Using XSLT with a WSDL Grounding

In cases where an XSLT (see Chapter III) script is used to generate an input message for a WSDL operation, values are passed to the WSDL script by means of variable/parameter bindings. Variables that appear in an atomic process precondition get bound to values when that precondition is evaluated, and those values also get bound to parameters that appear in an XSLT script. The XSLT script then can produce a WSDL input message that includes those values.

The precondition should be arranged so that all values required by the XSLT script are assigned either to input parameters or to local variables of the atomic process.

XSLT parameters should be defined using the URIs of the required input parameters and local variables. OWL-S allows that preconditions can be expressed in a variety of logic languages. The example in Listing 3 employs SWRL (http://www.w3.org/Submission/SWRL). The thing to notice about this example is that evaluation of this precondition binds local variables #Firstname, #Lastname, and #Id to values contained in the input #Booking. These same values are then plugged in to the XSLT script (as xsl:params) when it gets processed.

Web Service Modeling Ontology

According to its authors (Dumitru, Holger, & Keller, 2006), the Web service modeling ontology (WSMO) aims to achieve dynamic, scalable and cost-effective infrastructure, for electronic transactions in business and public administration. WSMO provides a

Listing 3. WSRL example

```
(?Booking :hasPassenger ?Passenger)
(?Passenger :hasFirstname ?Firstname)
(?Passenger :hasLastname ?Lastname)
(?Booking :hasId ?Id)

<!-- For simplicity we omit the definitions of Booking, Firstname,
   Lastname, and Id
   "congo" is the namespace prefix for the example
   ("http://www.example.org/congo")
   "congo_wsdl" is the namespace prefix for the WSDL spec
   "p" is the namespace prefix for owl-s/1.2/Process.owl
   "e" is the namespace prefix for owl-s/1.2/generic/Expression.owl
   "e" is the namespace prefix for owl-s/1.2/Grounding.owl
-->
<p:AtomicProcess rdf:ID="BookingInfo">
 <p:hasInput rdf:resource="#Booking">
 <p:hasLocal rdf:resource="#Firstname">
 <p:hasLocal rdf:resource="#Lastname">
 <p:hasLocal rdf:resource="#Id">
 <p:hasPrecondition>
  <e:Expression>
   <e:expressionObject parsetype="Collection">
   <swrl:IndividualPropertyAtom>
    <swrl:propertyPredicate rdf:resource="booking:hasPassenger"/>
    <swrl:argument1 rdf:resource="#Booking"/>
    <swrl:argument2 rdf:resource="#Passenger"/>
   </swrl:IndividualPropertyAtom>
   <swrl:IndividualPropertyAtom>
    <swrl:propertyPredicate
```

continued on following page

Listing 3. continued

```
           rdf:resource="booking:hasFirstname"/>
          <swrl:argument1 rdf:resource="#Passenger"/>
          <swrl:argument2 rdf:resource="#Firstname"/>
         </swrl:IndividualPropertyAtom>
         <swrl:IndividualPropertyAtom>
          <swrl:propertyPredicate
          rdf:resource="booking:hasFirstname"/>
          <swrl:argument1 rdf:resource="#Passenger"/>
          <swrl:argument2 rdf:resource="#Lastname"/>
         </swrl:IndividualPropertyAtom>
         <swrl:IndividualPropertyAtom>
          <swrl:propertyPredicate rdf:resource="booking:hasId"/>
          <swrl:argument1 rdf:resource="#Booking"/>
          <swrl:argument2 rdf:resource="#Id"/>
         </swrl:IndividualPropertyAtom>
        </e:expressionObject>
       </e:Expression>
      </e:hasPrecondition>
     </e:AtomicProcess>
     <g:WsdlAtomicProcessGrounding>
      <g:owlsProcess rdf:resource="#BookingInfo>
      <g:wsdlInput>
      <g:XSLTInputMessageMap>
      <grounding:wsdlMessagePart rdf:datatype="&xsd;#anyURI">
       congo_wsdl:BookingInfoMessagepart
      </grounding:wsdlMessagePart>
      <g:xsltTransformationString>
      <![CDATA[
      <xsl:stylesheet version="1.0"
       xmlns:xsl="http://www.w3.org/1999/XSL/Transform"
       xmlns:congo="http://www.example.org/congo">
       <xsl:param name="congo:Firstname"/>
       <xsl:param name="congo:Lastname"/>
       <xsl:param name="congo:Id"/>

      <xsl:template match="/">
       <Booking>
        <Passenger>
         <xsl:value-of select="$congo:Firstname"/>
         <xsl:value-of select="$congo:Lastname"/>
        </Passenger>
        <Id>
         <xsl:value-of select="$congo:Id"/>
```

continued on following page

Listing 3. continued

```
      </Id>
      </Booking>
    </xsl:template>
   </xsl:stylesheet>
  ]]>
  </g:xsltTransformationString>
  </g:XSLTInputMessageMap>
 </g:wsdlInput>
</g:WsdlAtomicProcessGrounding>
```

framework and a language, for semantically describing all relevant aspects of Web services, in order to facilitate the automatic discovering, composition and invocation, of e-services over the Web. WSMO consists of four main elements:

- *Ontologies*, which provide the terminology used by other WSMO elements,
- *Web service* descriptions, which describe the functional and behavioral aspects of a Web service,
- *Goals* that represent user objectives, and
- *Mediators*, which aim at automatically handling interoperability problems between different WSMO elements.

According to its authors, WSMO aims to integrate the basic Web design principles, the Semantic Web, as well as design principles for distributed, service-oriented computing on the Web. WSMO uses ontologies as the data model throughout, meaning that all resource descriptions, as well as all data interchanged during service usage, are based on ontologies. WMSO supports multiple ontologies, because service consumers may exist in specific contexts, which will not be the same as for available Web services. For example, a user may wish to book a holiday according to preferences for weather, see-sights and so on, whereas Web services will typically cover airline travel and hotel availability.

WSMO distinguishes between a service and a Web service. A Web service is a computational entity which is able (by invocation) to achieve a users goal. A service, in contrast, is the actual value provided by this invocation WSMO provides means to describe Web services that provide access (searching, buying, etc.) to services.

Language for Defining WSMO

WSMO is a metamodel for Semantic Web services related aspects. The meta-object facility (MOF) specification (http://www.omg.org/**mof**/) introduced in the last chapter, is used to specify this model. MOF defines an abstract language and framework for specifying, constructing, and managing technology neutral metamodels.

MOF defines a metadata architecture consisting of four layers, namely:

- The *information layer* that contains the data to be described.
- The *model layer* that contains the metadata that describes data in the information layer.
- The *metamodel layer* that contains the descriptions that define the structure and semantics of the metadata.
- The *meta-metamodel layer* that contains the description of the structure and semantics of meta-metadata.

So, according to the MOF layers, WSMO corresponds to the metamode layer which describes how Web services (defined at the model layer) should be structured. The actual data produced and exchanged by the Web services correspond to the information layer.

WSMO Top-Level Elements

According to its authors, WSMO identifies four top-level elements as the main concepts that have to be described in order to describe Semantic Web services.

- *Ontologies* that provide the terminology used by other WSMO elements to describe the relevant aspects of the domains of discourse.
- *Web services* that describe the computational entity providing access to services that provide some value in a domain. These descriptions comprise the capabilities, interfaces and internal working of the Web service. All these aspects of a Web service are described using the terminology defined by the ontologies.
- *Goals* that represent user desires that can be fulfilled by executing a Web service. Ontologies can be used for the domain terminology to describe the relevant aspects. Goals model the user view in the Web service usage process.
- Finally, *mediators* that describe elements that overcome interoperability problems between different WSMO elements. Mediators are used to resolve incompatibilities on the data, processes and protocols levels, of Web services.

Web Service Descriptions

According to the WSMO Consortium (DERI Innsbruck at the Leopold-Universitat Innsbruck, Austria, DERI Galway at the National University of Ireland, Galway, Ireland, BT, The OPen University, and SAP AG), WSMO Web service descriptions consist of functional, nonfunctional and behavioral aspects of a Web service. A Web service is characterized by several nonfunctional properties. The most important of them are briefly mentioned below. Nonfunctional properties of services will also be discussed in Chapter VIII.

- *Accuracy*, which represents the error rate generated by the Web service.
- *Financial* (i.e., cost-related and charging-related properties of a Web service), which may include service-usage billing policies (e.g., per request or delivery, per unit of measure or granularity, etc.), the settlement model used (transactional vs. rental), contracts, payment obligations, and payment instruments.
- *Network-related quality of service* (QoS), covering characteristics such as network delay and message loss.
- *Performance* (i.e., how fast a Web service request can be completed). Performance can be measured in terms of throughput, latency, execution time, and transaction time.
- *Reliability*, which represents the ability of a Web service to perform its functions (to maintain its Web service quality). It can be measured by the number of failures of the Web service in a certain time interval.
- *Robustness*, which represents the ability of the Web service to function correctly in the presence of incomplete or incorrect inputs. It can be measured by the number of incomplete or incorrect inputs for which the Web service still function correctly.
- *Scalability*, which represents the ability of the Web service to process more requests in a certain time interval. It can be measured by the number of solved requests in a certain time interval.
- *Security*, the ability of a Web service to provide authentication, authorization data encryption and nonrepudiation (properties discussed more extensively in Chapter VIII).
- *Trust* which represents the trustworthiness of a Web service or an ontology.
- *Capability*, which defines the Web service by means of its functionality.

Semantic Web Services Framework

The Semantic Web services framework (SWSF; Battle et al., 2005a) published on-line by the Semantic Web services Initiative, builds loosely on OWL-S, to provide a more comprehensive framework, in the sense of defining a larger set of concepts. It also builds on a mature preexisting ontology of process modeling concepts, the process specification language (PSL; NIST, 1999). SWSF specifies a Web-oriented language, SWSL, with a logic programming layer, and, also, a first-order logic layer. It uses SWSL to define an ontology of service concepts (SWSO) and takes advantage of SWSL's greater expressiveness (relative to OWL-S), to more completely formalize the concepts.

Semantic Web Services Ontology

The Semantic Web services ontology (SWSO; Battle et al., 2005b), comprises two other ontologies: FLOWS, the first-order logic ontology for Web services; and ROWS, the rules ontology for Web services. The goal of FLOWS is to enable reasoning about the semantics underlying Web and other e-services, and how they interact with each other and with the real world. FLOWS does not aim for a complete representation of Web services, but rather to provide the semantic of service behavior. However, FLOWS specifications can be mapped ("grounded") into real Web services that use WSDL for messaging. The changing aspects of the real world are modeled abstractly, using the notion of *fluents*. These are first-order logic predicates and terms that can change value over time. The FLOWS model provides the infrastructure for representing messages between services, with the focus being is on the semantic content of a message, rather than, for example, the syntax of how that content is packaged into a SOAP formatted message. FLOWS also provides constructs for modeling the internal processing of Web services.

FLOWS can be used for reasoning about essential aspects of Web service behavior, in order to support of supporting automated discovery, composition, and verification, and mapping declarative specifications of services to executable specifications. FLOWS captures the salient, functional elements of various models of Web services found in the literature and in industrial standards. In FLOWS, an emphasis is placed on enabling the formal representation and study of the following formalisms, among others (Battle et al., 2005b).

- Semantic Web services, including the OWL-S model of atomic processes, their inputs, outputs, preconditions and effects, and the WSMO ontology for describing the intended goals of Web services.

- Various process models for combining atomic services, including the OWL-S process model, BPEL (see Chapter IV), and others.

- Standards, such as WSDL BPEL, WSCL, WS-Choreography, and, more broadly, Service Oriented Architectures.

FLOWS represents an attempt to extend the work of OWL-S, to incorporate a variety of capabilities not present in OWL-S. As already mentioned in this chapter, OWL-S provides an ontology of Web services to facilitate automated discovery, enactment and composition of Web services. However, OWL-S does not address interoperation with industry process modeling formalisms such as BPEL. As such, OWL-S concepts, like messages, are abstract.

FLOWS is defined as a family of *extensions to PSL*, the Process Specification Language that has been standardized as ISO 18629 (NIST, 1999). FLOWS extends aspects of PSL with Web service-specific concepts. A primary goal of FLOWS is to provide a formal basis for accurately specifying "application dmains", based broadly on the paradigms of Web services and/or services oriented architecture (SOA). Following the high-level structure of OWL-S, FLOWS has three major components: service descriptors, process model, and grounding (Battle et al., 2005b).

FLOWS Process Model

According to (Battle et al, 2005b), the FLOWS process model adds two fundamental elements to PSL, namely (1) atomic processes as found in OWL-S and (2) infrastructure for specifying various forms of data flow. FLOWS currently consists of six ontology modules that specify core semantics about the activities associated with a service, together with classes of composite activities that are used to express different constraints on the occurrence of services and their subactivities.

- *FLOWS-Core,* which views services as activities composed of atomic activities.

- *Control constraints,* which model basic constructs common to workflow-style process models. In particular, the control constraints in FLOWS include the concepts from the process model of OWL-S.

- *Ordering constraints,* which allow the specification of activities defined by sequencing properties of atomic processes.

- *Occurrence constraints,* which support the specification of nondeterministic activities within services.

- *State constraints,* which support the specification of activities whose activities are triggered by states (of an overall system) that satisfy a given condition.

- *Exception constraints,* which provide some basic infrastructure for modeling exceptions.

Table 1 lists the FLOWS ontologies and the concepts defined in those ontologies (Battle et al., 2005b).

FLOWS-Core

The FLOWS-Core process model is intended to provide a formal basis for describing any process model of Web services and service composition. As such, the underlying conceptual process model focuses on the most essential aspects of Web services and their interaction. The FLOWS-Core process model principles can be summarized as follows (Battle et al., 2005b):

1. A formal service is modeled as a conceptual object, and for each service there is exactly one associated complex activity. The complex activity may have one or more *occurrences*, each of which corresponds intuitively to a possible execution of *the service* (subject to the constraints in the relevant application domain theory).

Table 1. FLOWS concepts

The FLOWS process model ontology modules	
Module	**Major Concepts**
FLOWS-Core	Service AtomicProcess composedOf message channel
Control Constraints	Split Sequence Unordered Choice IfThenElse Iterate RepeatUntil
Ordering Constraints	OrderedActivity
Occurrence Constraints	OccActivity
State Constraints	TriggeredActivity
Exception Constraints	Exception

2. The atomic actions involved in service activities are discrete "occurrences" of "atomic activities" This includes (a) the activities that modify facts (e.g., plane reservations, financial transfers, modification to inventory databases); (b) activities that support aspects of transferring messages between Web services; and (c) activities that create, destroy, or modify channels.

3. Following the OWL-S approach, a primary focus in FLOWS-Core is on (*FLOWS*) *atomic processes* (i.e., on atomic activities that have input parameters, output parameters, preconditions, and conditional effects).

4. The flow of information *between Web services* can occur via message passing or via shared access to the same "real world" fluent (e.g., an inventory database, a reservations database). FLOWS-Core models *messages* as (conceptual) objects that are created and (possibly) destroyed, and that their life span has a non-zero duration. This follows the spirit of standards such as WSDL and BPEL.

5. FLOWS-Core includes the *channel* construct, which provides a convenient mechanism for giving some structure to how messages are transmitted between services. Intuitively, a channel holds messages that have been "sent" and may or may not have been "received".

6. The acquisition and dissemination of information *inside a Web service* is modeled as follows. Inputs are considered to be knowledge-preconditions, and outputs knowledge-effects. This means the needed input values must be known prior to an occurrence (i.e., execution) of an atomic process. In addition, following the occurrence of an atomic process, values of associated outputs are known (assuming appropriate conditions in the conditional effect are satisfied).

7. FLOWS-Core does not provide any explicit constructs for the structuring of processing inside a Web service. This is intentional, as there are several models for the internal processing in the standards and literature (e.g., BPEL, OWL-S and so on).

In FLOWS-Core, when interacting with Web services, humans, organizations, and other nonservice agents are often modeled as specialized formal services

In the remainder of this section we provide more details concerning the major concepts of FLOWS-Core, as specified in (Battle et al., 2005b).

Service

Associated with every service is an activity that specifies the process model of the service. We call these activities *service activities*. A service occurrence is an occurrence of the activity that is associated with the service.

Atomic Process

According to the authors of SWSO, a fundamental building block of the FLOWS process model for Web services is the concept of an atomic process. An atomic process is a PSL activity that is generally a subactivity of the activity associated with a service. An atomic process is directly invocable, has no subprocesses, and can be executed in a single step. Such an activity, can be used on its own to describe a simple Web service, or it can be composed with other atomic or composite processes (i.e., complex activities), in order to provide a specification of a workflow. Associated with an atomic process, are zero or more parameters that capture the inputs, outputs, preconditions, and effects (called *IOPEs*), of the atomic process.

FLOWS uses atomic processes to model both the domain-specific activities associated with a service, and the atomic processes associated with producing, reading and destroying the messages that are sent between Web services. SWSO distinguishes the following categories of atomic processes (according to http://www.daml.org/services/swsf/1.0/swso/):

1.   **Domain-specific atomic process:** This kind of atomic process is focused on accessing and possibly modifying domain-specific relations and fluents. It is not able to directly manipulate messages or channels, or, in other words, it cannot access or modify the service-specific relations and fluents concerned with messages or channels. In particular, this kind of activity is intended to model (a) the knowledge that a process needs to execute (i.e., the input parameter values), (b) the preconditions about domain-specific relations and fluents that must hold for successful execution, (c) the impact the execution of the activity has on domain-specific fluents, and (d) the knowledge acquired by execution. Occurrences of activities of this kind do not include anything concerning messages (i.e., producing, reading or destroying of them). The occurrences may implicitly rely on previous message handling activities (e.g., because it uses for its input knowledge that was acquired by previously reading a message).

2.   **Produce_Message:** Occurrences of activities of this kind create a new message object. If a channel is used for the transmission of this message, then immediately after the message is produced it will be present in that channel.

3.   **Read_Message:** Occurrences of activities of this kind are primarily knowledge producing. Specifically, immediately after a Read_Message occurrence information about the payload of the message will be known. Thus, there is a close correspondence between the treatment of output values from a domain-specific atomic process, and the treatment of the payload of a message resulting from a Read_Message occurrence.

4.   **Destroy_Message:** Occurrences of activities of this kind have the effect of destroying a message; after that time, the message cannot be read.

5. **Channel manipulation atomic processes:** Are used to create and destroy channels, and to modify their properties (what services can serve as source or target for the channel, and what message types can be transmitted across them).

Associated with each atomic process, are (multiple) input, output, precondition, and (conditional) effect parameters (IOPEs). The inputs and outputs are the inputs and outputs to the program that realizes the atomic process. The preconditions are any conditions that must be true of the world for the atomic process to be executed. In most cases, there will be no precondition parameters since most software (and therefore, Web services too), has no physical preconditions for execution, at least at the level at which we are modeling it. Finally, the conditional effects of the atomic process are the side effects of the execution of the atomic process. They are conditions in the world that are true following execution of the process (e.g., a flight was booked). Such effects may be conditional, since they may be subject to some constraint (e.g., whether a seat is available).

To relate IOPEs in FLOWS, the inputs and (conditional) outputs of an atomic process are considered to be knowledge preconditions and knowledge effects respectively. If a fluent is an input (output, respectively) of an atomic process then it is a knowledge precondition

FLOWS Example

Listing 4 shows the presentation syntax for an atomic process called *book_flight_ticket*. It has two inputs, *customer_id* and *flight_number*, and two outputs: (1) a confirmation of the request if there is an available seat for that flight and (2) a rejection, if the flight is fully booked. This simple atomic process also has one effect which is the debit of the customer's account (assumed to be on file and accessible through the customer_id) by the price of the ticket, if a seat is available on that flight. As with the majority of Web services, there are no (physical) preconditions associated with the execution of that atomic process. The process must merely know its inputs in order to execute.

Service IOPEs

According to the authors of SWSO, the IOPEs of the complex activity associated with a service, are not formally defined. Inputs, outputs, preconditions and effects are only specified for atomic processes. However, for purposes such as automated Web service discovery, enactment and composition, inputs, outputs, preconditions and effects of the complex activity that describes the full process model of the ser-

Listing 4. Atomic process in FLOWS

```
Book_flight_ticket  {
   Atomic
   input customer_id
   input flight_number
   output request_confirm(customer_id, bookingid)
   output (flight(flightnumber) and seat_available(flightid)) price(ticket)
   ouptput (not seatavailable(flghtnumber()) reject(customer_id,flight_number)
   effect (seat_available(flightnumber) debit(customer_id,price(ticket))
}
```

vice might need to be described. In some cases, these properties may be inferred from the IOPEs of the constituent atomic processes, producing IOPEs conditional on the control constraints defining the service. As an alternative to repeated inference, these *computed* IOPEs may be added to the representation of the complex activity defining the service.

The IOPEs for complex activities are systematically translated into ROWS using the SWSL-Rules language. They are commonly used for Web service discovery.

In general, the activity associated with a service can be decomposed into subactivities associated with other services, and constraints can be specified on the ordering and conditional execution of these subactivities.

Messages in FLOWS

A key aspect of the Web services standards we have seen so far in Chapter IV, including WSDL, BPEL, and WS-Choreography, is the explicit representation and use of messages. This fundamental approach to modeling data flow is largely absent from OWL-S. To enable the direct study of the semantic implications of messages, the FLOWS-Core ontology models them as explicit objects.

Associated with messages, are *message type* and *payload* (or "body"), and perhaps other attributes and properties. Messages are produced by atomic processes occurrences of kind Produce_Message. Every message has a *message type*, which is an object in the FLOWS ontology. Such message types will be associated with one or more (abstract) functional fluents, which provides information on how the payloads of messages of a given message type impact the service activity occurrences reading the message, and the preconditions of the service attempting to produce the message. As FLOWS-Core is agnostic about the form of message type a message, it could be an XML data type, a database schema, or an OWL-like class description of a complex object.

Channel

As mentioned before, *channels* are objects in the FLOWS-Core ontology, used as an abstraction related to message-based communication between Web services. A channel holds messages that have been sent and may or may not have been received. In FLOWS-Core, there is no requirement that a message has to be "sent" using a channel.

In FLOWS-Core, messages in transit may be associated with at most one channel. As part of an application domain, a channel might be associated with a single source service and single target service, or might have multiple sources and/or targets.

Channels might be predefined, or can be created/destroyed dynamically by atomic process occurrences in an application domain. For this reason, fluents are used to hold most of the information about channels.

Channels can be created and destroyed by services which correspond to human administrators, specialized, automated services which have essentially an administrative role, ordinary Web services, or atomic processes which are not associated with any service. In any of these cases, the following kinds of atomic processes are supported.

Control Constraints

Most Web services cannot be modeled as simple atomic processes. Instead, they are better modeled as complex activities that are compositions of other activities (e.g., other complex activities and/or atomic processes). The control constraints extension to FLOWS-Core provides a set of programming language style control constructs (e.g., sequence, if-then-else, iterate, repeat-until, split, choice, unordered), similar to those of BPEL that were discussed in Chapter IV, that provide a means of specifying the behavior of Web services as a composition of activities. Control constraints impose constraints on the evolution of the complex activity they characterize. As such, specifications may be partial or complete.

Grounding a Service Description in SWSO

In the context of Web Services, "grounding" means the establishment of a mapping between selected message-oriented constructs in a Web services ontology language and their counterparts in WSDL service descriptions.

The SWSO concepts for service description and the instantiations of these concepts that describe a particular service, are *abstract* specifications, in the sense that they do not specify the details of particular message formats, transport protocols, and network addresses by which a Web service is accessed. The role of the *grounding* is to provide these more concrete details. The Web services description language WSDL (see Chapter III), provides a well developed means of specifying these kinds of details, and is already in widespread use within the commercial Web services community. Therefore, we can ground a SWSO service description by defining mappings from certain SWSO concepts to WSDL constructs that describe the concrete realizations of these concepts. For example, SWSO's concept of message can be mapped onto WSDL's elements that describe messages. These mappings are based upon the fact that SWSL's concept of grounding is generally consistent with WSDL's concept of *binding*. As a result, it is straightforward to ground a SWSL service description to a WSDL service description, and thus take advantage of WSDL features that allow for the lower-level specification of details related to interoperability between services and service users.

According to its authors, SWSO groundings are deliberately decoupled from SWSO abstract service descriptions, so as to enable reusability. An abstract service specification (such as a flight booking service) can be coupled with one grounding in one context (say, when deployed by one travel agent) and coupled with a different grounding (when deployed by a second travel agent). The two travel agents would have completely distinct groundings, which could not only specify different network addresses for contacting their services, but could also specify quite different message (SOAP) formats.

Whereas a default WSDL specification refers only to XSD primitive data types, and composite data types defined using XSD, a SWSO/WSDL specification can refer to SWSO classes and other types defined in SWSO (in addition to the XSD primitive and defined types). These types can, if desired, be used directly by WSDL-enabled services, as supported by WSDL type extension mechanisms. In this case, the SWSO types can either be defined within the WSDL spec, or defined in a separate document and referred to from within the WSDL spec.

SWSO/WSDL grounding involves a complementary use of the two languages, and both languages are required for the full specification of a grounding (Battle et al., 2005b). This is because the two languages do not cover the same conceptual space. As with the case of OWL-S/WSDL discussed earlier on, the two languages *do* overlap, to a degree, since they both allow the specification of "types" associated with message contents. WSDL, by default, specifies the types of message contents using XML Schema (Chapter III), and is primarily concerned with defining valid, checkable syntax for message contents. SWSO, on the other hand, does not constrain syntax at all, but rather allows for the definition of abstract types that are associated with logical assertions in a knowledge base. WSDL/XSD cannot express the semantics associated with SWSO concepts. Similarly, SWSO has no means to define the syntax or to declare the binding information that WSDL captures. Thus, a SWSO/WSDL grounding uses SWSO types as the abstract types of messages declared in WSDL, and then relies on WSDL binding constructs to specify the syntax and formatting of the messages.

SAWSDL-Semantic Annotations for WSDL

SAWSDL is an alternative approach to adding semantic annotations to WSDL. As said earlier on, WSDL does not explicitly provide mechanisms to specify the semantics of a Web service. Semantic Annotations for WSDL (SAWSDL) have been proposed by standards organization W3C (Farrell & Lausen, 2006) Many of the concepts in SAWSDL, are based on an earlier effort called WSDL-S which is another W3C standard. SAWSDL is used to enhance and augment WSDL for the purposes of classifying, discovering, matching, composing, and invoking Web services. SAWSDL uses the two main ontology languages we discussed in this chapter, RDF and OWL, for representing ontologies. SAWSDL is used to annotate WSDL documents with semantic concepts for use in Web service discovery, matching and composition. These annotations that can be added to a WSDL are meant to add semantic clarity to WSDL elements, by pointing to concepts in a semantic model that describes the larger context. They help understand whether a service matches clients' requests at a semantic level.

Defining Annotations to Publish a Web Service

A Web service can be semantically annotated with categorization information that can be used to publish it in a service registry. SAWSDL uses an extension mechanism called *modelReference* to add this categorization information to Web services. This categorization information could be used when automatically publishing services in registries such as UDDI (see Chapter III).

If a categorization semantic model already exists (e.g., a taxonomy), then a *modelReference* element could be defined either on an interface or on an operation of a Web service to point to a particular categorization in the taxonomy. For example, if a taxonomy for flight bookings operations (i.e., enquire, create booking, modify booking, etc.) was created as in Listing 5, then the WSDL interface of an item Seat-AvailabilityCheck could be annotated with that taxonomy information as shown in Listing 6.

WSDL interface could be annotated with categorization information that could be used in publishing a Web service (e.g., into a service registry).

Adding Categorization Information by Defining a Taxonomy

Some taxonomies may not provide direct URIs for their categories and may require multiple pieces of information to identify the categories. In such a case, users can define such information as per the requirements and associate a *modelReference* to point to such user-defined taxonomic information (see http://www.w3.org/TR/2006/WD-sawsdl-guide-20060928/).

Defining Annotations for use in Matching and Composing Web Services

One of the main motivations for SAWSDL specification is to provide mechanisms using which semantic annotations can be added to WSDL documents so that these semantics can be used to help automate the matching and composition of Web services. There are three mechanisms that SAWSDL uses to achieve that:

- **Matching Web service interfaces using a shared ontology:** The differences in the vocabulary used by the two services to represent their interfaces may

Listing 5. A taxonomy to organize Web services related to flight booking

```
@prefix rdf: <http://www.w3.org/1999/02/22-rdf-syntax-ns#> .
@prefix rdfs: <http://www.w3.org/2000/01/rdf-schema#> .
@prefix owl: <http://www.w3.org/2002/07/owl#> .
@prefix : <http://www.w3.org/2002/ws/sawsdl/spec/.../ FlightBookingServiceClassification #> .

 <http://www.w3.org/2002/ws/sawsdl/spec/.../FlightBookingServiceClassification#> rdf:type
owl:Ontology .
 :FlightBookingServices rdf:type owl:Class .
 :BookingModification rdf:type owl:Class;
  rdfs:subClassOf : FlightBookingServices.
 :SeatAvailabilityCheck rdf:type owl:Class;
  rdfs:subClassOf : FlightBookingServices.
 :TicketBooking rdf:type owl:Class;
  rdfs:subClassOf : FlightBookingServices.
 :BookingInquiry rdf:type owl:Class;
  rdfs:subClassOf : FlightBookingServices.
 :BookingTracking rdf:type owl:Class;
  rdfs:subClassOf : FlightBookingServices.
```

Listing 6. WSDL annotated with semantic information

```
...
<wsdl:interface name="CheckAvailabilityRequestService"
 sawsdl:modelReference="http://www.w3.org/2002/ws/sawsdl/spec/.../
FlightBookingServiceClassification#">
 ...
</wsdl:interface>
 ...
```

get in the way of making a match. A matching engine may not have sufficient information to identify them as related terms, unless explicitly specified. Semantic annotations, in cases such as these, could be quite helpful. In the simple case, if there were to be a common semantic model that one can use to annotate the WSDLs of the requester and the service provider, then a semantic engine could use this information to match the two Web services. In this approach, both WSDL documents are annotated with concepts from the same semantic model. A semantic engine can infer this relationship during Web service interface matching by parsing and reasoning over this semantic model.

- **Matching Web service interfaces with ontology mediation.** Ontologies might not always be shared between the requester and service provider domains. The vocabulary differences may result in two different ontologies used to describe the same domain. In such case, one can create a mediating ontology by capturing the relationships between the concepts used in the different ontologies. When a mediating ontology is available, then the semantic annotations extracted from the request and the advertisement WSDL can be matched using such a mediating ontology. Just as in the previous technique, a semantic matching engine can be applied to reason over these relationships during Web service interface matching (see Figure 4).

Composing Web Services with SAWSDL

Semantic annotations can also be used to compose Web services. This can be achieved by simply extracting the semantic annotations from the request, and all the advertised WSDLs and using the relationships in the mapping ontology to match the corresponding concepts.

Figure 4. Ontology mediation

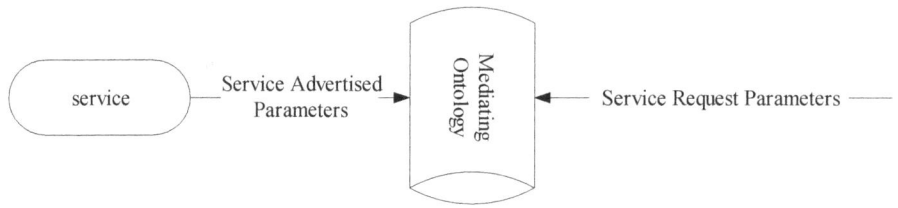

Composing Web Services Using Ontology Reasoning

Semantic annotations can also be used to compose Web services with ontology reasoning. Sometimes, even semantic annotations cannot help match a request with an advertisement, because there is no relationship between two concepts in a mapping ontology. In such cases, a third ontology might be used that bridges the concept definitions in the original ontologies, using other concepts. Web service composition can be achieved using the relationships between concepts in an ontology, even when the semantic annotations on the services do not match directly.

However, there may still be mismatches at the data level that would need to be addressed and captured to enable the invocation of a Web service. In the following section, we discuss the mechanisms defined in SAWSDL to capture such data transformation maps (known as *schema mappings*) to enable Web service invocation.

Defining Schema Mappings to Enable Web Service Invocation

Consider the example where a client/requester may have a first name and last name among its data, while the advertisement service requires a full name. In this case, when the client invokes the Web service of the service provider, the data values of *firstName* and *lastName* need to be concatenated in the message to the advertisement Web service to pass the correct values for the *fullName* element.To facilitate the association of such types of data transformations with Web services, SAWSDL provides a mechanism called *schemaMapping*. A *schemaMapping* concept is provided to allow the specification of transformation functions on the WSDL elements to map instance data defined by that XML schema document to the semantic data of the concepts in a semantic model. Conversely, it allows the specification of transformation functions that map the semantic data of ontological concepts to the instance data values that adheres to the XML schema document that is being annotated. In the former case, the transformation functions are referred to using the extensibility attribute *liftingSchemaMapping*, and in the latter case it is called *loweringSchemaMapping*. These kinds of mappings are useful in general, when the structure of the instance data does not correspond directly to the organization of the semantic data. Also, these types of mappings can be used to generate mediation code to support invocation of a Web service.

Semantic Web Services Execution Environment (SWSEE)

A *Semantic Web Services Execution Environment*, or execution engine, is a software system that enacts processes described using some process model defined in languages such as OWL-S, SWSO, and so on. This system needs to incorporate a knowledge base that contains the relevant service descriptions, and manages the service execution. A SWSEE plays the role of a service provider that is, manages the communications associated with a service from the provider's point of view, a service consumer, or both. When acting as a service provider, a SWSEE will need to accept a WSDL input message, extract the needed pieces of information from its content, and enter them into the knowledge base. In addition, a service-providing SWSEE will need to generate outputs by pulling information from its knowledge base and formatting it into appropriate WSDL-conformant output messages.

Conversely, when acting as a service consumer (invoker), a SWSEE will need to invoke a remote Web service. SWSEE will need to produce a WSDL-conformant message to send to the remote service. This message will be an input from the WSDL perspective, but an output from the SWSEE perspective in this scenario. Following that, it may need to receive a return message from the WSDL service. A SWSEE will need to make a run-time selection and binding to a particular WSDL service. Thus, the role of a grounding to WSDL would be to provide a SWSEE with the information it needs at runtime to handle (both send and receive) messages associated with WSDL service descriptions. To do this, it must provide the following things:

1. Mappings between the ontology language and WSDL elements that specify message patterns.

2. Mappings between abstract message types and the concrete message types declared in WSDL.

3. Specification of a method for translating from an abstract message type to the corresponding concrete message type.

4. Specification of a method for translating from a concrete message type to the corresponding abstract message.

Benefits from Using Ontologies in Service Engineering

In this section we summarize the benefits that result from employing ontologies in service engineering. Such benefits refer to enhanced capabilities to identify, design, and execute service descriptions, enhanced by ontology-based semantic descriptions (Tetlow et al., 2006). These are explained next.

Domain-Specific Reasoning Capability at Run Time

This benefit refers to the ability to reason about the service semantics at runtime (execution time), rather than merely its syntactic information. This, for example, makes possible to check the actual behavior of the service versus its static definition (semantics), and detect any deviations from it.

Support for Dynamic Binding of Web Services

With the use of ontologies, abstract service descriptions can be mapped to concrete ones at run time, by reasoning about properties of the concrete services (using ontologies), and selecting the most suitable candidate service.

Separate Domain Specific Knowledge from Application Specific Data Models

Ontologies allow the conceptual (implementation independent) representation of a company's information resources without the need to resort to for example, data definition languages.

Provide Central Point of Reference for all Application Semantics

Different applications that implement the underlying service logic or act as service consumers share a common semantic model, i.e., the service ontologies. This enhances application interoperability and reduces the risk of semantic incompatibility between applications.

Modeling of Services on Diverse Layers

The SOA approach requires models for the different views on the business and technologic aspects of the concept. Ontologies help to describe and organize these different perspectives and select service models that are appropriate for each service engineering task.

Reuse of Business Services

Software reuse today comes mainly in the shape of customizable enterprise application packages, such as enterprise resource planning software. This allows companies to reuse business functions implemented in software. Reuse of lower level software components has not been very widespread due to incompatible standards and the lack of integration of reuse within mainstream software development environments. However, reuse of software service logic has better chances of success, as the granularity of the service components is much higher than that of software components (such as Java classes) and, therefore, more close to the likely reuse requirements of an organization.

Preventing Loss of Information when Mapping Between Models

By encapsulating service semantics, ontologies allow the correct mapping between different service models, for example, from a business level service orchestration defined as a UML activity diagram, to a Web service level orchestration in BPEL.

Use Ontologies to Model Extended Service Descriptions

Extended properties of services such as nonfunctional properties and qualities (reliability, robustness, etc.), can be described with ontologies as seen in this chapter.

Modeling Service Domains

Business services are often industry specific. Ontologies can be defined to organize services across different industry domains. Such service classifications can share common aspects (i.e., for finer granularity services) and thus allow service reuse across domains.

Modeling the Data in SOA Environments

For SOA to be scaleable to enterprise level, semantic data modeling is required. An ontological approach allows data type to be modeled, instantiated, and managed.

Mapping Ontologies to Executable Service Models

Ontologies allow service models at different layers to coexist. At the same time, ontologies allow these models to be integrated and thus be transformable into each other. Thus, by using ontologies, business service models can be mapped into formal and executable orchestration models.

Chapter Summary

Semantic description of Web services is an ongoing research activity. While the semantic expressivity of current ontology languages is rich and flexible, they still suffer from limitations. For example as we saw earlier on, the OWL-S profile model duplicates the descriptions embodied in the rest of WSDL (namely input and outputs), which leads to duplicated definitions for describing the same service. Second, ontologies assume that everyone uses the same ontology language for representing ontologies, which may not always be the case. It would be better, if service designers were allowed to annotate their Web services with their choice of modeling language (such as UML or OWL-S). This is significant, since the ability to reuse existing domain models expressed in modeling languages like UML can greatly alleviate the need to model separately semantics. In this way, a service developer, who is going to design service descriptions for use by potential clients, can take advantage of the complementary strengths of different specification languages. To create the abstract service specification, the developer can make use of one of the service ontologies that provide more expressiveness than the XML Schema Definition (XSD). To create a concrete service realization, the developer can reuse the extensive work done in WSDL (and related languages such as SOAP), and software support for message exchanges based on WSDL declarations, for various protocols and transport mechanisms.

In the next chapter, we demonstrate how an ontology supported model-driven service engineering method can be used to develop executable service descriptions from domain service models.

References

Battle, S., Bernstein, A., Boley, H., Grosof, B., Gruninger, M., Hull, R., et al. (2005a). Semantic Web services framework (SWSF) overview. Retrieved March 15, 2007, from http://www.w3.org/Submission/SWSF/

Battle, S., Bernstein, A., Boley, H., Grosof, B., Gruninger, M., Hull, R., et al. (Eds.). (2005b). *Semantic Web services ontology (SWSO)* (Version 1.0). Retrieved March 16, 2007, from http://www.daml.org/services/swsf/1.0/swso/

Cutlip, R. (2004). *Ontology-based Web services for business integration.* Retrieved March 15, 2007, from http://www.alphaworks.ibm.com/tech/owsbi

Dumitru, R., Holger. L., & Keller, U. (Eds.). (2006, October 21). *D2v1.3. Web service modeling ontology (WSMO)* (Final draft). Retrieved March 15, 2007, from http://www.wsmo.org/TR/d2/v1.3/

Farrell, J., & Lausen, H. (Ed.). (2006). *Semantic annotations for WSDL and XML schema (SAWSDL).* Retrieved March 15, 2007, from http://www.w3.org/TR/sawsdl/

Gruber, T. (2007). *What is an ontology?* Retrieved March 15, 2007, from http://www-ksl.stanford.edu/kst/what-is-an-ontology.html

Martin, D., Burstein, M., Hobbs, J., Lassila, O., McDermott, D., McIlraith, S., et al. (2007). *OWL-S: Semantic markup for Web services.* Retrieved March, 16 2007, from http://www.ai.sri.com/daml/services/owl-s/1.2/overview/

NIST. (1999). *Process specification language PSL.* Retrieved March 15, 2007, from http://www.mel.nist.gov/psl/

Tetlow, P., Pan, J. Z., Oberle, D., Wallace, E., Uschold, M., & Kendall, E. (Eds.). (2006). *Ontology driven architectures and potential uses of the Semantic Web in systems and software engineering.* Retrieved March 15, 2007, from http://www.w3.org/2001/sw/BestPractices/SE/ODA/

W3C. (1999). *Resource description framework (RDF).* Retrieved March 15, 2007, from http://www.w3.org/RDF/

W3C. (2004). *Web ontology language (OWL).* Retrieved March 15, 2007, from http://www.w3.org/2004/OWL/

Chapter VII

A Methodology for Model-Driven Service Engineering Based on IDEF

Introduction

Chapter II introduced universal service concepts (i.e. concepts that apply to any type of organization and service). In that chapter, we argued that services are so ubiquitous, that it is hard to think of any organization that does not offer services of some sort to internal (i.e., its own departments, divisions, employees) or external consumers (customers, partners). Yet, despite its ubiquity, a service is often hard to pinpoint and describe, even by its own providers. There are several reasons for this apparent difficulty to conceptualize a service, such as:

- Services are not tangible; unlike physical products, there are usually no tangible deliverables in a service.

- A service description is often intertwined with those of its constituting ingredients (i.e., the resources that are consumed by the service and the processes that deliver it). Nevertheless, services are conceptually distinct from both processes and resources as we shall see later on in this chapter.

- There are usually multiple organizational departments, staff roles, and other company actors that collectively deliver the service. Often though, none of them has a complete and accurate picture of the service.

- External resources or services may be employed as part of the overall service. This makes the service even harder to understand and describe due to these external dependencies.

Of course, one might question the need to have formal models of services. Without a doubt there are many organizations that deliver services to customers successfully, without ever having to create formal models of their services. This question essentially leads to a more general one: what is the use and purpose of formal business models and more precisely, computer-based formal business models.

Since the early days of computing, computer models of businesses with varying scope, granularity, and utility have been proposed. From the original data-processing applications to subsequent sophisticated material requirements planning (MRP), and then to enterprise resource planning (ERP) systems, computer models have been used to describe and automate the essential functions of an organization.

Historically, modeling emphasis shifted from data processing to the modeling of the data itself, next to combined modeling of functions and data as objects and finally, to the modeling of complete sequences of business operations that together make up business processes. Methods such as SSADM, information engineering, the various dialects of object-oriented modeling and recent business process modeling languages such as BPN are the historical records of attempts to create computer-based organization models.

Business engineering is a term coined to describe the use of information technology as a tool to engineer an organization. Business engineering is inextricably linked to the creation and use of (formal) computer models of the business. Advocates of business engineering have proposed a variety of business-modeling methods and notations, with each approach offering unique strengths and weaknesses. Today, there exists a plethora of models, notations and methodologies for business engineering offered by software houses, IT, and business consultants. Some of them are an integral part of the software solution offered by the particular vendor. Others are more generic and can support several software tools and IT systems. This situation naturally begs the question as to which is the right model/method for business engineering.

In the context of this book, this question can be rephrased as "which is the right model/method for engineering a service-oriented organization" (i.e., for realizing its business services using IT).

Progress in business services engineering has taken place in a bottom-up fashion with the advent of technologies first for (Internet-based) e-services, which where then followed by the more standardized technologies of Web services (as discussed in Chapters III and IV). This phenomenon has, however, left organizations that want to embark on service engineering with the practical problem of how to link what their business people, customers, and partners perceive as services, with what their IT departments think as service implementations, and ultimately with the technologies they have at their disposal. There appears to be a significant gap between the business and the IT view of what is a service. However, as service technology has evolved from the IT side, it is high time that the business side of services catches up.

The main challenge for service modeling is to identify those services that attribute mostly to the organizational value creation. This will in turn enable the development of software applications that promote organizational abilities to employ strategies effectively and to create value for various shareholders.

This chapter provides a systematic, practical approach that answers the following questions that are often faced by the business modelers:

- Where to find the services.
- How to make sure that the discovered services are the right ones.
- How to decide at what level of granularity to model services.
- How to include in the model all essential aspects of services without getting bogged down in detail.
- How to achieve continuity between business and electronic services in a way that preserves the semantics of the former in the latter.
- How to automate the process of services engineering to achieve higher productivity and higher quality of realized services.

The chapter is structured as follows: In the next section, we outline the features of services and service modeling that distinguish them from processes and process modeling. Next, we provide formal underpinnings for services, based on principles of systems theory. By viewing business services as systems, we gain a robust yet flexible theoretical framework for understanding business organizations, their functions and their value creation mechanisms. Based on a systemic approach of the organization, we can specify techniques, tools and methodologies for identifying, modeling, and designing services of any kind and for any type of organization. The next sections contain the core of the proposed method for service identification and modeling. This is based on the IDEF family of languages. By utilizing the semantic underpinnings of IDEF together with the MDA and ontology paradigms, we illustrate a method to automatically transform models of business services to software services and execute them on different platforms. This we argue, bridges the business and IT domains, preserves the semantics and requirements of business services in software, provides resilience to the rapid change in service technologies, increases productivity and maximizes the return of the investment in service realization technologies.

Service Models

Service modeling, unlike process modeling, is still in its infancy. Far more business analysts and software designers are familiar with process modeling techniques than with service modeling. However, this leads to the temptation to treat services as processes, both conceptually as well as for modeling purposes. Yet, there are fundamental differences between the two, as we will argue.

Services are not processes; therefore, by focusing on the modeling of the latter rather than the former, we loose the main benefits of the service orientation paradigm, such as the ability to reason in terms of services while ignoring the mechanisms used in their implementation. Being able to abstract a service from the processes that realize it does offer several advantages. For example, by abstracting from the process implementation details, we are able to think of new variants of the services that apply perhaps to different types of customers or delivery channels.

We conclude therefore that the contemporary business modeling approaches place their emphasis on processes, and that we need alternative that explicitly model the service and distinguish it from its realization mechanism, the process.

The information systems and software engineering communities have produced over the years several modeling notations and methodologies for software systems. Some of these methodologies that cater for the more abstract models of software can potentially be useful for the modeling organizations (i.e., services). Entity relationship models for example, are a notation that can describe not only information entities and their relationships, but also the static structure of an enterprise. In fact, such an entity relationship modeling technique called IDEF1X will be employed later in this chapter.

Recent Web service modeling standards such as WSDL and BPEL (discussed in Chapters III and IV) are, without doubt, essential for describing in detail service functionality in terms of expected inputs, produced outputs (WSDL), or procedural aspects of Web services coordination (BPEL).

Thus, in principle, combinations of the previously mentioned models should be sufficient for representing the information resources manipulated by a service as well as the processes that deliver them. Yet, as we argued in Chapter VI, such models still fall short of capturing completely the essence and semantics of a business service.

Before we get to the stage of modeling the services in the precise detail required by SOAP and BPEL, we need to deal with methodological problems such as how to find candidate services, decide their utility, and, finally, design them in terms of processes, systems, people, and other resources of the organization. Methodologies such as IDEF, information engineering, SSADM and others, provide some useful constructs for analyzing and representing services. The issue of course is how to mix and match modeling concepts notations and techniques, out of the large repository of methods and notations that 40-odd years of systems analysis have left us with. These are some suggestions as to the types of models that we require for service modeling:

- Information entities used and consumed by the service. These need to be modeled at varying degrees of abstraction, as enterprise-level entities are bound to be stable but their computer presentations (e.g., database tables) are far more volatile. Later on in this chapter, we show an approach to information modeling based on IDEF1X language.

- Organization models, showing roles and skills of the organization staff and departments that will participate in the delivery of the service.

- Service coordination models that show how simpler services are combined to realize more complex ones. This should include all the enterprise IT systems that participate. Our approach utilizes the IDEF0 method for this purpose (IDEF, 2007b). This is explained further later on in this chapter.

- Models of the service consumer(s): Here, customer profile models might prove useful. In this book we are not concerned with approaches for customer profiling, behavior modeling, and so on, however, there are many service design theories (from the customer perspective) as well as IT systems (e.g., customer relationship management-CRM systems) that propose theoretical and practical customer profile models.

The next section provides a service identification method that answers the question about where to start looking for services in an organization. The approach proposed here views the service as a network of collaborating organization resources that deliver concrete or intangible benefits to some consumers. This provides guidelines for modeling the service from the organization *resource perspective* (i.e., what resources/capabilities do we have that our customers value?), which leads to the *process perspective* (and how do we coordinate our resources/capabilities into useful services?).

However, once such services are discovered and their business purpose validated, they must be designed in terms of orchestrations of human and other tangible and intangible resources of the organization. In this manner, we move from an abstract view of the services to concrete service *realization* models. This is where, according to our opinion, a gap exists currently between the business and the IT perception of services. Businesses view the service in terms of consumer expectations, capabilities, added-value benefits, and so on. IT people view services as a programmatic model of invoking a series of Web services that invoke and use enterprise data and applications. Our solution is to bridge this gap by using the same language to describe the business service models and their (programmatic) execution in software. However, business-level service models cannot be directly executed in software without adding additional information to them that allows them to be executed by some software platform. Essentially, we are basing this approach on the MDA paradigm (see Chapter V) that proposes the transformation of computer independent business models (CIBM) to platform-independent (PIM) and then to platform-specific ones (PSMs). Our approach uses the IDEF languages for creating both CIBMs and PIMs. PSMs can then be generated for the desired e-services technology. This avoids loosing the continuity between the business services and their executable equivalent, when there is a handover of services from the business to the IT department.

A Systemic View of Business Services

Our approach to service identification and modeling is based on a tried and tested modeling notation that has been used for over 30 years, called *IDEF.* While new modeling notations can be invented fairly easily, it is not this book's intention to propose yet another modeling formalism. On the same token, we do not agree with the current trend of taking existing modeling notations and rebadging them *service modeling.* In this section, we argue that IDEF provides semantics (based on systems theory) that are close to business services. More specifically, we use two modeling methods from the IDEF family of methods, IDEF0 (2007b) and IDEF1X (IDEF, 2007a).

IDEF0, already introduced in Chapter I, is based on the structured analysis and design technique (SADT), a graphical approach to system description, proposed by Douglas T. Ross in the early 1970s. An IDEF0 activity diagram contains one or more levels of decomposition of a process. Boxes within a diagram show the sub-processes of the parent process named by the diagram. Arrows between the boxes show the flow of products between processes (see Figure 1).

At the highest level of abstraction, (Level 0) a process is modeled in terms of inputs, outputs, controls and mechanisms:

- Inputs denote the triggers that will cause the initiation of the process.
- Outputs are the outcome of the process.
- Controls are the methods, procedures, standards, and so on constraining the execution of the process.

Figure 1. Process model in IDEF0 notation

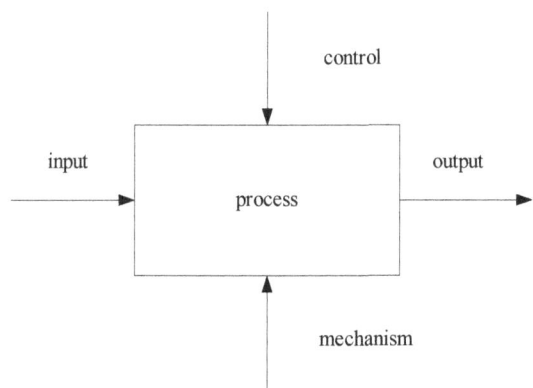

- Finally, mechanisms are the actor roles and other resources such as equipment used in the provision of the service.

The main construct of the metamodel is the Activity. An IDEF0 model is composed of a number of activities. According to the level of decomposition, the activity can represent the whole process, a subprocess or an atomic activity. Each activity has the following properties:

- Inputs and outputs, representing the messages exchange between activities.
- Controls, that constrain the execution of activities depending on value comparison and on activity states, for example, price > 5.00 and activity "issue invoice" has completed. Controls act as preconditions for the execution of an activity.
- Mechanisms, which can be software applications or personnel roles that are responsible for executing the activity; for example, an "accountant" role can execute the activity "issue invoice."

Each IDEF0 activity is described using the following information:

- An identifier, which provides each activity in the model with a unique identity. Identifiers are labeled as A_n or $A_{n.m}$, where n is the level of decomposition and m is the number of the activity within that level.
- A name, which must be self-descriptive.
- A description of what the activity does, as well as other related information.

- Activity synchronization, which constrains the activity's execution, depending on other activities' states; for example, the "issue invoice" can only be executed after both activity "purchase request" and activity "purchase approval" have been completed.

- Control synchronization. This is used to express the relation between the controls of the activity. For example, the activity "issue invoice" can have two controls. Control 1: "value of invoice < 1000" and control 2: "supplier credit status > 0." In this case we may have the following control synchronizations, according to the business process: ["Control 1" and "Control 2"] or ["Control 1" or "Control 2"], and so on.

As a function modeling language, IDEF0 has the following characteristics:

1. It is comprehensive and expressive, capable of graphically representing a wide variety of business operations in manufacturing and other types of enterprises to any level of detail.

2. It is a coherent and simple language that allows rigorous and precise expressions that promote consistency of usage and interpretation.

3. It enhances communication among analysts, architects, developers, managers, and users through its ease of learning and its emphasis on hierarchical exposure of detail.

4. It is well-tested and proven through many years of use by large organizations such as the United States Air Force and other government agencies as well as by private industry.

5. It can be generated by a variety of computer-based tools; several commercial products specifically support development and analysis of IDEF0 diagrams and models.

IDEF0 models are ideal tools for representing organizational processes because:

- Decomposition of processes and activities provide a natural way to business people to categorize and construct hierarchies of their business processes. Decomposition is a great metaphor to employ in the development of business models that support business agility. Separation of concerns starts at the business level and then propagates across the decomposition diagrams.

- Assignment of role to each activity through the concept of mechanism is another intuitive modeling technique for business people.

- Apart from flow between activities, which can be expressed clearly with the concepts of input and output, control and mechanism constructs can also be used in an IDEF0 model, to enrich the semantics of the less observable aspects of business services. These include collections of beliefs and preferences, schemas, and knowledge networks of business collaborations, along with preconditions and effects of the activities (i.e., feedback).

- Logical knowledge can also be depicted via control and mechanisms in order to capture nonlinear relationships between business subsystems, intuitive theories about the business, etc.

- Feedback is a very important notion that IDEF0 can effectively capture, as it leads to more dynamic models. Feedback loops simulate the decision and action situations that characterize real-world business processes.

IDEF0 therefore provides a flexible business process model which allows us to describe complex business-process models that include rich semantics and business knowledge. In this way, we have a full view of the Web services a business process utilizes and how they relate to each step of B2B collaborations. The benefit from this approach is the semantic integrity across the various business models.

IDEF0 models therefore can help to visualize major aspects of complex business activities. More importantly, as we will demonstrate in the rest of this chapter, IDEF0 can act as a service modeling method due to its capability to decompose activities and depict interactions and resource exchanges between activities. With IDEF0, we can effectively represent reusable activities that can be used in multiple business processes

IDEF and Business Services

IDEF0 provides suitable constructs on which to base service-specific semantics without resorting to an entirely new notation. The core modeling construct of IDEF0, *function,* implies the delivery of a capability (i.e., a service). The second central service concept (introduced in Chapter II), closely linked to capabilities, is the one called *resource.* Thus, capabilities are obtained by manipulating resources in a way that ultimately delivers value to customers.

In our approach, an IDEF0 model is not a procedural specification of how a service should be delivered. Instead, it is a declarative description of what are the capabilities that the service delivers and how these are constrained (depend upon) the availability of resources. Thus, an IDEF0 network of services provides a business-oriented specification of what the service is expected to provide without resorting to the description of procedural implementations of such services. This is consistent with the notion that services are neither programs (procedures) nor processes. A banking loan service, for example, is not the transformation of loan applications into loans. Instead, services such as loans involve the coordination of various banking resources (mainly information based), in two-way interactions between the bank and the customer, with the aim to transfer a financial resource (a loan) to the customer subject to constraints such as contracts/agreements.

Capabilities cannot be realized without the availability of resources. Thus, it is important to understand what resources are required to support the various capabilities. In this chapter, we propose a practical method for capturing and modeling information about resources using a member of IDEF family of modeling languages called IDEF1X. This is presented in detail in the next section.

Capabilities are delivered by *mechanisms* (in IDEF0 speak), which are systems deployed in the enterprise that manipulate resources. Some mechanisms can be implemented as Web services. Mechanisms that are more complex are implemented by other types of systems (e.g., legacy ones) that might implement Web service interface(s) or adopt some other technology/standard.

Thus, an IDEF0 service model describes the coordinated delivery of capabilities by Web services and other systems. A service execution environment is a BPEL (see Chapter IV) or other software environment that can execute a service model. However, as argued already, an environment for the execution of business services requires more than the syntactic descriptions of Web service orchestrations (i.e., as present in a BPEL program); it requires semantic descriptions of the executed services, the resources they manipulate and the rules and constraints they abide by (Chapter VI).

Apart from reaping all the benefits of model-driven development (Chapter V), the construction of a formal but executable model of an organization's services in IDEF can be a goal onto itself. Such a model can be used to verify, validate, and monitor the services performance against targets such as service-level agreements (see Chapter VIII). One desirable capability of a service model is *traceability* (i.e., the ability to trace each concrete service to the business services that it realizes). This is important for several reasons:

- In order to ensure that the realized services implement the business requirements, policies etc.

- In order to be able to pinpoint changes that will need to be made to the e-services, according to business level changes.

- In order to reuse existing services to support new business services.

The remaining of this chapter illustrates how this service design approach works. As stated already, a systemic approach to modeling business organizations facilitates dealing with several level of abstraction. For this reason, systems theory introduces hierarchical levels of abstraction in the analysis of business services. Subsequently,

Figure 2. Elements of a business service

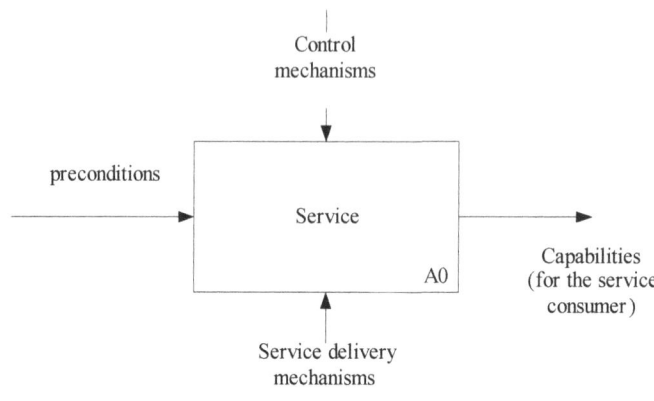

the transformation process of the business system is perceived as the coordination of a network of services organized in the context of a hierarchy.

In modeling the business service of the organization from a systems theory perspective, we consider business service as a system of interconnected *resources, controls,* and *mechanisms.* The notation we employ is shown in Figure 2, with the service represented as a rectangle and the incoming and outgoing arrows showing dependencies, controls, mechanisms and outputs of the service.

Inputs to the service are all the conditions that must be established to be able to deliver the service. This can include the outputs (capabilities) from other services. In turn, the output of the service is a set of capabilities delivered to a consumer (who can be another service).

Controls are elements that constrain the availability of the service by dictating under which conditions the service will be delivered, and may refer to some contract or *service-level agreement.* The difference between inputs and controls is that inputs are preconditions or prerequisites required for the delivery of a service, while controls are rules and constraints about when and how the service will be made available. Such rules and constraints may be expressed in terms of other services. *Mechanisms* are the physical means by which services are delivered; in other words, it is the systems (IT, human-based, or other) used in delivering the service.

To illustrate further the service concepts, Figure 3 shows the model of a medical consultation service. For the service to be delivered, a number of preconditions must be satisfied. For example, the patient must have made an appointment, turn up for the appointment, see an available doctor, and so on. The service requires the use of resources such as patient data, medical test results, medical notes, and possibly others. The output of the service is a diagnosis of the patient's medical condition, which represents the valuable service outcome for the patient (service consumer).

Figure 3. Example of a medical consultation business e-service

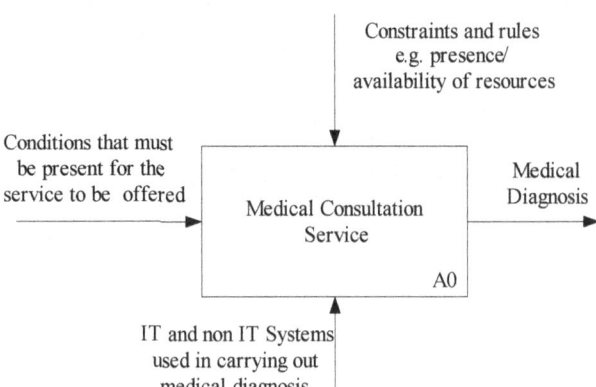

The service is controlled by the medical procedure followed, which depends on the exact nature of the consultation. The output of the service may be used in the provision of another service, such as a postconsultation appointment to discuss the results. The mechanisms used to implement the service are the doctor, medical centre, consultation room, other medical and computer equipment, and so on. In other words, the medical consultation service is realized by the participating roles (doctor, nurses, other staff) that interact and coordinate with each other and with the patient and utilize the employed resources (e.g., medical equipment).

Tables 1 through 5 further clarify the semantics of service elements by providing examples for each one of them.

Identifying Services with IDEF0

A service therefore can be considered to be a coordinated manipulation of organization resources by systems that ultimately deliver a capability/benefit to some consumer (i.e., something that is valued by some customer). A service requires the presence, availability, and coordination of interactions that are often complex in nature, of a network of resources, actors and process steps.

As the service consists of interacting elements such as resources and processes, it is important to think of it as a system of interconnected elements. According to systems theory, a system is more than the sum of its parts. Rather than reducing a system therefore to the properties of its elements, systems theory focuses on the interactions of and relations between the parts which connect them into a whole.

Table 1. Types of service resources

Service Resource Type	Explanation	Example
Availability of an information resource	A form that must be completed	A sales order
Availability of a physical resource	An employee of the service provider is available	A bank teller
Availability of a digital information resource	Data from a computer system must be available	A sales software application

Table 2. Types of service output (capability, customer perceived value/benefits)

Service Output Type	Explanation	Example
Informational	Customer obtains requested information from the service	A customer receives stock price information from a Web service
Access to a company noninformational resource	Customer is granted access resources belonging to the service provider	A customer is allocated a seat on a flight
Transactional (state change)	The customer enters in a transaction with the service provider, which results in a recognized *state of affairs* for the customer	Customer receives a degree from a university (customer's state of affairs changes from *student* to *graduate* after the completion of the service

Table 3. Types of service mechanisms

Service Mechanism Type	Explanation	Example
A person	Person performing the activity	A bank teller
A hybrid (manual/mechanical/IT) system	Any machinery used by service provision companies	A paper ticket printing machine
A software-based system	A software system	A Web service

Table 4. Types of service controls

Service control type	Explanation	Example
A procedure manual	An operations manual used by company staff	A telesales script describing the sequence of interactions between the sales agent and the client
Change of state of some resource	An authorization/approval	A sale is authorized
The outcome of another service	Outcome of the performance of another service	A service request has been declined

Table 5. Types of service interfaces

Type of Service Interface	Explanation	Example
Physical, direct interaction	Consumer interacts face to face with the interface	Customer at a hotel reception
Customer interacting with a human actor over a communications network	Customer interacts with a company employee over a communications network, such as telephone network	Customer making a hotel reservation over a phone
IT application-based interface over a network	Customer interacts with a software application of the company	Customer making a room reservation over the Internet using a Web browser
Physical interface to the customer	The customer interacts directly with a physical (tangible) interface	The interface of a ticket printing machine
IT controlled remote interface	The customer interacts with this interface via a program over a network	A Web service interface

Services therefore need to be understood and modeled in their own right, independent from the resources and processes that realize them. In practical terms, this means that a method for identifying and modeling services must treat them as *first class* entities, not as the mere results of their constituting elements.

Systems theory (Checkland, 1981) emphasizes that real systems are open to, and interact with, their environments. Systems concepts include *system-environment boundary, input, output, process, state, hierarchy, goal-directedness*, and *information*. Systems theory can be applied to the modeling and understanding of organizations. Thus, the same systemic concepts and principles underlie the different organizational processes (marketing, finance, accounting, logistics, etc.) providing a basis for their unification. Systemic concepts are used to narrow the complexity of an organizational entity and to focus on its critical elements.

To model e-services, we must adopt a systems perspective of the service-centered organizations and analyze them separately from the environment by defining their boundaries. Organizational boundaries are defined with respect to the organizational *goals* and the environmental *constraints*. Organizational goals express the expectations of various stakeholders about the ability of the organization to transform inputs to valuable outputs. They are used to perform gap analysis, through feedback handling mechanisms, between actual and desired states of delivered value (i.e., it is similar to single- and double-loop organizational learning processes (Argyris & Schön, 1996). Environmental constraints affect organization requirements for the delivered value (service) and the inputs that may be used to deliver this value. Both organizational goals and environmental constraints define the scope of the organization.

Figure 4. A systemic perspective of business services

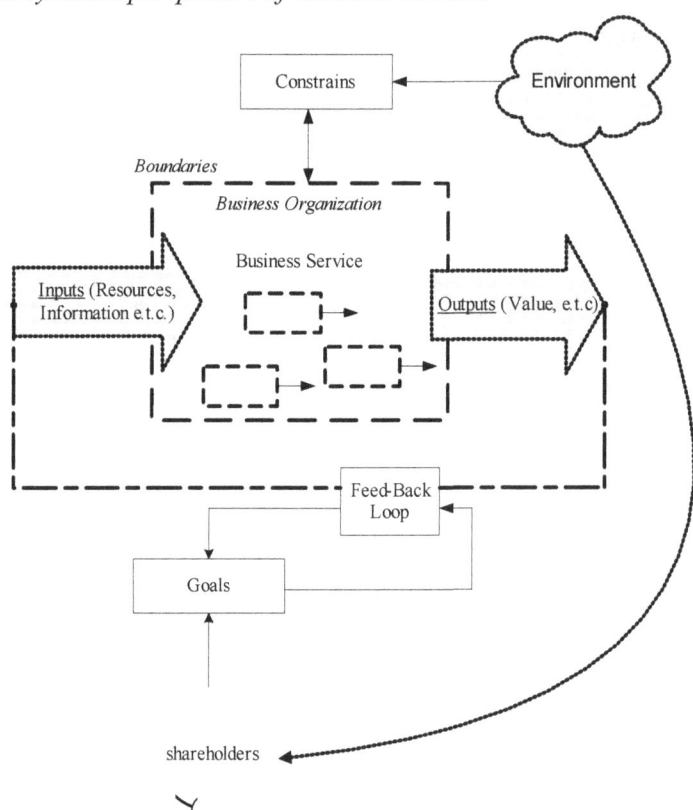

IDEF0/1 can provide a modeling baseline for service-centered organizations and a methodological tool to integrate value creation with architectural modeling. This is possible because IDEF0/1 enables the application of systems theory concepts on modeling modern business environments. Systems theory is a cross sectional discipline that can be used by both management experts and IS practitioners, to resolve organizational complexity. The main management concern is to identify the value creation mechanisms behind business processes. On the other hand, IS practitioners are interested in modeling business services and developing applications that support the management's informational requirements.

According to systems theory, each service is a system within a larger organizational system. A service mobilizes resources to provide capabilities to other services or to external consumers. IDEF0/1 can facilitate and formalize the previously mentioned procedure by providing semantic tools required to apply systems theory in practice and by modeling business services at a logical rather a physical level. In applying

IDEF0/1 to the modeling purposes of e-services, the IDEF building block (called *function*) becomes the service. A service has inputs, which are the preconditions for the provision of a capability. Such preconditions might refer to availability of other services that this service depends upon. Services are controlled by procedures, contracts, agreements and other similar constructs. This is required as professional organizations provide standardized and repeatable services rather than one-off and ad hoc ones. The mechanisms used to deliver the service are IT infrastructure (systems, Web services) that manipulate resources to deliver the expected outcome. Finally, service has an output, namely, the delivered capability, which is defined by business goals and requirements, consumer (customer) expectations, and so on. Such output can become input to another service. Note that IDEF0/1 provides the ability to expand the aforementioned analysis. For instance, multiple inputs/outputs may be defined for the same service or the latter may be considered as a part of a wider network of services.

Service design is the creative phase that involves selecting out of the complex networks of possible resource/capability networks, those combinations that are deemed to provide added benefit to the consumer. Although, in general, an organization can combine its resources in almost unlimited ways, only some of these combinations will make sense and offer added value to a customer. Therefore, the modeling effort must focus on identifying within the complex network of interrelated resources those ones that meet criteria of added value/benefit to the customer.

To identify the capabilities that the service needs to deliver, we can employ both *resource-driven* and *capability-driven* approaches. A resource-driven approach attempts to answer the question "which of our available resources can be transformed/combined and be made available to our customers in a way that offers them capabilities?" Such resources can include information/physical assets of the company, or particular skills and knowledge of its employees.

Figure 5. The IDEF0 model for service

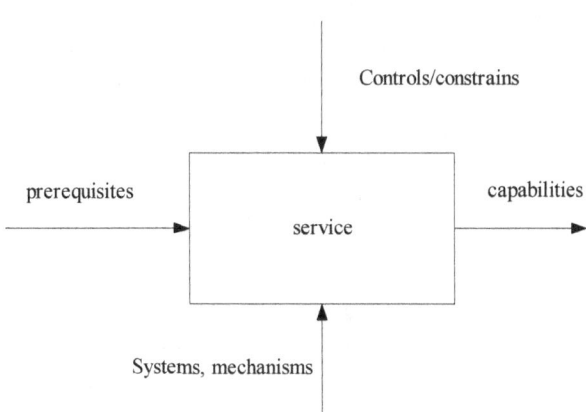

A customer requirements-driven approach, on the other hand, answers the question: "How can we meet the customer requirements for a specific service given our available resources (i.e., personnel, skills, other physical and intangible assets)?"

Through marketing, customer opinion surveys, or by looking at the competition, the organization could, for example, identify demand for a particular service. This, in turn, can be met using a network of collaborating company resources. Designing this network equals designing the business service.

In the resource-driven approach, first, the resources that will be used for the service are defined, and then the way that they will interact is defined in an IDEF0 model.

In the customer requirements-driven approach, customer service capabilities are first defined, and then the services (and associated resources) to deliver them as well as the interactions between such services are modeled. In this top-down approach, a service is gradually decomposed into a network of atomic services. Once we decide that a service is atomic, we then need to specify the mechanism to deliver it. This mechanism can be a manual procedure, an automated one (using computer applications including Web services), or a mixed one.

In the *bottom-up* service design approach, existing organization services are aggregated into composite services. The idea here is that although on their own such services may not be of value to the customer, once combined, they become value-adding ones.

Business strategy (i.e., a formal action plan for achieving goals) is a good starting point for identifying services. Achievement of these goals requires that organization has effectively utilized its resources in order to produce outputs (i.e., products, services, goods) that satisfy a wide range of shareholders. This implies that the organization has created and delivered superior value to its environment. For this reason, in Figure 6 business strategy and goal are considered as control variables of the service process. The linkage between strategy and services is the cornerstone for classifying the role of services and identifying those important for achieving goals and generating organizational value.

If we attempt to represent the linkage between business services and strategy by using IDEF semantics, we must focus on *feedback handling*. Feedback handling analyzes delivered capabilities (i.e., output of service) and determines constraints that filter delivered capabilities.

Further feedback handling may be modeled using IDEF0. For feedback handling, input is the *service states*. Desired service states are determined by the strategy of the organization. The outputs of controller are the *constraints,* the *service scope,* and *goals.*

The identification of services is therefore an ad hoc and iterative procedure. Out of many potentially candidate service designs, the most suitable ones must be identified, using their importance in delivering capabilities and value creation as the selection

Figure 6. The feedback handling of a service

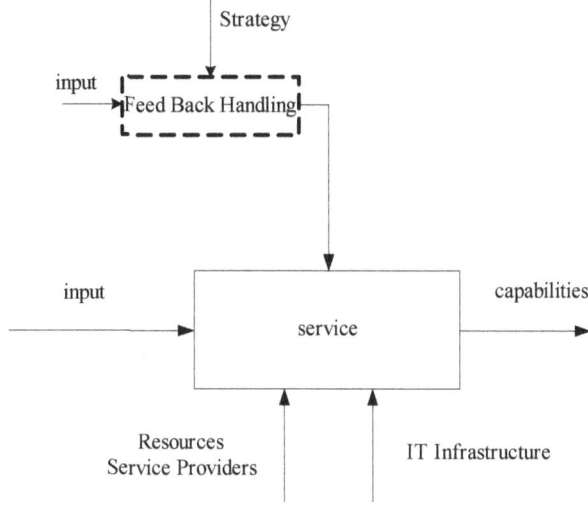

Figure 7. IDEF0 model for feedback handling

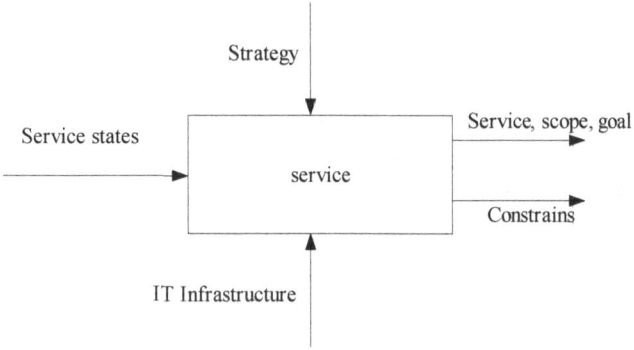

criterion. To judge the relative importance of delivered capabilities for each service, we must focus on business strategy and goals.

Service Design

In a nutshell, the strategy we employ in our service modeling approach is to initially conceptualize the service based on business value adding models, trying to

Figure 8. The decomposed medical consultation service

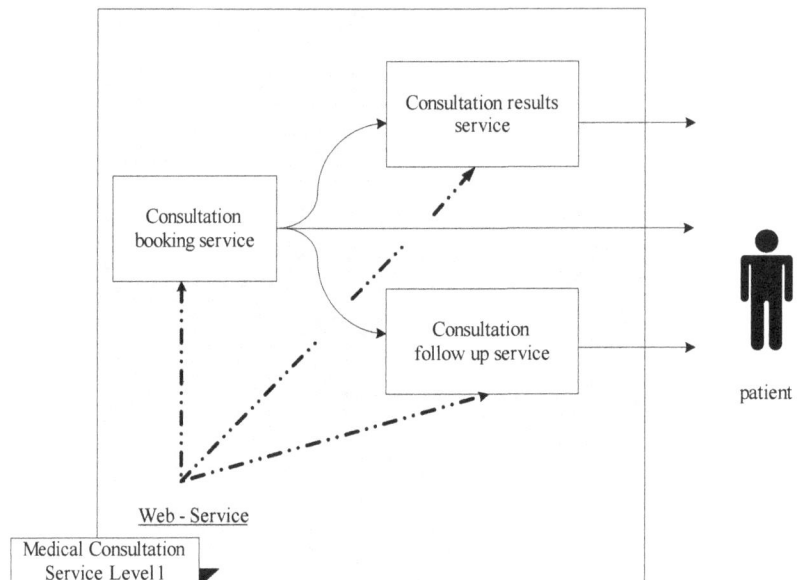

abstract from any specific processes that realize the service, and then to gradually add more detail to the service descriptions through a series of successive models. A service that is deemed composite (i.e., realized as a coordination of other services) is decomposed in a more detailed IDEF0 diagram. Once we get to a level where it is clear how a service will be realized (i.e., via a software system, a manual business process, an atomic or complex Web service, etc.), decomposition stops.

As with all hierarchical system decomposition methods, it is sometimes difficult to know when to stop decomposing. An informal rule to apply in such cases is that, once it is clear that a service is delivered by a single system (person, IT, or other system) (i.e., without reliance upon other services), decomposition stops.

Applying the proceding to the medical diagnosis service example of Figure 3, as this service is realized by a variety of systems and resources, it needs to be decomposed into finer levels of detail. Thus, the medical diagnosis service can be decomposed into services for booking an appointment, having the diagnosis carried out, receiving/viewing the diagnosis results and possibly others. Services such as booking an appointment and receiving the diagnosis results, deal primarily with information resources and thus can be totally realized by IT systems and offered as e-services (e.g., Web services). Figure 8 shows the medical consultation service of Figure 3 decomposed into a network of three services. It may be decided at this stage, that each of these services will be realized by a Web service mechanism thus, no further decomposition is required. In subsequent sections, we will see how such services are automatically transformed to Web services using an MDD approach (see Chapter V).

During the initial modeling stages therefore, the service descriptions remain deliberately abstract. At these stages we identify:

- The *context* of the service: the organization area that will be responsible for the service, the service scope, and the service boundaries/environment.

- The *perspective* of the service: whether the service is modeled from the perspective of the provider or the consumer.

- The *types of resources* that participate in the service; at this stage these only need to be identified at an abstract level.

- The *capabilities* that the service needs to deliver, without yet considering the details about such capabilities will be implemented.

Level 0 models of services will then undergo a number of decompositions that allow us eventually to derive atomic services. Web services correspond to lowest level atomic services in an IDEF0 model. In IDEF0 models, we have complete traceability of the Web services a business e-service exposes. Such approach benefits from the continuity between the whole business process and the constituting Web services.

Additionally, this method allows us to capture and maintain *service knowledge*. Service knowledge is organization specific and ultimately, relates to organizational goals and values and to models of the customer/consumer. Such knowledge can become lost once services are encoded in software. By providing concepts such as control and mechanism, IDEF0 facilitates the representation of knowledge, which is at the core of business services. Having all the business rules that govern service provision encoded as controls and mechanisms, provides a very flexible way to access and revise them in the IDEF0 model.

The following table summarizes the purpose of the different modeling levels in service design. Apart from cases of very simple services, it is unlikely that a business service will be modeled in sufficient detail within a single level. Another issue to consider is the granularity of services that we expose. The use of coarse-grained capabilities for external consumption is recommended, whereas fine-grained services might be used inside the enterprise. For example, a coarse-grained service might be the complete processing for a given process model while a number of fine-grained services might result in the same goal. With the use of IDEF0, coarse-grained services are recommended for external consumption, as they guarantee that the service requester will use the service in a consistent manner, and their use meet the requirements for integration with the consumer.

IDEF0 Diagram Level	Name	Purpose
0	Service context diagram	Shows the service at the highest level of abstraction
Levels 1, 2, ...	Intermediate-level service network diagram	These optional levels are required only if the service is very complex and needs to be understood at various levels of abstraction
Lowest level	Detailed service network diagram	Shows atomic capabilities and the mechanisms that realize them

Modeling the Service Resources: The IDEF1X Methodology

To pick up from where the previous section left, an IDEF0 service model depicts services together with the resources they utilize. As we have already explained, some (or even all) of the mechanisms that deliver the service and handle only information resources will be automated. These mechanisms will need to manipulate information resources whose logical structure and relationships will need to be modeled. At this stage, modeling will be done at a logical rather than physical level, as we are not yet concerned about the physical format of the data (e.g., as paper documents, files, database records, etc.) that realize the information resources. For information modeling, we employ IDEF1X, another standard related to IDEF0 that, however, instead of focusing on function modeling (as IDEF0 does), is used to produce an information model representing the structure of information needed to support the functions of an organization (IDEF1X, 2007). With IDEF1X, we model the following types of information:

Entities, which are objects of the organization, either real or abstract, and have properties. In general, an entity is something about which specific characteristics

Figure 9. Concepts of IDEF1x models

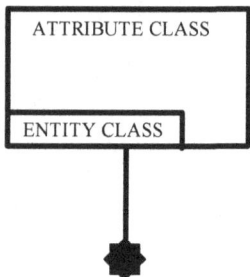

are known. Each entity has identifiable properties called *attributes* that can be used to describe the entity. Each entity is an individual member of some *entity class*. Entity classes also have specific properties of their own and relate to an individual set of circumstances.

An entity class represents the kinds of things that are known in common, about a collection of individual entities with similar properties. Each of these individual entities, which are members of the entity class employee, has its own unique characteristics, but these characteristics are similar in that they apply to each entity in the same way. An entity class represents information that is known about a collection of individual entities with similar properties and are one of the primary building blocks of the information model.

A *relationship* is an association between two entities. Such association must be meaningful (*make sense*) in the organization and must be something that we are interested to know about. Often, one entity can relate to many other entities. The information model expresses these relationships as a relation class. A relation class describes the way in which members of an entity class relate to members of another (or other members of the same) entity class. Additional IDEF1X models specify the minimum and maximum numbers of entity occurrences on each side of an association

Figure 10 shows the notation used to specify relation classes between entity classes. Numbers and the *N* and *M* characters indicate the number of entity occurrences on

Figure 10. Symbols for relations in IDEF1x

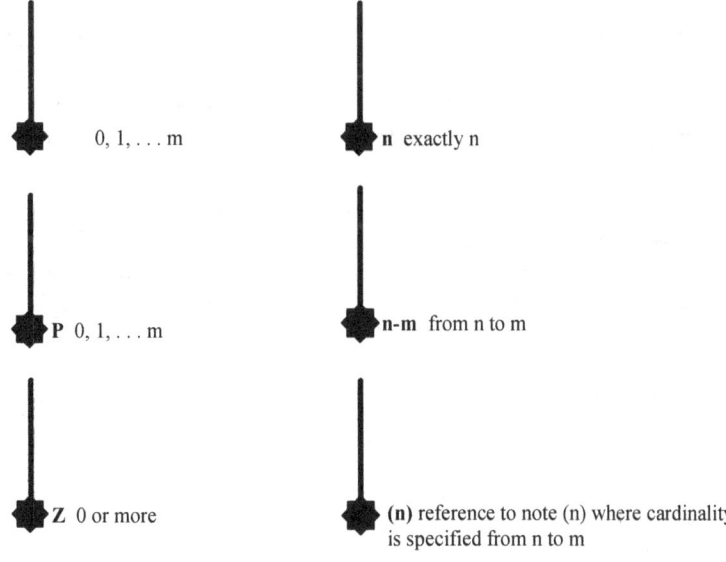

Figure 11. An IDEF1 information model for a medical consultation

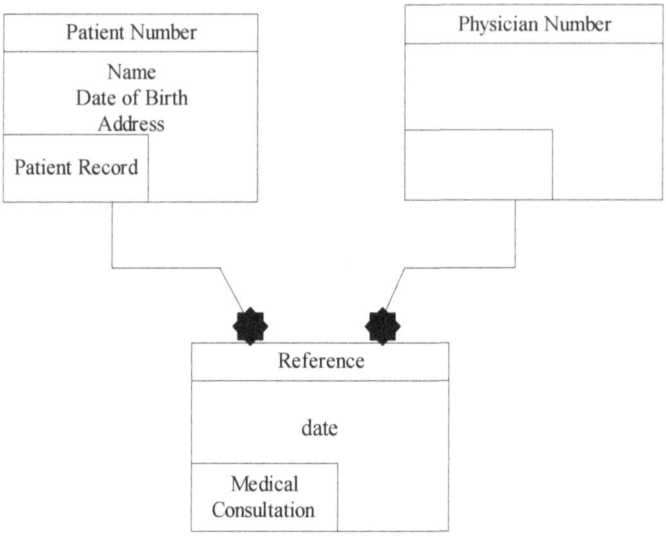

each side of the relation. For example, a line with *0,1* on both sides means that at most one entity occurrence must appear on each side of the relationship.

An entity class diagram focuses attention on a single entity class, which is called the *subject*. The subject entity class is surrounded by other entity classes that share some relation class with it. Only entity classes that have a direct relation class linking them to the subject entity class may appear on an entity class diagram.

The following IDEF1X entity class diagram demonstrates the use of IDEF to describe the logical structure of the information resources used in a medical service. The diagram focuses on the information resource, used in a medical consultation service. This information resource has attributes such as 'reference' and 'date' and is linked to exactly one *Patient Record* entity (the record of the patient for whom the consultation is about) and one physician (the one who carries out the consultation). It can be noted from the diagram, that a single *medical consultation* patient record can be associated with many consultations and also, that a physician can carry out many consultations. Logical information structures captured in IDEF1X notation will eventually be mapped to XML in a way explained in the next section.

An IDEF1X Modeling Approach

To construct a model of the organization's information using IDEF1X, we need to catalog the concepts (like in a data dictionary) appearing in a business domain and create a model of the domain. Thus, in building an information model, the following tasks are carried out:

1.   Catalog the concepts/terms
2.   Capture the constraints that govern how those terms can be associated with each other in that domain
3.   Build a model

The information modeling process therefore consists of the following five activities.

- **Organizing and scoping:** The organizing and scoping activity establishes the purpose, viewpoint, and context for the information modeling project. This is dictated by the scope of the service modeled in IDEF0 modeling activity.
- **Data collection:** During data collection, raw data needed for the project are acquired from sources such as documents, forms, databases, and so on.
- **Data analysis:** Data analysis involves analyzing the data to facilitate extraction of relevant terms.
- **Initial model development:** The initial development activity develops a preliminary information model in IDEF1X from the data gathered.
- **Model refinement and validation:** The model is refined and validated to complete the development process.

Figure 12. Different types of classification

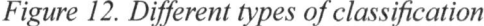
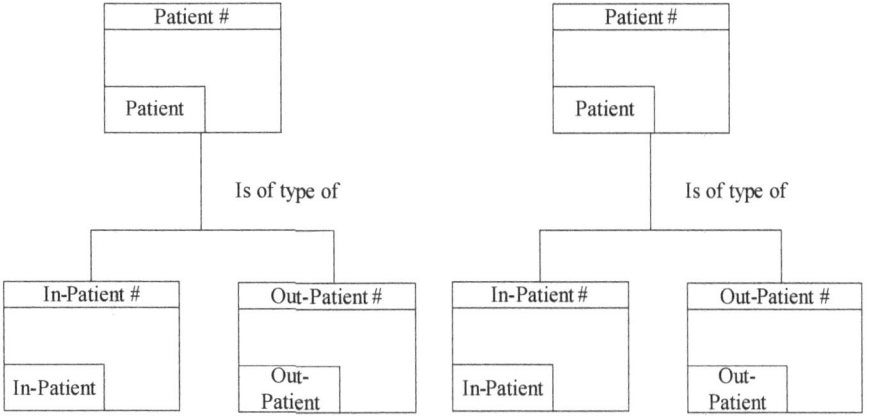

The purpose of the IDEF1X model is not just to identify and describe unrelated information entities of the organization but to relate them in meaningful ways and to organize them in classifications/taxonomies in order to enhance understanding and reuse. The following modeling techniques can be employed towards that end.

Entity Classifications

Classifications provide mechanisms for humans to organize knowledge into logical taxonomies. Of particular importance are two types of classification: *description subsumption* and *natural kind* classification. In description subsumption, the defining properties of the top-level kind in the classification, as well as those of all its subtypes, constitute necessary and sufficient conditions for membership in that kind. Conversely, natural kind classification does not assume there are rigorously identifiable necessary and sufficient conditions for membership in the top-level kind. The difference between the two types of classification is illustrated in Figure 12.

Composition

Compositions serve as mechanisms to represent graphically the *part-of* relation. In particular, this capability enables users to express facts about the composition of a given kind of entity.

As the diagram in Figure 13 shows, a patient record consists of a part with personal patient data and a part with medical patient data.

Figure 13. Composition

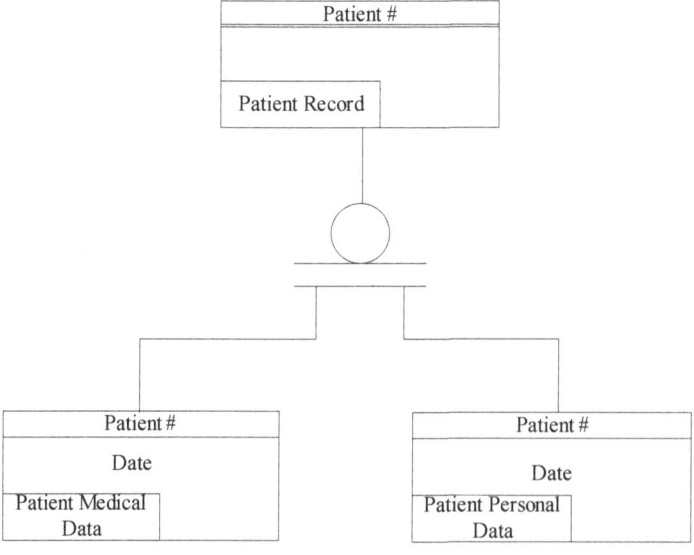

Copyright © 2008, IGI Global. Copying or distributing in print or electronic forms without written permission of IGI Global is prohibited.

Entity States and State Transitions

Although IDEF1X does not explicitly support the modeling of entity states, it is often useful to be able to show visually the possible states an entity can be in at any time and the allowed transitions between them. We achieve that by adding a semicolon, followed by the state name inside the entity name box. Transitions between states are shown using arrows connecting the different states. The direction of the arrow is the direction of the transition. For example, in Figure 14 a patient can be in either the *hospitalized* state or in the *discharged* state.

Mapping and Transforming IDEF Service Models

The previous sections were concerned with the derivation of IDEF0 and IDEF1X service models. This is largely a manual (i.e., human-driven activity) that aims to scope and bound the service and identify and describe all service elements in sufficient levels of detail. However, as we argued already, service engineering must be based on automated techniques if the targets of productivity, efficiency, and quality must be met. Thus, the following sections show how the IDEF0, IDEF1X, and associated artifacts derived are automatically transformed into computer-specific artifacts so that eventually they can be executed in some target environment(s).

Figure 15 shows three transformation domains:

- The *business models of services* described in IDEF0 and IDEF1X. These correspond to higher level service models.

Figure 14. Example object state transition schematic

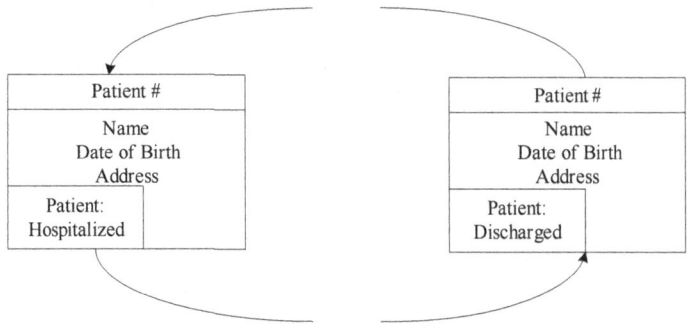

- The *decomposed service models* in terms of atomic services. These are still expressed in IDEF0 and IDEF1X but are expressed in a computer rather than a business viewpoint.

- The *software services domain*. This consists of software artifacts such as interface descriptions, configuration files, programs (code) and target execution on some software platform.

The methods and techniques for mapping across the above domains are detailed below.

Mappings Between Service and Computing Domains

Mapping from the service domain to the computing domain shows how a service capability is provided by a system (called the *mechanism*), which can be a computing system, including Web services. Since several technologies can be used to implement a capability mechanism, the mappings between service and computing domains must be done via a number of intermediate models. The reason for that is that we do not want to restrict unnecessarily our solution to a single execution environment or technology. By specifying the mechanism functionality in a program-

Figure 15. Service transformation domains

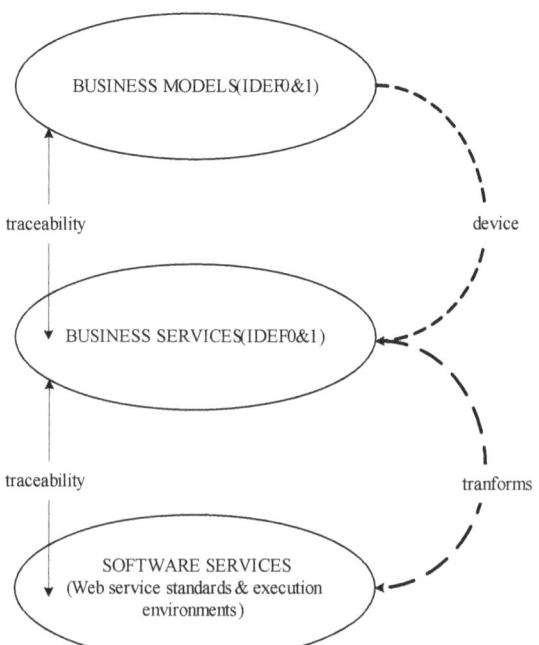

ming language/platform independent manner, we are able to encapsulate existing systems within Web services and/or to generate Web services code for both different service execution environments from the same model.

This is in essence the MDD approach of creating and transforming a succession of computing models, that was presented in Chapter V. Concerning mappings from PIMs to PSMs, the situation with respect to what is the best service execution platform is still not clear. Several such environments are available, belonging to one of the two competing camps (.NET and EJB). For organizations that want to preserve their investment in service modeling, it is not wise to commit to a specific environment that makes subsequent changes of environment more difficult. Thus, for a truly flexible service realization approach we need to maintain different PSMs reflecting the different architectures of .NET and EJB.

Mapping Business Service Models to Platform-Independent (Realizable) Service Models

In general, the mapping from computational-independent model (CIM) to platform-independent model (PIM) is the critical step in representing the business in the software model in an adequate way. The effectiveness of the CIM model affects the capability of the system to represent the real business behavior.

PIMs serve as generic models that are able to capture the specification of business services, which have been identified beforehand in computational-independent models. PIM models employ usually visual notations such as the activity diagram of UML and the business process modeling notation (BPMI, 2007). UML and BPMN raise the level of abstraction order to provide adequate understanding of the problem domain model. However, notations such as UML are, arguably, more suitable for building computational models (PIMs) rather than CIMs. For example, the activity diagrams of UML are not very good for describing *systemic* concepts needed to represent services, such as hierarchical decompositions, inheritance and feedback loops (i.e., structures and behaviors common across all types of organizations).

When modeling an enterprise, analysts need to carry out modeling in parallel across several layers or viewpoints such as business process, IT applications, software components, and so on. Such levels can be quite detailed. For example, a Java-based IT system can be made of application servers, which in turn execute Enterprise Java Bean components, which in turn are made of Java objects, made of byte code instructions. Since each of these levels corresponds to one or more PSM models, the question is, what is the sufficient number of models required to capture all program independent and program specific information of the intended system?

This book argues that for modeling and realizing business services, it is important to employ models and abstractions (i.e., CIMs) that are conceptually close to the problem domain (i.e., business services) but that also lead to natural mappings to computer specific models (PIMs and PSMs) (i.e., to service execution models). Our argument is that a modeling approach such as IDEF0 (supported by IDEF1X) is the ideal vehicle for representing and mapping both CIM and PIMs. Since both CIMs and PIMs can be expressed in IDEF notation, we avoid the semantic mismatches and other problems that are likely to occur when mapping between two different notations; for example, BPMN and UML. Ultimately, this results in the design and deployment of flexible service-oriented systems that expose a more dynamic and realistic behavior with respect to the business environment within which they operate.

Mapping a business service model to a Web service specification such as WSDL involves mapping the input parameters of a service to WSDL input messages and the output parameters to WSDL output messages. WSDL defines port types, which own operations. Operation definitions reference, but do not own, message definitions, with some messages playing the role of input parameters for the operation, and some playing the role of output parameters. The XML formats of the message payloads can be derived by applying an information model mapping (such as XMI), since all of the input and output parameter types of the business service's IDEF definition are contained in the IDEF1X information model.

Figure 16 shows the XSD schema for an IDEF0 service model in a graphical format, while Listing 2 shows the same in text format. From this description, WSDL definitions can be generated automatically.

Mapping from a business domain to a service domain shows how a business service can be decomposed into a network of realizable services. Using the IDEF0 method, business services are decomposed into networks of such coordinated services and resources. The reverse mapping (i.e., from the service domain to the business domain) can also apply (i.e., existing resources and capabilities can be reused to deliver multiple business services).

Transforming IDEF PIM to PSM

As described previously, a service identification and modeling project using IDEF0 will end with a model comprising a network of atomic services, each realized by a single mechanism. We can say, therefore, that an IDEF-based service approach starts with a CIM that is subsequently gradually transformed to PIMs as we carry out hierarchical decomposition. Thus, this approach creates multiple PIM models that enable the description of services at multiple levels. Each service level shows a network of dependencies. PIM to PSM to technology mappings are discussed below.

As explained in Chapter V, a key aspect of MDA is that a PIM model (describing what a service needs to provide) is transformed into a PSM model (describing how a service execution platform will provide it), which itself can be mapped to different actual (target) execution environments. Thus, the description of the business logic that the mechanism implements, together with the configuration files of the service execution platform must be generated. Earlier on, we defined three mapping levels: the business service level, the Web service level, and the software system level. In each level, we transform a PIM into a PSM that we map to the technology corresponding to the given level. In the business service level, there is no PSM model as the business services are defined in a technology neutral way (IDEF0). An IDEF mechanism at a sufficiently abstract level, can be manual, automated or a mixture of both. It is only when the mechanism is decomposed in subsequent levels that we decide whether this is a Web service or a (manual or computer-based) system. Once we identify mechanisms at the Web service level, we are able to generate the service description documents (WSDL) used for describing the service interfaces from an IDEF model as we saw earlier. At the same time, from the specification of the business logic, we can specify software components (i.e., Java or .NET) classes

Figure 16. XSD met-model for an IDEF0 business service

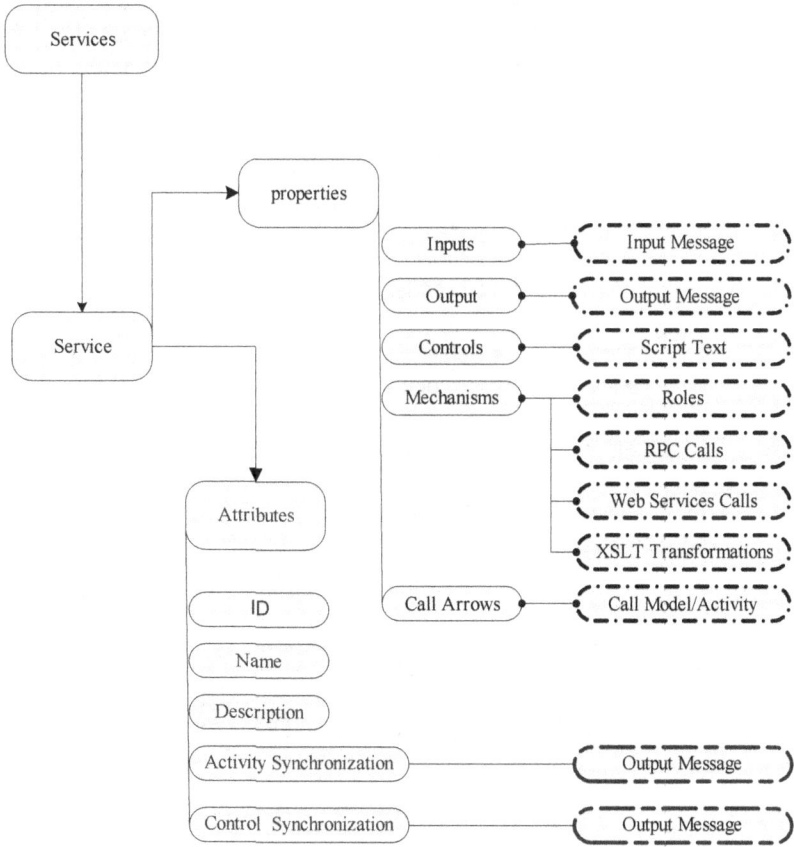

Listing 2. XSD for an IDEF0 business service

```xml
<?xml version="1.0" encoding="UTF-8"?>
<xs:schema xmlns:xs="http://www.w3.org/2001/XMLSchema" elementFormDefault="qualified">
    <xs:complexType name="ServicesType">
        <xs:sequence>
            <xs:element name="Service" type="ServiceType" maxOccurs="unbounded"/>
        </xs:sequence>
    </xs:complexType>
    <xs:complexType name="ServiceType">
        <xs:sequence>
            <xs:element name="Inputs" type="InputsType"/>
            <xs:element name="Outputs" type="OutputsType"/>
            <xs:element name="Controls" type="ControlsRefType"/>
            <xs:element name="Mechanisms" type="MechanismsRefType"/>
            <xs:element name="CallArrows" type="CallArrowsRefType"/>
        </xs:sequence>
        <xs:attribute name="ID" type="xs:string" use="required"/>
        <xs:attribute name="Name" type="xs:string" use="required"/>
        <xs:attribute name="CodeName" type="xs:string" use="required"/>
        <xs:attribute name="Description" type="xs:string" use="required"/>
        <xs:attribute name="PendingJobInfo" type="xs:string" use="required"/>
        <xs:attribute name="ActivitySynch" type="xs:string" use="required"/>
        <xs:attribute name="ControlSynch" type="xs:string" use="required"/>
    </xs:complexType>
    <xs:complexType name="CallArrowType">
        <xs:sequence>
            <xs:element name="Model"/>
            <xs:element name="Activity"/>
            <xs:element name="LinkedServer"/>
            <xs:element name="TimeOut"/>
            <xs:element name="RemoteProgID"/>
            <xs:element name="RemoteSystemID"/>
        </xs:sequence>
        <xs:attribute name="ID" type="xs:string" use="required"/>
    </xs:complexType>
    <xs:complexType name="CallArrowsType">
        <xs:sequence>
            <xs:element name="CallArrow" type="CallArrowType" maxOccurs="unbounded"/>
        </xs:sequence>
    </xs:complexType>
    <xs:complexType name="CallArrowsRefType">
        <xs:sequence>
            <xs:element name="CallArrow" type="ItemType"/>
        </xs:sequence>
```

continued on following page

Listing 2. continued

```
</xs:complexType>
<xs:complexType name="ControlType">
    <xs:sequence>
        <xs:element name="Name"/>
        <xs:element name="CodeName"/>
        <xs:element name="Condition"/>
    </xs:sequence>
    <xs:attribute name="ID" type="xs:string" use="required"/>
</xs:complexType>
<xs:complexType name="ControlsType">
    <xs:sequence>
        <xs:element name="Control" type="ControlType" maxOccurs="unbounded"/>
    </xs:sequence>
</xs:complexType>
<xs:complexType name="ControlsRefType">
    <xs:sequence>
        <xs:element name="Control" type="ItemType" maxOccurs="unbounded"/>
    </xs:sequence>
</xs:complexType>
<xs:complexType name="InputsType">
    <xs:sequence>
        <xs:element name="Schema" type="ItemType" maxOccurs="unbounded"/>
    </xs:sequence>
</xs:complexType>
<xs:complexType name="ItemType">
    <xs:attribute name="ID" type="xs:string" use="required"/>
</xs:complexType>
<xs:complexType name="MechanismType">
    <xs:sequence>
        <xs:element name="Name"/>
        <xs:element name="Description"/>
        <xs:element name="Type"/>
        <xs:element name="ProgID"/>
        <xs:element name="Method"/>
        <xs:element name="Arguments"/>
        <xs:element name="Roles"/>
        <xs:element name="XSLT"/>
        <xs:element name="SOAP_URL"/>
        <xs:element name="SOAP_ServiceName"/>
        <xs:element name="SOAP_ServicePort"/>
        <xs:element name="SOAP_ServiceInput"/>
        <xs:element name="HTTP_URL"/>
        <xs:element name="HTTP_Header"/>
```

continued on following page

Listing 2. continued

```
              <xs:element name="HTTP_Inputs"/>
              <xs:element name="HTTP_Synchronous"/>
              <xs:element name="HTTP_Username"/>
              <xs:element name="HTTP_Password"/>
              <xs:element name="HTTP_Timeout"/>
          </xs:sequence>
          <xs:attribute name="ID" type="xs:string" use="required"/>
      </xs:complexType>
      <xs:complexType name="MechanismsType">
          <xs:sequence>
              <xs:element name="Mechanism" type="MechanismType"
maxOccurs="unbounded"/>
          </xs:sequence>
      </xs:complexType>
      <xs:complexType name="MechanismsRefType">
          <xs:sequence>
              <xs:element name="Mechanism" type="ItemType" maxOccurs="unbounded"/>
          </xs:sequence>
      </xs:complexType>
      <xs:complexType name="OutputType">
          <xs:sequence>
              <xs:element name="Schema" type="ItemType"/>
          </xs:sequence>
      </xs:complexType>
      <xs:complexType name="OutputsType">
          <xs:sequence>
              <xs:element name="Schema" type="ItemType"/>
          </xs:sequence>
          <xs:attribute name="RuntimeMainOutput" type="xs:string" use="required"/>
      </xs:complexType>
      <xs:element name="Process">
          <xs:complexType>
              <xs:sequence>
                  <xs:element name="EntityPool" type="EntityPoolType"
maxOccurs="unbounded"/>
                  <xs:element name="Activities" type="ActivitiesType"
maxOccurs="unbounded"/>
              </xs:sequence>
              <xs:attribute name="ID" type="xs:string" use="required"/>
              <xs:attribute name="Name" type="xs:string" use="required"/>
              <xs:attribute name="CodeName" type="xs:string" use="required"/>
              <xs:attribute name="Description" type="xs:string" use="required"/>
              <xs:attribute name="Puspose" type="xs:string" use="required"/>
```

continued on following page

Listing 2. continued

```
                <xs:attribute name="Viewpoint" type="xs:string" use="required"/>
            </xs:complexType>
        </xs:element>
        <xs:complexType name="SchemaType">
            <xs:sequence>
                <xs:element name="Name"/>
                <xs:element name="Description"/>
                <xs:element name="XSD"/>
            </xs:sequence>
            <xs:attribute name="ID" type="xs:string" use="required"/>
        </xs:complexType>
        <xs:complexType name="SchemasType">
            <xs:sequence>
                <xs:element name="Schema" type="SchemaType" maxOccurs="unbounded"/>
            </xs:sequence>
        </xs:complexType>
        <xs:complexType name="EntityPoolType">
            <xs:sequence>
                <xs:element name="Schemas" type="SchemasType"/>
                <xs:element name="Controls" type="ControlsType"/>
                <xs:element name="Mechanisms" type="MechanismsType"/>
                <xs:element name="CallArrows" type="CallArrowsType"/>
            </xs:sequence>
        </xs:complexType>
</xs:schema>
```

that implement parts of the business logic. Using the code-generation techniques described, we can then generate the code for these components.

Transforming Resources to Data Definitions Using Ontologies

As is shown, IDEF1X is a method that models the company's information resources that are manipulated by mechanisms. In IDEF1X, these resources are modeled as objects (classes) described in terms of data and operations that may be performed on the data. An IDEF1X model is therefore an *ontology* (see Chapter VI) of an organization's resources. Object classes can be incorporated within *larger* object classes (i.e., superclasses), as required by the business logic. Conversely, special

Figure 17. Service model transformations

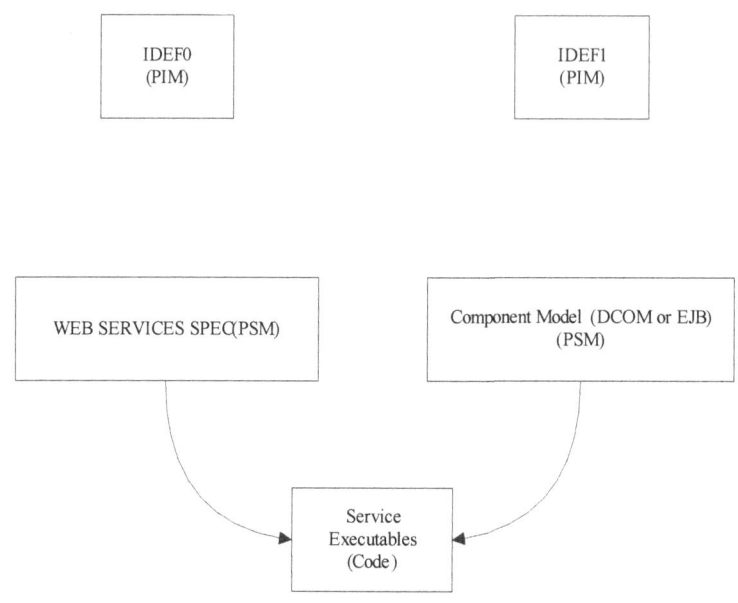

Figure 18. Entity to XSD mapping

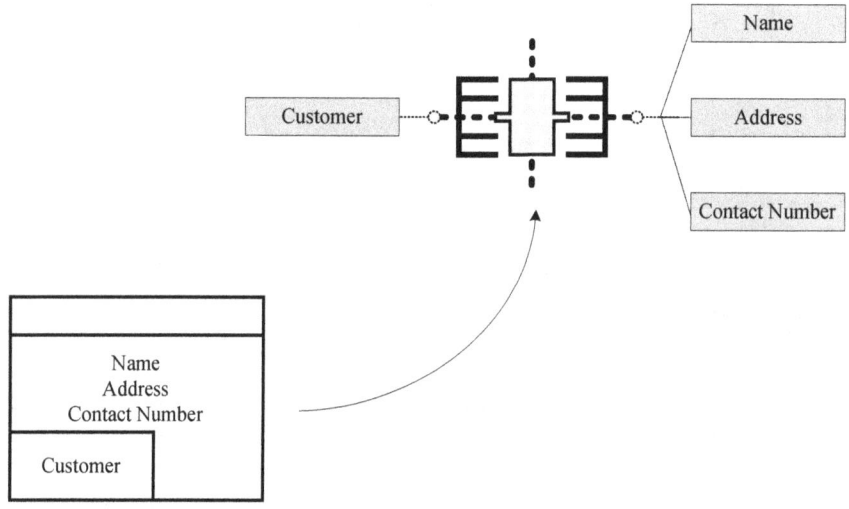

Figure 19. Mapping between two XSDs

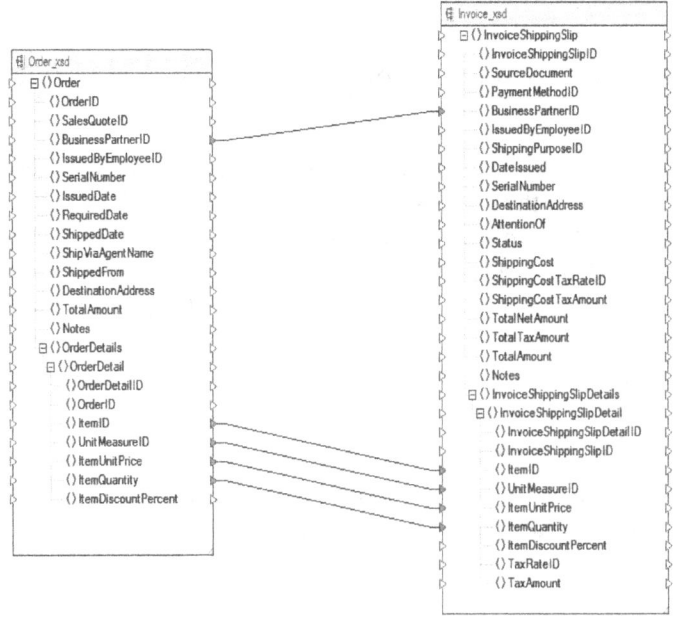

cases of a more general object class are referred to as subclasses. The advantage of defining object classes in a hierarchy is that specialized objects share all of the properties and operations of the more general classes through a mechanism called *inheritance*. Web services however return output which is encoded as payload within a SOAP formatted message (see Chapter III). The payload in a SOAP message however is an XML document, not an object. Thus, there needs to be a mechanism for transforming the objects captured in IDEF1X into XML documents. This can be achieved by using the MDD technique of *model mapping*. IDEF1X objects are transformed to XML schemas using a mapping (described in a *metamodel*) of object elements (such as the object's name, attributes, and methods) to corresponding elements of an XML schema. Figure 18 shows an example of an IDEF1X object *customer* and its corresponding XML (XSD) schema. The customer XSD is shown in graphical notation for convenience. More detailed metamodels for generating data artifacts will be presented in Chapter IX.

Transformation of information resources from one type to another can be automated in a similar way (i.e., by using mappings of the input XML schema to the output XML schema. Such mappings are defined in the *XSLT* language (see Chapter III). Figure 19 shows mapping of two business documents, *order* XSD to an *invoice* XSD (i.e., the mappings between the inputs and outputs of a Web service that receive customer orders as inputs and produces invoices as outputs). The visual mappings shown in Figure 19 are used by the modeling tools to generate XSLT code (see Chapter III).

Scripting the Service Logic

As already explained in Chapter V, a common technique to generate the software modules that realize the business logic is through user-defined templates. A template can share variables and trigger the processing of other templates, therefore allowing the user to define arbitrary flows of the generation process precisely. Templates consist of two types of content: static and dynamic. Dynamic content is expressed in a scripting language and is enclosed between the [% and %] delimiters. Everything that exists outside those delimiters is considered *static content*. Dynamic content populates the static content with data from the models.

For example, consider the script of Listing 3. This template is used to generate a Java class definition. When the script inside the template is executed, the names within the delimiters will be substituted for the actual names of the Java class and of its attributes.

Service Controls: Using a Rule Language to Define Control Logic

Although the control element of an atomic service can be defined using programming language control structures (such as conditional, choice, switch statements, etc.) within the components (e.g., the class methods) that implement the business logic, it is advantageous in most situations to avoid such encapsulation of control knowledge. Controls essentially implement business rules and constraints that specify how a service will be delivered. It is good practice to separate the decision of under what circumstances a service is delivered from the functional implementation of the service logic. To separate service control from service logic, we can employ technologies such as rule-based languages and *constraint satisfaction systems*.

Listing 3. Example template for code generation

```
public class [%=class.name%] {
[%for each attribute in class.attribute%]
private [%= attribute.type] [%= attribute.name %];
[%next%]
}
```

Listing 4. An OCL rule/constraint

```
context Order
inv: self. value > 10
```

In a rule-based language, each control is implemented as a set of rules stating *preconditions* or *triggers* that must be in place before the service is executed. In a constraint-based approach, the execution of a particular service will be tied to a number of constraints that must be satisfied for the service to be allowed to execute. Both rules and constraints are essentially logic expressions described in terms of the service input and output fields and also, in terms of the service *state,* that when evaluated result in *true* or *false.*

A rule, for example, used by a Web service that creates invoices could state that the value of the order must be at least 10 dollars. This rule is based on the input parameters of the Web service (as described in its WSDL). As rules of this type can change relatively frequently (when, for example, a company reviews its policies) it is good practice to define them outside the service, i.e. outside the XML schemas describing its WSDL. A *rule processor (engine)* can be used to execute such rules or check the constraints. In order to decide if a Web service will be executed, the rule engine will execute all applicable rules, and only if they are satisfied the service can proceed with its execution. Rule engines can thus become parts of a service execution environment. Listing 4 shows how such rule can be expressed in the OCL language (OMG, 2003). Object constraint language (OCL) is part of the OMG's family of languages for model-driven architecture (Chapter V).

Another issue in service realization involves the implementation of service orchestrations. In our approach, services orchestrations are modeled using the IDEF0 notation. This allows us to use systems theory and to view services independently from the processes and resources that deliver them. Alternatively, the services network can be described in a Web service coordination language, such as BPEL (Chapter IV), and executed automatically by a suitable program known as an *engine.* Such engines are discussed in more detail in the next chapter.

Today, as technologies for Web services execution have matured significantly in terms of both standards and implementation/execution platforms, there is a plethora of commercial platforms that fall into two main camps: the Java-based one (J2EE) and the Microsoft one (.NET based). A new type of platform for service execution and management called *service bus* will be discussed in the following chapter. Despite their relative sophistication, such environments fail to maintain the traceability of lower level technical services to the business services that they realize. This limitation is caused largely by the historical evolution of Web services, which as we have already seen (see Chapter III), happened *bottom up*. Web services grew from areas such as distributed system programming and remote procedure calls, with the standards for service descriptions following later on. At the time of writing this text, there are no standards as such for specifying and designing service-based systems. The most popular notation for software design, UML, is frequently employed in Web service projects for specification and design; however, UML does not provide any specific support for service realization projects.

Service realization projects can of course be approached as conventional software projects that undergo the phases of requirements, specification, design, and coding. The main problem with this approach is the gap that will exist between the models used for specification and design and the corresponding code. Such an approach will fail to capture the fact that a Web service is a realization of a higher level business service. Thus, a Web service model must be linked to the business service model that it realizes. If we capture the relations between the two models in a precise (formal) way, then we can potentially automate the process of deriving Web service models from business service models, in other words, the process of automatically realizing business services.

Generating Web Services Graphical User Interfaces (GUIs)

Although Web services are typically consumed by software applications rather than humans, sometimes it is necessary to invoke a Web service through a browser similarly to requesting and viewing an HTML page. A user therefore can interact with a Web service by simply pointing a browser at the Web service's URL. To fully utilize a Web service via a graphical user interface (GUI), support for flexible form navigation, variable-size lists, and dynamically enumerated options is required. Each screen of the user interface will be tied to a particular WSDL operation of the Web service. In addition, *virtual* WSDL operations that are compositions of several WSDL operations or just one WSDL operation with default values can be defined. A virtual operation's GUI can be simpler and more intuitive than GUIs for single WSDL operations. A virtual operation composes one or more WSDL operations (possibly using default values for some parameters) to construct a new Web service operation.

This is similar to a database, where data is stored in base tables, upon which views are defined; to a database user, a view is essentially no different from a base table. Similarly, a virtual operation is defined on operations and can be used just like any other operation.

There are several technologies for automatically generating GUIs from Web service descriptions (Kassoff, Kato, & Mohsin, 2003). For example, SOAPClient. com (http://www.soapclient.com/) introduced a Web services description language

(WSDL)-based WSGUI generator that uses WSDL definitions. Essentially, the GUIs were simple HTML forms consisting of text input boxes, labelled by the WSDL part to which they corresponded. Another proposal for generating GUIs for Web services is Web service user interface WSUI (http://www.wsui.org/doc/wsui). WSUI allows the creation of a user interface component for a Web service and facilitates assembling UI components.

Listing 5 shows part of the code that allows a customer to invoke a price quotation service. The generated GUI would look like the one in Figure 20, once appropriate stylesheets are added to the code of Listing 6 to define the formatting and page layout features.

Listing 5. XML code to generate a GUI for quotation request service

```xml
<?xml version="1.0" encoding="UTF-8"?>
<deployment
xmlns="http://.../wsgui"
xmlns:fdns="urn:Quotationrequest"
xmlns:xsl="http://.../XSL/Transform">
<wsdl href="http://.../Quotation.wsdl" />
<stylesheets>
<stylesheet name="input"
href="http://.../quotation_input.xsl" />
<stylesheet name="output"
href="http://.../quotation_output.xsl" />
</stylesheets>
<pages>
<page name="Quotation Request service"
inputStylesheet="input"
outputStylesheet="output"
operations="getQuotation" />
</pages>
<operations>
<operation name="getQuotation"
wsdlService="fdns:Quotationservice"
wsdlPort="QuotationPort"
wsdlOperation="getQuotation">
<submit>
<label>Submit</label>
</submit>
</operation>
</operations>
```

continued on following page

Listing 5. continued

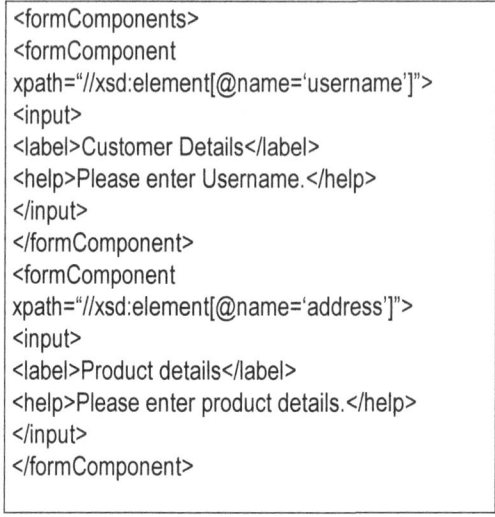

```
<formComponents>
<formComponent
xpath="//xsd:element[@name='username']">
<input>
<label>Customer Details</label>
<help>Please enter Username.</help>
</input>
</formComponent>
<formComponent
xpath="//xsd:element[@name='address']">
<input>
<label>Product details</label>
<help>Please enter product details.</help>
</input>
</formComponent>
```

Figure 20. Part listing of code to generate a Web service GUI for quotations

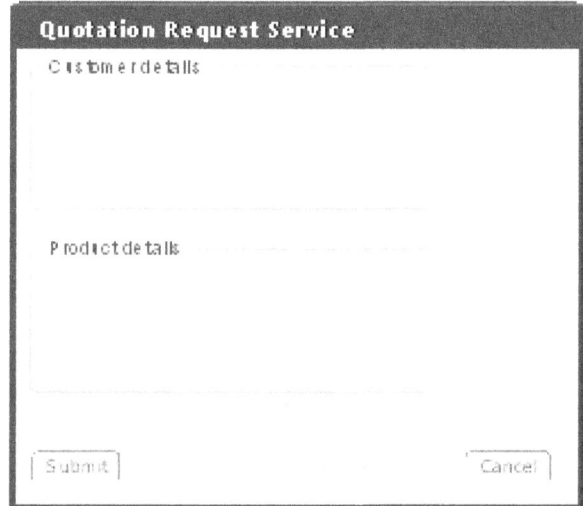

IDEF Service Ontologies

One of the key advantages of the approach defined in this chapter, is that the constructed IDEF service models are not merely visual or syntactic descriptions of business services but full-blown ontologies that capture the semantics of the service and of its context (i.e., the business domain of the service). This is in accordance with the paradigm of service-oriented architecture. Rather than providing software objects for a developer to reuse, our IDEF derived service-oriented method exposes services that both business users and developers can access. Apart from facilitating shared understanding between business users and software experts, service ontologies

Figure 21. An ontology of business and software services

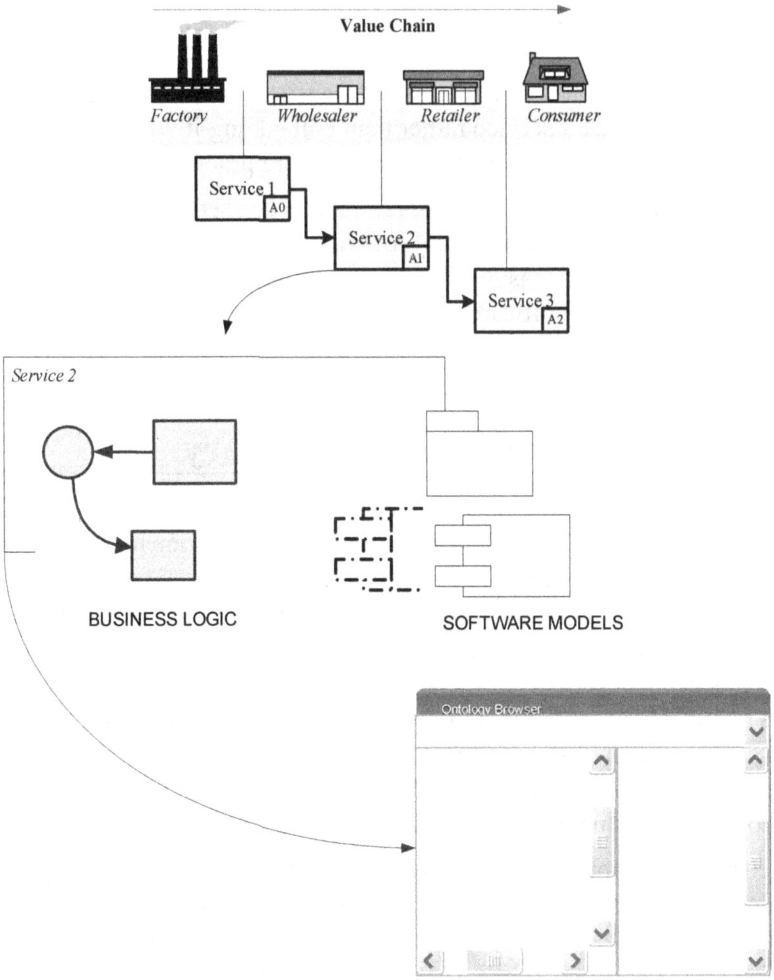

provide a pragmatic approach to reuse. Object-based reuse is riddled with problems, as it is difficult, for example, to get everybody to agree what a *customer* object class is and is not. In a service-oriented approach, there is no common *Customer* class but instead services such as *CreateCustomer, UpdateCustomer, DeleteCustomer*, and so on. Therefore, there is no need for everyone to agree on a single definition of *Customer*. Instead, any service consumer that needs to access services for customers must conform to the definition of customer the services expose. If a consumer's view of *Customer* is different, it must, somehow, map that view into the definition exposed by the service it wants to access. In Chapter V, we saw how this can be achieved using shared ontologies, mapping between ontologies, and mediating ontologies. While agreeing on a common notion of customer might be nice, it is not required for the client to reuse services. Changes to service to meet expectations of clients can still be problematic, although only externally visible changes are a concern for clients. Unlike object reuse through inheritance, changing the internal implementation of a service will not affect clients who depend on this service. There is no need for strict enforcement of reuse rules. If a service client needs to access a customer related service, the only way to do it in a well-designed SOA environment is via the service interface. Also, because this approach exposes the business rules and controls of a service rather than embedding it within the service logic, it makes reuse of business logic significantly more practical.

Figure 21 visualizes the ontology-driven approach to service engineering by showing an environment where business and software experts can use ontology tools (ontology editors, browsers, reasoners, etc.) to discover, reuse, and compose services at either the business or software levels, with full traceability between the two.

Chapter Summary

This chapter described a model-driven approach to service identification modeling and realizationbased on the IDEF modeling languages. The approach starts with a computation-independent model (CIM) of the business service derived from organization value chain thinking that is refined over several iterations into a platform-independent model (PIM) network of services, resources, mechanisms, and rules required to provide the service. Subsequently, platform-specific model (PSM) map specifications of service capabilities to the architecture of the targeted service execution environment and end with implementation of the Web services and other supporting programs required for service coordination.

In general, the mapping from computational-independent model to platform-independent model is the critical step in representing the business in the software model in an adequate way. The effectiveness of the CIM model affects the capability of the system to represent the real business behavior. Platform-independent models serve as generic models that are able to capture the specification of business services, which have been identified beforehand in computational-independent models.

In this chapter, we have argued that IDEF provides the conceptual underpinnings and semantics to move from CIM (business services) to their executable realizations (PIMs) in a seamless manner. When creating an enterprise services model, analysts need to carry out modeling in parallel at different levels of detail, such as business process, IT applications, software components, and so on.

This chapter has argued that for modeling and realizing business services, it is important to employ models and abstractions (i.e., CIMs) that are conceptually close to the problem domain (i.e., business services) but that also lead to natural mappings to computer specific models (PIMs and PSMs) (i.e., to service execution models). Our argument is that a modeling approach such as IDEF0 (supported by IDEF1X) is the ideal vehicle for representing and mapping both CIM and PIMs. Since both CIMs and PIMs can be expressed in IDEF notation, we avoid the semantic mismatches and other problems that are likely to occur when mapping between two different notations, for example BPMN and UML. Ultimately, this results in the design and deployment of flexible service-oriented systems that expose a more dynamic and realistic behavior with respect to the business environment within which they operate.

Regarding mappings from PIMs to PSMs, the situation with respect to what is the best service execution platform is still not clear. Several such environments exist, that belong to one of the two competing camps (.NET and EJB). It is not always wise to commit to a specific environment, as that makes subsequent changes of environment more difficult. Thus, for a truly flexible service realization approach we might need to be able to generate different PSMs reflecting the different architectures of the various service execution environments. This is possible using the IDEF driven approach as presented in this chapter.

The method proposed in this chapter offers therefore several benefits:

- The service design and implementation is inextricably linked to high-level business goals and/or customer driven requirements.
- There is traceability between such high-level goals/requirements and concrete service realizations.
- Services can be specialized/adopted by developing alternative service designs, whilst still maintaining reference to the original high level
- A service can be improved by for example substituting its interface for a more effective one or adding more control or better knowledge to make the service more effective.

- The service model can be simulated in a suitable simulator in order to measure and understand some of its properties.

- The service model can be directly fed as input to a service execution environment (*engine*).

- Some of the capabilities or even whole services can be outsourced. The service model can make clear the service interfaces to the partner to whom the service is outsourced.

    - Productivity gains: Software productivity is a barrier to realizing business benefits with computer technology. By automating the production of service-based software, we enable companies to reap the benefits brought by electronic service delivery.

    - Easier adaptation: Adapting features of the delivered service effectively means changing the requirements for the corresponding Web services.

    - Easier to prove and maintain backward and forward traceability between business services and Web services. Consumers of services need guarantees and assurances that the services are provided, according to certain quality criteria. It is important for both providers and consumers to be able to verify that these are enforced by the executable (Web) services.

The service realization approach that this chapter has presented ensures continuity from the business services to their technological implementation as Web services. To ensure such continuity, it is important to employ an automated approach that transforms business services to executable services. The model-driven development paradigm (MDA/MDD) provides the concepts tools and techniques for model driven realization of services. With MDA, the discovered services are transformed into intermediate, platform independent, capability descriptions that can be automatically realized in a target environment based on Java or .NET. However, being able to quickly generate Web services from any business-level service, if uncontrolled, can lead to an explosion of Web services that is difficult to manage.

Up to now, service modeling and design has either been dealt with in a high-level business-oriented manner (e.g., service strategies, theories on customer perception of service quality, etc.) or in a low-level IT manner (Web services). The method described in this chapter bridges the gap that exists in the middle. Services are neither business processes nor computer artifacts, thus, neither business process modeling formalisms such as BPN or software modeling notations such as UML, as suitable for modeling services. A systemic view of services can bring together management and IT perspectives for the purposes of services modeling.

References

Argyris, C., & Schön, D. (1996). *Organizational learning II: Theory, method and practice*. Reading, MA: Addison Wesley.

Badica, C., & Fox, C. (2002). *A formal IDEF-based notation for business process modeling*. Paper presented at the 14th International Conference on Advanced Information Systems Engineering, Toronto, Ontario, Canada.

BPMI. (2007). *Business process modeling notation (BPMN)*. Retrieved March 15, 2007, from http://www.bpmn.org/

Checkland, P. (1981). *Systems thinking, systems practice*. New York: Wiley.

IDEF. (2007a). *IDEF1X information modeling method*. Retrieved March 15, 2007 from http://www.idef.com/IDEF1X.html

IDEF. (2007b). *Integration definition for function modeling (IDEF0)*. Retrieved March 15, 2007, from http://www.idef.com/idef0.html

Kassoff, M., Kato, D., & Mohsin, W. (2003, September). Creating GUIs for Web services. *IEEE Intelligent Computing*. 66-73.

OMG. (2003). *UML 2.0 OCL specification*. Retrieved March, 15, 2007, from www.omg.org/docs/ptc/03-10-14.pdf

Section IV

Service Deployment
Execution and Management

Chapter VIII

Service Deployment Execution and Management

Introduction

This chapter is concerned with concepts, technologies, and standards for deploying, executing, and managing services. In previous chapters, we have argued that the design of the service must strive for a balance between offering to customers what they want and creating potential for developing additional revenue generating services. We have already established that, although not all possible types of services can be delivered to the consumers in an electronic form, information needed for the coordination and mobilization of the core service resources can be digitized and offered as a support service. In Chapter II, we explained that support services which attach to a core business service are information-based in the sense that they help the consumer locate, evaluate, and access the offered service. Effectively, such services add value to the main business service.

The Internet allows us to deliver services in a cost-effective manner. Even if the core business service cannot be delivered through electronic channels, most of its supporting (information-based) services can. Supporting services are used to assist the consumer in locating, evaluating, and consuming the core service, according to the service life cycle shown in Chapter II. In this chapter, however, we will examine service technologies and standards, which mainly use the Internet to deploy and manage services for the consumers. Such standards refer primarily to Web services, as this is the prevalent technology for implementing e-services.

Environments for Consumption and Provision of Services

Increasingly, service execution environments deal not only with the provision, production, and management but also with the consumption of services. Although consumption and provision of services are separate (and loosely coupled, by the definition of services), Web services increase the integration between the two.

Today, most consumption of e-services is via portals accessed using Web browsers; but rich clients (which are programs that have capabilities beyond simple browsing) are also growing in popularity. Rich-client consumers of e-services often use portals as the glue that brings together the management of the resultant environment. Leading services platforms include technologies and architectures that provide value in bringing together consumption with the provision of e-services, while maintaining the benefits of loose coupling (Smith, Abrams, Sholler, Plummer, & Cantara, 2005).

With the ubiquity of the Internet and the Word Wide Web, delivering services electronically has numerous advantages for providers and consumers alike. The power of the Internet and the Web for reaching customers has been proven in every business function from marketing to after-sales support and in every business domain. Providing an e-service to consumers over the Web traditionally has meant the following things:

- A Web site containing HTML pages with service information and metainformation. Metainformation is effectively a directory of services available on the Web site and instructions on how to access them, such as the UDDI discussed in Chapter III. The Web site is hosted by a Web server which is an application that serves clients (typically Web browsers) with the Web pages they request using standard communication protocols (typically the HTTP protocol)

- A Web browser used by the consumer to access the pages of the service provider's Web site

- The ability of the Web server and the Web browser to communicate by exchanging messages that are transmitted using the standard Internet protocols (typically HTTP over TCP/IP).

Each Web page will typically contain information that can be viewed by the consumer and perhaps the ability for two-way interaction between the consumer (through the Web browser) and the Web site. Two-way interactions may include facilities such as consumer logging to the Web site and transactional capabilities. Logging in allows the Web site to identify the consumer in order to help him/her select the most suitable service or to customize a service. Transactional capabilities include the ability of the consumer to pay for the offered service via online payment facilities. A transactional capability requires in addition the Web site being linked to some databases of the company and perhaps also to other systems of the provider company that deal with payments, billing, and so on.

While these Web sites would had been sufficient in the past for providing e-services, the 21st century has seen the emergence of different type of technologies that can provide the means for deploying and consuming e-services, collectively known as *Web service execution platforms*. Before we look in detail into what are Web services platforms and how they can provide the infrastructure for the design and delivery of e-services, we need to consider the current technology and market forces that led to their rapidly growing popularity.

The conventional Web server/Web browser technology combination is by now quite mature and has proved its usefulness in situations where a person needs to access information stored in HTML pages of a Web site. In many cases, viewing this information equals receiving the service. A flight information service, for example, published by an airline, allows its customers to search for and view information about a specific flight or flights. However, things change once we stop making the assumption that the consumer of the service will always be a person. If the consumer of the service is not human, then an HTML-based delivery of the service may not be ideal, as programs cannot *see* the contents of an HTML page. Other programs may find it difficult to separate the content from the presentation information and therefore to understand the contents of an HTML page. Thus, service information needs to be structured in a way that is intelligible to other programs. In Chapter VI, we proposed *ontologies* as a mechanism to achieve that (i.e., as a way to add more semantic information [*meaning*] to the service descriptions).

We already argued in earlier chapters that, to offer a service, a company often has to mobilize not only its own resources but also those of its partners. The company uses such resources as an *external* type of service. Airlines, for example, use the services of the airports (to obtain parking space for their planes, terminals for their passengers, catering services, etc.). Therefore, we concluded that, in order to provide a service, a company must use (and sometimes coordinate) a whole network of services (either its own or those of its partners). However, to connect to an external service, the Web browser/HTML combination might not be ideal as the services need to interact at the machine (i.e., by two computers exchanging data with each other) rather than at a human level. In Chapter IV, we saw languages such as BPEL used for composing and coordinating services. BPEL service orchestrations, however, cannot be executed on a simple Web browser; they require a special execution environment, or *engine.*

With the widespread use of mobile communications, service consumers are increasingly *mobile.* It is no longer safe to make the assumption that the consumer of the e-service will sit behind a personal computer at a fixed location. Consumers may wish to receive the service while on the move. In such cases, the consumer can be virtually anywhere and use a mobile device that ranges from a fairly unsophisticated mobile phone to a significantly more advanced PDA. Again, because of the nature of such devices (small screen, a small or nonexistent keyboard), the HTML/Web browser solution might not be ideal or even feasible for delivering the service.

We come therefore to the conclusion that the delivery of an e-service needs to assume that the consumer is not always a human but possibly another software program, and that the service needs to be delivered not only through a Web browser running on a personal computer, but possibly to other devices that can be mobile.

With the necessity of allowing both provider and consumer of an e-service to be software programs, the following become essential requirements:

- **To be able to provide business services:** *That is,* services published at a level of abstraction that corresponds to real-world activity and recognizable business function. This level has to go beyond the programmatic representations of Web service information (e.g., as in a WSDL description).

- **Separation of interface from implementation:** The interface, as opposed to the implementation of the service, should be designed in a manner that the consumer has no visibility of the implementation. Services are offered at a business-level of abstraction, which renders the interface a business interface, and this generally means a contract, which is expressed in XML (see Chapter II).

- **Contract-based integration:** The importance of the existence of a formal contract cannot be overestimated. The formal contract is the instrument that allows the consumers to implement virtual and dynamic partnerships, minimize dependencies to specific partners, maximize adaptability, have a choice of services, and more easily change provider.

- **Generic service interfaces:** With a view to ease the management from the consumer's viewpoint and management of supply risk. If a company is dependent upon a few key service providers, this represents a potential risk. This leads to a design goal of making service specifications as general as possible, which of course might conflict with performance objectives.

- **Common business language:** Shared between the provider and consumer and used for describing the permitted sequences of messages between the communicating parties.

- **A services vocabulary:** A vocabulary from which the messages are constructed. This has to be shared between the provider and consumer so that they understand each other.

- **A network transport:** For delivering messages between providers and consumers.

The diagram shown in Figure 1 provides a full life-cycle view of the service engineering process. This service life cycle does not imply any particular transition between the stages or a top-to-bottom approach. It depicts the need to communicate and share information in two dimensions (CBDI Forum, 2005):

- Across the life-cycle phases: Between participants in provisioning or consumption. There is a need to ensure traceability of the service across life-cycle stages. For example, to ensure that the deployed service is consistent with the analysis specification or that the service design meets the SLA obligations.

- Between participants: The service provider and service requestor (and other participants such as intermediaries) need to share information at various points in the life cycle (e.g., the *business analysts* of both *service provider* and *service consumer* exchanging information on a service requirement).

Figure 1. Service lifecycle

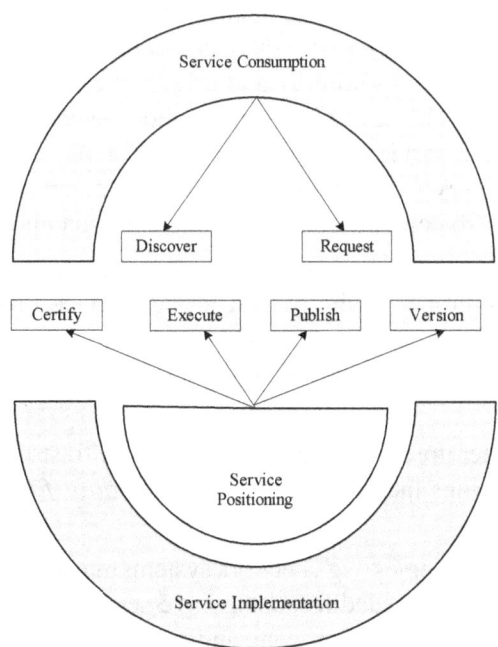

Managed Service Delivery

In Chapter III, we looked at the main ingredients of Web services (XML, WSDL, UDDI, SOAP), essentially, specifications and protocols on which the basic e-service concepts (resource, interface, contract, etc.) can be mapped. However, such concepts do not consider explicitly the management of e-services. E-services, like all other business services and processes, need to be managed. Simply delivering the service to its consumers without some monitoring and control point that manages the state of the service and its consumption does not make much sense in a business context. Providing an e-service means essentially opening up the company's resources to external access. Without some kind of mechanism for controlling the availability of such resources (i.e., for *securing* the provision of the service), the business can become exposed to all types of risk. Even in cases where the service is delivered internally (i.e., consumed within the same organization that provides the service), it makes sense to limit its availability to only authorized business roles or business areas. Knowing the actual usage patterns of the service (i.e., who consumes it as well as the level of such consumption) allows the effectively planning of the service and the resources it utilizes. Even if the service is provided *for free*, it is essential to have some kind of usage logging facility. Obviously, such facility is essential when the service is provided on a fee basis.

From the service consumer viewpoint, managing the service delivery is equally important. In the case of a paid service, for example, the consumer needs to know that the billing received is correct. If the service fails to be delivered to the required standards (or fails to be delivered at all), the consumer needs to locate the cause of the failure as being with the provider, the communication network or with its own systems. The consumer's security and privacy concerns must also be addressed in service delivery. The security of information owned by the consumer and used in consuming the service (e.g., its payment details) need to be guaranteed. The consumer's privacy (i.e., the knowledge of what services it consumes and how) should also be protected from being available to unauthorized third parties.

Service providers therefore will have to manage security, control access rights and accounting, monitor availability, and broker service requests to the appropriate systems that implement the service. Other requirements include the need to manage service aggregation and dynamic configuration in the case of complex composite services.

This chapter, therefore, will discuss the needed infrastructure for service delivery, which means things like *technologies, functionality, facilities,* and *platform environments.*

Whilst other technologies (e.g., network systems management methods) can provide some of the features needed for managing e-services, it is Web services platforms that currently offer a rapidly growing and maturing set of technologies for e-service management. Of course, Web services are actually a special type of e-service—one concerned with the provision of a remote computing capability. Nevertheless, their management infrastructure can support other types of e-services as well.

In Chapter II, we drew an analogy between e-services infrastructure and the ones for plumbing, water, gas, and electricity in a typical domestic dwelling. A network of gas pipes and supply points makes possible, for example, the installation of heating and cooking systems. Similarly, the electrical wiring and access points (electrical sockets, etc.) allow electrical appliances to be connected and used. Meters installed on the consumer's gas and electric network ensures that the consumer can be billed by the electric or gas company (the service provider) according to consumption. For something to be called *service infrastructure,* it needs to provide basic services and guarantees for the performance and availability of such services similar to service-level agreements

We divide such infrastructure into the following:

- **Service management infrastructure:** This is essential from both the supplier and consumer perspectives, in order to ensure adaptations to the service, enforcement of contracts, billing, auditing, and other similar purposes. At the same time, this infrastructure must cater for service performance, reliability, modularity, integration with existing systems, and so on.

- **Service security infrastructure:** This is infrastructure that ensures the contents of the service, the delivery channels, and the service resources are protected from unauthorized access and interference and that privacy requirements of the service consumer are met.

Figure 2 illustrates the concept of managed service delivery. Monitoring and security enforcement nodes are inserted between the e-service and its consumers. These nodes are discussed in more detail next.

Web Services Management (WSM)

WSM covers a range of function that includes monitoring, tracking, and service modification (Arora et al., 2005). Service providers that offer service level agreements need to be able to track activity from the consumer end across to the provider end, plus at all intermediate nodes (i.e., for services that incorporate other external services). Management of Web services is defined as a set of capabilities for discovering the existence, availability, health, and usage as well the control and configuration of service elements such as service interface and contract descriptions, the systems that implement or support the service as well as the service itself.

Figure 2. The concept of managed service delivery

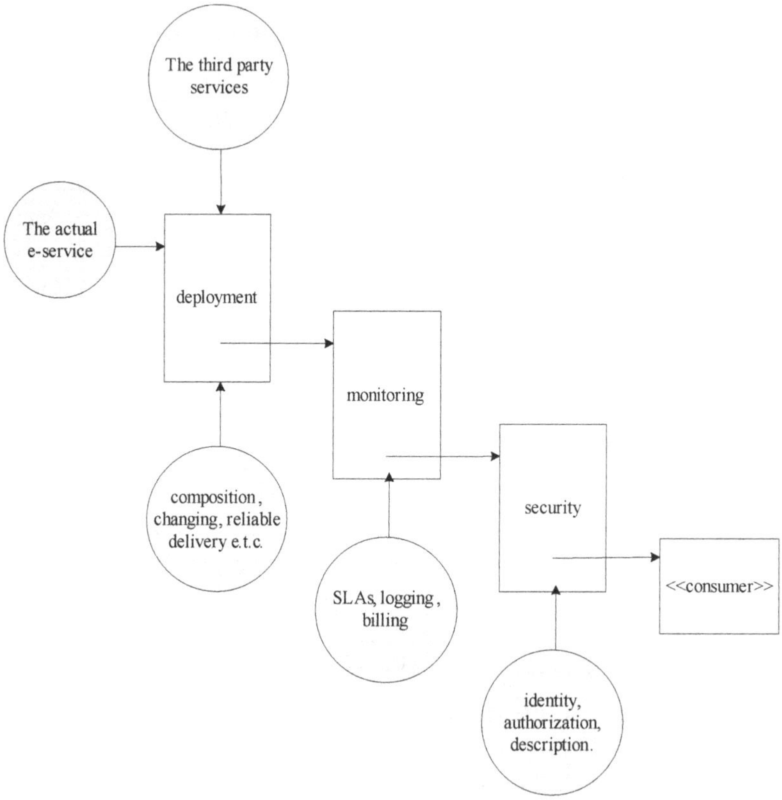

Concepts necessary for understanding and managing a service such as managed resource life cycle are discussed below.

Managed Resource

A deployed (managed) resource is a resource that exists in the physical world. There are many kinds of deployed resources, including agents, services, and descriptions. A deployed resource has a physical location, such as a file in a computer or a process executing on a computer. A deployed resource may realize a service.

Service Life Cycle

A *life cycle* is a set of states and transition paths between them for an e-service. The life cycle of the service can be explicitly described so that it can be managed. Service life cycle, as discussed in Chapter II, needs to be defined from both the provider and consumer perspectives. To manage the life cycle of a service, *event* descriptions are used. These are messages that indicate a problem, a life cycle state change, or a state change. State change events occur whenever life cycle state transitions happen. A request processing event description indicates that the state of a request has been changed and should include the previous state and the transition time. The event may also include any context associated with the request, reply, or failure message and any part or the complete content of these messages. Event descriptions provide valuable information for managers and can be used to calculate many of the service management metrics discussed below.

Service Management Metrics

Management metrics are atomic, unambiguous information about the performance of a system. For manageability metrics, the information is used for management purposes. The value of the metric captures the information at a point in time. Generally, these values are numeric, but they may be textual as well. Measurements are calculated with a formula based on metrics (e.g., average response time during the last hour of execution). A managed element should allow any available metrics and measurements to be reported according to configurable time intervals.

Monitoring Service Usage

Service providers need to remain in control of who uses the service as they want to know the consumers' needs, possibly bill them, and be able to communicate with them so that they can coordinate changes. However, if the provider keeps tight control over the usage of a service, they may constrain its use. One way of overcoming this need to control usage is to implement an enhanced *logging service*. Every time the service is used, a message is logged which records the basic usage data. To complement the logging service, a usage reporting service can be added that allows both provider and prospective and actual consumers to know the level of usage. By combining log and the internal service registry information, such information can be made quite usable. A further enhancement would be to log information that would allow the provider to log not only the usage but also the identity of the consumer. This would then permit communications on matters such as upgrade issues.

Service Version Control

The issue of service version control is important in any publicly accessible service (i.e., where not all the identities of the service consumers will be known to the service provider in advance). Service providers need to change the interfaces to their services (e.g., to improve the service), making it more flexible or easy to access and so on. For example, an airline might decide to add a new parameter to its seat reservation service to allow the passengers to specify seating requirements (i.e., a seat near the window or the aisle of the aircraft). Usually, the provider will provide a new interface for the parameter, and it probably will not keep the old interface available. It is very difficult for service providers to maintain backwards compatibility, so often they don't (Orchard, 2002). The reason is that to implement the new service, the databases, application logic, and other parts of the service have all changed, and to maintain backwards compatibility is difficult. When this happens, generally, the service consumer application will cease to work. The provider's interface is expecting another parameter in the service request, which the client software isn't providing. In the worst scenario, the provider simply changed the interface and didn't give any advance warning to the consumer. This is what typically happens in the Web service provider market today. In such situations, the consumer must undertake a change process to discover the new parameter, perhaps changing interface and logic to collect and pass on the parameter. Depending upon the complexity, the consumer's service may be down for an unknown amount of time, perhaps weeks or months.

In e-services, the interface change problem is increased, because a service upgrade may affect a large number of services that are on many different and separate consumer machines. The consumer of an updated service, in general, cannot download an update, uninstall, or reinstall the service. The only solution to the problem of upgrading services and therefore affecting existing client software today is through the use of contracts. A typical contract will state that the service provider must give 60 days notice of interface change, with test accounts available for testing available within 30 days. But even then, ultimately, each and every client must upgrade their software that accesses the service. The key concept though is that part of the contract between the service provider and the consumer is the treatment of versioning of interfaces.

Quality-of-Service (QoS) Contracts

Quality-of-service contracts quantify the expected behavior of the e-service or offer the means to negotiate the parameters of the service. The quality-of-service contract can be specified statically by enumerating the features the service provider server will respect. Alternatively, a more dynamic solution can be implemented that conducts negotiations between the service consumer and its server. Common examples of quality-of-service parameters that may be exposed by a server are maximum response delay, average response, quality/precision of the result, and result throughput.

Service Quality, Monitoring, and Support

Some of the real-world issues of Web service delivery have to do with contract negotiation, billing, security, provisioning, and version control. Any commercial Web service must provide some specification of these capabilities. The service provider will simply provide these to the general world via a registry such as the UDDI, discussed in Chapter III. The specifications for the various capabilities of the service are also collected during this negotiation process.

It is an essential requirement of providers to monitor the performance of the Web services. Monitoring the performance of Web services is not about monitoring the technology components that support the service but is about monitoring the service as it is consumed by the consumer and building up a picture of the different types of consumers that exist within their business. By actively managing Web services, the organization can control the interaction of their resources from a business perspective, thereby aligning their e-service offerings with business objectives.

Service Infrastructure Scalability and Extensibility

A major goal for any service infrastructure is that it is inherently scalable and extensible. This goal is broken down into the following critical success factors: modularity and extensibility, reliability, and peer-to-peer interaction. These critical success factors are considered next.

Modularity and Extensibility

A service infrastructure must be modular (i.e., consisting of self-contained components of appropriate granularity). This in turn facilitates the overall conceptual integrity of the infrastructure and its easy comprehension. Message structures, service interfaces, and so on, must be explicitly identified and potentially described using description languages such as WSDL and its semantic extensions (see Chapter VI). Minimal assumptions must be made by the service consumer about the required components to realize the services. Another advantage of modularity is extensibility. New modules offering added or improved functionality to the service can be easily integrated (*plugged-in*) to the infrastructure by obeying agreed interface protocols.

Peer-to-Peer Interaction

To support services interacting with each other in a peer-to-peer style, the infrastructure must allow services to have persistent identity, must permit descriptions of the capabilities of services and must support flexibility in the discovery of services by each other. Services must be allowed to communicate with each other using a very general concept of message exchange. Typical examples of message exchange pattern are request-response, publish-subscribe, and event notification. A service wishing to use a peer-to-peer style interaction may use, for example, a publish-subscribe pattern for message exchange. According to the publish-subscribe pattern, services publish notifications to which other services subscribe. Thus, services that are interested in the output of a particular service get notified when this becomes available. In Chapter IV, we stated that services have semantics that may be identified in a service description and that may be expressed in an ontology service description language. The description of the semantics of a service, and for more advanced agents, the description of the service contract itself, permits agents implementing services to determine the capabilities of other peer agents. This, in turn, is a critical success factor in the architecture supporting peer-to-peer interaction of services. Finally, the fact that services have descriptions means that these descriptions may be published in discovery agencies and also retrieved from such agencies. In effect, the availability of explicit descriptions enables services and agents to discover each other automatically as well as having these hard-coded.

Service Reliability

The goal of service reliability is to both reduce the error frequency for interactions and, where errors occur, to provide a greater amount of information about the cause and nature of the error. In the context of e-services, we can address the issues of reliability at three distinct levels:

- Reliable and predictable interactions between services,
- Reliable and predictable delivery of services, and
- Reliable and predictable behavior of individual service providers and consumers.

The highest level of reliability identified here refers to the choreographies of the interactions between service consumers and providers (see Chapter IV). In effect, reliability at this level becomes a measurable property of the descriptions of choreographies (W3C, 2004). Assuming that the infrastructure is reliable, and assuming that the services are reliable, choreographies must describe situations in which the composed service will behave in predictable ways.

The reliability of the individual service providers and consumers is depends on how services are realized (implemented). Reliability at this level is enhanced by service providers adopting deployment platforms that have strong management capabilities. The reliability of the infrastructure services refers to the reliability of the messaging infrastructure and the discovery infrastructure; the former is often referred to as *reliable messaging*. In general, this refers to a predictable behavior of service related to the delivery of the messages involved with the service. Message reliability entails assurance for the sender of the message that a given message has been received by its intended receiver and that the message has been received exactly once.

Knowing if a message has been received correctly allows the sender to take compensating action in the event the message has not been received. At the very least, the sender may attempt to resend a message that has not been received. The general goal of reliable messaging is to define mechanisms that make it possible to achieve these objectives with a high probability of success in the face of inevitable but unpredictable network, system, and software failures. The goals of reliable messaging can be made more explicit by considering the issues related to multiple receptions of a message and message intermediaries. If there is an intermediary, does the sender want to know whether the message got to the intermediary or to the intended end recipient? Does the receiver care whether it receives a message more than once? Protocols and specifications, such as Web services reliable messaging protocol (OASIS, 2005) and Web services reliability (OASIS, 2004b) can be implemented to obtain reliable message based communications at the SOAP protocol level.

Contracts

As service provider and consumers have contractual obligations to each other, an acceptable message conforming to the correct format of the message needs to be planned and designed appropriately. Such contracts are usually specified as XML schemas (see Chapter III). Only messages that satisfy this contract will be acceptable.

Fault Tolerance

Fault tolerance is a major concern since faults are not easily discovered in loosely coupled service architectures. The need to identify the fault lines and taking measures to resolve the issues is important. Essentially, faults fall into one of the two categories: *business* faults and *system* faults. Business faults occur when the parameters or operations of the service have changed and, hence, either the sending service or the receiving service has changed or the business rules have changed. System faults occur due to infrastructure-level failures, which are usually purely technology related. Business-level fault can be prevented by refining the message schema and capturing inconsistencies when the contents of a message are validated against the schema. System-level faults occur due to various reasons related to infrastructure, such as network failures or server downtimes. For this reason, a service execution platform needs to implement some fault collection mechanism to anticipate these faults and develop automated mechanism to handle them (Poozhikunnel, 2007).

Message Monitoring

Message monitoring is as important as message fault tolerance. A message observer service can be implemented to check all the messages that flow through the system. Any time a fault occurs, the service will raise an event to notify any systems subscribing to the service, and it can then process the information appropriately.

Network Monitoring

Monitoring of the network is also an important task that can be done by sending test messages that could be checked at periodic intervals. The verification can be done based on the time, load, and authenticity of the test message transmitted. This is done because any messages from the services may not be accountable due to the loosely coupled nature of services.

Service Security

Overview of Service Security

E-services and Web service in particular have characteristics that make its security needs different than those of other software applications:

- Loose coupling between the service provider and service consumer.
- Usage of XML to describe exchanged messages and metadata.
- Highly-focus on interoperability.
- Platform- and programming-language neutral.
- A variety of transport protocols, with HTTP the most common but not the only one.

- Multiple (third) parties might be involved in the provision of a service, if the service is composed from other ones.

Some of the characteristics of a Web service that make it especially vulnerable to security attacks include the following:

- Interactions are performed over the Internet using transport protocols that are usually allowed through network firewalls and thus can penetrate a network's first line of defense.
- Communication is often initiated by service consumers who have no prior relationship with the service provider.
- The message format is text based (not binary).

There are several well-defined aspects of application security that, when properly addressed, help to minimize the security threats. These include *authentication, authorization, integrity, confidentiality,* and *nonrepudiation* (Vasiu, Mackay, & Warren, 2003).

E-Service Security Requirements

E-services can be accessed via widely accepted standards, such as HTTP and XML, that were not originally conceived with security in mind. Since these are based on message exchanged between provider and consumer over the Internet, there are always security risks, as messages could be stolen, lost, or modified. E-services therefore have security implications in (at least) the following areas:

1. First, by implementing computer to computer services, there is great potential for malicious entities to find and exploit loopholes before they are closed. So, when processes are automated, business processes can fail for unforeseen reasons that automation actually exacerbates.
2. Separating service provision and consumption and making them platform independent requires a new security infrastructure. With e-services, consumers and providers need to be treated *asymmetrically* (i.e., the provider needs to identify consumers and the consumer needs to identify providers). Since consumers and providers are implemented as automated exchanges between programs, risks can be introduced. For example, it needs to be verified that consumers have the authority to enter into a specific transaction.

3. Collaborations with third-party Web service providers introduce elements that are not completely under the control of the primary service provider. Vulnerabilities introduced by greater flexibility and more third-party dependencies might include:
   - Customers get services to which they are not entitled, or for which they haven't paid the correct price.
   - Employees can execute services (or access company resources) without proper authorization.
   - Third-party services providers charge excessive amounts for inadequate or unwanted services.
   - Valuable company resources assets (including information) are degraded or stolen.

Four security requirements must therefore be addressed to ensure the safety of information exchange among service providers and consumers:

1. *Confidentiality,* which guarantees the exchanged information is protected against eavesdroppers.
2. *Authentication,* which guarantees access to business applications and data are restricted to only those who can provide the appropriate proof of identity. In other words, authentication is the process of verifying that a potential partner in a business transaction is authorized of representing a person or organization
3. *Integrity,* which refers to assurance that the message was not modified accidentally or deliberately in transit.
4. *Nonrepudiation,* which guarantees the sender of the message cannot deny having sent it.

All the aforementioned requirements can be satisfied by encrypting the communicated data. However, apart from encryption, we also have to consider the protection of resources such as data and applications so that only appropriate entities are allowed to access particular resources. The fifth requirement is therefore:

5. *Authorization,* which establishes whether or not an entity can access a particular resource.

Table 1 is based on a report called *Security Challenges, Threats, and Countermeasures,* produced by the Web services Interoperability Organization (WS-I, 2005).

Copyright © 2008, IGI Global. Copying or distributing in print or electronic forms without written permission of IGI Global is prohibited.

Table 1. Security challenges, threats, and countermeasures

Challenge	Threats	Countermeasures
Identify and authenticate service providers or consumers	Altered messages, eavesdropping, forged claims, unauthorized replay of messages	-HTTPS with X.509 server authentication -HTTP client authentication (Basic or Digest) -HTTPS with X.509 mutual authentication of server and user agent -OASIS SOAP Message Security
Identify and authenticate the origin of data	Altered messages, eavesdropping, forged claims, unauthorized replay of messages	-OASIS SOAP Message Security -MIME with XML Signature/XML Encryption -XML Signature
Data integrity (including transport data integrity and SOAP message integrity)	Message alteration, replay	-SSL/TLS with encryption enabled -XML Signatures (as profiled in OASIS SOAP message security)
Data confidentiality (including transport data confidentiality and SOAP message confidentiality)	Confidentiality	-SSL/TSL with encryption enabled -XML Signatures (as profiled in OASIS SOAP message security)
Message Uniqueness	replay of message parts, replay, denial of service	-SSL/TLS between the node that generated the request and the node that is guaranteeing

Techniques in the XML encryption and XML digital signature to secure SOAP messages and attachments suggested in the above table will be discussed in the remaining sections of this chapter.

Web Services Security Initiatives and Organizations

The following organizations work on Web services security specifications, guidelines, and techniques:

- The World Wide Web Consortium (W3C)
- Organization for Advancement of Structured Information Standards (OASIS)
- Web Services Interoperability Organization (WS-I)

These organizations and bodies are developing specifications related to Web services security. WS-I creates profiles that recommend what to implement from various specifications and provides direction on how to implement the specifications. The following sections briefly discuss the specifications and profiles being developed by each organization.

W3C Specifications

W3C develops the following protocols guidelines and specifications related to Web services security:

- **XML Encryption (XML-Enc):** This specification provides requirements for XML syntax and processing for encrypting digital content, including portions of XML documents and protocol messages (W3C, 2001).

- **XML Digital Signature (XML-Sig):** This specification proposes an XML compliant syntax used for representing the signature of Web resources and portions of protocol messages and procedures for computing and verifying such signatures (W3C, 2002a).

- **XML Key Management Specification (XKMS):** The specification specifies protocols for distributing and registering public keys, suitable for use in conjunction with the W3C recommendations for XML Signature and XML Encryption (W3C, 2001).

OASIS Specifications

OASIS drives the development, convergence, and adoption of e-business standards. OASIS is working on the following specifications related to Web services security (OASIS, 2004a).

- **Web Services Security (WSS)—SOAP Message Security:** This specification describes enhancements to SOAP messaging for message integrity, message confidentiality, and message authentication. The objective of this specification is to accommodate a wide variety of security models and encryption technologies. This specification also defines an extensible, general-purpose mechanism for associating security tokens with message content as well as how to encode binary security tokens, a framework for XML-based tokens, and how to include opaque encrypted keys.

- **Security Assertion Markup Language (SAML):** The SAML specification defines an XML-based mechanism for secure business-to-business (B2B) and business-to-consumer (B2C) e-commerce transactions. SAML defines an XML framework for exchanging authentication and authorization information. SAML uses XML-encoded security assertions and XML-encoded request/response protocol and specifies rules for using assertions with standard transport and messaging frameworks. SAML provides interoperability between disparate security systems. SAML can be applied to single sign-on, distributed transactions, and authorization services.

- **eXtensible Access Control Markup Language (XACML):** The XACML specification defines a common language for expressing security policy. XACML defines an extensible structure for expressing authorization policies in XML. A common policy language, when implemented across an enterprise, allows the enterprise to manage the enforcement of all the elements of its security policy in all the components of its information systems.

WS-I Specifications

The Web Services Interoperability Organization (http://www.ws-i.org/) promotes Web services interoperability across platforms, operating systems, and programming languages. WS-I creates, promotes and supports generic protocols for the interoperable exchange of messages between Web services. WS-I creates profiles, for the various Web services specifications created by W3C, OASIS, and others. WS-I is working on the following profiles related to Web services security (WS-I, 2007).

- **Basic Security Profile (BSP):** The Basic Security Profile provides guidance on the use of WS-Security and the User Name and X.509 security token formats.
- **REL Token Profile:** The REL Token Profile is the interoperability profile for the Rights Expression Language (REL) security token that is used with WS-Security.
- **SAML Token Profile:** This is the interoperability profile for the security assertion markup language (SAML) security token that is used with WS-Security.

Technologies for E-Services Security and Privacy

Based on this list of standards and recommendations, in the following sections we will focus on three areas that relate to XML document encryption, secure messaging, and access control, namely:

- Public key infrastructure and key management technologies for XML.
- Transport security (SOAP message security).
- Security assertions and the SAML language.

Public Key Infrastructure and Key Management

Several existing security standards, such as SSL, can be employed in e-services security, together with new emerging standards such as XML digital signatures. With these technologies, safe information exchange among service provider and consumers can be ensured.

To address the issue of authenticating the public key representing a given entity for purposes of encryption and digital signature. Since in general we cannot be sure that the public key is authentic (i.e., that it really represents the entity whose name is on it), the public key infrastructure (PKI) process provides a basis to ensure the authenticity of public keys. The process that ensures key authenticity is *key management*, which consists of *key registration* and *key retrieval*. The XML Key Management Specification (XKMS), published by W3C, aims to simplify the key management process (W3C, 2001). There are two major components of XKMS: the *XML Key Information Service Specification* (XKISS) and XML *Key Registration Service Specification* (XKRSS). One of the main goals of XKMS is to complement other emerging W3C standards, such as XML Digital Signature and XML Encryption (see previous section). One of the important aspects of XKMS is that key management functions are provided in terms of Web services. In this way, complex certificate processing logic does not need to be embedded into applications. Furthermore, key management can be administered at a single point within an entire enterprise. This is advantageous for simplifying management of an enterprise's security.

Authorizations to protect resources by giving appropriate permissions to the accessing entities and PKI and XKMS (XML Key Management Services are also discussed in subsequent sections of this chapter).

Transport Security

This concerns security technologies that specifically address information exchange between consumer and provider using SOAP messaging (see Chapter III). At the *message* transport level, we have a collection of security technologies such as HTTP Basic Authentication and Secure Socket Layer (SSL). SOAP security provides transportagnostic security measures. More specifically, we can use digital signatures, encryption, and security assertions for SOAP messages. The most popular security method on the Internet is a combination of HTTP Basic Authentication and SSL. This method is widely used in many e-commerce Web sites because the configuration is fairly simple, but it still provides a security-level adequate for small transactions.

HTTP Basic Authentication is often called *password authentication.* A requester includes the following header in the HTTP request:

Authorization: Basic credential

The credential is simply username/password encoded using the encoding system Base64, thus making the password easily decodable. Therefore, basic authentication alone is not secure at all and should be combined with SSL. Secure socket layer is a protocol for transmitting data in a secure way using encryption methods. SSL can fulfill three of the five security requirements mentioned earlier, namely *confidentiality, authentication,* and *integrity.* HTTPS is a secure version of the HTTP protocol over SSL. In order to establish a secure communication channel, the server and client have to authenticate each other. With SSL, the client can authenticate the server (server authentication) and vice versa (client authentication). Currently, client authentication is not common because it requires clients to have certificates issued by a certificate authority. Instead, client authentication is often performed using basic authentication. However, in future e-services, not only human clients but also business applications will make requests, so mutual authentication by SSL will become more common.

SOAP Security

The two main components of SOAP security (OASIS, 2004) are the SOAP Digital Signature and SOAP Encryption. For XML message exchanges between two parties, a digital signature provides a means to prove that the sending party created the message. Listing 1 shows a digitally signed document. The SOAP Signature specification defines how to embed the Signature element in SOAP messages as a header entry. All or part of a SOAP message can be signed. Furthermore, if a message has attachments, they can also be signed. However, there are at least two problems in the SOAP messaging approach (Nakamur, Hada, & Neyama, 2002). By definition, SOAP messaging can include intermediaries, and any of them could be owned by organizations other than the service requester or the service provider. The first problem is that any of these third parties may need to read the message. Inherently, transportlevel security solutions like SSL assume that communication occurs only directly between two parties. The second problem is that SSL encrypts the whole message, while often, a user may want to encrypt only parts of the message. SOAP encryption can resolve such problems.

Listing 1 shows a SOAP digital signature example adapted from a W3C specification.

Authorization

Authorization means granting permission to access resources based upon access rights. The purpose is to control access to resources such as Web services, databases, and so on. The most basic implementation of this approach is the *access control list* (ACL), which defines a mapping from entities to resources that can be accessed by each entity. A more advanced model is *rolebased access control* (RBAC), which maps entities to roles and then roles to resources. This model simply adds one extra layer of abstraction to the ACL model. The most familiar authorization is URL authorization that is performed by Web servers (Nakamur et al., 2002).

Security Assertions

Security technologies reviewed so far are concerned with performing authorization on a single party. However, in an open e-services market, many unknown consumers may need to access services. In this case, it is not possible to set up user names and passwords in the e-services server configuration for every possible entity. In order to address authorization in such cases, the idea of a security assertion has been proposed. The *security assertion markup language* (SAML) (OASIS, 2006) defines an XML document layout specifying the following security assertions: *authentication assertion, attribute assertion,* and *decision assertion.* These assertions are produced by their respective authorities. In some cases, the authorities can be located within the same company that hosts the e-service, but they could be located anywhere else on the Internet. To facilitate interoperability of assertions, SAML is defined in an XML format.

Listing 1. SOAP digital signature example

```
<SOAPENV:Envelope
xmlns:SOAPENV="http://schemas.xmlsoap.org/soap/envelope/">
<SOAPENV:Header>
<SOAPSEC:Signature SOAPENV:actor="" SOAPENV:mustUnderstand="1"
xmlns:SOAPENV="http://schemas.xmlsoap.org/soap/envelope/"
xmlns:SOAPSEC="http://schemas.xmlsoap.org/soap/security/200012">
<dsig:Signature xmlns:dsig="http://www.w3.org/2000/09/xmldsig#">
<dsig:SignedInfo>
<dsig:CanonicalizationMethod
Algorithm="http://www.w3.org/TR/2001/RECxmlc14n20010315"/>
<dsig:SignatureMethod
Algorithm="http://www.w3.org/2000/09/xmldsig#rsasha1"/>
```

continued on following page

Listing 1. continued

```
<dsig:Reference URI="#43871">
<dsig:Transforms>
<dsig:Transform
Algorithm="http://www.w3.org/TR/2000/CRxmlc14n20001026"/>
</dsig:Transforms>
<dsig:DigestMethod
Algorithm="http://www.w3.org/2000/09/xmldsig#sha1"/>
<dsig:DigestValue>... Base64encoded Digest Value...
</dsig:DigestValue>
</dsig:Reference>
</dsig:SignedInfo>
<dsig:SignatureValue>
... Base64encoded Signature Value...
</dsig:SignatureValue>
<KeyInfo xmlns="http://www.w3.org/2000/09/xmldsig#">
... Key Info is specified here
</KeyInfo>
</dsig:Signature>
</SOAPSEC:Signature>
</SOAPENV:Header>
<SOAPENV:Body>
<ServiceX xmlns="http://AServiceProvider.com/ServiceX"
id="12121" submitted="20030506">
...
</ServiceX>
</SOAPENV:Body>
</SOAPENV:Envelope>
```

A security assertion document is therefore similar to a ticket, in the sense that the identity of the carrier is not authenticated by the receiver. This implies the possibility of a single signon for distributed, multi party e-services. Furthermore, the ticket idea also ensures the anonymity of the service consumer, because the consumer does not have to reveal its identity to the target service. Standardized security assertions can benefit the e-services market because it will no longer be necessary for every provider to manage authentication information for every consumer they provide services to. By having trusted third parties to play the role of assertion authorities, an openended, more flexible, and more scaleable eservices infrastructure will become possible (Nakamur et al., 2002). Standardized security assertions via conventions like SAML can make such infrastructure feasible.

Web Service Transactions

Web service coordination was discussed in Chapter IV, in the context of business-process coordination. In this section, we will see how coordination of services can be handled by a service management infrastructure. In general, business activity coordination refers to coordinating activities of different partners. Activities can be classified as *atomic* or *long running*. During the execution of activities of a business process exceptions may occur and these must be handled by the coordination infrastructure. Compensating actions may also be invoked in the event of an error. A compensating action is used to *undo* a previous action in order to bring the whole process back to a consistent state. Generally, business activities have the following characteristics:

- They may consume many resources over a long duration.

- There may be a significant number of atomic transactions involved.

- Responding to a request may take a long time as human approval, or some other activity, may have to take place before a response can be sent.

- In the case where an exception requires an activity to be undone, abort is typically not sufficient. Exception handling mechanisms may require business logic, for example, in the form of a *compensation task*, to reverse the effects of a previously completed task (Cabrera et al., 2005c).

- Participants in a business activity may have different trust relationships with the others.

The above characteristics imply some requirements and constraints for the infrastructure for activity coordination:

- All state transitions within the business process must be reliably recorded,

- A consistent view of state must be maintained between the coordinator and participant.

- Notifications regarding state changes are transmitted as individual messages to achieve end-to-end agreement coordination for long-running activities.

Atomic transactions are all-or-nothing type of activities in the sense that all operations defined within the scope of an atomic transaction must succeed for the whole transaction to succeed (Bhiri, Godart, & Perrin, 2004). Prior to committing a transaction, the actions taken by the participants are only tentative (i.e., not persistent/final). When an application finishes, it requests the coordinator to determine the outcome for the transaction. The transaction coordinator determines if there were any processing failures by asking the participants to vote. If the participants all vote that they were able to execute successfully, the coordinator commits all actions taken. If a participant votes that it needs to abort, or a participant does not respond at all, the coordinator aborts all actions taken. Commit then makes the tentative actions final, while abort rolls back the tentative actions as if they had never happened. An atomic transaction manager environment is therefore very useful for distributed applications as it provide consistent failure and recovery actions

Specifications and standards for coordination both at the atomic transaction level and for longer business process transactions have been proposed by IBM, BEA Systems, Microsoft, Arjuna, Hitachi, and IONA. These coordination specifications are explained in the next section.

WS-Coordination

The WS-Coordination specification (Cabrera et al., 2005c) describes an extensible framework for providing protocols that coordinate the actions of distributed applications, including those that need to reach consistent agreement on the outcome of distributed activities. The WS-Coordination specification defines an extensible framework for defining coordination types. This specification describes a framework for a coordination service (or coordinator) which consists of the following component services:

- An *activation* service with an operation that enables an application to create a coordination instance or context.
- A *registration* service with an operation that enables an application to register for coordination protocols.
- A coordination type-specific set of coordination protocols.

The framework defined in this specification enables an application service to create a context needed to propagate an activity to other services and to register for coordination protocols. The framework enables business process management, workflow managements and other systems as discussed in Chapter IV, to hide their proprietary protocols and to operate in a heterogeneous environment. This specification also describes a definition of the structure of context and the requirements for propagating context between cooperating services. WS-Coordination therefore describes an extensible framework for providing protocols that coordinate the actions of distributed applications. Such coordination protocols are used to support a number of applications, including those that need to reach consistent agreement on the outcome of distributed activities. Additionally, this specification describes a definition of the structure of context and the requirements for propagating context between cooperating services.

WS-BusinessActivity

The WS-BusinessActivity specification (Cabrera et al., 2005b) provides the definition of the business activity coordination type that is to be used with the coordination framework described in the WS-Coordination specification above. The specification defines two specific agreement coordination protocols for the business activity coordination type:

- *BusinessAgreementWithParticipantCompletion*
- *BusinessAgreementWithCoordinatorCompletion*

WS-BusinessActivity uses WS-Coordination and extends it to support business activities. It does this by adding constraints to the protocols defined in WS-Coordination and by defining its own coordination protocols that provide the following:

- A business application may be partitioned into *business activity scopes*. A business activity scope is a business task consisting of a general-purpose computation carried out by a collection of Web services that require a mutually agreed outcome.
- Nested scopes, which allow a business application to select which child tasks are included in the overall outcome processing. For example, a flight application might solicit an estimate from a number of travel agents and choose a quote or bid based on lowest cost.
- Allow a business application to catch an exception thrown by a child task, apply an exception handler, and continue processing, even if something goes wrong. When a child completes its work, it may be associated with a compensation that is registered with the parent activity.
- A participant task may decide to exit a business activity and allows business programs to delegate processing to other participants. In contrast to atomic transactions, the participant list is dynamic and a participant may exit the protocol at any time without waiting for the outcome of the protocol.
- It allows a participant task within a business activity to specify its outcome directly without waiting for a request from the coordinator. This is useful when a task fails so that the notification can be used by a business activity exception handler to modify the goals and drive processing in a timely manner.

- It allows participants in a coordinated business activity to perform tentative operations as a normal part of the activity. The result of such tentative operations may become permanent before the activity is complete and may require compensation actions. Such a feature is critical when the joint work of a business activity requires many operations performed by independent services over a long period of time.

WS-AtomicTransaction

The WS-AtomicTransaction specification (Cabrera et al., 2005a) supports the coordination of atomic transactions and is to be used within the extensible coordination framework described in the WS-Coordination specification above. The specification defines three specific agreement coordination protocols for the atomic transaction coordination type: *completion, volatile two-phase commit,* and *durable two-phase commit.* These can be used for building applications that require consistent agreement on the outcome of atomic transactions (i.e., of short-lived distributed activities that have the all-or-nothing property). This specification defines the following protocols for atomic transactions.

- **Completion:** The completion protocol initiates commitment processing. The completion protocol is used by an application to tell the coordinator to either try to commit or abort an atomic transaction. After the transaction has completed, a status is returned to the application. Based on each protocol's registered participants, the coordinator begins with Volatile 2PC, and then proceeds through Durable 2PC. The final result is signaled to the initiator.
- **Two-Phase Commit (2PC):** The 2PC protocol coordinates registered participants to reach a commit or abort decision, and ensures that all participants are informed of the final result. The 2PC protocol has two variants:
- **Volatile 2PC:** Participants managing volatile resources such as a cache should register for this protocol.
- **Durable 2PC:** Participants managing durable resources such as a database should register for this protocol.

Under the 2PC Protocol *t*he coordinator accepts the following messages:

- **Commit:** Upon receipt of this notification, the coordinator knows that the participant has completed application processing and that it should attempt to commit the transaction.

- **Rollback:** Upon receipt of this notification, the coordinator knows that the participant has terminated application processing and that it should abort the transaction.

Under the 2PC completion protocol, the initiator accepts the following messages:

- **Committed:** Upon receipt of this notification, the initiator knows that the coordinator reached a decision to commit.
- **Aborted:** Upon receipt of this notification, the initiator knows that the coordinator reached a decision to abort.

Under the 2PC completion protocol, the participant accepts the following messages:

- **Prepare:** Upon receipt of this notification, the participant knows to enter Phase 1 and vote on the outcome of the transaction. If the participant does not know of the transaction, it must vote to abort. If the participant has already voted, it should resend the same vote.
- **Rollback:** Upon receipt of this notification, the participant knows to abort, and forget, the transaction. This notification can be sent in either Phase 1 or Phase 2. Once sent, the coordinator may forget all knowledge of this transaction.
- **Commit:** Upon receipt of this notification, the participant knows to commit the transaction. This notification can only be sent after Phase 1 and if the participant voted to commit. If the participant does not know of the transaction, it must send a *committed* notification to the coordinator.

In Phase 2 of the 2PC, the coordinator accepts the following messages:

- **Prepared:** Upon receipt of this notification, the coordinator knows the participant is prepared and votes to commit the transaction.
- **ReadOnly:** Upon receipt of this notification, the coordinator knows the participant votes to commit the transaction and has forgotten the transaction. The participant does not wish to participate in Phase 2. Upon receipt of this notification, the coordinator knows the participant has aborted, and forgotten, the transaction.
- **Committed:** Upon receipt of this notification, the coordinator knows the participant has committed the transaction.

- **Replay:** Upon receipt of this notification, the coordinator may assume the participant has suffered a recoverable failure. It should resend the last appropriate protocol notification.

Architectures for Managed Service Delivery

Chapter VII described a model-driven approach for realizing business services. One of the main advantages of this approach is that you don't loose continuity between the business service and its implementation, the Web service. Should the business service need to change, the model transformation steps can ensure that the Web service can be automatically reimplemented too. However, there is another issue that emerges when trying to apply this approach to a real business context: A real organization offers dozens and even possibly hundreds of services. Even if the approach described in Chapter VII is followed for each high-level business service, the outcome would be thousands of lower level services (i.e., Web services) organized into several networks. Even with model-driven generation support, the resulting outcome would be a nightmare: many thousands of Web service implementing programs that need to be maintained individually. Furthermore, it is likely that many of such programs and services share a large degree of commonality, since a single lower level service can often support more than one higher level ones. However, if service realization is done in a nonsystematic way, it is not possible to detect such commonalities and thus utilize the opportunity to reuse service realizations. The uncontrolled explosion in the number of services can therefore do nothing else but result in maintenance chaos and in lost opportunities for reuse (i.e., cost-savings and productivity improvements). It is clear that a framework for *governance* is needed to control service development across the whole enterprise.

Service-oriented architecture (SOA) is an architectural style that promotes business process orchestration of enterprise-level business services (Lublinsky & Tyomkin, 2003). According to the SOA philosophy, systems are assembled from loosely coupled collection of services. SOA promises business agility, flexibility, reduced development time, and cost reduction. SOA essentially advocates that:

- Services should be reusable
- Services should be loosely coupled by removing unnecessary dependencies to implementation technologies
- Services should be easily integrated with other software both the service provider's own as well as that of the consumer's

SOA has three main elements:

- **Services:** In SOA, services are business driven, coarse grained, process centric, stateless, loosely coupled, and distributed. These services are available within and across the enterprise. Services are defined by an interface, which consists of a set of parameters and communication protocols. Open communication protocols such as SOAP (Chapter III) are used for data transfer.
- **Business process:** Business process executes a set of enterprise services in a specific order to achieve the required business functionality.
- **Organization:** Organization is responsible for creating, using, and maintaining the SOA architecture.

We can apply these SOA concepts to model service architectures that separate concerns, provide flexibility by loose coupling, and enable different services to be aggregated or composed into higher level services. An SOA architecture provides a useful layer of abstraction and composition that aggregates low-level implementation services into more meaningful business services. A layered SOA architecture plays a key role in ensuring that composite services and required resources are loosely coupled. Additionally, the architecture provides the infrastructure to support all layers. In summary, an SOA architecture:

- Hides the detail in each layer from the others: Each layer can be implemented using different technology and each layer can have different ownership.
- Virtualizes the provided services.
- Supports federation of services.
- Offers agility via loose coupling across layers.
- Supports change and control of change within layer.
- Provides separation of concerns via layering abstractions.
- Provides separation of specialized solutions from generic resources.

Relationship of SOA to Other Software Technologies

Service-oriented architecture (SOA) is a relatively new proposal. Despite its conceptual and practical significance, though, the SOA concept is not totally original; it can be traced to previous software architectures, theories, and practices for distributed system design, programming methods, and similar areas. SOA is also

Figure 3. SOA elements

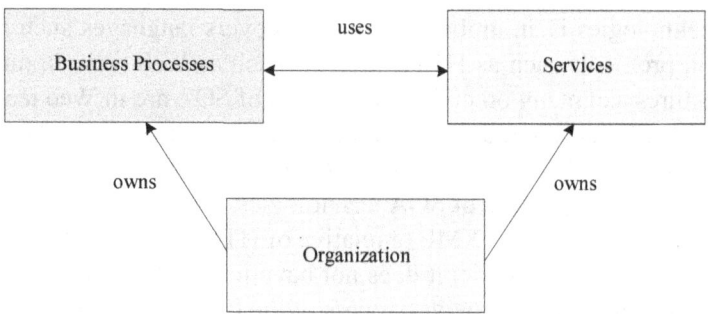

being positioned as a *meta-architecture* (i.e., an architectural framework that can be used as guidance for the development of other software architectures). In this respect, things like *SOA systems, tools,* or *applications* are implemented using other technologies with SOA used as guidance for their architecture and behavior. Web services, of course, are the technology that comes closest to realize the philosophy of SOA. However, Web services and SOA are not going to replace other software systems and technologies overnight. Thus, in this section we attempt to give some suggestions as to how SOA can coexist with such other approaches and technologies in harmony, and possibly even enhance and improve them. We have identified the following technologies and categories of systems as particular important and therefore in need to be positioned with respect to SOA: *object orientation, enterprise systems, distributed systems, Web technologies,* and *mobile technologies.*

SOA and Object Orientation

Object-oriented software has now become a mainstream software technology due to the popularity of languages such as Java and methodologies such as UML. We will not discuss object-oriented principles in detail, as there are many excellent books on object-oriented systems. Amongst the key characteristics of object orientation is the concept of *objects as autonomous units,* the concept of *interface to an object,* and the concept of *encapsulating object methods and data within the object itself.* Although Web services are not objects and, as a mater of fact, are implementation technology *agnostic,* there are benefits in using objects to realize Web services, as they both share the aforementioned principles. This is shown in Table 2.

SOA and Web Technologies

Web technologies is an umbrella term that covers languages such as HTML, Javascript, protocols such as HTTP, systems such as Web servers, multitiered Web architectures and many others. As the origins of SOA are in Web technologies, we need to clearly understand their commonalities and differences. Web technologies such as HTTP and HTML predate SOA and Web services. Even more, it can be said that the underpinning of SOA technologies, such as Web services, are indeed Web technologies such as XML (a relative of HTML) and HTTP. Of course, since SOA is technology agnostic, it does not have to rely on Web technologies for its realization. However, the pervasiveness of the Internet and the Web means that to grow in popularity amongst organizations, SOA principles need to be implemented using Web technologies

SOA and Other Distributed Software Technologies

Distributed software technologies allow software entities (e.g., objects or applications) to communicate, invoke each other, and exchange data over a network. Examples of such technologies include remotely invoking Java objects (RMI) and an architecture/specification for distributed object-oriented systems called *CORBA* (OMG, 2007). The main problem with these technologies is that the communicating software entities must be *compatible* with each other (e.g., Java objects can only communicate with other Java objects). SOA, on the other hand, does not make any assumptions as to how the services are implemented. Because such technologies predate SOA, they are more mature in several areas, such as, for example, the management of the distributed objects life cycle. Thus, their technologies have the potential to shape and influence areas of SOA that are still evolving.

Table 2.

SOA strengths	Object orientation strengths	SOA+object strengths
Service independence, service interface	Object identity, object interface, encapsulation	Service implementation that preserves key service semantics

Table 3.

SOA Strengths	Web Technology Strengths	SOA+Web Strengths
All main SOA strengths	Ubiquitous, 'light weight'	Web as the vehicle for SOA

SOA and Enterprise Systems

Systems such as *enterprise resource planning* (ERP), *customer relationship management* (CRM), and *supply chain management* (SCM) automate a large percentage of enterprise activities and processes. They are critical for the enterprise and thus need to be positioned with respect to SOA. **SOA**, on the other hand, is a complete rethinking of how systems are analyzed, designed, built, integrated, and managed, and this, of course, includes packaged enterprise applications like ERP. SOA has the potential to further open up such systems and make their functionality available to both the organization and its partners. However, the cost of reengineering existing enterprise systems to make them SOA compliant may be prohibitive. Thus, a more realistic approach might be to replace older systems when retired with standardized SOA compliant service components.

SOA and Mobile Technologies

Mobile computing and *mobile communications* are two areas that are rapidly converging with traditional mobile devices (telephones) becoming more computer-like and mobile computer devices such as PDAs acquiring mobile phone capabilities. Organizations must expect that more and more of their customers will want to access their services using mobile devices. While nothing specific in the SOA philosophy distinguishes mobile service consumers from non-mobile ones, the peculiarities of mobile service consumption (e.g., the mobility of the service consumer, the limited capacity of mobile phones, etc.) must be taken into account. Thus, the dimension of mobility must be taken into consideration in the continuing evolution of the SOA approach.

Table 4.

SOA Strengths	Distributed Technology Strengths	SOA+DT Synergies
Technology independence protocols	Robust protocols, Embedded Security, life-cycle management	DT influence maturation of SOA areas such as security, transaction management and life-cycle management

Table 5.

SOA strengths	Enterprise Systems strengths	SOA+enterprise systems synergies
Openness	Wide coverage of business functionality	Expose more business functionality/services to where needed

Table 6.

SOA Strengths	Mobile Strengths	SOA+Mobile Synergies
-	Consume services from anywhere (mobility)	Mobile enabled SOA

Service Bus

Application frameworks provide a platform for design, development, assembly, deployment, execution, and monitoring of applications built on multitiered distributed application model. Leading application frameworks (Microsoft .NET and J2EE-based ones) currently provide extensive support for Web services execution and management. Competition between J2EE and .NET is bound to continue for several more years. Ultimately, though, as both approaches will be compliant with core services standards, competition and co-petition between such frameworks is likely to lead to faster adoption of Web services standards, and to the creation of efficient robust and scalable Web service development and execution environments.

A *service bus* is a Web services execution platform (i.e., an integrated software environment that enables the development, execution, and management of Web services; Lublinsky & Tyomkin, 2003). A Web service execution platform must exhibit the following characteristics:

- Must be able to provide a run-time environment for Web services. Typically, this will be via a built-in application server, portal server, and so on.

- Has functionality required to produce or develop Web services and service-oriented architecture solutions via the capabilities of an integrated service definition and composition environment. In a Web services platform, the integration with the rest of the infrastructure is more important than advanced functionality alone.

- Is capable of managing Web services/SOA and applications that use Web services in terms of providing basic security and governance, but it does not have to have full Web services management or framework capabilities. Use of Web services to manage entities (e.g., management using Web services) does not suffice. Most of these offerings have some management capability but do not offer all the capabilities of management-focused products.

SOA services are able to request services and respond to requests to/from each other. Thus, communication takes place over the service bus.

A service bus consists of the following systems:

- **Business process engine:** Allows business processes to be available externally.
- **Service locator:** Allows the service to be externally visible.
- **Business service:** Encapsulates the actual business functionality with an interface.
- **Utility service:** Supports company's main business functionality (see Chapter II). This service is available to clients.
- **Infrastructure service:**   Provides infrastructure support for the business services (see Chapter II).

The SOA implementation of a service bus introduces two data-related models:

- Data model for the service implementation.
- Dictionary for service messaging, defining communication semantics of SOA. It is derived from the data model to make it easier and simpler.

The technology architecture for SOA is described next:

The architecture consists of three main parts: Development tools, infrastructure, and run-time support.

Figure 4. A service bus

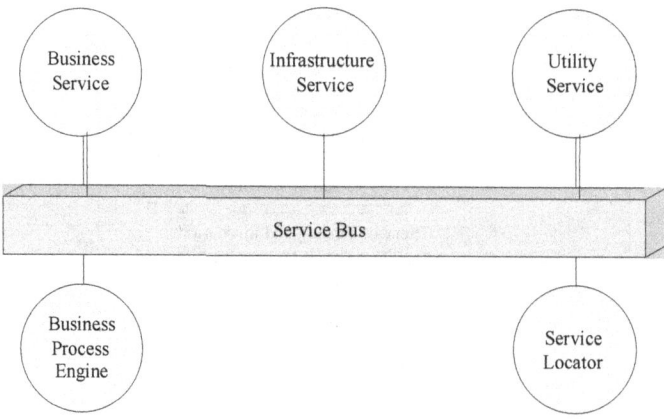

- *Development* tools include tools, processes, methodologies, and patterns required to design Web services.

- *Infrastructure* provides basic infrastructure support for the services run time, which consists of service development, infrastructure and configuration, service run time and support, and service binding and invocation.

- *Service run time and support* refers to service quality support and service versioning support.

In the typical IT environment of a large company, services are deployed across heterogeneous environments; enabling these services to communicate and synchronize with each other is a critical task. As services are built on top of other services by aggregation/composition and orchestration (see Chapter IV), each service would need to respond to request messages from other services. This would mean that these messages have to be transported to these services asynchronously with a high-level of fault tolerance. Moreover, any new service should be able to subscribe or be able to publish their interface using the platform without creating a new transport mechanism. Service interoperation therefore must be based on XML and SOAP messaging standards (see Chapter III). Systems built under the SOA guidelines must be able to support SOAP messages. Nonstandard systems will need to be adopted to provide SOAP messaging. Additionally to SOAP, the family of W3C WS-* specifications (WS-Security, WS-Routing, WS-Addressing, WS-Referral, WS-Timestamp) can be used. SOAP messages will implement the WS-* standards as part of their payload. The *message header* of a SOAP message contains any contextual, processing and or security information while the *body* of the message will contain the actual payload.

Figure 5. Service deployment architecture

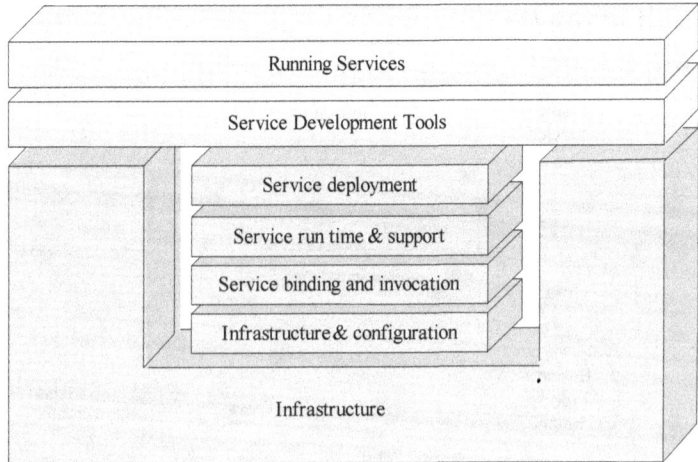

Platforms usually implement request/response service listeners that can be realized via a combination of message queuing, file transfer, remote database access, or Web services technologies. A background process running on the service platform constantly monitors the listeners to obtain the message. After the message is read, it is routed to the appropriate location (the requester or endpoint) using one of the following routing techniques (Poozhikunnel, 2007).

Itinerary-based routing. In itinerary-based routing mechanism, the message will contain a list of addresses it would need to visit. This list is in the metadata and is carried with the message. A service bus has several end points, and this message would visit each one of those and will be forwarded on by their invocation mechanism. This would mean there is no central routing mechanism and that each end-point reference will determine the next step. The benefit is the routing is distributed and hence a dependence on centralized routing is eliminated and single point failure is prevented. There are added benefits of having several different end points, at times with specialized end point, each with different levels of orchestration. These messages can also be modified at different end points. This increases the flexibility of the service bus functionality.

Content-based routing. Content-based routing mechanism is when a message is routed based on it content. The content is evaluated by an XML Xpath (see Chapter III) expression. The message will then be forwarded to the appropriate end point. In this approach, the routing mechanism is a central router that evaluates each message and takes the necessary action to forward the messages to the endpoints that have subscribed to this message. The benefit of a content-based routing is that there is a centralized mechanism for all the routing. The disadvantage is this can be a single point of failure. However, the benefits of single point of maintenance and also that the messages can be totally ignorant of the end point are the added advantages. Moreover, when messages flow across, they can be sent to all the subscribers and if there is a failure at any end point references it can be quickly and easily identified.

Service bus platforms can realize both types of routing mechanisms with the choice of routing based on careful evaluation of the existing systems in the organization and the resources available.

A Service Architecture Example: Designing E-Services for an Airline

Cheap Flights Airline is a fictitious airline company that has decided to offer its customers the benefit of planning and booking flights through a Web-based e-service. Cheap Flights Airline is trying to achieve three key goals through the development and deployment of their Web services:

- Allow customers to submit travel itineraries to its Web site,
- Automatically procure appropriate airline reservations for customer itineraries, and
- Automatically return confirmation on all reservations back to the customer once processing of the itinerary is complete.

As part of this application, Cheap Flights recognizes that the ability to allow business partners and customers programmatic access their services through a Web services interface—thereby allowing the customer or partner to loosely integrate the airline's services into their business travel processes—will give them a significant strategic advantage and help them to streamline their business. When the customer's itinerary cannot be wholly met by Cheap Flight's available flights and routes, flights of partner airlines will be used. Thus, Cheap Flights needs to access the reservation systems of other airlines on behalf of its customers and make bookings.

Cheap Flights realizes, therefore, that, in order for this solution to work, it must have a way to integrate its itinerary processing coordinate with those of other airlines with which it does business. This fact highlights several distinct challenges.

- Cheap Flights must have a way to connect the customer-facing Web service it wants to externalize with the business process it wishes to automate and integrate with its business partners.
- Each partner must externalize a means of allowing Cheap Flights to directly integrate its business processes into the partner's reservation system.
- Cheap Flights must be able to ensure the reliability and dependability of the entire process.
- Cheap Flights must be able to coordinate the activities of each individual partner in order to properly ensure that the customer's itinerary is satisfactorily processed.

Next we will outline a method for designing simple (informational) and more complex (transactional) services for the airline.

In previous chapters we saw that a business service is really an ensemble of lower level services that help a customer locate, select, possibly customize, and eventually consume the service. These support services are ultimately dealing with information about the resource, its location, terms of the offered service, and so on. When this information does not cause a change in the state of the provider's resources (e.g., such as the booking of a seat), we call such services *simple information services.*

In contrast, when the service may result in the change of the state of some of the provider's resources, it is called *transactional.* One of the main reasons that we need to distinguish between simple informational and transactional services is that, for a start, the latter are far more complex to implement. Let us look first at a simple information service whose purpose is to provide the consumer with information related to the business service. So, in the context of Cheap Flights Airline, an information service may provide information about the airline's flight timetable. As we saw in the previous chapters, in order to identify such services we need to think in terms of what the consumer wants to know about the provided service, and how we can assist him to consume the service.

As we already argued in this book, services are essentially capabilities acquired through the consumption of resources (i.e., Chapters I, II, and VII). For physical resources, essential information includes that of time and location. Thus, for flight information services, the location of the flight (i.e., country, city, airport, terminal, departure gate) together with the flight time, constitute important information. Other important information relates to the status of the service. A service can at anytime be in one of possible states (i.e., available, scheduled for consumption, canceled, in-progress, rescheduled, completed or retired). It is important for the consumer to be aware of the state of the service at anytime. Therefore, information services need to have access to the process(es) that realize the service, because such processes have the required information about the service and its status. Prior to the departure of the flight, it is the ground operations center that has information about the status of the flight. Once airborne, it is the flight crew that can provide information about the ongoing progress of the flight. Naturally, as we said, even such processes need to obtain outside information in order to ascertain or predict the status of the service. Thus, the ground operations centre needs information from the airport flight centre about availability of take of time slots.

Information, whether it is provided through services or otherwise, has several unique properties. First, it has to be valid otherwise it is useless or in extreme cases even dangerous. Second, it has to be reliable to a degree its consumer is comfortable with. Thirdly it has to be timely for time critical services. Finally, it has to be secure to the extent determined by the criticality of the information. Information whose unavailability, corruption, or late availability can lead to threat in lives or significant financial losses must be secured in the best possible way. Less critical information must be protected in the most feasible way.

In the design of the information service we need to take al the above factors into account. Thus, we need to question the validity and reliability of the information source, its timeliness, and whether it can be tampered with maliciously or unintentionally on the way between its origin and point of provision.

Based on these requirements, Figure 6 depicts the architecture of a system to support a flight information system service for Cheap Flights Airline. The diagram assumes that the service is published and accessed by using Web services standards such as WSDL, UDDI, and SOAP, as discussed in Chapter III.

Figure 6. Architecture for realizing a flight's information service

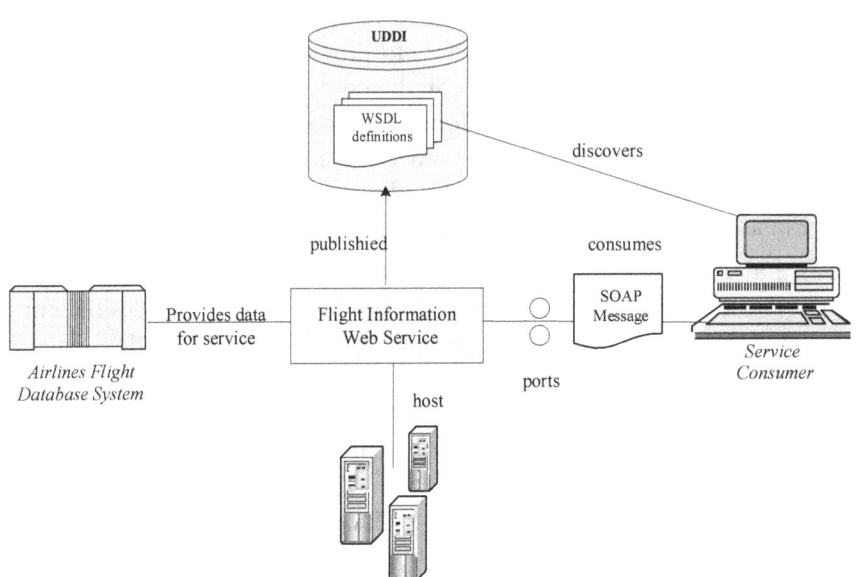

Transaction Services Infrastructure for Cheap Flights Airline

We will turn our attention now to transaction-based services. Such services usually have more complex requirements for QoS features, including security, reliability, and exception handling. To support these services, developers must define extensions to the basic Web services specifications using protocols for transactions, as defined earlier in this chapter. For example, they might need specific SOAP header entries to carry a message's transactional context and security context.

This type of services requires two-way flow of information between the service and its consumer. The information-based service is *stateless*. The service is consumed instantaneously in a *request-response* mode and then the service terminates. However, the transaction-based service needs to have a *stateful* behavior. This happens because transactions are atomic units of interaction between parties. Each unit will contain several of actions from both the supplier and the client side. All these actions need to succeed in order for the transaction to be successful. Even if one of the actions fails, the whole transaction must fail and previous actions must be rolled back. In the flight booking example, the booking of a flight involves a complicated sequence of steps, which include locating the flight's departure and destination, the flight's date, entering names and numbers of passengers, paying for the cost of the flight, and so on. If a flight booking involves multiple airlines and their reservation systems, then the activities that take place will need to be coordinated across all the involve parties. If any of such activities fail to execute during the transaction the whole transaction of flight booking must be cancelled. Compensating actions may need to take place at several participating systems. For example, if a multiple booking transaction involved in sequence the reservation systems of airlines A, B, C, and D (airline A being the coordinator of the transaction), and for some reason activities of airline D failed (a booking cannot be made for some reason), compensating actions must be performed on the systems of A, B, and C.

There are many reasons (*multiple points of failure*) why a transaction such as the above can fail to complete:

- The flight cannot accommodate the customer (consumer) requirements (e.g., because of not enough available seats).
- There is a communications failure and the connection between the service and the consumer becomes lost.
- The consumer's payment is rejected.
- The consumer decides to abandon the transaction.

By using the atomic transaction coordination protocols such as 2PC (two-phase commit) described earlier on, a multiple booking transaction can be performed in a manner that satisfies consistency, security, and integrity of the used resources. By applying the 2PC protocol, for example, each participating airline can provisionally commit a reservation. When all participating airlines report a successful booking, the transaction coordinator initiates the second phase of the transaction and instructs the participants to make the booking permanent (i.e., commit the transactional change to their databases). If for any reason any of the participants fails to commit, the whole transaction is rolled back and any state changes are undone.

The outcome of a successful transaction is the creation of a booking in the company's flight reservation system. The service needs to inform the outcome of the transaction to the consumer by returning a code (e.g., *confirmed, not confirmed, aborted*) and either a unique identifier for the booking (such as a booking reference number), or some indication for the reason of the failure.

A good service design should also retain some of the information created during the (failed or aborted) transaction to allow the consumer to return to it at a later stage to complete the transaction. In the case of flight booking, the service could retain the passenger requirements and information and give a reference number to the consumer to allow him to retrieve the transaction information and start a new one. The diagram of Figure 7 shows how a Web services coordination manager can manage transactional services that involve not only the airline's booking system but also those of other airlines.

Figure 7. Architecture for realizing transactional services

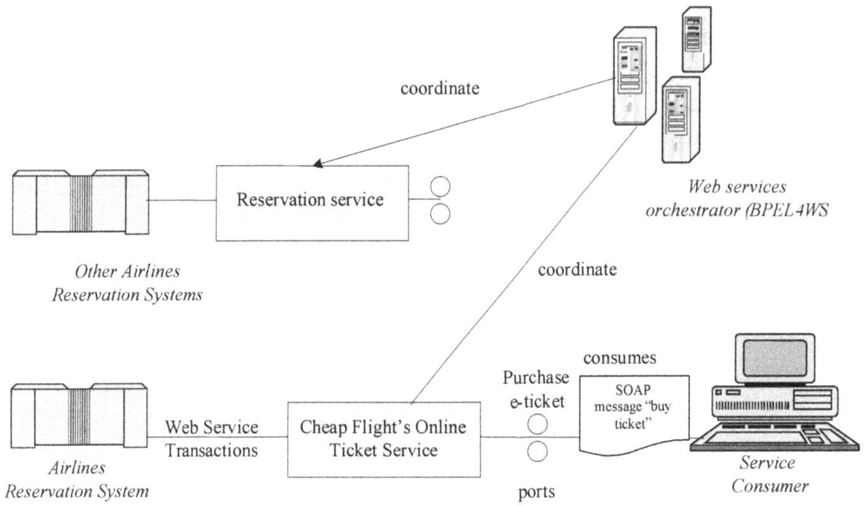

Chapter Summary

This chapter has introduced several software technologies architectures and standards for delivering, managing, and securing services. It has reviewed the still-maturing umbrella of Web service technologies for service management and security. However, Web services are still very much oriented towards the programming viewpoint of service, where service is a program (function) that can be executed by users remotely. While an e-service can be delivered through a Web server and accessed by a Web browser, increasingly users will want to consume e-services not directly (i.e., by accessing information on a Web page), but indirectly through the use of *assistants* (agents) (i.e., software applications that can search and consume services on behalf of their owners).

Sometimes, the service server itself will initiate the delivery of the service in a proactive way. An important issue therefore is how to design the mode of interaction between the consumer and the service provider. In Chapter II, we assumed that this is initiated by the consumer who searches for services, evaluates them, and eventually selects the one they desire. Effectively, we implied that service delivery is initiated by the consumer. However, it is possible to have a proactive approach to service delivery where the provider offers the service, not *on demand,* but according to an understanding and prediction of when the consumer will require the service and how.

Proactive rather than reactive service delivery means that it is not the consumer that contacts the service interface, but vice versa (i.e., the service itself will contact the consumer through an interface that belongs to the consumer). An analogy from the conventional services market is that of car servicing. Typically, it is the customer who must initiate a service of his car. However, many modern cars have systems that detect when the car requires a service and inform their owners (e.g., by flashing lines on the dashboard). This can be seen as an example of proactive service delivery.

Today's technologies for delivering electronic services are stronger in consumer-driven (reactive) modes and not as matured yet in proactive mode. This is because they stem from concepts of distributed programming, where the service is a remote program (procedure), that needs to be invoked (as and when needed) by other programs, which are the consumers of the service.

Other issues that concern service development and delivery from the provider perspective have primarily to do with efficiency, performance, reliability, and security. From the consumer perspective, the main issues are ease of access, ease of selection and customization, performance reliability, and security, depending on the nature of the offered service.

This chapter has been concerned with the requirements of a technical infrastructure for supporting e-services at an enterprise level. While the management of e-services that are offered internally to the enterprise or to a small number of known and trusted partners can be done in an ad hoc way, the delivery of e-services to an open market of consumers needs to be managed in a systematic way. The e-service provider needs to manage security, control access rights, monitor the delivery of the offered service and enforce existing quality contracts. At the same time, the e-services infrastructure needs to be flexible, reliable, and extensible. In this chapter, we have seen standards and specifications for e-service management proposed by standards organizations, such as W3C. At the same time, the market for commercial e-service management platforms is rapidly growing. However, whether companies go for an in-house or off-the-shelf approach to building their e-services infrastructure, they need to ensure a technology-neutral service bus, based on open standards, such as XML. This will ensure that the infrastructure will cope with changing business requirements and will integrate with those of other business partners and collaborators as service delivery will become increasingly distributed and multiparty.

Thus, this chapter also dealt with the concept of governing the realization of services through an architectural framework called *SOA*. SOA views the whole organization as delivering a set of services that comply with the same standards regarding their behavior and life cycle (identification, sharing, delivery, and so one). Because SOA impacts the software architecture of the whole organization, a positioning of SOA with respect to other important information technologies was also done in this chapter. The final issue that needs to be considered is how to realize the SOA concept using service execution and management environments/platforms. In the next chapter, we will see a representative service execution environment.

References

Arora, A., Cohen, J., Davis, J., Dutch, M., Golovinsky, E., Hagiwara, Y., et al. (2005, June). *Web services for management (WS-Management)*. Retrieved March 16, 2007, from http://developers.sun.com/techtopics/Web services/management/WS-Management.June.2005.pdf

Bhiri, S., Godart, C., & Perrin, O. (2004). A transaction-oriented framework for composing transactional Web services. In *Proceedings of the 2004 IEEE International Conference on Services Computing (SCC'04)* (pp. 654-663).

Cabrera, L. F., Copeland, G., Feingold, M., Freund, R. W., Freund, T., Johnson, J., et al. (2005a). *Web services atomic transaction (WS-AtomicTransaction, Version 1.0)* Retrieved March 15, 2007, from ftp://www6.software.ibm.com/software/developer/library/WS-AtomicTransaction.pdf

Cabrera, L. F., Copeland, G., Feingold, M., Freund, R. W., Freund, T., Johnson, J., et al. (2005b, August). *Web services business activity framework (WS-BusinessActivity, Version 1.0)*.Retrieved 15 March 2007, from ftp://www6.software.ibm.com/software/developer/library/WS-BusinessActivity.pdf

Cabrera, L. F., Copeland, G., Feingold, M., Freund, R. W., Freund, T., Johnson, J., et al. (2005c, August). *Web services coordination (WS-Coordination, Version 1.0)*. Retrieved 15 March 2007, from ftp://www6.software.ibm.com/software/developer/library/WS-Coordination.pdf

CBDI Forum. (2005). *Service life cycle*. Retrieved March 15, 2007, from http://www.cbdiforum.com/public/events/workshops/Communicating_SOA.php

Kreger, H. (2001, May). *Web services conceptual architecture (WSCA 1.0)*. IBM Software Group.

Lublinsky, B., & Tyomkin, D. (2003, October). Dissecting service-oriented architectures. *Business Integration Journal*, 52-58.

Nakamur, Y., Hada, S., & Neyama, R. (2002). Towards the integration of Web services security on enterprise environments. In *Proceedings of the 2002 Symposium on Applications and the Internet (SAINT) Workshops* (pp. 166-175).

OASIS. (2004a, March). *Web services security: SOAP message security 1.1 (WS-Security 2004, OASIS Standard 200401)*. Retrieved March 16, 2007, from http://docs.oasis-open.org/wss/v1.1/

OASIS. (2004b, November 15). *WS-reliability 1.1 OASIS standard* (Document identifier: wsrm-ws_reliability-v1.1-spec-os). Retrieved March 16, 2007, from http://docs.oasis-open.org/wsrm/ws-reliability/v1.1

OASIS. (2005, February). *Web services reliable messaging protocol (WS-ReliableMessaging)*. Retrieved March 16, 2007, from http://download.boulder.ibm.com/ibmdl/pub/software/dw/specs/ws-rm/ws-reliablemessaging200502.pdf

OASIS. (2006). *Security assertion markup language (SAML)* (Version 2.0, Technical Overview Working Draft 10, 9 October 2006). (Document identifier: sstc-saml-tech-overview-2.0-draft-10). Retrieved March 17, 2007, from http://www.oasis-open.org/committees/documents.php?wg_abbrev=security

OMG. (2007). *OMG's Corba Web site.* Retrieved August 19, 2007, from http://www.corba.org/

Orchard, D. (2002). *Web services pitfalls.* Retrieved August 23, 2007, from http://www.xml.com/pub/a/ws/2002/02/06/webservices.html

Pallos, M. S. (2001, December). Service-oriented architecture: A primer. *EAI Journal*, 32-35.

Poozhikunnel, J. (2007). *Building an enterprise service bus to support service-oriented architecture.* Retrieved August 19, 2007, from http://www.15seconds.com/issue/050519.htm

Sleeper, B. (2003). *Toward the service-oriented enterprise.* Retrieved March 15, 2007, from http://www.Web servicespro.com/Web servicespro-69-20030903TowardstheServiceOriented Enterprise.pdf

Smith, D. M., Abrams, C., Sholler, D., Plummer, D. C., & Cantara, M. (2005). *Magic quadrant for Web services platforms* (Gartner research publication date 2005, ID No. G00129507). Retrieved August 23, 2007, from http://www.logidexassetcenter.com/resources/analyst_files/magic_quadrant.pdf

Vasiu, L., Mackay, D., & Warren, M. (2003). *The tri-dimensional role of information security in e-business: A managerial perspective.* Retrieved March 15, 2007, from http://www.hicbusiness.org/BIZ2003Proceedings/Lucian%20Vasiu.pd

W3C. (2001). *XML key management specification (XKMS).* Retrieved March 15, 2007, from http://www.w3.org/TR/xkms/

W3C. (2002a). *XML encryption syntax and processing: W3C recommendation 10 December 2002.* Retrieved March 16, 2007, from http://www.w3.org/TR/xmlenc-core/

W3C. (2002b). *XML-signature syntax and processing: W3C Recommendation 12 February 2002.* Retrieved March 16, 2007, from http://www.w3.org/TR/xmldsig-core/

W3C. (2002c). *Web service choreography interface (WSCI, 1.0).* Retrieved March 15, 2007, from http://www/w3/org/TR/2002/NOTE-wsci-20020808

W3C. (2004). *Web services architecture.* Retrieved March 15, 2007, from http://www.w3.org/TR/ws-arch/

W3C. (2007). *Web services conversation language (WSCL, 1.0).* Retrieved August 8, 2007, from http://www.w3.org/TR/wscl10

WS-I. (2005). *Security challenges, threats and countermeasures (Version 1.0, Final material date: 2005/05/07)*. Retrieved March 16, 2007, from http://www.ws-i.org/Profiles/BasicSecurity/SecurityChallenges-1.0.doc

WS-I. (2007). *Basic security profile (Version 1, Approval draft 2007-02-20)*. Retrieved March 16, 2007, from http://www.ws-i.org/Profiles/BasicSecurity-Profile-1.0.html

Chapter IX

A Platform for Model-Driven Service Engineering

Introduction

Having discussed concepts and requirements for managed service delivery in the last chapter, we have now completely covered the whole service engineering life cycle, namely *identification, modeling, design, realization, deployment*, and *management*. More specifically, so far, we have dealt with the following issues:

* Service concepts and fundamentals (Chapter II).

* Formalized service semantics and service metamodels (Chapter V).

* Service derivation from business models described in the IDEF0/IDEF1X languages (Chapter VII).

* Service realization by model-driven transformations of business services to executable Web services (Chapters VI and VII).

* Environments and platforms for service execution and management (Chapter VIII).

This chapter introduces a *service engineering platform* (CLMS) that caters for all the phases of the service engineering life cycle. Although complete coverage of the service life cycle is important, currently, few software environments and platforms manage it, with the majority of such environments dealing with just service execution (delivery). It is nevertheless important to have a single environment/platform that handles the whole service life cycle with seamless transition between phases (CBDI Forum, 2005). To deal with these requirements, the CLMS platform adopts a model-driven approach (see Chapter VI). More specifically, the platform seamlessly links business service specification models to realizable services and manages the delivery of the latter in an environment that monitors services execution. Moreover, this approach ensures that alternative service deployment techniques (e.g., *proactive* as well as *reactive* service delivery systems) and service execution environments can be accommodated. This is of particular importance today, with service engineering still evolving and with new service paradigms and competing technologies appearing all the time.

The chapter is organized as follows. The next section discusses the rationale and motivation behind the conception of the CLMS platform. After that, we introduce the platform's architecture in terms of major subsystems. Next, we present the service engineering method associated with the CLMS platform. This is essentially an approach derived from the methodology that was presented in Chapter VII, modified to accommodate the requirements and constraints of the available technologies for service realization. Finally, will illustrate the environment at run time (i.e., when services are deployed, executed, and managed). The CLMS platform will be used again in Chapter X to illustrate a step-by-step method for service realization in the accounts receivable/payable financial domain.

Platform Overview and Philosophy

The CLMS platform allows the modeling (specification), design, realization, deployment, and management of business services using software technologies that include, but are not restricted to, Web services. The CLMS platform adopts a model-driven philosophy for the realization of the service, with different metamodels guiding and automating activities (e.g., modeling, specification, code generation) and driving the generation of software artifacts. There are currently no systematic approaches for deriving enterprise service-oriented architectures. A top-down or bottom-up analysis of an enterprise's data or processes will probably fail to reveal all important services. We argue that a systemic view of the enterprise provides an effective mechanism for identifying and modeling services and, more importantly, for linking and tracing services to business processes and activities.

Key Features in CLMS Platform

At the core of the CLMS platform is an IDEF0 processing engine with the ability to execute IDEF0 service descriptions. Recalling from Chapter VII that at the lowest level of decomposition an IDEF0 model is a network of atomic services, where each service is provided either by a uniquely identifiable system/application or by an atomic (Web) service that has yet to be realized. This network of services, therefore, corresponds to a platform-independent model (PIM) of a realized business service. CLMS platform is capable of executing this PIM model natively or by converting it to a service orchestration description in a language such as BPEL (see Chapter IV). To be able to execute the PIM at run time, the atomic Web services need to be implemented together with interfaces to other (non-Web service) external systems. If such atomic Web services exist and are available to the CLMS run-time environment, then all that needs to be done is to automatically generate appropriate client interfaces based on the service WSDL descriptions.

Another main component of CLMS platform is the enhanced service modeling environment, based on extensions to the well-established standards of the IDEF0/IDEF1X modeling languages (see Chapter VII) and the W3C XML schema (see Chapter III). The IDEF0/IDEF1X editors automatically generate XML definitions of the IDEF models. In addition to allowing the programmatic manipulation of such models, the use of XML schema allows the capturing of service semantics in a platform-neutral manner. This, in turn, allows generation of software artifacts for alternative software platforms and technologies (UML, Java, .NET, etc.).

One of the key features of the CLMS platform, therefore, is that it is agnostic of the underlying software service technologies. Thus, current Web services standards, but also future ones, can be accommodated. Other key features of the CLMS platform include:

Openness, based on Web service standards. More specifically, the extensible mark-up language (XML), simple object access protocol (SOAP), Web service description language (WSDL) and other standards discussed in Chapter III are supported, to enable interoperability across various technical platforms. In addition to basic Web service standards, CLMS platform supports extensible stylesheet language transformation (XSLT; Chapter III) with an integrated XSLT engine. By employing such technologies, business service functionality can be transformed to and exposed as a Web service.

Security within heterogeneous environments. It protects applications and Web services from unauthorized use by incorporating technologies for authorization, privacy, and integrity (see Chapter VIII). The platform supports current Internet security standards (reviewed in Chapter VIII), such as secure HTTP (HTTPS), secure socket layer (SSL), and lightweight directory access protocol (LDAP) as well as single-sign-on (SSO) capabilities and central user management.

Comprehensive service design, development, deployment, and continuous change support. CLMS platform ensures services can be managed and configured from a central location. It provides a centrally managed environment and a wide choice of tools for planning, development, deployment, and administration of services.

Platform Architecture

In this section, we present the core and supporting components of CLMS platform. CLMS platform follows the principles of service-oriented architecture (SOA) which, as was stated in Chapter VIII, is a philosophy for prototyping, developing, and maintaining software systems as networks of services. The CLMS platform helps the developer to concentrate on the business logic of the service through IDEF0 modeling, rather than spending effort and time in maintaining user interface, data access code, and so on.

The CLMS platform architecture focuses primarily on the development of services following the SOA architectural model and provides the necessary tools and environment to specify, design, and orchestrate Web services. This is done with the IDEF modeling standard (see Chapter VII), model-driven service generation (see Chapter V), and appropriate run-time execution context supporting transactions, logs, and error handling (see Chapter VIII).

An examination of most business applications today reveals several common types of functionality and components used in e-service provision. For example, in most situations there is a need for a user authentication service, used as part of an authorization and access control component that determines whether the user is authorized to access a particular service. Such services, as explained in Chapter II, are called *infrastructure services*, and they are distinguished from the core e-services that provide business-related functionality. To speed up e-service development, the CLMS platform provides an infrastructure and a predefined set of services that helps the developer to accelerate the development of business e-services while, at the same time, minimizing the errors or the need to write custom logic.

The main components of the CLMS platform are the following:

Listener Web Service

This is an interface that allows the CLMS platform to be invoked by client applications. The listener component acts as a Web service that accepts and responds to messages encoded inside SOAP envelopes (see Chapter III).

Figure 1. CLMS platform architecture

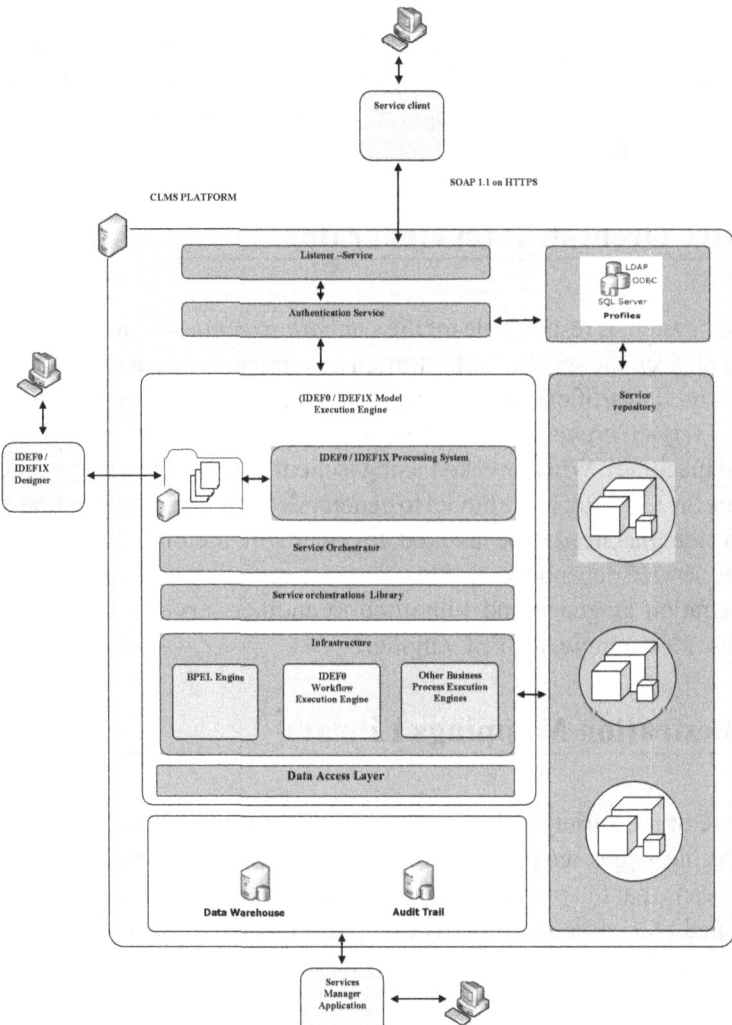

Authentication Services

The CLMS platform provides a number of support services to its clients over the Internet. One of such services is an authentication service that can be integrated with third party technologies such as LDAP based servers (Koutsonikola & Vakali, 2004). This means that the *authentication service* authenticates potential clients of the CLMS platform services using a user name and password mechanism.

IDEF0/IDEF1X Processing System

This is the core component of the CLMS platform. This component is responsible for executing orchestrations of services expressed either as an IDEF0 model or in an alternative orchestration language. It comprises a number of subsystems, detailed in the next section.

Service Orchestration Generator

This subsystem is responsible for the *symbolic execution* of an IDEF0 service model. In this respect, the service orchestration generator is similar to constraint-based reasoners, used in artificial intelligence, or to ontology reasoners, discussed in Chapter V. The *service orchestrator* is also comparable to a virtual machine (e.g., the Java virtual machine). When invoked using a client request, the service orchestrator will execute the IDEF0 service model to generate a complete orchestration description of the services that need to be invoked, together with their input and output parameters and the service dependencies. This can be executed *natively* or converted to a target orchestration language and submitted to another service execution environment, such as, for example, a BPEL engine.

Orchestration Mappings Library

Because of the variety of business process coordination (choreography, orchestration) technologies see (Chapter IV), CLMS adopts a multitechnology perspective. This means that the platform independent IDEF0 orchestration descriptions can be translated to a particular process execution language specification, such as BPEL, according to mappings defined in this library.

Workflow Execution Engine (IDEF0 Workflow Engine)

The CLMS platform has its own workflow engine that executes process orchestration models defined in IDEF0. The functionality provided by the IDEF0 based workflow engine is described in the following.

Accept Envelope

Accept envelope is the basic service exposed by the workflow. As was described previously, the *Accept Envelope* service takes an XML file as input that complies with

Listing 1. Empty SOAP envelope

```xml
<?xml version="1.0" encoding="ISO-8859-7"?>
<SOAP-ENV:Envelope SOAP-ENV:encodingStyle="http://schemas.xmlsoap.org/soap/
encoding/" xmlns:SOAP-ENV="http://schemas.xmlsoap.org/soap/envelope/">
        <SOAP-ENV:Header>
                <Role/>
                <User/>
                <Action/>
                <ProgID/>
                <ProgID_Description/>
                <PendingJob/>
                <InstanceID/>
                <SystemID/>
                <ReferenceASP/>
                <LinkedServer>
                        <LinkedServerInstanceID/>
                        <InitiatorsSystemID/>
                        <LinkedServer/>
                        <InitiatorsListener/>
                </LinkedServer>
        </SOAP-ENV:Header>
        <SOAP-ENV:Body/>
</SOAP-ENV:Envelope>
```

a specific XML schema. This XML file is called *SOAP envelope*, because it complies with the SOAP syntax rules. An empty SOAP envelope is shown in Listing 1.

In general, the *header* of this document contains all the workflow related data, while the *body* contains the XML document that corresponds to a business structure that a client sends to workflow engine (e.g., invoice data).

An example of a SOAP envelope filled with data is shown in Listing 2:.

The SOAP Envelope in Lising 2 is submitted to the workflow's listener. If the activity completes without any problems, the returned SOAP envelope is shown in Listing 3.

If an error occurs during the service execution, the returning envelope contains in its body some fault information, which describe the source of the fault (Listing 4).

Service Engineering Using the CLMS Platform

The service engineering approach used in conjunction with the CLMS platform is domain model driven. Domain modeling activities are analogous to requirements analysis and design steps in traditional software engineering. The primary language used for domain modeling is *IDEF0*. This language is used by domain experts and users initially but also by software architects, designers, developers, and testers in later stages to describe abstractions of a business service domain. The development approach is reuse-based, in the sense that models are not always built from scratch, but existing IDF0 and IDEF1X service ontologies are combined, extended, and instantiated. IDEF browser tools allow the selection of specific model components (e.g., service control or mechanisms descriptions) using a system-service-component

Listing 2. SOAP envelope containing data

```
<?xml version="1.0" encoding="ISO-8859-7"?>
<SOAP-ENV:Envelope SOAP-ENV:encodingStyle="http://schemas.xmlsoap.org/soap/
encoding/" xmlns:SOAP-ENV="http://schemas.xmlsoap.org/soap/envelope/">
        <SOAP-ENV:Header>
                <Role>Administrator</Role>
                <User>demoUser</User>
                <Action>Execute</Action>
                <ProgID>Resources.CUSTOMER.CUSTOMER_INSERT</ProgID>
                <ProgID_Description/>
                <PendingJob/>
                <InstanceID/>
                <SystemID>{24D50F9883144088934A53CD8FBA06EE29122005114929}
</SystemID>
                <ReferenceASP>RemoteIP: 127.0.0.1  Resource: /TestDemo/forms/
Customer.asp</ReferenceASP>
                <Username>test</Username>
                <Password>test</Password>
                <LinkedServer>
                        <LinkedServerInstanceID/>
                        <InitiatorsSystemID/>
                        <LinkedServer/>
                        <InitiatorsListener/>
                </LinkedServer>
        </SOAP-ENV:Header>
        <SOAP-ENV:Body>
                <Customer>
```

continued on following page

Listing 2. continued

```
                              <CustomerID>-1</CustomerID>
                              <Code/>
                              <Name>A Name</Name>
                              <TaxOfficeID>-1</TaxOfficeID>
                              <TaxOfficeName/>
                              <TaxReferenceNumber>3453443534</TaxReferenceNumber>
                              <DateEntered>13/1/2006</DateEntered>
                              <LastModified>13/1/2006</LastModified>
                              <SQLTimestamp/>
               <ApplicationID>{24D50F9883144088934A53CD8FBA06EE29122005114929}</
ApplicationID>
                              <LanguageCode>English</LanguageCode>
                       </Customer>
                 </SOAP-ENV:Body>
           </SOAP-ENV:Envelope>
```

classification approach. Developers then use the resulting domain models to generate user interfaces and business control logic. In contrast to many traditional software development methodologies, where analysis and design only leads to intermediate artifacts (e.g., UML models), this approach employs the same models throughout stages such as analysis, design, implementation, testing, and at run time. The ontologies defined in the early phases determine the functionality of components (e.g., COM, Java, .NET) in implementation, while, at the same time, the original design models remain accessible when the application is executing. The logic captured in

Listing 3. Returned SOAP envelope

```
<SOAP-ENV:Envelope SOAP-ENV:encodingStyle="http://schemas.xmlsoap.org/soap/
encoding/" xmlns:SOAP-ENV="http://schemas.xmlsoap.org/soap/envelope/">
         <SOAP-ENV:Header>
               <Role>Administrator</Role>
               <User>demoUser</User>
               <Action>Execute</Action>
               <ProgID>Resources.CUSTOMER.CUSTOMER_INSERT</ProgID>
               <ProgID_Description/>
               <PendingJob/>
               <InstanceID>1101</InstanceID>
               <SystemID>{24D50F9883144088934A53CD8FBA06EE29122005114929}<
/SystemID>
```

continued on following page

Listing 3. continued

```
                <ReferenceASP>RemoteIP: 127.0.0.1  Resource: /TestDemo/forms/
Customer.asp</ReferenceASP>
                <LinkedServer>
                        <LinkedServerInstanceID/>
                        <InitiatorsSystemID/>
                        <LinkedServer/>
                        <InitiatorsListener/>
                </LinkedServer>
        </SOAP-ENV:Header>
        <SOAP-ENV:Body>
                <Customer>
                        <CustomerID>2</CustomerID>
                        <Code/>
                        <Name>A Name</Name>
                        <TaxOfficeID>-1</TaxOfficeID>
                        <TaxOfficeName/>
                        <TaxReferenceNumber>3453443534</TaxReferenceNumber>
                        <DateEntered>13/1/2006</DateEntered>
                        <LastModified>13/1/2006</LastModified>
                        <SQLTimestamp/>
        <ApplicationID>{24D50F9883144088934A53CD8FBA06EE29122005114929}</
ApplicationID>
                        <LanguageCode>English</LanguageCode>
                </Customer>
        </SOAP-ENV:Body>
</SOAP-ENV:Envelope>
```

Listing 4. Envelope with fault information

```
<SOAP-ENV:Envelope SOAP-ENV:encodingStyle="http://schemas.xmlsoap.org/soap/
encoding/" xmlns:SOAP-ENV="http://schemas.xmlsoap.org/soap/envelope/">
        <SOAP-ENV:Header>
                <Role/>
                <User/>
                <Action/>
                <ProgID/>
                <ProgID_Description/>
                <PendingJob/>
                <InstanceID/>
                <SystemID/>
```

continued on following page

Listing 4. continued

```
                    <ReferenceASP/>
                    <LinkedServer/>
            </SOAP-ENV:Header>
            <SOAP-ENV:Body>
                    <SOAP-ENV:Fault>
                            <FaultCode>3421</FaultCode>
                            <FaultString>Customer code invalid.</FaultString>
                            <FaultActor>CUSTOMER</FaultActor>
                            <FaultActivity>Resources.CUSTOMER.CUSTOMER_
INSERT</FaultActivity>
                            <FaultLinkedServer/>
                            <FaultLinkedServerActivity/>
                            <FaultCallArrowSourceActivity/>
                            <FaultCallArrowTargetActivity/>
                    </SOAP-ENV:Fault>
            </SOAP-ENV:Body>
    </SOAP-ENV:Envelope>
```

the IDEF models can then be exploited during model verification and validation. Also, because IDEF models are given explicit run-time semantics, reasoning services are used at run time for their execution.

The CLMS approach follows the MDD paradigm that, as explained in Chapter V, is widely regarded as being able to deliver the next great leap in software development productivity. MDD aims to bridge the gap between models and code and specifies a way of generating executable code for multiple platforms from one single platform-independent model. MDD introduces new levels of abstraction, which allows designers and developers to concentrate on implementing the specified requirements, instead of spending valuable time adapting the system to a specific platform and environment. Since systems are modeled independent of the target platform, the ability to reuse at the specification or design level is significantly enhanced.

The CLMS platform implements a service engineering method that is domain modeling driven and conforms to the MDD paradigm. The six basic stages of this methodology are outlined in Figure 2.

The methodology encompasses the notion of continuous business service engineering. For that reason, the stages form a cycle representing the cyclic process of change:

Scoping → Architecting → Modeling → Building → Deploying → Managing → Scoping.

Figure 2. Enterprise systems semantics methodology

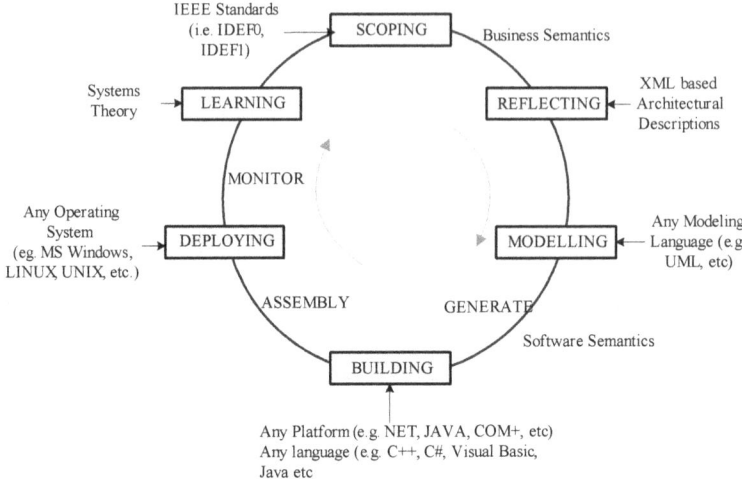

Figure 3. Process model in IDEF0 notation

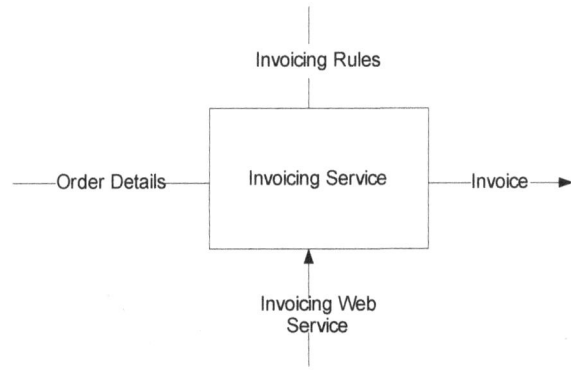

In the following sections, each of these stages will be analyzed in detail.

Methodology. Stage 1: Scoping

For the scoping stage, IDEF0-based and IDEF1X-based modeling techniques are used in parallel. Figure 3 shows a business service as represented in Level 0 of an IDEF0-based model.

IDEF0-based models produced at this stage capture and represent the dynamics of business services and can be used to derive flexible and adaptable process orchestrations. In this way, IDEF0-based models enable the service improvement activity of Stage 6.

IDEF1X-Based Models

IDEF1X-based models (introduced in Chapter VII) capture information about the entities involved within the scope of an enterprise. IDEF1X was conceived as a method for organizations to analyze and clearly state their information resource management needs and requirements. Rather than a database design method, IDEF1X is an analysis method used to identify the following:

1.   Information collected, stored, and managed by the enterprise.
2.   Rules governing the management of information.
3.   Logical relationships within the enterprise reflected in the information.
4.   Problems resulting from the lack of good information management.

IDEF1X-based models identify the information objects of the solution, their relation, and their characteristics. An example of an IDEF1X model is shown in Figure 4.

IDEF1X-based models are used as a basis for the software artifacts that are created during the software generation process.

Figure 4. IDEF1 example

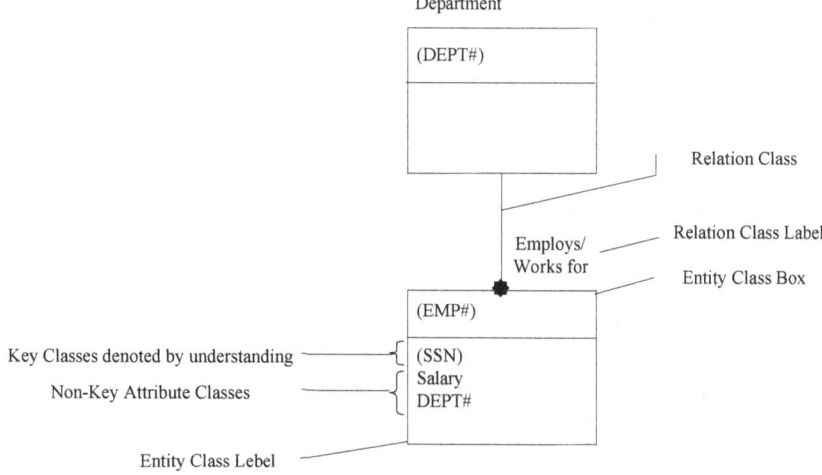

Figure 5. Service deployment architectures

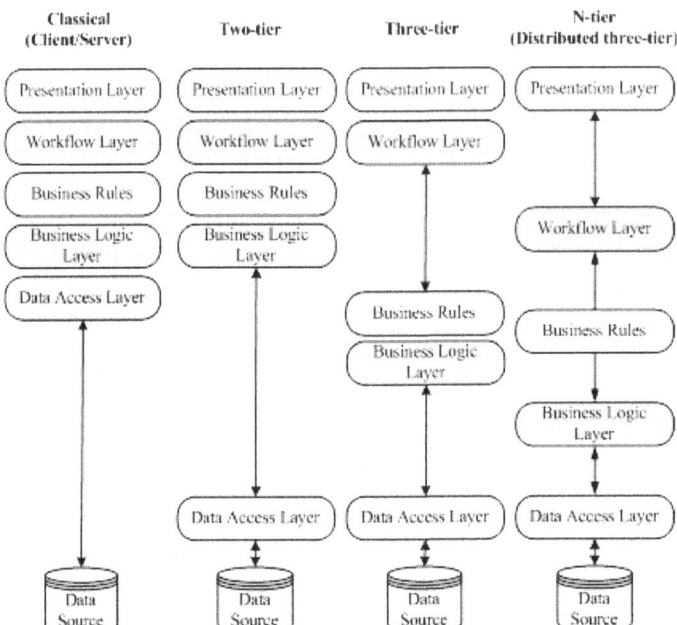

Methodology. Stage 2: Service Architecting

During this stage, the architecture of the system that delivers the discovered service is decided. Designers may choose, for example, between classical client server architecture, 2-tier, 3-tier, or n-tier architecture (see Figure 5).

The architectural phase is concerned with the major subsystems that will provide the service. These may include:

- **The presentation layer (subsystem):** If the service consumer is human, the service will be accessible via some kind of user interface, such as a Web portal. Such interface can be automatically generated from service descriptions, as it will be explained in subsequent sections.

- **The business logic layer subsystem:** This will contain the system(s) that will implement the business logic of the service. Such systems can be based on the CLMS IDEF execution engine or on an alternative service execution environment. In turn, this environment will have to execute on top of a computing platform, such as Windows (e.g., .NET), Unix (e.g., Java, J2EE), and so on (Miller, 2003).

- • **The data access tier (subsystem):** This tier contains all sources of data used or produced by the service. Such data correspond to the IDEF1X model descriptions obtained in Stage 1 (modeling). Data schema definitions and manipulations can be automatically generated for the target storage technology (e.g., a relational database management system). The mechanism to achieve that explained in more detail in the next section.

In addition to the above main tiers, intermediate tiers of *middleware* systems may be added, if required. This decision is determined by the environment in which the service is deployed and the nature of the service (e.g., transactional, proactive, reactive, etc.). An event-based notification tier may, for example, be required for services that are proactive (i.e., serve clients on a proactive rather than on a demand-driven mode).

Methodology. Stage 3: Service Modeling

Following the MDD philosophy and the selected architecture from the previous stage, this stage involves the generation of appropriate metamodels (i.e., XML schemas that encode the specifications of the various components to be deployed).

If, for example, we choose a 3-tier architecture, we need to encode:

1. The database characteristics (tables, relations);
2. The business logic; and
3. The user interface requirements, with appropriate XML schemas.

Modeling stage also involves creating the business object models, based on the IDEF1X models captured in the scoping stage and creating the software artifacts templates, which will facilitate the code generation. Figure 6 presents the deliverables of this stage (1-3).

The completion of modeling stage provides all the appropriate information to proceed with building and deploying the solution.

Methodology. Stage 4: Building

As the Internet and its related technologies grow, and organizations seek to integrate their systems across departmental and organizational boundaries, service-based approaches to building solutions have evolved. From the consumer's perspective,

Figure 6. CLMS approach to model driven service engineering

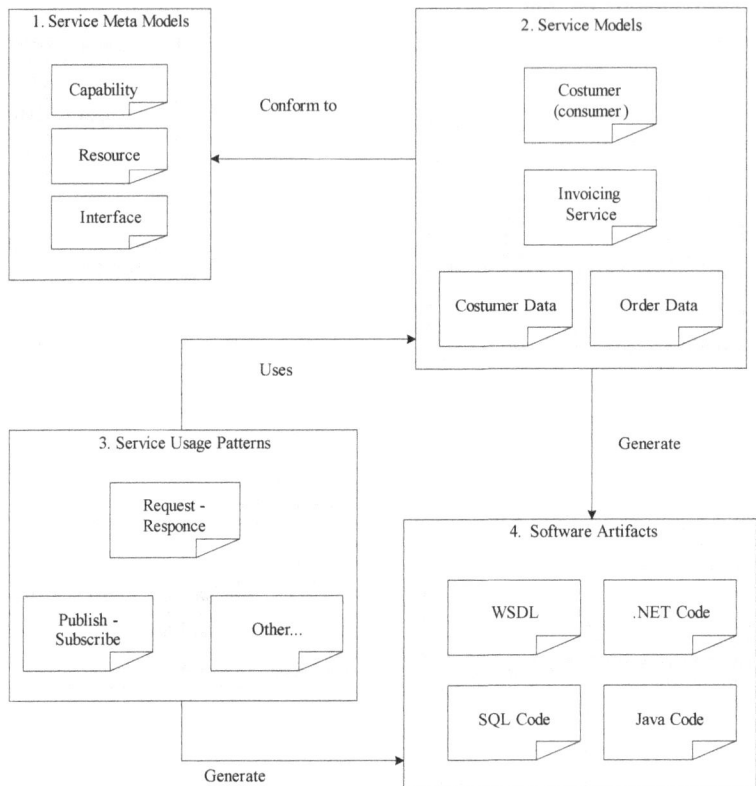

services are conceptually similar to traditional components, except that services encapsulate their own data and are not, strictly speaking, part of their applications; rather, they are used by their applications. Applications and services that need to be integrated may be built on different platforms, by different teams, on different schedules, and may be maintained and updated independently. Therefore, it is critical to implement communication between them with the least coupling possible (see Figure 7).

It has become widely accepted that an application should be divided into components providing presentation, business, and data services (see Figure 8). Components that perform similar types of functions can be grouped into layers that, in many cases, are organized in a stacked fashion so that components *above* a certain layer use the services provided by it, and a given component will use the functionality provided by other components in its own layer and from other layers *below*, to perform its work.

Figure 7. Application components separated in to layers

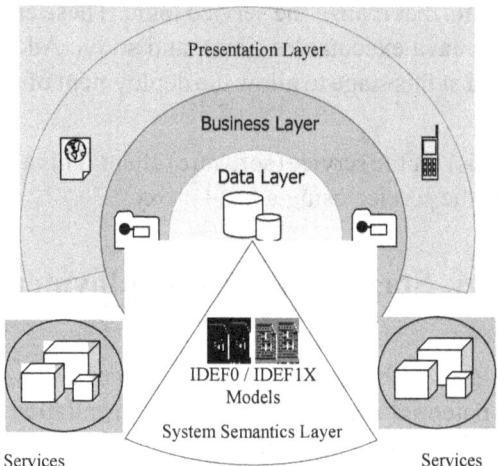

This partitioned view of an application can be also applied to services. From a high-level view, a service-based solution can be considered to comprise multiple services, each communicating with the others by message exchanges. Conceptually, the services can be considered as components of the overall solution. However, internally, each service is made up of software components, just like any other application, and these components can be logically grouped into presentation, business, and data services. Services contain logic components that orchestrate the business tasks they perform, business components that implement the actual business logic of the service, and data access components that access the service's data store. In addition, services expose their functionality through service interfaces, which handle the semantics of exposing the underlying business logic. The definition of the set of messages that must be exchanged with a service in order for the service to perform a specific business task constitutes a contract. A service interface acts as a façade that exposes the business logic implemented in the service to potential consumers (see Chapter II). An application may also call other services through service agents, which communicate with the service on behalf of the calling client application.

The building stage involves generating the software artifacts that comprise the service, bearing in mind the target service execution environment(s). Such artifacts will typically include:

- • The service specification (in WSDL).

- • Components that realize the service logic. These can be realized as Windows DLL files, Java executables (jars), and so on. Additional configuration files are created at this stage to allow the deployment of such components on target platforms.

- • Code (stubs) for the service (software) client. This allows the client application to invoke the service using a local proxy.

Methodology. Stage 5: Service Deployment

The *deployment stage* is the final configuration of the system in order to be ready for use by its potential users. It involves the installation and configuration of the developed solution to the target platform (e.g., a .NET or Java environment running under Windows, Unix, etc.). Several configurations and technologies may be combined. A typical service deployment architecture is depicted in Figure 8.

Figure 8. CLMS platform architecture

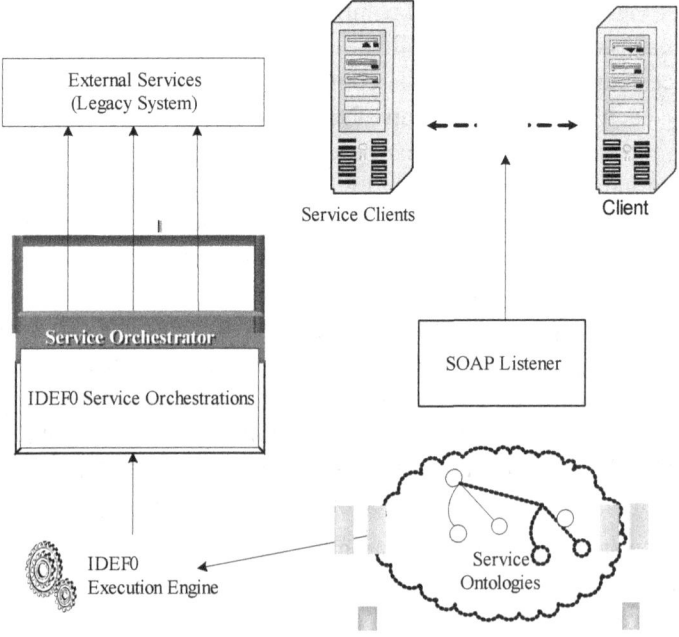

Methodology. Stage 6: Service Adaptation and Improvement

The adaptation and improvement stage is the most dynamic stage of the methodology. It includes the monitoring, management, and improvement of the service, according to changing customer requirements or business conditions. Due to the dynamic nature of businesses, it is crucial for any organization and any enterprise to be able to adapt its services with the minimum time required and the least effort.

With the adoption of the IDEF0-based models, this process can take place on the fly and with minimal disruption on the running activities. This is feasible, because IDEF0-based constructs that are used for modeling business services can be easily extended and altered, causing no change to existing business processes. Therefore, having IDEF0-based models at the core of business services enables the adaptation process to take place in a smooth and efficient way.

The architecture of the service run-time environment, comprising the subsystems previously presented, is depicted in Figure 9.

Figure 9. Enterprise systems server's architecture

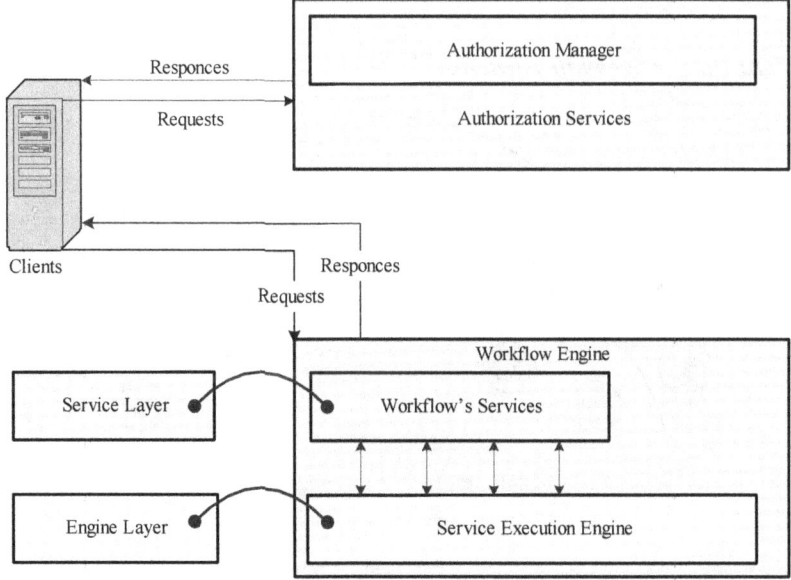

Model-Driven Generation of Service Artifacts

In Chapter V, we introduced model-driven architecture (MDA) as an instance of model-driven development (MDD). In MDD, models are the primary source of an application. All other artifacts, such as code, tests, and documentation are (mostly) automatically derived and generated from models.

The CLMS platform has adopted MDD in all stages of application development, from UI code to data access layer code. In this way, CLMS platform has the potential to greatly reduce the cost of solution development and improve the consistency and quality of applications. Rather than repeatedly applying technical expertise manually when building application artifacts, the expertise is encoded directly in *code templates*. This has the advantages of both consistency and maintainability. A modified code template can be reapplied rapidly to generate application artifacts that reflect a change in the implementation architecture.

Code templates used in the CLMS platform follow widely accepted design patterns and encapsulate the skills knowledge and expertise of its developers. A core metamodel of the CLMS platform, used for deriving many software artifacts is called *Master/Detail*. This metamodel describes an abstract one-to-many relation between entities, database tables, and UML classes, depending on the application context. Master/Detail is capable of supplying the necessary metadata to the code

Figure 10. Services infrastructure

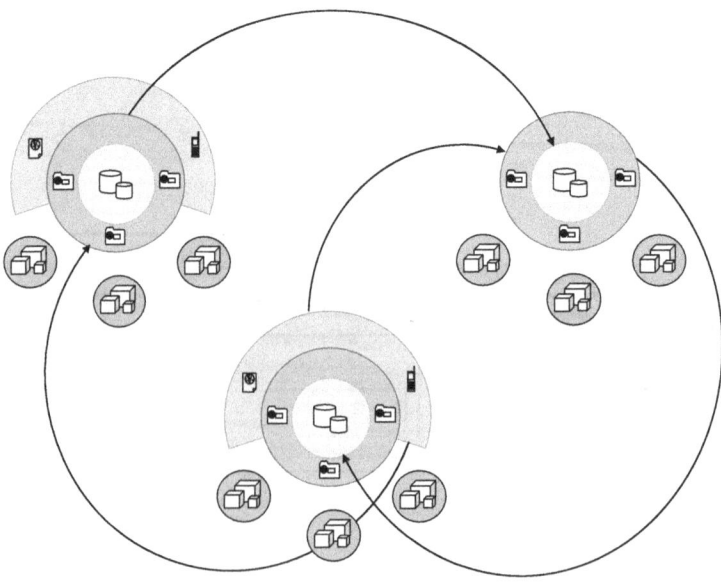

generation engine in order to generate plug-n-play software artifacts. The generated software artifacts can be the following:

- **UI web forms:** The generated Web form implements the model-view-controller design pattern, with built-in client-side validation and business logic. Upon submission, the form requests the execution of the appropriate IDEF0 activity.

- **UI related code snippets:** These include automatic menu/commands creation, business objects list/query management, and so on.

- **Data access layer components:** Data access layer components that support transactions, object pooling targeting most popular database servers (SQL server 2000, Oracle, MySQL).

- **Business rules:** Business rules *code* and *logic* can be generated automatically based on metadata, the Master/Detail model holds. Business rules code can perform a wide range of operations, comparisons, assignments, exception throwing, and is capable of operating on business objects.

CLMS Coding Facility: Implementing MDD Using XML Technologies

Metamodeling

CLMS MDD uses XML schemas as metamodeling language. XML dialects are also being used as domain-specific modeling languages for a variety of problem domains, for example, *business process execution language* (Andrews et al., 2003); *Web modeling language* (WebML, 2007); and the *eXtensible architecture description language* (XADL, 2007). Metamodels define rules that models must conform to. Additionally, XML schema-based metamodels support inheritance, reuse, and constraints. In the context of the CLMS approach to MDD, XML schemas can fully express the necessary properties, data type constraints, and rules that models must conform to. Throughout the code generation stage, the CLMS platform makes extensive use of formally specified (using XSDs) metamodels from which software artifacts can be automatic generated. The main metamodels employed are explained below.

Figure 11. CLMS platform architecture

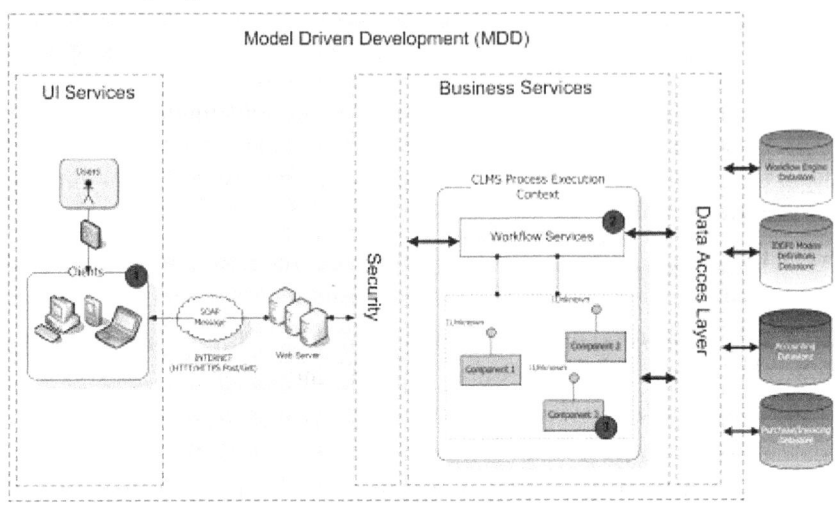

Figure 12. "Master/Detail' metamodel

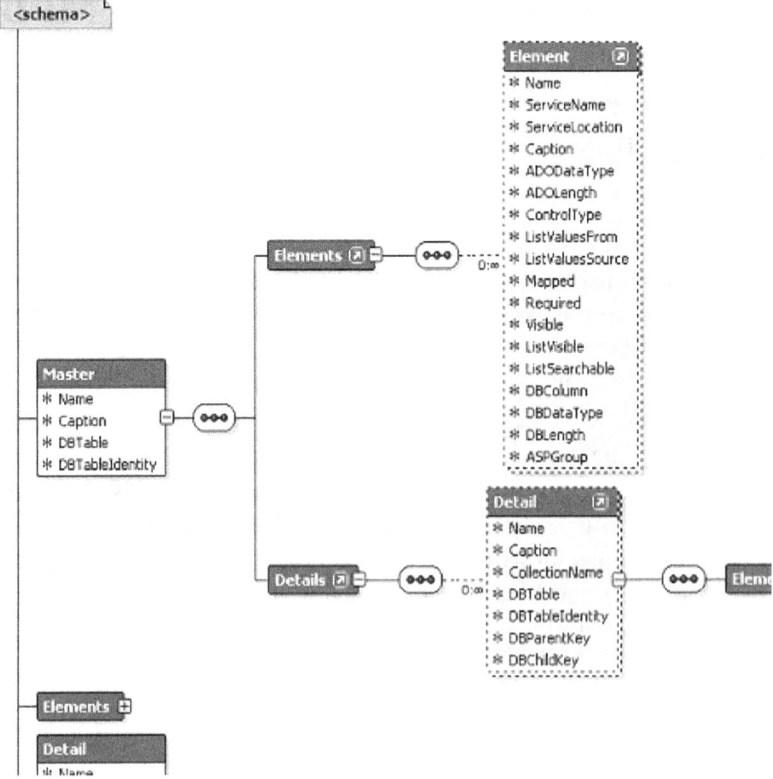

Master/Detail Metamodel

As we already described, this metamodel contains an abstract one-to-many relation between entities, which can be database tables or UML object classes, depending on the application context. This metamodel is capable of supplying the necessary metadata to the code-generation engine in order to generate software artifacts. Figure 12 shows the Master/Detail XML schema metamodel.

The main concepts in this metamodel are:

- **Master:** A complex type that usually maps a database table, IDEF1X entity, or UML class that has one-to-many relation with a *Detail* entity.
- **Detail:** A complex type that usually maps a database table, IDEF1X entity, or UML class that has many-to-one relation with the *Master* entity.
- **Service:** A complex type that usually maps a database view, IDEF1X entity, or UML class that has one-to-one relation with the *Master* or *Detail* entity. The *Service* entity is generally used to describe foreign key constraints and supports helper operations such as LookUp functions, based on foreign keys.
- **Element:** A complex type that usually maps a Database column, IDEF1X attribute, or UML class property. Each *Master*, *Detail*, or *Service* entity can have an arbitrary number of user-defined unmapped *Element* elements, if this is required to achieve specific code-generation results, like calculated fields or dummy read-only fields.

Artifacts derived from the Master/Detail metamodel include:

- Stored procedures
- Data access layer business objects
- XML schemas describing the *Master*, *Detail*, and *Service* entities
- XML document instances

Business Rules Metamodel

This metamodel describes business rules and is capable of producing business logic code. Business logic is expressed as *if-then* pairs of actions, and the vocabulary used can be defined as operations on:

- Business object's properties and methods

Figure 13. "Master/Detail' model composition

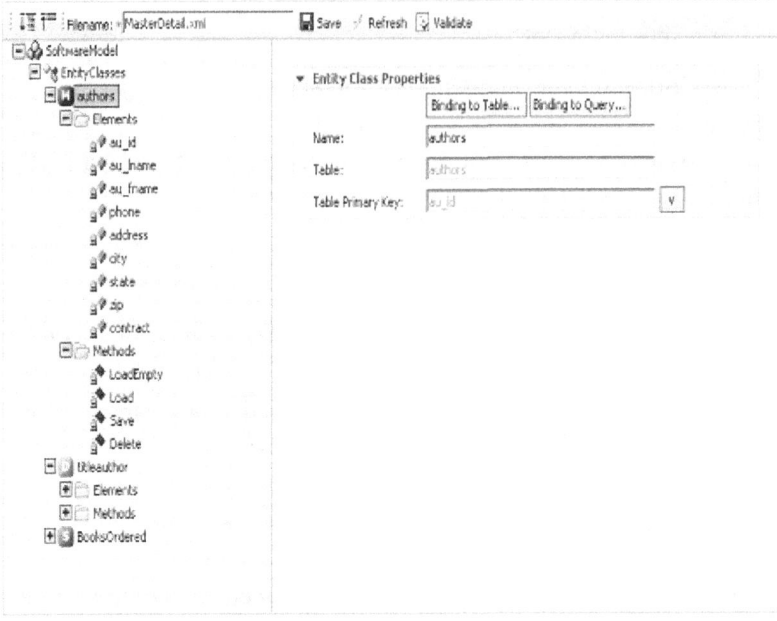

- Select, Insert, Update, Delete operations on database table columns
- XPath (see Chapter III) functions on XML document instances
- Built-in system functions (e.g., Date(), Time(), Concat(), etc.)

Artifacts derived from the business rules metamodel include software components exposing its set of rules as methods

Web Form Metamodel

This metamodel works together with, and depends on, the Master/Detail metamodel. *Web form* metamodel describes the UI layout and operational aspects of a Web form that is capable of collecting information at run time from the end user in order to generate valid XML document instances of XML schemas.

Generated artifacts derived from Web form metamodel are:

- HTML Web forms
- HTML helper forms, supporting the functionality of theHTML Web form (e.g., lookup pick lists)

- HTML list and query management Web forms (e.g., form that displays the list of Customers, Orders, etc.)

Modeling

Model composition is performed using a tree-like graphical structure that provides enhanced usability features. Moreover, the user is able to check the models for *wellformedness* and validity against their metamodels and navigate to the source of possible inconsistencies.

Code Generation

Generation of software artifacts is achieved through user-defined templates. A template can share variables with and trigger the processing of other templates, therefore allowing the user to define arbitrary flows of the generation process precisely.

Templates consist of two types of content: *static* and *dynamic*. Dynamic content is expressed in a scripting language and is enclosed between the [% and %] delimiters. Everything that exists outside those delimiters is considered to be *static* content. Dynamic content populates the static content with data from the models.

In order to access the information contained in models, the simplest approach would be to script the XML document object model (DOM) directly. Neverthe-

Figure 14. "Web Form' model composition

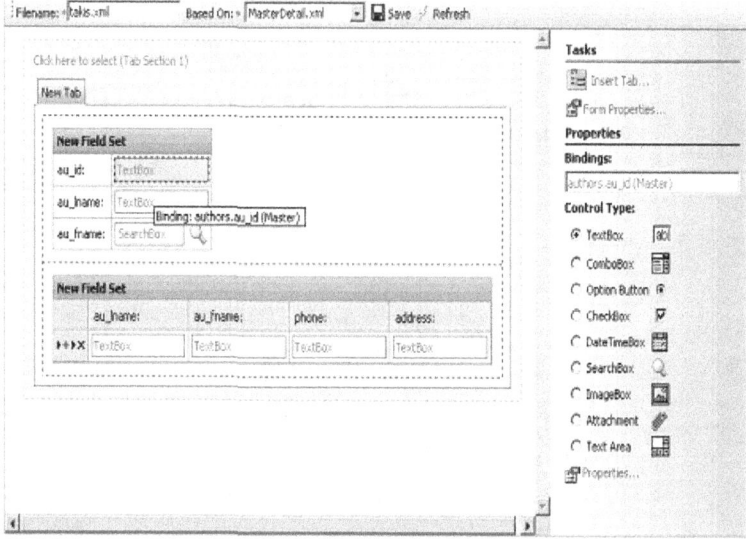

Figure 15. "Business Rules' model composition

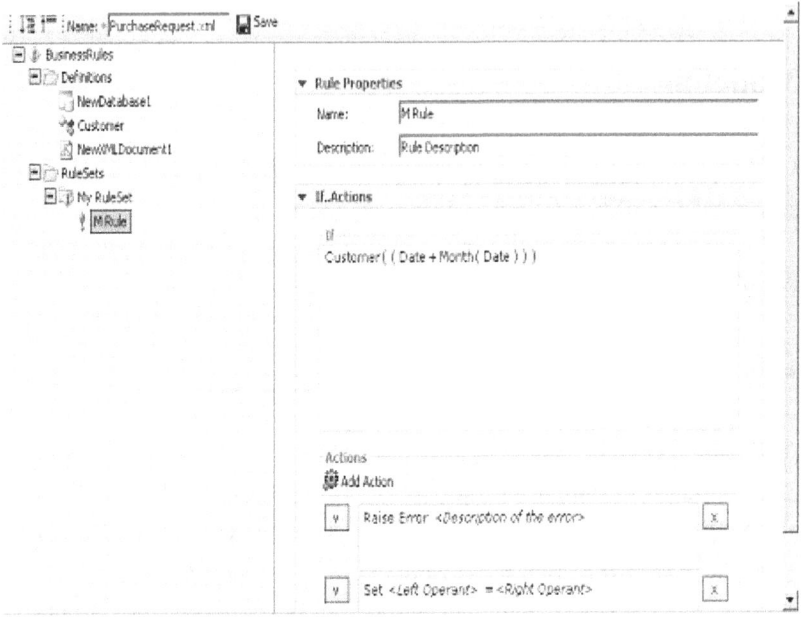

Figure 16. Example showing the interactions across the platform

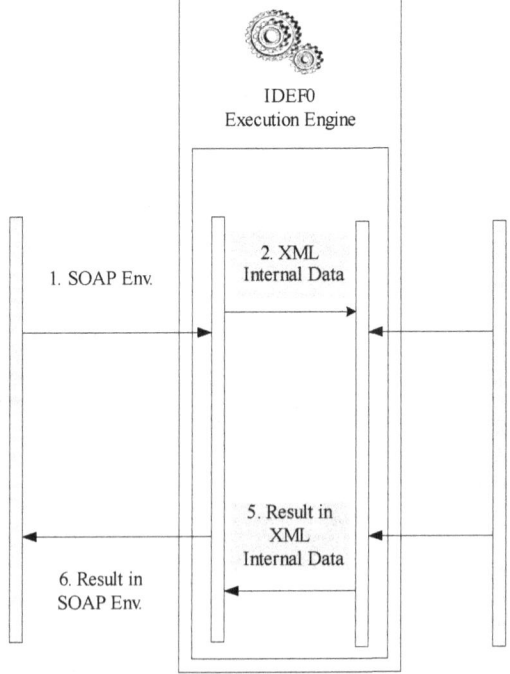

less, this would insert DOM-specific code in the templates, making authoring and maintenance more difficult. For this reason, the CLMS platform provides utilities for wrapping/exposing the user-defined metamodels as complete object models that can be scripted and referenced through the templates, making the scripting code more brief and elegant. For example, in order to generate a simple .NET class from a *Master* entity, we only need the following script:

```
      class [%=Master.Name%]
  {
    [%for each Element in Master.Elements %]
      private [%=Element.DataType] m_[%=Element.Name%];
    [%next%]
  }
```

Template script using the Master/Detail object model

A Service Runtime Example

This example demonstrates how the components of the CLMS platform collaborate to provide services to clients. A client wants to invoke a business service on a CLMS enterprise systems server. The interaction begins when the client sends to the CLMS listener a request which, as explained in previous section, is in the form of a SOAP envelope. When the listener receives the request, it transforms it to an internal XML format and forwards it to the workflow's core engine. The engine extracts the identifier of the request and requests the CLMS authorization manager of the corresponding IDEF0 service model. CLMS server manager returns the model's path, and the engine loads and executes the service model to fulfill the client's request. After execution is completed, the engine sends to the listener the result in an internal XML format, which the latter transforms into a SOAP envelope and sends back to the client. The whole process described above, with all the interactions, is depicted in Figure 16.

Chapter Summary

This chapter has presented an example of a service engineering platform that combines model-driven characteristics with semantic consistency and platform interoperability. First, we argued that service engineering platforms need to facilitate service-oriented thinking, because of the complex feedback type interrelationships of services with other systems both internal to the business as well as external. By relying on principles of model-driven development, the platform supports the methodical design of the data and processing elements of the Web services and the automatic generation of all the artifacts (WSDL, scripts, data schemas) necessary for deploying the services. A unique feature of the service engineering platform introduced in this chapter, is that it blends SOA and MDD principles and allows complete business systems to be modeled and realized in a service-oriented manner, ensuring continuity from the business to the software technology domains.

In this chapter, we proved that the realization of business services in software is a viable proposition if model driven approaches are used. However, this requires appropriate and powerful service metamodels that transform the business-oriented service models to executable services, taking into account software architectural patterns and Web service execution technologies. The next chapter will present a complete case study of services realization that uses the CLMS platform.

References

Andrews, T., Curbera, F., Dholakia, H., Goland, Y., Klein, J., Leymann, F., et al. (2003). *Business process execution language for Web services (Version 1.1)*. Retrieved March 16, 2007, from http://xml.coverpages.org/BPELv11-May-052003Final.pdf

CBDI. (2003). *Service architecture and optimal J. CBDI report.* Retrieved March 15, 2007, from www.cbdiforum.com

Koutsonikola , V., & Vakali, A. (2004). LDAP: Framework, practices, and trends. *IEEE Internet Computing, 8*(5), 66-72.

Miller, G. (2003). NET vs. J2EE. *Communications of the ACM, 46*(6), 64-67.

Samtani, G., & Sadhwani, D. (2002). *Web services and application frameworks working together.* Retrieved March 15, 2007, from http://www.Web servicesarchitect.com/content/articles/samtani04.asp

XADL. (2007). *XADL 2.0 highly extensible architecture description language for software and systems.* Retrieved March 17, 2007, from http://www.isr.uci.edu/projects/xarchuci/

WebML. (2007). *The Web modeling language.* Retrieved March 17, 2007, from http://www.Web ml.org/Web ml/page3.do?ctx1=EN

Chapter X

A Case Study of Business Service Realization:
Account Receivables—Account Payables

Introduction

Having discussed a method for service realization in Chapter VII, the service methodology that was first outlined in the Introduction of this book is now complete. We have covered the following, so far:

- Service concepts and fundamentals (Chapter II).

- Service identification from business models and modeling, using the IDEF0/IDEF1X notations (Chapter VII).

- Service realization using the MDA transformation of business services to executable Web services (Chapter V).

- Environments for service execution and management (Chapter IX).

This chapter demonstrates how the above aforementioned concepts and methods can be applied to the analysis design and implementation of real business services.

The business domain that we have chosen, *accounts payable/accounts receivable* (A/R-A/P), is pervasive, but by no means trivial. In this chapter, we approach this traditional accounting domain from a fresh, service-oriented perspective, by following the steps of the approach presented in the previous chapters, to show how services can be realized. We finally implement the modeled services using the CLMS service engineering platform that was first introduced in Chapter IX.

Background

The *general ledger* approach for the development of information systems (IS) that support business transaction cycles has several limitations. It emphasizes the accounting informational perspective (Cushing & Marshal, 1994) of the operational environment, ignoring its multidimensional aspects and its underlining dynamic nature. General ledger approach focuses on the integration of accounting information extracted from various processes and imposes an architectural paradigm that:

1. Relies on interfaces to retrieve information from different processes of the operational environment. These interfaces capture only the information required to support general ledger procedures.

2. Provides no *prudence* at the operational environment. *Operational environment* is a set of processes organized towards the achievement of an organizational purpose. General ledger approach originates in the accounting discipline to provide information to several interest groups, under specific rules (i.e., GAAPs, IAS, etc.). Subsequently, its flexibility to serve alternative purposes is rather limited.

3. Ignores the interactions developed between business processes and thus provides no means to handle the complexity of systems dynamics.

4. Perceives information systems as an entity that is separate from the main organization. Information systems are considered to be part of the organizational control mechanisms and, therefore, they are distinguished by the organization itself.

This architectural approach results in static IS applications with minimum ability to integrate business processes and to aid management in handling dynamic environments. This is in contrast to the requirements of contemporary management. Managers operate within continuous evolving enterprise environments and thus, the formulation of the strategic path is not a monolithic procedure but something that is constantly being adapted, according to the varying environmental and organiza-

Figure 1. The general ledger approach

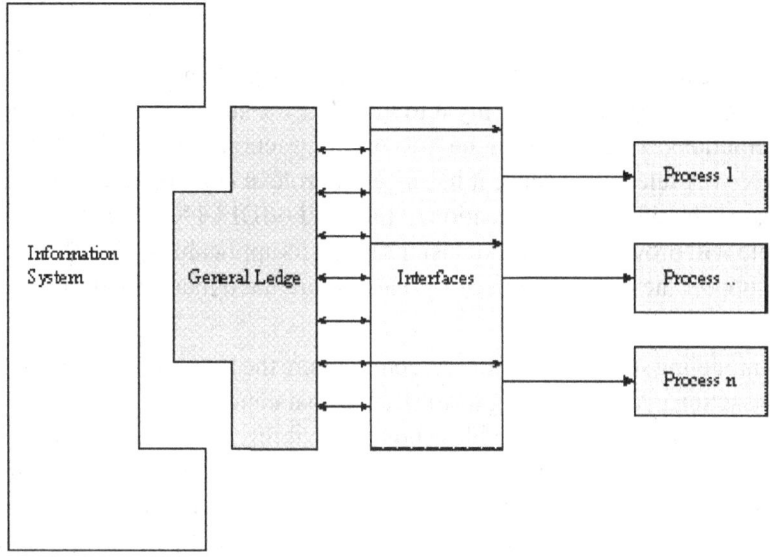

tional parameters. This implies an adaptation process, which is usually referred to as *organizational learning*, and which is the key to corporate survival and success. The strategic role of IS infrastructure is to support this adaptation process, since it can be used to integrate business processes by acting as:

a. The informational dimension of the operational environment,

b. A communication channel across the organizational boundaries, and

c. A tool employed by different organizational teams for task performance monitoring.

However, general ledger approach provides a rather limited methodological framework for developing IS infrastructure to serve the above strategic role.

To address the requirements for integrating business processes, we must model, initially, the business transaction cycles. Modeling business processes is essential because:

1. It provides visualizations of the operational environment, its processes and their interactions. Interactions are considered to be the exchange of resources and information between the processes, subprocesses, and activities for a specific cause.

2.   It helps to understand the role of the IS infrastructure within the operational environment and how it is integrated with the businesses processes.

To address modeling requirements for the business transaction cycles, we adapt the IDEF0 language and we apply it to visualize the subprocesses, activities, and their interactions in the context of the A/R-A/P transaction cycle. The A/R-A/P transaction cycle was selected because it has a central role at contemporary business environments. Therefore, the application of the IDEF0/IDEF1X at the A/R-A/P transaction cycle will provide useful conclusions about its applicability and its appropriateness to support the development of IS that capture the dynamic aspects of the business environments.

By modeling service semantics, we can capture the important aspects of the A/R-A/P transaction cycle without ignoring details that concern its dynamic nature. Furthermore, IDEF0/IDEF1X provides enough flexibility to adjust the analysis to varying degrees of organizational complexity. This is possible because, as we already stated in previous chapters, IDEF0/IDEF1X provides the conceptual framework to apply general systems theory (Chekland, 1981) thinking to the IS infrastructure and so to deal with the dynamic complexity of the system.

As argued in previous chapters, general systems theory through IDEF0/IDEF1X introduces a number of concepts in the process modeling, that reduce the complexity of real environments, using as criterion the scope of the system (i.e., organization). These concepts include:

1.   *Input-output*, which represents the flow of resources and information between processes in the context of interactions between processes.
2.   *Processes*, which are sets of activities collaborating towards the achievement of a specific goal.
3.   *Feedback loop handling mechanisms*, which associate the inputs of a process with its outputs, and may concern a single process or a set of processes.

The identification of the feedback loop mechanisms of the organization is the framework for integrating business processes in the context of the IS infrastructure. Feedback loop mechanisms associate the inputs of a specific process with its outputs and diagnose gaps between actual and desired states of outputs. The desired states of outputs are extracted by the goal of each process, the business rules and prior knowledge. Thus, the interactions between the processes are filtered and directed through a gap analysis, in order to create the desired results for the organization. Having visualized the feedback loop mechanisms, IS infrastructure can be an coordinator of the interactions and a valuable administrative tool for implementing corporate policies and strategies.

Figure 2. Systems theory applied to general ledger

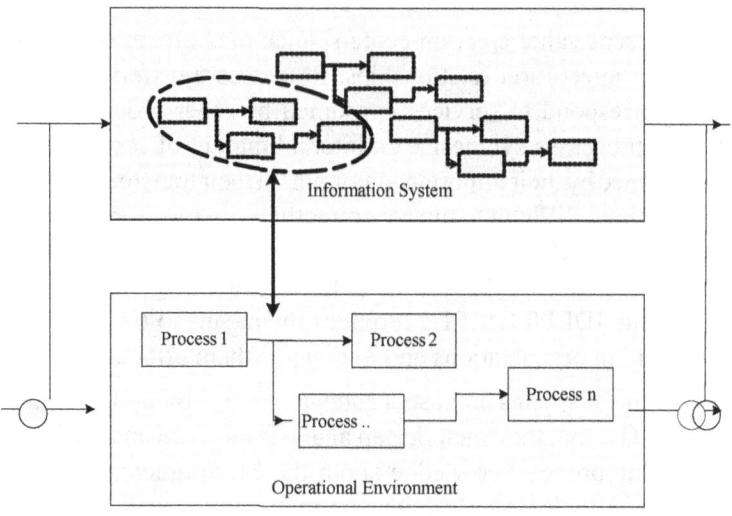

Figure 3. Feedback loops

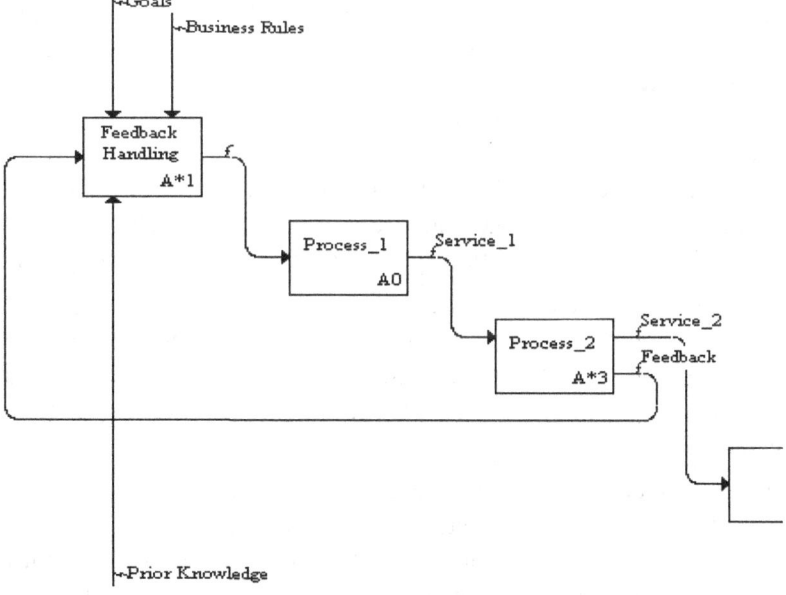

Finally, the visualization of the feedback loop mechanisms and their incorporation in an IS architectural paradigm can support the management of value creation mechanism and organizational learning.

Processes represent value creation centers since they are associated with a scope and involved in interaction relationships. Processes transform inputs to valuable outputs that correspond to services consumed by other processes. Subsequently, organizational processes synthesize an internal market of services whose value is directly determined by their importance as inputs at their transformation mechanisms. However, it is rather difficult to manage directly those transformation mechanisms. Alternatively, feedback loop mechanisms establish a typology of input-outputs allowing the production of the desired outputs by altering the inputs of a process. Subsequently, the IDEF0/IDEF1X provides the means to trace the value creation mechanisms within organizations and to manage them effectively.

Feedback loop mechanisms are also a gateway to improving learning effects. This stems from the fact that they include gap analysis mechanisms. The outcome of the gap analysis is improved knowledge about the environmental responses towards specific actions. This learning mechanism may be managed and improved by IS developed under the dictations of the IDEF0/IDEF1X.

Introducing the A/R-A/P Transaction Cycle

Contemporary business environments consist of complex amalgams of entities and processes, which interact within the context of business transactions (Colantoni, Manes, & Whinston, 1971). Business transaction cycles comprise the operational environment of organizations and can be broadly grouped into four basic categories: *revenue, expenditure, financial* and *production*. The revenue cycle encompasses the marketing-related activities of the firm. The financial cycle concerns financing and investing activities. The expenditure cycle includes purchasing goods/services and assets. Finally, the production cycle involves the production process.

Each operating cycle interfaces with the others. For instance, production planning relies on the information from the marketing department regarding sales forecast. Subsequently, many business transactions expand across the boundaries of several operating cycles, such as *account receivables* and *account payables* transaction cycle.

Accounts receivables (A/R) are the money owed by customers (individuals or corporations) to the organization in exchange for goods or services that have been delivered or used but not yet paid for (e.g., the value of the issued invoices or shipments that have not yet been paid). They usually come in the form of operating lines of credit and are typically due within a relatively short time period, ranging from a few days or weeks to a year.

Accounts payable (A/P) are debts that must be paid off within a given time period, in order to avoid defaulting. Thus, the purpose of the A/R-A/P transaction cycle is to provide goods/services and to keep track of these charges on credits and the corresponding payments.

In order to keep track of unsettled receipts and payments, A/R-A/P transaction cycle must support at least:

1. The registration (posting) of outgoing and incoming invoices, usually originating in separate sales and purchasing systems.

2. The registration of outgoing and incoming payments, usually received through a bank or other external settlement agency.

3. The matching of the payments against the invoices.

4. Identification of business differences with customers and suppliers that have lead to discrepancies between debts and payments.

5. The registration of adjustments or corrections that arise as a result of resolving differences with debtors and creditors (customers and suppliers).

Understanding the dynamics of A/R-A/P transaction cycle has significant impact on the financial wealth of organizations. Account receivables represent a large proportion of their working capital, especially in commercial organizations. In a similar way, the account payables is the value in shipments or invoices received that have not been paid and is likewise an important liability. If an organization fails to implement the A/R-A/P transaction cycle efficiently, it may cause imbalances between cash inflows and outflows undermining the financial credibility of the organization.

The A/R-A/P transaction cycle has also a strategic role, since it provides the basis for the establishment of the input/output relationships of the organization with the environment, thus the opportunity for service exchanges with the environment. The new opportunities presented by thinking of the A/R-A/P transaction cycle in service terms are discussed in the next section.

The Importance of Modeling the A/R-A/P Transaction Cycle

The predominant perception of managers that A/R-A/P related information is extracted exclusively from the accounting recording systems has imposed *general ledger* as the central transaction recording process of A/R-A/P transaction cycle. General ledger is the record to which monetary transactions (debits and credits) are posted and is the final record from which financial statements are prepared. However, adopting a general ledger approach at the core of the development effort for information systems support for A/R-A/P transactions serves only to satisfy the accounting information requirements imposed by financial authorities. This approach overemphasizes the accounting informational perspective, ignoring inherent characteristics of the A/R-A/P transaction cycle and their potential managerial implications.

The A/R-A/P transaction cycle is a critical element of the operational environment and therefore provides services derived from combining processes, activities, resources, and information to other cross-boundaries processes. It establishes dynamic relationships that can barely be described by focusing only at their informational perspective. A general ledger also captures only a part of this information, since:

1. Most information elements have more fields. For instance, an A/R-A/P entry includes a due date, which is not included in the general ledger entry. These information elements are for the most part straightforward extensions of those found in the general ledger.

2. Services can include operations, which use this extended information. For instance, it is possible to retrieve transactions based on their settlement status.

3. Additional, specific services can support the A/R-A/P functions of reconciliation and the discovery of differences with respect to trading partners.

4. The A/R-A/P provides limited support for storage and retrieval of entries, such as commitments, at earlier points in the transaction life cycle than traditional accounting.

It is obvious, therefore, that an IS infrastructure supporting the A/R-A/P transaction cycle cannot rely on the consolidation of information under the dictations of the traditional accounting paradigm. An IS infrastructure must address the service-oriented character of the A/R-A/P transaction cycle and the requirements to manage them under the conditions of servicing agents cross-boundaries (i.e., suppliers, customers, etc.).

A service-oriented approach to IS for A/R-A/P is a vehicle for improving management efficiency in modern competitive environments. Modeling the A/R-A/P processes in the context of the supporting IS infrastructure does not serve only to provide developers with abstract descriptions of the complicated environments in order to improve the life-cycle development of the IS. It should be incorporated as a functional characteristic of information systems operated by managers, so that it enhances their abilities to diagnose the problematic areas of A/R-A/P transaction cycle to draw the alternatives solutions and to select the optimum in the context of corporate strategic planning.

Modeling business services in A/R-A/P must therefore consider the following:

1. The flow of information and resources amongst activities and processes.
2. The mechanisms supporting the operation of an activity.
3. The role of organizational groups in the context of controlling operational activities and processes.
4. The feedback handling mechanisms used by organizational groups to manage the A/R-A/P transaction cycle.

Modeling A/R-A/P Services with IDEF0 and IDEF1X

IDEF0 and IDEF1X, as presented in Chapter VII, draw on the principles of general systems theory and provide constructs that can be used to resolve the complexity of systems and to contribute to the design of service-oriented applications for A/R-A/P, capable to operate within complex operational environments.

As we stated in Chapter VI, in general systems theory, organizations are perceived as real systems open to, and interacting with, their environments, which can acquire new properties through continual evolution. Rather than reducing an entity such as an organization to the properties of its parts or elements (i.e., departments or processes), systems theory focuses on the arrangement of, and relations between, the parts that connect them into a whole. This particular organization determines a system, which is independent of the concrete substance of the elements (e.g., people, information). Thus, the same concepts and principles of organization underlie the different disciplines (accounting, management, finance, learning theory, etc.), providing a basis for their unification. Such unification enables the development of an improved understanding of the organization and an expansion of the possibilities to integrate theories and techniques from a wide range of scientific fields (e.g., information systems, strategic management, operational research, organizational learning), in order to facilitate the management of modern organizations. Systems concepts include *system-environment boundary, input, output, process, activities, state, hierarchy, goal-directedness,* and *information flow.* On the other hand, IDEF0 and IDEF1X semantics include all the above concepts and enables us to describe organizations systems, to clarify the boundaries of processes allocated within them, and to model them by applying general systems theory. IDEF0 and IDEF1X semantics enable us to resolve the complexity of systems dynamics by separating those relationships that are crucial for the success of the organization to response at the organizational challenges. This can be achieved by determining the scope (i.e., strategic goals, mission) of the organization. Defining organizational scope is essential for clarifying the boundaries of processes in terms of interrelationships developed with respect to other internal processes or external entities. These interrelationships are associated with the organizational scope, because each process contributes to the achievement of the scope by directing its outputs properly. Such outputs are the services that organizational processes exchange between them at the context of organizational operational environment. Once the internal processes are determined, we can use a systems approach to describe their interrelationships.

A/R-A/P process modeling using IDEF0/IDEF1X is a case of applying general systems theory to an organization. In fact, by modeling the A/R-A/P-related processes, we can visualize the backbone of the operational environment for the organizations. For simplicity reasons, in the following sections we will examine accounts receivable and accounts payable processes separately. For each process, we analyze the subprocesses and activities using the IDEF-based approach we introduced in Chapter VII.

Service Identification in the A/R Process

From an accounting perspective, account receivables represent the portion of total sales that are expected to be collected in the direct future (i.e., usually, within a year). A/R processes provide further information, such as the date of transaction, the amount of account receivables, bad debts, and so on. Organizations use this information to structure and implement various management activities, such as working capital management, credit policies, stock management, and so on. Although this information is useful to evaluate the effectiveness of the aforementioned management activities, it is rather abstract to draw safe clues regarding the reasons causing the variability of this effectiveness. This requires analyzing A/R processes further in order to identify useful services.

The basic A/R processes are associated with the revenue cycle of the transaction-oriented enterprise cycle, since account receivables emerge as a result of the selling procedures. The processes involved at the revenue cycle are the following:

1. Sales order management
2. Sales invoicing
3. General ledger posting
4. Receivables collection
5. Shipping management

Sales Order Management

Sales order management is essentially a set of services regulated by controls and rules as to how salespeople record a sale. The services are executed in the following order:

1. A customer places a *purchase request.*

2. A salesperson then prepares a *sales order*, which is a record of the customer's purchase request.

3. Salespersons propose a *quotation* considering the sales order.

4. In case the *quotation is rejected*, salespersons formulate a new quotation proposal.

5. Once the quotation proposal is accepted, the sales order is *approved.*

The sales order management process thus relies on the dynamic exchange of information between salespersons and customers. Customers define their expectations and restrictions and salespersons try to satisfy them according to the marketing, strategic, promotional, and price policies imposed by their organization. When an agreement is reached and the sales order is approved, the restrictions imposed

Figure 4. A/R processes

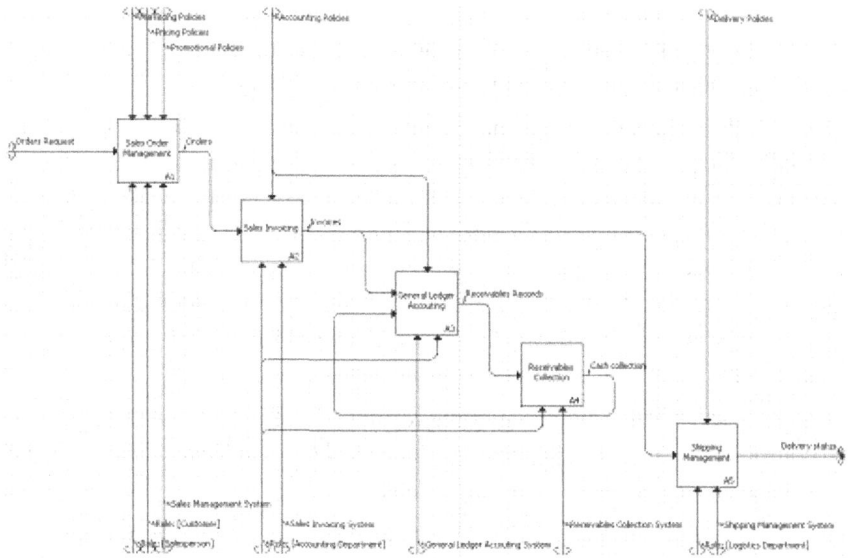

Figure 5. Sales order management diagram: [A-0]

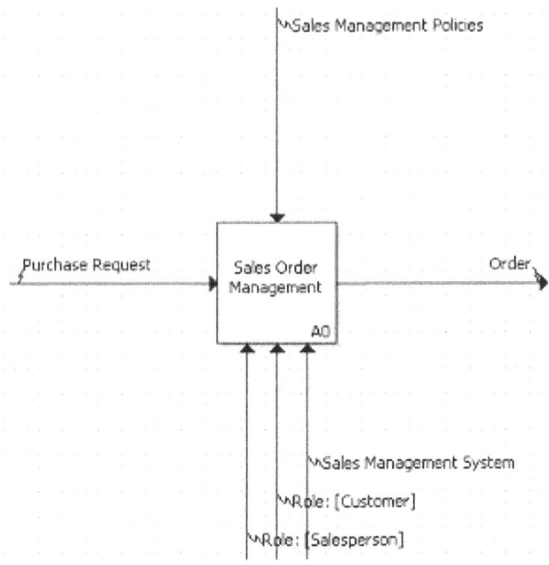

by both parties are finally met. This continuous exchange of information between salespersons and customers is modeled as a loop that is active until customer and salesperson reach an agreement. Such interaction between salespersons and customers can be modeled so that the customers can use one or more Web services to automate their requests and responses. We use the term *customers* to also include not only individual persons but whole organizations wishing to place an order. Thus, the service consumers are effectively the information systems of the customers, and the Web services automate the interaction with those systems.

IDEF0 Model: The sales order management service is modeled as shown in Figure 5. Initially, the process is modeled as service A0, taking as input a *Purchase Request* and producing as output an *Order*. The controls of the service are: *Marketing Policies, Pricing Policies, Promotional Policies, Purchase Request Policies, Sales Policies, Customers Policy* and *Quotation Policies*. Finally, the mechanisms that implement this service are the *Automated Recording Role,* the *Customer/Automated System,* the *Salesperson Role* and the *Sales Management Systems*. All these constructs will be used in the next levels of details of the service.

In Figure 6, sales order management is further decomposed in a number of services that comprise the service. These services are: *[A1] Record Sales Order, [A2] Provide Quotation,* and *[A3] Approve Sales Order*.

Service [A1] (*Record Sales Order*) takes as input the *Purchase Request* submitted by the customer. It validates it against the *Purchase Request Policies* imposed by the

Figure 6. Diagram [A0] sales order management

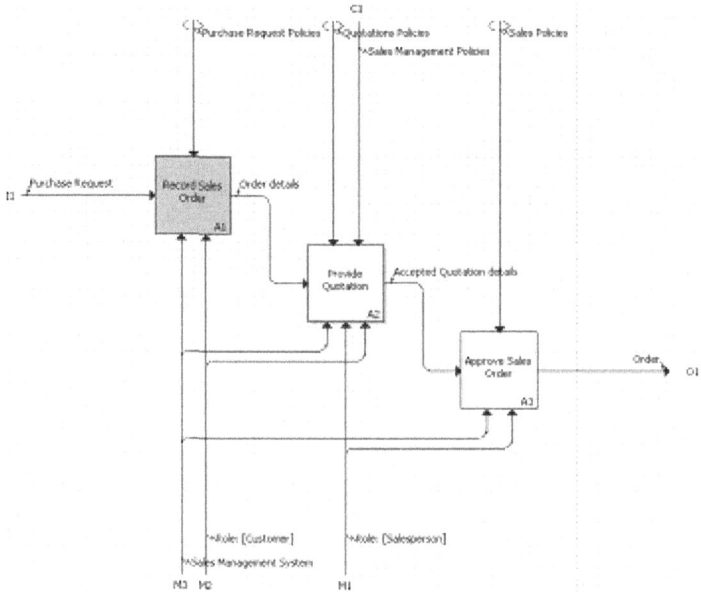

organization and, if the validation succeeds, the purchase request is automatically recorded in the internal system of the organization, using the software functions of the *Sales Management System*. After the completion of this service, the output *Order Details* provides input to the next service *Provide Quotation*. This service is a candidate service to be exposed as a Web service, because (a) it is concerned with the interaction of external entities (customers) with our system, and (b) it can be synchronous, as there is no human intervention during service execution. The *Role Automated Recording* implies the automatic execution (as a Web service) of this service.

Service [A2] (*Provide Quotation*) takes as input the *Order Details* produced by Service [A1] and uses a number of policies imposed by the organization and the software functions of the sales management system. Two kinds of roles are employed in this service: *Customer/Automated System* and *Salesperson*. The output of this service is *Accepted Quotation Details* that provides the input to the next service approve sales order.

This service is further decomposed in 3 services (i.e., it is not atomic, and therefore it is not a candidate service to be exposed as Web service). We will examine later on whether any of its component services can be exposed as a Web service.

Service [A3] (*Approve Sales Order*) takes as input the *Accepted Quotation Details* produced by service [A2] and validates it against the *Sales Policies* imposed by the

Figure 7. Diagram: [A2] provide quotation

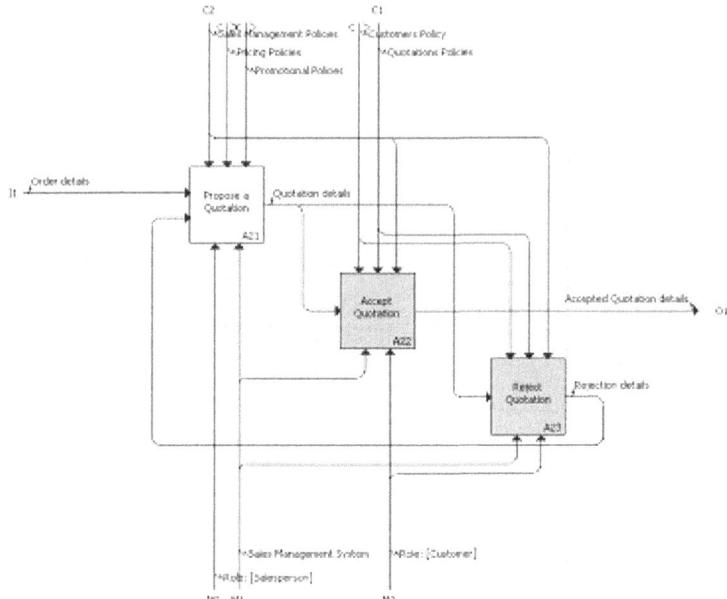

organization. In case the validation succeeds, the service uses the software functions of the *Sales Management System* in order to save internally the new status of the order. The service is performed by the role *Salesperson*, and its output is *Order*. However, as it concerns an internal function of the system, this is not a candidate service to be exposed as Web service.

After analyzing the services of *Diagram* [A0], we will now examine the decomposition of service [A2] (*Provide Quotation*). In the diagram of Figure 7, [A2] (*Provide Quotation*) is further decomposed in three services: [A21] (*Propose a Quotation*), [A22] (*Accept Quotation*), and [A23] (*Reject Quotation*).

Service [A21] (*Propose a Quotation*) takes as input the *Order Details*, uses the software functions of the sales management system, and by following the *Marketing, Pricing,* and *Promotional Policies*, produces the *Quotation Details* as output. The service is performed by a user that has the role of *Salesperson*. Moreover, as it concerns an internal function of the system, it is not a candidate service to be exposed as Web service.

Service [A22] (*Accept Quotation*), takes as input the *Quotation Details* produced by *Propose a Quotation* and validates it against the *Customers Policies* and *Quotations* imposed by the organization. If the validation succeeds, the accepted quotation is automatically recorded in the internal system of the organization using the software functions of the sales management system. The output produced is the *Accepted Quotation Details*. This service is a candidate service to be exposed as Web service, because (a) it is concerned with the interaction between external entities (customers) and the system and (b) it can be synchronous, as there is no human intervention in the service realization role *Customer/Automated System,* which implies automatic execution.

Service [A23] (*Reject Quotation*): This service takes as input the *Quotation Details* produced by *Propose a Quotation*, it validates it against the *Customers Policies* and *Quotations Policies* imposed by the organization and, if the validation succeeds, the rejected quotation is automatically recorded in the internal system of the organization, using the software functions of the sales management system. The output produced is the *Rejection Details* that acts as feedback to service *Propose a Quotation*. This service is a candidate service to be exposed as Web service, because (a) it is concerned with the interaction of external entities (customers) with the system, and (b) it can be synchronous, as there is no human intervention in the service realization role *Customer/Automated System*, which implies automatic execution.

Web Services: As discussed in the analysis of the business services, the candidate Web services of the sales order management process are:

1. A1 [Record Sales Order]
   Input: Purchase Request
   Output: Order Details
   Role: Salesperson
2. A22 [Accept Quotation]
   Input: Quotation Details
   Output: Accepted Quotation Details
   Role: Customer/Automated System
3. A23 [Reject Quotation]
   Input: Quotation Details
   Output: Rejection Details
   Role: Customer/Automated System

In order to realize these Web services, we need to carry out the following steps:

* Derive the information models of their inputs and outputs using the IDEF1X notation, as explained in Chapter VII. Recall from Chapter VII that the IDEF1X model for the top-level business service is derived after IDEF0 has completed.

The information model of the services will be a subset of the general IDEF1X model.

- From the IDEF1X model of the services, we derive the WSDL (see Chapter III) of the services (i.e., the service's *interface*).

- If the Web services collaborate to deliver the business service, then we draw an *interaction diagram* showing the collaboration between the Web services. This diagram will be used to automate the collaboration of services using a technology such as BPEL4WS (see Chapter IV).

- If the service simply transforms inputs to outputs, we define the XML (XSD) schemas of inputs and outputs and then define the XSLT transformations of the input XSD to the output XSD (see Chapter VII).

- For services involving more complex logic, we design the objects that will realize the business logic. Such objects will execute scripts such as the ones presented in Chapter VII. At this stage, we also implement any data-access logic required by the service.

- Finally, we deploy the service components (WSDL, BPEL4WS scripts, objects, database schemas, etc.) in a service execution environment which publishes the services interfaces on some kind of UDDI type of registry (see Chapter III) and handles client requests received as SOAP messages (see Chapter III).

The aforementioned steps are detailed in the following sections. The service execution environment used for the examples, CLMS platform, was discussed in Chapter IX.

Figure 8. First interaction diagram

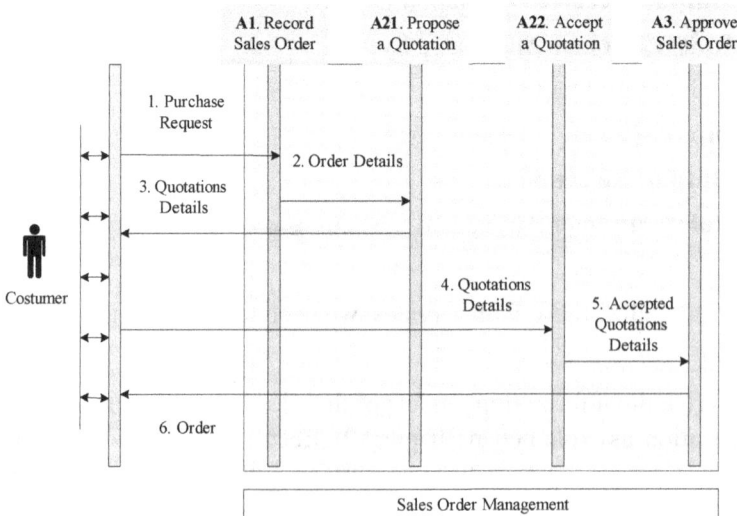

Service Design

Service Interaction Diagrams

In this section, we present the interaction diagrams that show the sequence of interactions between the service consumer and the Web services comprising the sale order management system. *Interaction diagrams* is a technique we borrow from object-oriented analysis and design methods (UML) to show how objects collaborate by exchanging messages. In our case study, IDEF0 activities play the role of the objects. There are three different interaction diagrams, showing the three different possible interactions:

1. **First case (Figure 8):** Customer submits a Purchase Request (step 1), and when he or she receives back the Quotation Details (step 3) the customer accepts the Quotation (step 4) and he or she receives back the placed order (step 6).

2. **Second case (Figure 9):** Customer submits a Purchase Request (step 1), and when he or she receives back the Quotation Details (step 3), the customer rejects the Quotation (step 4). When the sales order management system records the rejected quotation (Activity A23), based on the Customer's and Quotations Policies, it doesn't activate Activity A21 in order to make a new quotation proposal, and the interaction ends.

Figure 9. Second interaction diagram

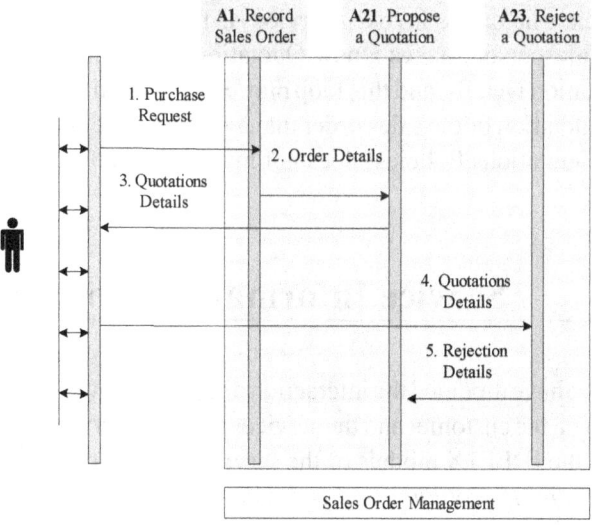

Figure 10. Third interaction diagram

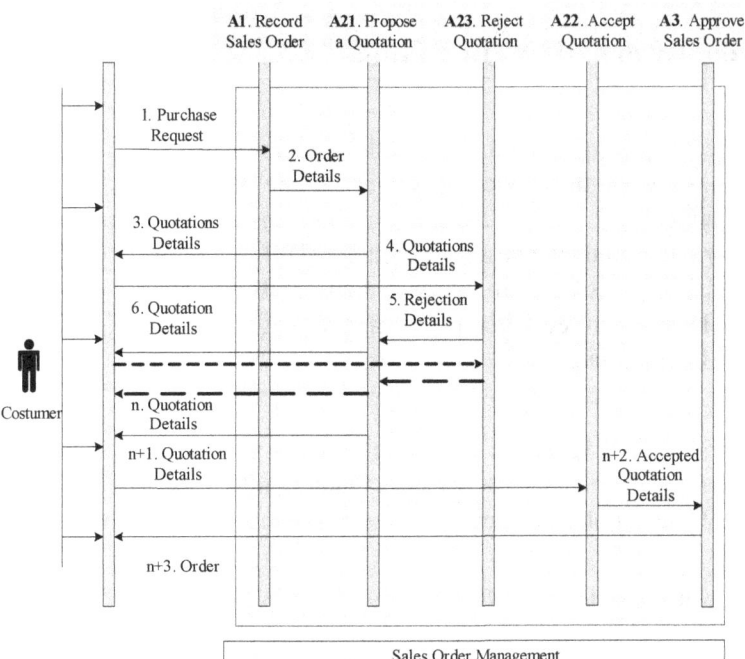

3.   **Third case (Figure 10):** Customer submits a Purchase Request (step 1), and when he or she receives back the Quotation Details (step 3), the customer rejects the Quotation (step 4). When the sales order management system records the Rejected Quotation (service A23), based on the Customer's and Quotations Policies, he or she invokes service A21 via the feedback loop (step 5 & step 6). Salesperson makes a new Quotation Proposal, the customer receives the Quotation Details, and this loop may continue until either the customer accepts the quotation or the sales order management system (based on the Customer's and Quotations Policies) does not invoke service A21.

Service Information Modeling

Now that we have modeled the interaction diagrams showing the sequence of interactions between the customer and the services of the sale order management system, we can define the IDEF1X models of the services' input and output resources, namely *purchase request, quotation,* and *order.*

As shown in Figure 11, *purchase request* has the *PurchaseRequestID* as the identity key, *DateIssued* as the date that the purchase request was issued, *SerialNumber* as a serial number of the purchase request, and a *CustomerID* that uniquely identifies the customer that has sent the purchase request.

The Detail section has the *PurchaseRequestDetailID* as the identity key, *PurchaseRequestID* as the foreign key of the Master section, *ProductCode* that uniquely identifies the product that the customer wish to buy, Quantity that specifies the quantity for the product that the customer wish to buy, and *DueDate* that specifies until when the customer wishes to have the products delivered.

As shown in Figure 12, *quotation* has *QuotationdID* as the identity key, *SerialNumber* as a serial number of the quotation, *DateIssued* as the date that the quotation was issued, a *PurchaseRequestID* that uniquely relates the quotation with a submitted purchase request, a *CustomerID* that uniquely identifies the customer that the quotation concerns, and a *Salesperson* that refers to the salesperson who made the quotation.

In the Detail section, it has the *QuotationdDetailID* as the identity key, *QuotationID* as the foreign key of the Master section, a *ProductCode* that uniquely identifies a product, *QuotedQuantity* that specifies the quantity quoted, *QuotedPrice* that specifies the price quoted, and *DeliveryDate* that specifies when the product with the quoted quantity and price will be delivered to the customer.

Figure 11. Purchase request's IDEF1X diagram

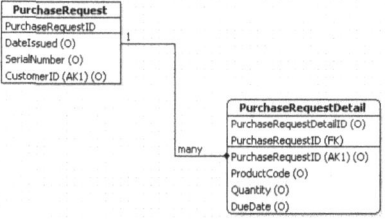

Figure 12. IDEF1 diagram for quotations

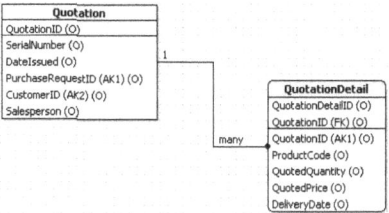

Figure 13. IDEF1X diagram for order

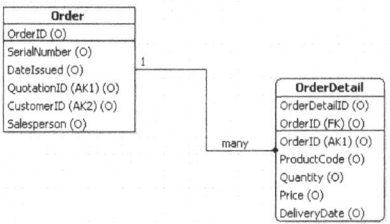

As shown in Figure 13, Order has *OrderID* as the identity key, *SerialNumber* as a serial number of the order, *DateIssued* as the date that the order was issued, a *QuotationID* that uniquely relates the order with a quotation, a *CustomerID* that uniquely identifies the customer that the order concerns, and a *Salesperson* that refers to the salesperson who is responsible for the order. In the Detail section, it has the *OrderDetailID* as the identity key, *OrderID* as the foreign key of the Master section, *ProductCode* that uniquely identifies a product, *Quantity* that specifies the ordered quantity, *Price* that specifies the price, and *DeliveryDate* that specifies when the product with the ordered quantity and the agreed price will be delivered to the customer.

Creating the Input and Output XSDs

In this section, we show the XSD models for the inputs and outputs of the identified Web services.

A1 [Record Sales Order] **Input:** Purchase Request

The input XSD is shown in Listing 1.
The Output: XSD **Quotation details** is shown in Listing 2.

Role: Salesperson
Web service A22 [Accept Quotation]
Input: Quotation details
Output: Accepted Quotation details

Listing 1. Input XSD for purchase requests

```xml
<?xml version="1.0" encoding="UTF-8"?>
<schema targetNamespace="http://www.clms-uk.com/PR" xmlns="http://www.w3.org/2001/
XMLSchema" elementFormDefault="unqualified" attributeFormDefault="unqualified">
        <element name="PurchaseRequest">
                <complexType>
                        <sequence>
                                <element name="PurchaseRequestID" type="int"/>
                                <element name="DateIssued" type="string"/>
                                <element name="SerialNumber" type="string"/>
                                <element name="CustomerID" type="int"/>
                                <element name="PurchaseRequestDetails">
                                        <complexType>
                                                <sequence>
                                                        <element name="Purchas
eRequestDetail" minOccurs="0" maxOccurs="unbounded">
                                                                <complexType>
                                                                <sequence>


        <element name="PurchaseRequestDetailID" type="int"/>

        <element name="PurchaseRequestID" type="int"/>

        <element name="ProductCode" type="string"/>

        <element name="Quantity" type="decimal"/>

        <element name="DueDate" type="date"/>
                                                                </sequence>
                                                                </complexType>
                                                        </element>
                                                </sequence>
                                        </complexType>
                                </element>
                        </sequence>
                </complexType>
        </element>
</schema>
```

This is shown in Listing 3.

Web service A23 [Reject Quotation]

Input: Quotation details

The input XSD is shown in Listing 2.

Listing 2. XSD for quotation details

```xml
<?xml version="1.0" encoding="UTF-8"?>
<schema targetNamespace="http://www.clms-uk.com/PR" xmlns="http://www.w3.org/2001/
XMLSchema" elementFormDefault="unqualified" attributeFormDefault="unqualified">
        <element name="Quotation">
                <complexType>
                        <sequence>
                                <element name="QuotationID" type="int"/>
                                <element name="SerialNumber" type="string"/>
                                <element name="DateIssued" type="string"/>
                                <element name="Salesperson" type="string"/>
                                <element name="CustomerID" type="int"/>
                                <element name="QuotationDetails">
                                        <complexType>
                                                <sequence>
                                                        <element
 name="QuotationDetail" minOccurs="0" maxOccurs="unbounded">
                                                                <complexType>
                                                                <sequence>

        <element name="QuotationDetailID" type="int"/>

        <element name="QuotationID" type="int"/>

        <element name="ProductCode" type="string"/>

        <element name="QuotedQuantity" type="decimal"/>

        <element name="QuotedPrice" type="decimal"/>

        <element name="DeliveryDate" type="date"/>

                                                                </sequence>
                                                                </complexType>
```

continued on following page

Listing 2. continued

```
                                                            </element>
                                                        </sequence>
                                                    </complexType>
                                                </element>
                                            </sequence>
                                        </complexType>
                                    </element>
</schema>
```

Output: Rejection details

The output XSD is shown in Listing 4.

Once all the XSDs of the inputs-outputs of the Web services have been defined, then the WSDL files are generated. This activity can be automatic if supported by a suitable IDEF0/IDEF1X Editor.

Listing 3. XSD for accepted quotation

```
<?xml version="1.0" encoding="UTF-8"?>
<schema targetNamespace="http://www.clms-uk.com/PR" xmlns="http://www.w3.org/2001/
XMLSchema" elementFormDefault="unqualified" attributeFormDefault="unqualified">
        <element name="AcceptedQuotation">
                <complexType>
                    <sequence>
                        <element name="QuotationID" type="int"/>
                        <element name="SerialNumber" type="string"/>
                        <element name="DateIssued" type="string"/>
                        <element name="Salesperson" type="string"/>
                        <element name="CustomerID" type="int"/>
                        <element name="QuotationDetails">
                            <complexType>
                                <sequence>
                                    <element
name="QuotationDetail" minOccurs="0" maxOccurs="unbounded">
                                        <complexType>
                                            <sequence>
```

continued on following page

Listing 3. XSD for accepted quotation (continued)

```
        <element name="QuotationDetailID" type="int"/>

        <element name="QuotationID" type="int"/>

        <element name="ProductCode" type="string"/>

        <element name="QuotedQuantity" type="decimal"/>

        <element name="QuotedPrice" type="decimal"/>

        <element name="DeliveryDate" type="date"/>
                                                    </sequence>
                                                </complexType>
                                            </element>
                                        </sequence>
                                    </complexType>
                                </element>
                            </sequence>
                        </complexType>
                    </element>
</schema>
```

Service Implementation

Now that we have defined the XSDs of the inputs-outputs of the Web services, we can generate the WSDL files using an IDEF0/IDEF1X Editor. The result is shown in Listing 5.

Implementing the A/R-A/P Services with CLMS Platform

In this section, we will show how the Web services offered to the customer and the sales order management system are implemented using the CLMS platform, which was described in Chapter IX.

Listing 4. XSD for rejected quotation

```xml
<?xml version="1.0" encoding="UTF-8"?>
<schema targetNamespace="http://www.clms-uk.com/PR" xmlns="http://www.w3.org/2001/
XMLSchema" elementFormDefault="unqualified" attributeFormDefault="unqualified">
        <element name="RejectedQuotation">
                <complexType>
                        <sequence>
                                <element name="QuotationID" type="int"/>
                                <element name="SerialNumber" type="string"/>
                                <element name="DateIssued" type="string"/>
                                <element name="Salesperson" type="string"/>
                                <element name="CustomerID" type="int"/>
                                <element name="QuotationDetails">
                                        <complexType>
                                                <sequence>
                                                        <element
name="QuotationDetail" minOccurs="0" maxOccurs="unbounded">
                                                                <complexType>
                                                                        <sequence>

        <element name="QuotationDetailID" type="int"/>

        <element name="QuotationID" type="int"/>

        <element name="ProductCode" type="string"/>

        <element name="QuotedQuantity" type="decimal"/>

        <element name="QuotedPrice" type="decimal"/>

        <element name="DeliveryDate" type="date"/>
                                                                        </sequence>
                                                                </complexType>
                                                        </element>
                                                </sequence>
                                        </complexType>
                                </element>
                        </sequence>
                </complexType>
        </element>
</schema>
```

The sequence of interactions between the service consumer and the Web services comprising the sale order management system are:

1.   Customer uses the *request for quotation service* Web service in order to submit their request (Figure 14)

Listing 5. Record sales order WSDL

```
<definitions xmlns:http="http://schemas.xmlsoap.org/wsdl/http/" xmlns:soap="http://schemas.
xmlsoap.org/wsdl/soap/" xmlns:s="http://www.w3.org/2001/XMLSchema" xmlns:s0="http://www.
clms.com/Web Service/" xmlns:soapenc="http://schemas.xmlsoap.org/soap/encoding/" xmlns:
tm="http://microsoft.com/wsdl/mime/textMatching/" xmlns:mime="http://schemas.xmlsoap.
org/wsdl/mime/" xmlns="http://schemas.xmlsoap.org/wsdl/" targetNamespace="http://www.clms.
com/Web Service/">
        <types>
                <schema targetNamespace="http://www.clms.com/Web Service/"
xmlns="http://www.w3.org/2000/10/XMLSchema">
                        <element name="PurchaseRequest">
                          <complexType>
                            <sequence>
                              <element
name="PurchaseRequestID" type="int"/>
                              <element name="DateIssued"
type="string"/>
                              <element name="SerialNumber"
type="string"/>
                              <element name="CustomerID"
type="int"/>
                              <element name="PurchaseRequest
Details">
                                <complexType>
                                  <sequence>
                                    <element
name="PurchaseRequestDetail" minOccurs="0" maxOccurs="unbounded">

        <complexType>

        <sequence>

        <element name="PurchaseRequestDetailID" type="int"/>

        <element name="PurchaseRequestID" type="int"/>
```

continued on following page

Listing 5. continued

```
            <element name="ProductCode" type="string"/>

            <element name="Quantity" type="decimal"/>

            <element name="DueDate" type="date"/>

            </sequence>

            </complexType>
                                                                    </element>
                                                                </sequence>
                                                            </complexType>
                                                        </element>
                                                    </sequence>
                                                </complexType>
                                            </element>
                                            <!--END Here goes the xsd of the Input of the Selected Activity-->
                            </schema>
            </types>
            <message name="SubmitEnvelopeSoapIn">
                    <part name="parameters" element="s0:PurchaseRequest"/>
            </message>
            <message name="SubmitEnvelopeSoapOut">
                    <part name="parameters"/>
            </message>
            <portType name="ActivityServiceSoap">
                    <operation name="SubmitEnvelope">
                            <input message="s0:SubmitEnvelopeSoapIn"/>
                            <output message="s0:SubmitEnvelopeSoapOut"/>
                    </operation>
            </portType>
            <binding name="ActivityServiceSoap" type="s0:ActivityServiceSoap">
                    <soap:binding style="document" transport="http://schemas.xmlsoap.org/
soap/http"/>
                    <operation name="SubmitEnvelope">
                            <soap:operation soapAction="http://www.clms.com/Web Service/
SubmitEnvelope" style="document"/>
                            <input>
                                    <soap:body use="literal"/>
                            </input>
                            <output>
                                    <soap:header message="SubmitEnvelopeSoapOut"
part="parameters" use="literal"/>
```

continued on following page

Listing 5. continued

```
                              <soap:body use="literal"/>
                    </output>
               </operation>
          </binding>
          <service name="RecordSalesOrder">
               <documentation>The location of the service is filled by the "Generate
WSDL" wizard</documentation>
                    <port name="ActivityServiceSoap" binding="s0:ActivityServiceSoap">
                         <soap:address location="http://www.clmsuk-com/Web services/"/>
                    </port>
          </service>
</definitions>
```

Listing 6. A22 [Accept Quotation] WSDL

```
<definitions xmlns:http="http://schemas.xmlsoap.org/wsdl/http/" xmlns:soap="http://schemas.
xmlsoap.org/wsdl/soap/" xmlns:s="http://www.w3.org/2001/XMLSchema" xmlns:s0="http://www.
clms.com/Web Service/" xmlns:soapenc="http://schemas.xmlsoap.org/soap/encoding/" xmlns:
tm="http://microsoft.com/wsdl/mime/textMatching/" xmlns:mime="http://schemas.xmlsoap.
org/wsdl/mime/" xmlns="http://schemas.xmlsoap.org/wsdl/" targetNamespace="http://www.clms.
com/Web Service/">
          <types>
                    <schema targetNamespace="http://www.clms.com/Web Service/"
xmlns="http://www.w3.org/2000/10/XMLSchema">
                              <element name="Quotation">
                                   <complexType>
                                        <sequence>
                                             <element name="QuotationID"
type="int"/>
                                             <element name="SerialNumber"
type="string"/>
                                             <element name="DateIssued"
type="string"/>
                                             <element name="Salesperson"
type="string"/>
                                             <element name="CustomerID"
type="int"/>
                                             <element name="QuotationDetails">
                                                  <complexType>
```

continued on following page

Listing 6. continued

```
                                                                      <sequence>
                                                                        <element
name="QuotationDetail" minOccurs="0" maxOccurs="unbounded">

        <complexType>

        <sequence>

        <element name="QuotationDetailID" type="int"/>

        <element name="QuotationID" type="int"/>

        <element name="ProductCode" type="string"/>

        <element name="QuotedQuantity" type="decimal"/>

        <element name="QuotedPrice" type="decimal"/>

        <element name="DeliveryDate" type="date"/>

        </sequence>

        </complexType>
                                                                    </element>
                                                                 </sequence>
                                                            </complexType>
                                                         </element>
                                                    </sequence>
                                                 </complexType>
                                         </element>
                              </schema>
                  </types>
                  <message name="SubmitEnvelopeSoapIn">
                        <part name="parameters" element="s0:Quotation"/>
                  </message>
                  <message name="SubmitEnvelopeSoapOut">
                        <part name="parameters"/>
                  </message>
                  <portType name="ActivityServiceSoap">
                        <operation name="SubmitEnvelope">
                              <input message="s0:SubmitEnvelopeSoapIn"/>
                              <output message="s0:SubmitEnvelopeSoapOut"/>
                        </operation>
```

continued on following page

Listing 6. continued

```
        </portType>
        <binding name="ActivityServiceSoap" type="s0:ActivityServiceSoap">
                <soap:binding style="document" transport="http://schemas.xmlsoap.org/
soap/http"/>
                <operation name="SubmitEnvelope">
                        <soap:operation soapAction="http://www.clms.com/Web Service/
SubmitEnvelope" style="document"/>
                        <input>
                                <soap:body use="literal"/>
                        </input>
                        <output>
                                <soap:header message="SubmitEnvelopeSoapOut"
part="parameters" use="literal"/>
                                <soap:body use="literal"/>
                        </output>
                </operation>
        </binding>
        <service name="AcceptQuotation">
                <documentation>The location of the service is filled by the "Generate
WSDL" wizard</documentation>
                <port name="ActivityServiceSoap" binding="s0:ActivityServiceSoap">
                        <soap:address location="http://www.clmsuk-com/Web services/"/>
                </port>
        </service>
</definitions>
```

Listing 7. A23 [Reject Quotation] WSDL

```
<definitions xmlns:http="http://schemas.xmlsoap.org/wsdl/http/" xmlns:soap="http://schemas.
xmlsoap.org/wsdl/soap/" xmlns:s="http://www.w3.org/2001/XMLSchema" xmlns:s0="http://www.
clms.com/Web Service/" xmlns:soapenc="http://schemas.xmlsoap.org/soap/encoding/" xmlns:
tm="http://microsoft.com/wsdl/mime/textMatching/" xmlns:mime="http://schemas.xmlsoap.
org/wsdl/mime/" xmlns="http://schemas.xmlsoap.org/wsdl/" targetNamespace="http://www.clms.
com/Web Service/">
        <types>
                <schema targetNamespace="http://www.clms.com/Web Service/"
xmlns="http://www.w3.org/2000/10/XMLSchema">
                        <element name="Quotation">
                                <complexType>
```

continued on following page

Listing 7. continued

```
                                        <sequence>
                                            <element name="QuotationID"
type="int"/>
                                            <element name="SerialNumber"
type="string"/>
                                            <element name="DateIssued"
type="string"/>
                                            <element name="Salesperson"
type="string"/>
                                            <element name="CustomerID"
type="int"/>
                                            <element name="QuotationDetails">
                                                <complexType>
                                                    <sequence>
                                                        <element
name="QuotationDetail" minOccurs="0" maxOccurs="unbounded">

        <complexType>

        <sequence>

        <element name="QuotationDetailID" type="int"/>

        <element name="QuotationID" type="int"/>

        <element name="ProductCode" type="string"/>

        <element name="QuotedQuantity" type="decimal"/>

        <element name="QuotedPrice" type="decimal"/>

        <element name="DeliveryDate" type="date"/>

        </sequence>

        </complexType>
                                                        </element>
                                                    </sequence>
                                                </complexType>
                                            </element>
                                        </sequence>
                                    </complexType>
                                </element>
```

<label>navigation</label>
continued on following page

Listing 7. continued

```
                    </schema>
            </types>
            <message name="SubmitEnvelopeSoapIn">
                    <part name="parameters" element="s0:Quotation"/>
            </message>
            <message name="SubmitEnvelopeSoapOut">
                    <part name="parameters"/>
            </message>
            <portType name="ActivityServiceSoap">
                    <operation name="SubmitEnvelope">
                            <input message="s0:SubmitEnvelopeSoapIn"/>
                            <output message="s0:SubmitEnvelopeSoapOut"/>
                    </operation>
            </portType>
            <binding name="ActivityServiceSoap" type="s0:ActivityServiceSoap">
                    <soap:binding style="document" transport="http://schemas.xmlsoap.org/
soap/http"/>
                    <operation name="SubmitEnvelope">
                            <soap:operation soapAction="http://www.clms.com/Web Service/
SubmitEnvelope" style="document"/>
                            <input>
                                    <soap:body use="literal"/>
                            </input>
                            <output>
                                    <soap:header message="SubmitEnvelopeSoapOut"
part="parameters" use="literal"/>
                                    <soap:body use="literal"/>
                            </output>
                    </operation>
            </binding>
            <service name="RejectQuotation">
                    <documentation>The location of the service is filled by the "Generate
WSDL" wizard</documentation>
                    <port name="ActivityServiceSoap" binding="s0:ActivityServiceSoap">
                            <soap:address location="http://www.clmsuk-com/Web services/"/>
                    </port>
            </service>
</definitions>
```

Figure 14. Invoking the request quotation service

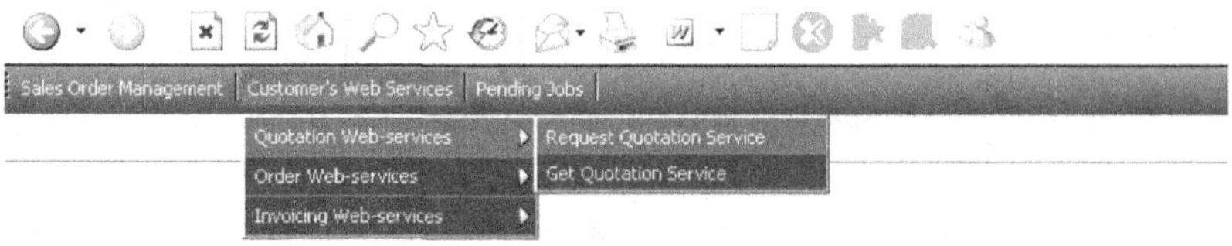

Figure 15. SOAP envelope generation

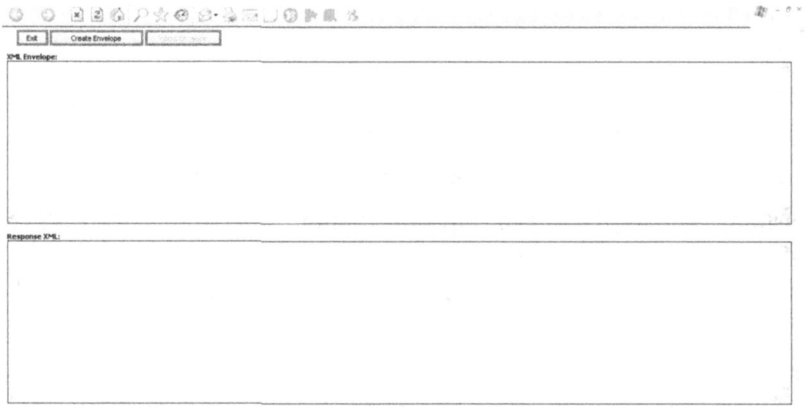

Figure 16. SOAP payload

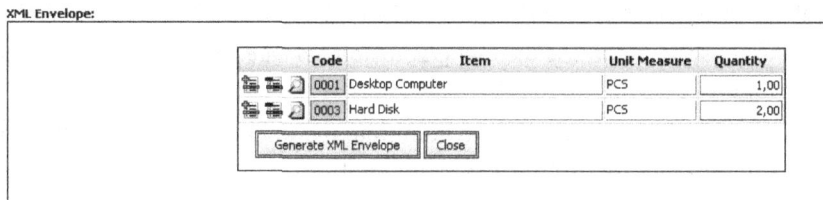

In Figure 15, we see the interface through which the customer generates the SOAP envelope that he will submit to the Web service.

Customer fills in a number of items that he wants to request quotation for (Figure 16).

Listing 8. Generated SOAP envelope

XML Envelope:

```
     view plain | print | copy to clipboard
 1   <SOAP-ENV:Envelope SOAP-ENV:encodingStyle="http://schemas.xmlsoap.org/soap/encoding/" xmlns:SOAP-ENV="http://schemas.xmlsoap.org/soap/envelope/">
 2     <SOAP-ENV:Header>
 3       <Role>Accountant</Role>
 4       <User>harry</User>
 5       <Action>Execute</Action>
 6       <ProgID>ERPCommerce.SALESQUOTE_MG.SALESQUOTE_INSERT</ProgID>
 7       <ProgID_Description/>
 8       <PendingJob></PendingJob>
 9       <InstanceID/>
10       <SystemID>{51E5742F674C4E67A66A0403F0DE1F5426120061461S}</SystemID>
11       <ReferenceASP>RemoteIP: 88.218.11.74  Resource: /BusinessServicesDemo/forms/CustReqSalesQuote.asp</ReferenceASP>
12       <LinkedServer>
13         <LinkedServerInstanceID/>
14         <InitiatorsSystemID/>
15         <LinkedServer/>
16         <InitiatorsListener/>
17       </LinkedServer>
```

After finishing, he or she presses the *Generate XML Envelope* button, and the *XML Envelope* text area shows the SOAP envelope that is ready to be sent (Listing 8).

The SOAP envelope that will be submitted is shown in Listing 9.

Customer presses the *Submit Envelope* button, and the SOAP envelope is submitted to the Web service. The response is shown in the *Response XML* text area. The interface also shows what the Quotation Token is; in our example, the value 58 (Figure 17).

The SOAP envelope that the customer receives back is shown in Listing 10.

Now that the request for quotation has been submitted, if we check at the pending jobs of the system, we find that a Salesperson has to create a new Quotation (Figure 18).

A Salesperson click on the pending job and, in the following interface, he or she has to create the new quotation, based on the requested quotation from the customer.

The Salesperson completes the Unit price for the quoted items and clicks on the *Save & Send* button.

Now the customer can use the *Get Quotation Service* in order to retrieve the Quotation (Figure 21).

In Figure 22, the customer has to complete the quotation token (with value 58, in our example), in order to retrieve the quotation.

The retrieved SOAP envelope that contains the quotation is shown in Listing 11.

Now the Customer may examine the quotation and may decide to place an order or not.

If he or she decides to submit an order based on the quotation, the Customer uses the *Submit Order Service* (Figure 23).

Listing 9. Submitted SOAP envelope

```
<SOAP-ENV:Envelope SOAP-ENV:encodingStyle="http://schemas.xmlsoap.org/soap/
encoding/" xmlns:SOAP-ENV="http://schemas.xmlsoap.org/soap/envelope/">
        <SOAP-ENV:Header>
                <Role>Accountant</Role>
                <User>harry</User>
                <Action>Execute</Action>
                <ProgID>ERPCommerce.SALESQUOTE_MG.SALESQUOTE_INSERT</
ProgID>
                <ProgID_Description/>
                <PendingJob/>
                <InstanceID/>
                <SystemID>{51E5742F674C4E67A66A0403F0DE1F54261200614615}</
SystemID>
                <ReferenceASP>RemoteIP: 88.218.11.74  Resource: /
BusinessServicesDemo/forms/CustReqSalesQuote.asp</ReferenceASP>
                <LinkedServer>
                        <LinkedServerInstanceID/>
                        <InitiatorsSystemID/>
                        <LinkedServer/>
                        <InitiatorsListener/>
                </LinkedServer>
        </SOAP-ENV:Header>
        <SOAP ENV:Body>
                <SalesQuote>
                        <SalesQuoteID>-1</SalesQuoteID>
                        <OrderID>-1</OrderID>
                        <OrderSerialNumber/>
                        <OrderDateIssued/>
                        <BusinessPartnerID>35</BusinessPartnerID>
                        <PartnerCode/>
                        <PartnerName>Demo Customer</PartnerName>
                        <TaxData/>
                        <Address/>
                        <City/>
                        <Area/>
                        <PostalCode/>
                        <Country/>
                        <PhoneNumber1/>
                        <PhoneNumber2/>
                        <IssuedByEmployeeID>-1</IssuedByEmployeeID>
                        <SerialNumber/>
                        <SeriesID>-1</SeriesID>
                        <SeriesName/>
```

continued on following page

Listing 9. continued

```xml
<SeriesDescription/>
<DateIssued/>
<TotalAmount>0,00</TotalAmount>
<Notes/>
<FiscalYearID>3</FiscalYearID>
<Void>0</Void>
<Temporary>-1</Temporary>
<SQLTimestamp/>
<ApplicationID>{51E5742F674C4E67A66A0403F0DE1F54261200614615}</ApplicationID>
<Employee>
        <Code/>
        <FirstName/>
        <LastName/>
</Employee>
<SalesQuoteDetails>
        <SalesQuoteDetail>
                <SalesQuoteDetailID>-1</SalesQuoteDetailID>
                <SalesQuoteID>-1</SalesQuoteID>
                <ItemID>13</ItemID>
                <ItemDetailID>-1</ItemDetailID>
                <UnitMeasureID>26</UnitMeasureID>
                <UnitMeasureName/>
                <UnitMeasureDecimalPlaces>0</UnitMeasureDecimalPlaces>
                <ItemQuantity>1</ItemQuantity>
                <ItemUnitPrice>0,00</ItemUnitPrice>
                <ItemDiscountPercent>0,00</ItemDiscountPercent>
                <Item>
                        <Code/>
                        <Name/>
                        <DetailCode/>
                        <DetailName/>
                        <Description/>
                        <RetailUnitPrice>0,00</RetailUnitPrice>
                        <WholeUnitPrice>0,00</WholeUnitPrice>
                        <Discontinued>0</Discontinued>
                        <Assembled>0</Assembled>
                        <Serialised>0</Serialised>
```

continued on following page

Listing 9. continued

```
MinimumQuantityRequired>                              <MinimumQuantityRequired>0</

                                                      <ReorderQuantityLevel>0</
ReorderQuantityLevel>
                                                      <SalesUnitMeasureID>-1</
SalesUnitMeasureID>
                                                      <SalesUnitMeasureName/>
                                                      <PurchaseUnitMeasureID>-1</
PurchaseUnitMeasureID>
                                                      <PurchaseUnitMeasureName/>
                                                      <StockUnitMeasureID>-1</
StockUnitMeasureID>
                                                      <StockUnitMeasureName/>
                                                      <SalesTaxRateID>-1</
SalesTaxRateID>
                                                      <TaxRate>
                                                              <TaxRateName/>
                                                              <TaxRateCode/>
                                                              <TaxPercent>0,00</
TaxPercent>
                                                      </TaxRate>
                                                      <Balance>0</Balance>
                                              </Item>
                                      </SalesQuoteDetail>
                                      <SalesQuoteDetail>
                                              <SalesQuoteDetailID>-1</
SalesQuoteDetailID>
                                              <SalesQuoteID>-1</SalesQuoteID>
                                              <ItemID>16</ItemID>
                                              <ItemDetailID>-1</ItemDetailID>
                                              <UnitMeasureID>26</UnitMeasureID>
                                              <UnitMeasureName/>
                                              <UnitMeasureDecimalPlaces>0</
UnitMeasureDecimalPlaces>
                                              <ItemQuantity>2</ItemQuantity>
                                              <ItemUnitPrice>0,00</ItemUnitPrice>
                                              <ItemDiscountPercent>0,00</
ItemDiscountPercent>
                                              <Item>
                                                      <Code/>
                                                      <Name/>
                                                      <DetailCode/>
                                                      <DetailName/>
```

continued on following page

Listing 9. continued

```
                                              <DetailName/>
                                              <Description/>
                                              <RetailUnitPrice>0,00</
RetailUnitPrice>
                                              <WholeUnitPrice>0,00</
WholeUnitPrice>
                                              <Discontinued>0</Discontinued>
                                              <Assembled>0</Assembled>
                                              <Serialised>0</Serialised>
                                              <MinimumQuantityRequired>0</
MinimumQuantityRequired>
                                              <ReorderQuantityLevel>0</
ReorderQuantityLevel>
                                              <SalesUnitMeasureID>-1</
SalesUnitMeasureID>
                                              <SalesUnitMeasureName/>
                                              <PurchaseUnitMeasureID>-1</
PurchaseUnitMeasureID>
                                              <PurchaseUnitMeasureName/>
                                              <StockUnitMeasureID>-1</
StockUnitMeasureID>
                                              <StockUnitMeasureName/>
                                              <SalesTaxRateID>-1</
SalesTaxRateID>
                                              <TaxRate>
                                                   <TaxRateName/>
                                                   <TaxRateCode/>
                                                   <TaxPercent>0,00</
TaxPercent>
                                              </TaxRate>
                                              <Balance>0</Balance>
                                    </Item>
                              </SalesQuoteDetail>
                        </SalesQuoteDetails>
                        <LanguageCode>English</LanguageCode>
                  </SalesQuote>
            </SOAP-ENV:Body>
</SOAP-ENV:Envelope>
```

Figure 17. Web service response

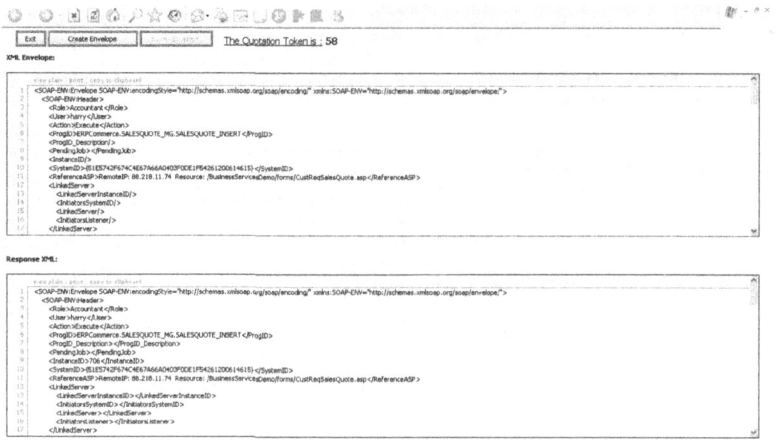

Listing 10. Received SOAP envelope

```
<SOAP-ENV:Envelope SOAP-ENV:encodingStyle="http://schemas.xmlsoap.org/soap/
encoding/" xmlns:SOAP-ENV="http://schemas.xmlsoap.org/soap/envelope/">
        <SOAP-ENV:Header>
                <Role>Accountant</Role>
                <User>harry</User>
                <Action>Execute</Action>
                <ProgID>ERPCommerce.SALESQUOTE_MG.SALESQUOTE_INSERT</
ProgID>
                <ProgID_Description/>
                <PendingJob/>
                <InstanceID>706</InstanceID>
                <SystemID>{51E5742F674C4E67A66A0403F0DE1F54261200614615}</
SystemID>
                <ReferenceASP>RemoteIP: 88.218.11.74  Resource: /
BusinessServicesDemo/forms/CustReqSalesQuote.asp</ReferenceASP>
                <LinkedServer>
                        <LinkedServerInstanceID/>
                        <InitiatorsSystemID/>
```

continued on following page

Listing 10. continued

```
                    <LinkedServer/>
                    <InitiatorsListener/>
            </LinkedServer>
        </SOAP-ENV:Header>
        <SOAP-ENV:Body>
            <SalesQuote>
                    <SalesQuoteID>58</SalesQuoteID>
                    <OrderID>-1</OrderID>
                    <OrderSerialNumber/>
                    <OrderDateIssued/>
                    <BusinessPartnerID>35</BusinessPartnerID>
                    <PartnerCode/>
                    <PartnerName>Demo Customer</PartnerName>
                    <TaxData/>
                    <Address/>
                    <City/>
                    <Area/>
                    <PostalCode/>
                    <Country/>
                    <PhoneNumber1/>
                    <PhoneNumber2/>
                    <IssuedByEmployeeID>-1</IssuedByEmployeeID>
                    <SerialNumber/>
                    <SeriesID>-1</SeriesID>
                    <SeriesName/>
                    <SeriesDescription/>
                    <DateIssued/>
                    <TotalAmount>0,00</TotalAmount>
                    <Notes/>
                    <FiscalYearID>3</FiscalYearID>
                    <Void>0</Void>
                    <Temporary>-1</Temporary>
                    <SQLTimestamp/>
                    <ApplicationID>{51E5742F674C4E67A66A0403F0DE1F5426120
0614615}</ApplicationID>

                    <Employee>
                            <Code/>
                            <FirstName/>
                            <LastName/>
                    </Employee>
                    <SalesQuoteDetails>
                            <SalesQuoteDetail>
                                    <SalesQuoteDetailID>32</
```

continued on following page

Listing 10. continued

```
/SalesQuoteDetailID>
                                    <SalesQuoteID>58</SalesQuoteID>
                                    <ItemID>13</ItemID>
                                    <ItemDetailID>-1</ItemDetailID>
                                    <UnitMeasureID>26</UnitMeasureID>
                                    <UnitMeasureName/>
                                    <UnitMeasureDecimalPlaces>0</
UnitMeasureDecimalPlaces>
                                    <ItemQuantity>1</ItemQuantity>
                                    <ItemUnitPrice>0,00</ItemUnitPrice>
                                    <ItemDiscountPercent>0,00</
ItemDiscountPercent>
                                    <Item>
                                            <Code/>
                                            <Name/>
                                            <DetailCode/>
                                            <DetailName/>
                                            <Description/>
                                            <RetailUnitPrice>0,00</
RetailUnitPrice>
                                            <WholeUnitPrice>0,00</
WholeUnitPrice>
                                            <Discontinued>0</Discontinued>
                                            <Assembled>0</Assembled>
                                            <Serialised>0</Serialised>
                                            <MinimumQuantityRequired>0</
MinimumQuantityRequired>
                                            <ReorderQuantityLevel>0</
ReorderQuantityLevel>
                                            <SalesUnitMeasureID>-1</
SalesUnitMeasureID>
                                            <SalesUnitMeasureName/>
                                            <PurchaseUnitMeasureID>-1</
PurchaseUnitMeasureID>
                                            <PurchaseUnitMeasureName/>
                                            <StockUnitMeasureID>-1</
StockUnitMeasureID>
                                            <StockUnitMeasureName/>
                                            <SalesTaxRateID>-1</
SalesTaxRateID>
                                            <TaxRate>
                                                    <TaxRateName/>
                                                    <TaxRateCode/>
```

continued on following page

Listing 10. continued

```
                                                      <TaxPercent>0,00</
TaxPercent>
                                              </TaxRate>
                                              <Balance>0</Balance>
                              </Item>
                      </SalesQuoteDetail>
                      <SalesQuoteDetail>
                              <SalesQuoteDetailID>33</
SalesQuoteDetailID>
                              <SalesQuoteID>58</SalesQuoteID>
                              <ItemID>16</ItemID>
                              <ItemDetailID>-1</ItemDetailID>
                              <UnitMeasureID>26</UnitMeasureID>
                              <UnitMeasureName/>
                              <UnitMeasureDecimalPlaces>0</
UnitMeasureDecimalPlaces>
                              <ItemQuantity>2</ItemQuantity>
                              <ItemUnitPrice>0,00</ItemUnitPrice>
                              <ItemDiscountPercent>0,00</
ItemDiscountPercent>
                              <Item>
                                      <Code/>
                                      <Name/>
                                      <DetailCode/>
                                      <DetailName/>
                                      <Description/>
                                      <RetailUnitPrice>0,00</
RetailUnitPrice>
                                      <WholeUnitPrice>0,00</
WholeUnitPrice>
                                      <Discontinued>0</Discontinued>
                                      <Assembled>0</Assembled>
                                      <Serialised>0</Serialised>
                                      <MinimumQuantityRequired>0</
MinimumQuantityRequired>
                                      <ReorderQuantityLevel>0</
ReorderQuantityLevel>
                                      <SalesUnitMeasureID>-1</
SalesUnitMeasureID>
                                      <SalesUnitMeasureName/>
                                      <PurchaseUnitMeasureID>-1</
PurchaseUnitMeasureID>
                                      <PurchaseUnitMeasureName/>
```

continued on following page

Listing 10. continued

```
                                                <StockUnitMeasureID>-1</
StockUnitMeasureID>

                                                <StockUnitMeasureName/>
                                                <SalesTaxRateID>-1</
SalesTaxRateID>
                                                    <TaxRate>
                                                        <TaxRateName/>
                                                        <TaxRateCode/>
                                                        <TaxPercent>0,00</
TaxPercent>
                                                    </TaxRate>
                                                    <Balance>0</Balance>
                                        </Item>
                                </SalesQuoteDetail>
                        </SalesQuoteDetails>
                        <LanguageCode>English</LanguageCode>
                        <CreatePending>true</CreatePending>
                </SalesQuote>
        </SOAP-ENV:Body>
</SOAP-ENV:Envelope>
```

Figure 18. Pending Jobs for accountant

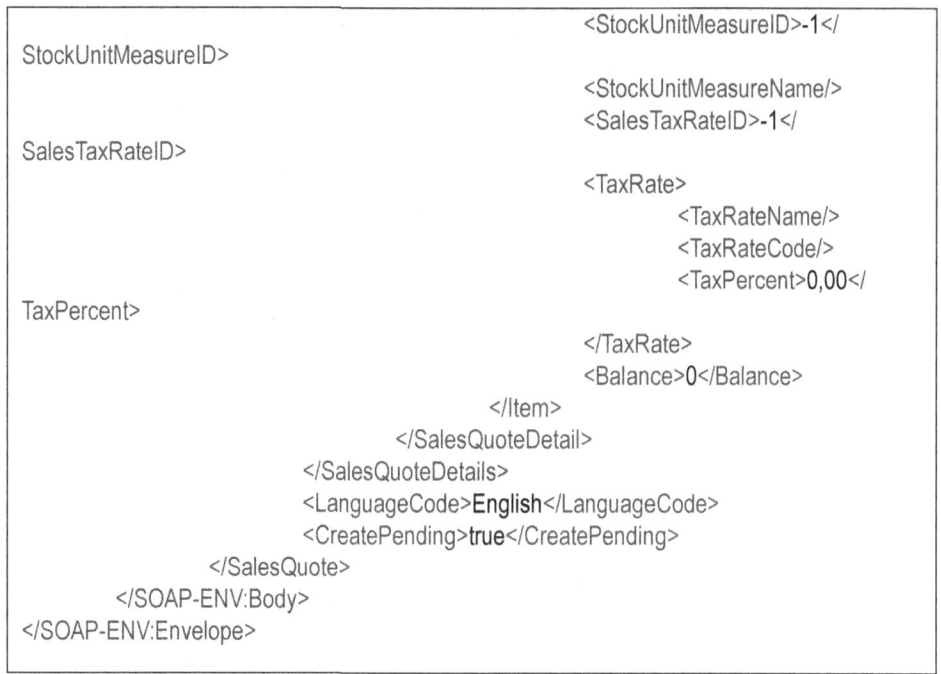

In Figure 24, the Customer fills in the Quotation token, clicks on the *Get Quotation* button in order to retrieve the quotation, and then clicks on the *Submit As Order*, in order to submit the retrieved quotation to the *Submit Order Service*.

Now that the Order has been submitted, if a Salesperson checks the pending jobs of the system, he or she will find that there is a Pending Order (Figure 25).

Figure 19. Screen for customer quotation request

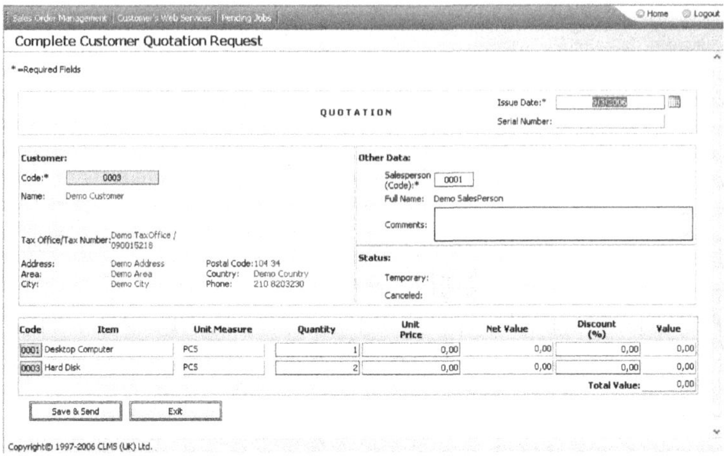

Figure 20. Creating a new quotation

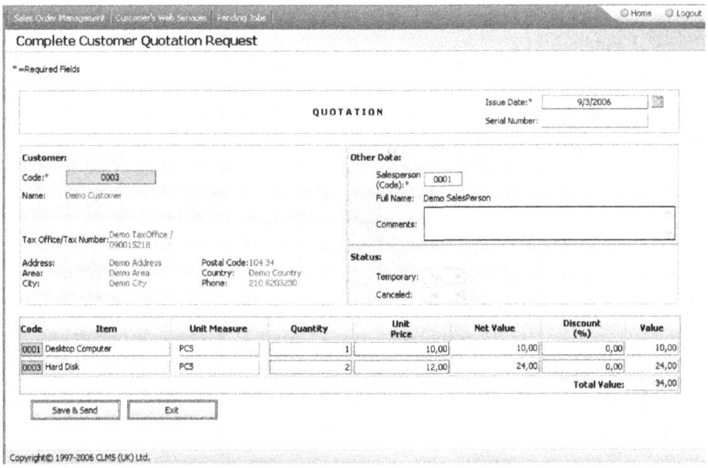

Figure 21. Invoking get quotation service

Figure 22. Retrieving a quotation

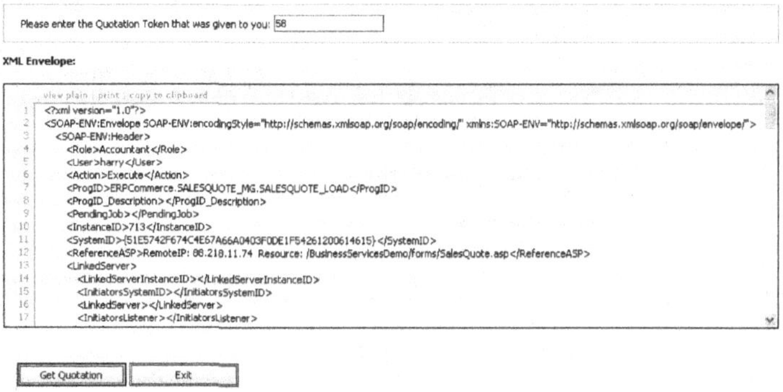

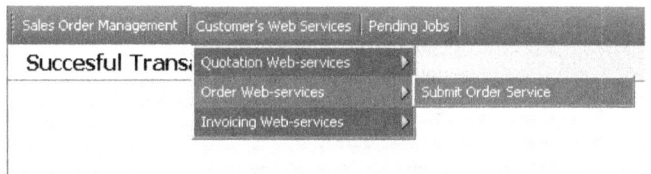

Figure 23. Invoking submit order Web service

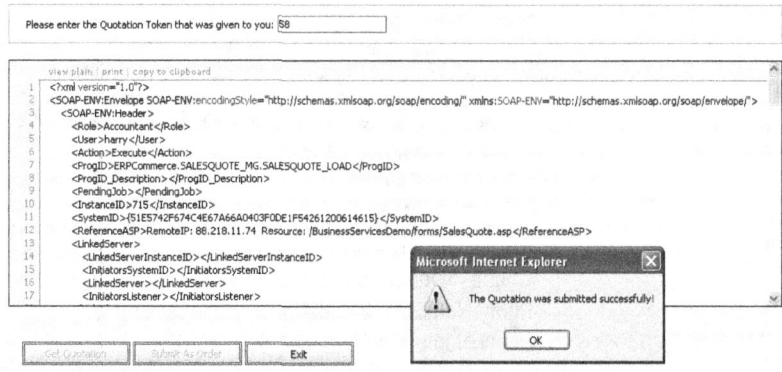

Figure 24. Submitting a quotation

Listing 11. SOAP envelope containing quotation

```
<?xml version="1.0"?>
<SOAP-ENV:Envelope SOAP-ENV:encodingStyle="http://schemas.xmlsoap.org/soap/
encoding/" xmlns:SOAP-ENV="http://schemas.xmlsoap.org/soap/envelope/">
        <SOAP-ENV:Header>
                <Role>Accountant</Role>
                <User>harry</User>
                <Action>Execute</Action>
                <ProgID>ERPCommerce.SALESQUOTE_MG.SALESQUOTE_LOAD</
ProgID>
                <ProgID_Description/>
                <PendingJob/>
                <InstanceID>713</InstanceID>
                <SystemID>{51E5742F674C4E67A66A0403F0DE1F54261200614615}</
SystemID>
                <ReferenceASP>RemoteIP: 88.218.11.74  Resource: /
BusinessServicesDemo/forms/SalesQuote.asp</ReferenceASP>
                <LinkedServer>
                        <LinkedServerInstanceID/>
                        <InitiatorsSystemID/>
                        <LinkedServer/>
                        <InitiatorsListener/>
                </LinkedServer>
        </SOAP-ENV:Header>
        <SOAP-ENV:Body>
                <SalesQuote>
                        <SalesQuoteID>58</SalesQuoteID>
                        <OrderID>-1</OrderID>
                        <OrderSerialNumber/>
                        <OrderDateIssued/>
                        <BusinessPartnerID>35</BusinessPartnerID>
                        <PartnerCode>0003</PartnerCode>
                        <PartnerName>Demo Customer</PartnerName>
                        <TaxData>Demo TaxOffice / 090015218</TaxData>
                        <Address>Demo Address</Address>
                        <City>Demo City</City>
                        <Area>Demo Area</Area>
                        <PostalCode>104 34</PostalCode>
                        <Country>Demo Country</Country>
                        <PhoneNumber1>210 8203230</PhoneNumber1>
                        <PhoneNumber2/>
                        <IssuedByEmployeeID>1</IssuedByEmployeeID>
                        <SerialNumber>0019</SerialNumber>
                        <SeriesID>92</SeriesID>
```

continued on following page

Listing 11. continued

```
<SeriesName/>
<SeriesDescription>Χωρίς Σειρά</SeriesDescription>
<DateIssued>9/3/2006</DateIssued>
<TotalAmount>34,00</TotalAmount>
<Notes/>
<FiscalYearID>3</FiscalYearID>
<Void>False</Void>
<Temporary>False</Temporary>
<SQLTimestamp>00000000000FFEF3</SQLTimestamp>
<ApplicationID>{51E5742F674C4E67A66A0403F0DE1F5426120
0614615}</ApplicationID>

<Employee>
        <Code>0001</Code>
        <FirstName>Demo</FirstName>
        <LastName>SalesPerson</LastName>
</Employee>
<SalesQuoteDetails>
        <SalesQuoteDetail>
                <SalesQuoteDetailID>34</
SalesQuoteDetailID>
                <SalesQuoteID>58</SalesQuoteID>
                <ItemID>13</ItemID>
                <ItemDetailID>-1</ItemDetailID>
                <UnitMeasureID>26</UnitMeasureID>
                <UnitMeasureName>PCS</
UnitMeasureName>
                <UnitMeasureDecimalPlaces>0</
UnitMeasureDecimalPlaces>
                <ItemQuantity>1,00</ItemQuantity>
                <ItemUnitPrice>10,00</ItemUnitPrice>
                <ItemDiscountPercent>0,00</
ItemDiscountPercent>
                <Item>
                        <Code>0001</Code>
                        <Name>Desktop Computer</
Name>
                        <DetailCode/>
                        <DetailName/>
                        <Description/>
                        <RetailUnitPrice>60,00</
RetailUnitPrice>
                        <WholeUnitPrice>0,00</
WholeUnitPrice>
```

continued on following page

Listing 11. continued

```
Discontinued>                              <Discontinued>False</

                                           <Assembled>False</Assembled>
                                           <Serialised>False</Serialised>
                                           <MinimumQuantityRequired>0</
MinimumQuantityRequired>
                                           <ReorderQuantityLevel>0</
ReorderQuantityLevel>
                                           <SalesUnitMeasureID>26</
SalesUnitMeasureID>
                                           <SalesUnitMeasureName>PCS</
SalesUnitMeasureName>
                                           <PurchaseUnitMeasureID>26</
PurchaseUnitMeasureID>
                                           <PurchaseUnitMeasureName>PCS
</PurchaseUnitMeasureName>
                                           <StockUnitMeasureID>26</
StockUnitMeasureID>
                                           <StockUnitMeasureName>PCS</
StockUnitMeasureName>
                                           <SalesTaxRateID>18</
SalesTaxRateID>
                                           <TaxRate>
                                               <TaxRateName>Φόρος
19%</TaxRateName>
                                               <TaxRateCode>0001</
TaxRateCode>
                                               <TaxPercent>19</
TaxPercent>
                                           </TaxRate>
                                           <Balance>999964</Balance>
                                       </Item>
                                   </SalesQuoteDetail>
                                   <SalesQuoteDetail>
                                       <SalesQuoteDetailID>35</
SalesQuoteDetailID>
                                       <SalesQuoteID>58</SalesQuoteID>
                                       <ItemID>16</ItemID>
                                       <ItemDetailID>-1</ItemDetailID>
                                       <UnitMeasureID>26</UnitMeasureID>
                                       <UnitMeasureName>PCS</
UnitMeasureName>
                                       <UnitMeasureDecimalPlaces>0</
```

continued on following page

Listing 11. continued

```
UnitMeasureDecimalPlaces>
                                    <ItemQuantity>2,00</ItemQuantity>
                                    <ItemUnitPrice>12,00</ItemUnitPrice>
                                    <ItemDiscountPercent>0,00</
ItemDiscountPercent>
                             <Item>
                                    <Code>0003</Code>
                                    <Name>Hard Disk</Name>
                                    <DetailCode/>
                                    <DetailName/>
                                    <Description/>
                                    <RetailUnitPrice>0,00</
RetailUnitPrice>
                                    <WholeUnitPrice>0,00</
WholeUnitPrice>
                                    <Discontinued>False</
Discontinued>
                                    <Assembled>False</Assembled>
                                    <Serialised>False</Serialised>
                                    <MinimumQuantityRequired>0</
MinimumQuantityRequired>
                                    <ReorderQuantityLevel>0</
ReorderQuantityLevel>
                                    <SalesUnitMeasureID>26</
SalesUnitMeasureID>
                                    <SalesUnitMeasureName>PCS</
SalesUnitMeasureName>
                                    <PurchaseUnitMeasureID>26</
PurchaseUnitMeasureID>
                                    <PurchaseUnitMeasureName>PCS
</PurchaseUnitMeasureName>
                                    <StockUnitMeasureID>26</
StockUnitMeasureID>
                                    <StockUnitMeasureName>PCS</
StockUnitMeasureName>
                                    <SalesTaxRateID>18</
SalesTaxRateID>
                             <TaxRate>
                                    <TaxRateName>Φόρος
19%</TaxRateName>
                                    <TaxRateCode>0001</
TaxRateCode>
                                    <TaxPercent>19</
```

continued on following page

Listing 11. continued

```
                                                    <TaxPercent>19</
TaxPercent>
                                                </TaxRate>
                                            <Balance>999833</Balance>
                                        </Item>
                                    </SalesQuoteDetail>
                                </SalesQuoteDetails>
                            </SalesQuote>
                        </SOAP-ENV:Body>
                    </SOAP-ENV:Envelope>
```

Figure 25. Pending jobs for accountant

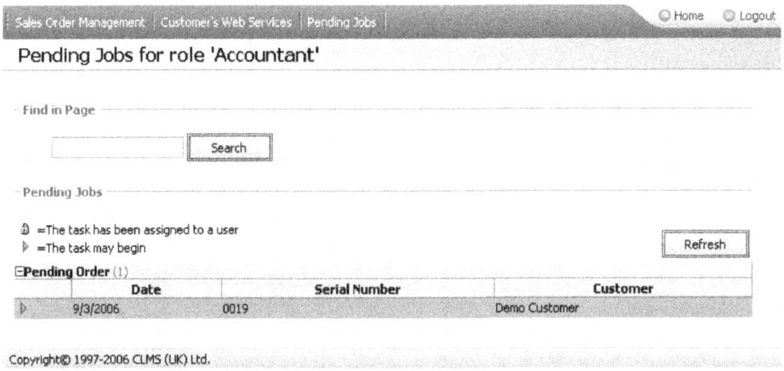

Figure 26. Saving order

Figure 27. List of pending jobs

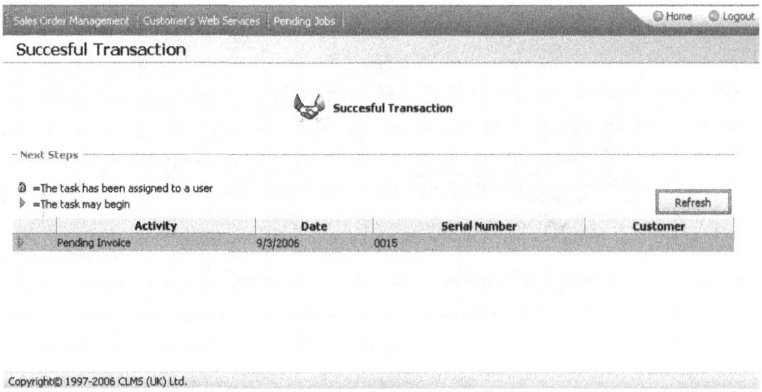

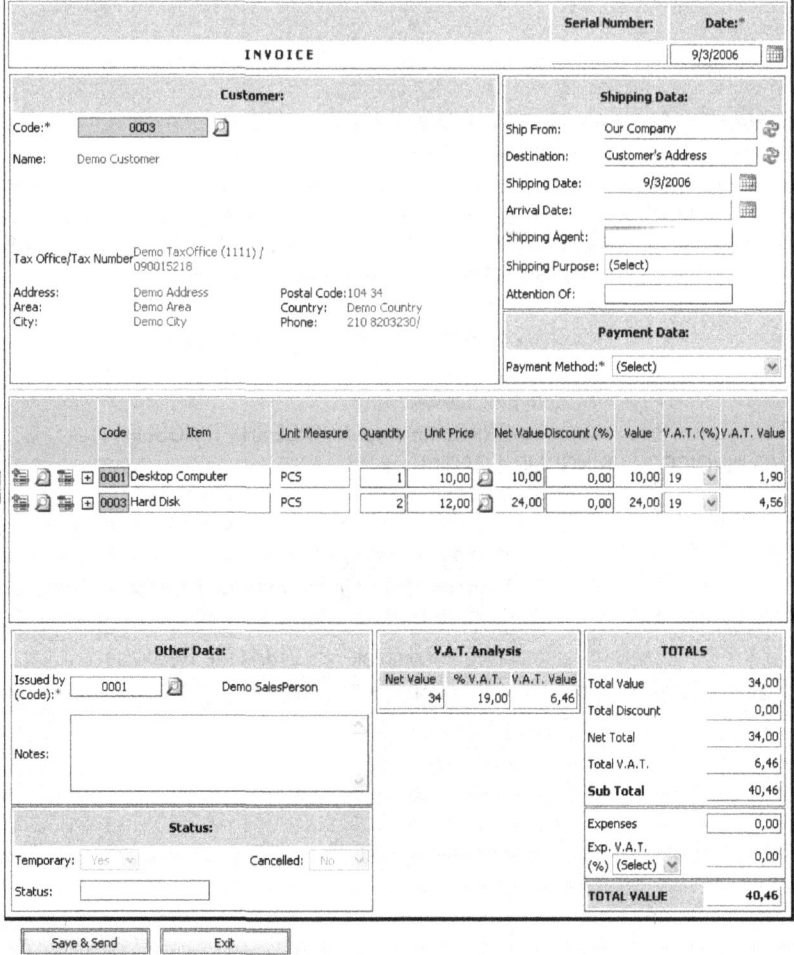

Figure 28. Saving and sending invoice

Figure 29. Invoice retrieved

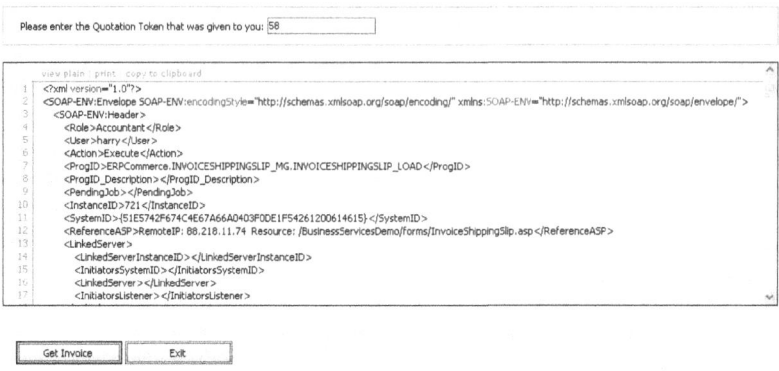

Listing 12. Get invoice service response

```
<?xml version="1.0"?>
<SOAP-ENV:Envelope SOAP-ENV:encodingStyle="http://schemas.xmlsoap.org/soap/encoding/"
xmlns:SOAP-ENV="http://schemas.xmlsoap.org/soap/envelope/">
        <SOAP-ENV:Header>
                <Role>Accountant</Role>
                <User>harry</User>
                <Action>Execute</Action>
                <ProgID>ERPCommerce.INVOICESHIPPINGSLIP_
MG.INVOICESHIPPINGSLIP_LOAD</ProgID>
                <ProgID_Description/>
                <PendingJob/>
                <InstanceID>723</InstanceID>
                <SystemID>{51E5742F674C4E67A66A0403F0DE1F54261200614615}</
SystemID>
                <ReferenceASP>RemoteIP: 88.218.11.74  Resource: /
BusinessServicesDemo/forms/InvoiceShippingSlip.asp</ReferenceASP>
                <LinkedServer>
                        <LinkedServerInstanceID/>
                        <InitiatorsSystemID/>
                        <LinkedServer/>
                        <InitiatorsListener/>
                </LinkedServer>
```

continued on following page

Listing 12. continued

```
            </SOAP-ENV:Header>
            <SOAP-ENV:Body>
                <InvoiceShippingSlip>
                    <InvoiceShippingSlipID>39</InvoiceShippingSlipID>
                    <Void>False</Void>
                    <SourceDocument>SalesOrder</SourceDocument>
                    <SeriesID>-1</SeriesID>
                    <SeriesName/>
                    <SeriesDescription/>
                    <PaymentMethodID>1</PaymentMethodID>
                    <BusinessPartnerID>35</BusinessPartnerID>
                    <PartnerCode>0003</PartnerCode>
                    <PartnerName>Demo Customer</PartnerName>
                    <TaxData>Demo TaxOffice / 090015218</TaxData>
                    <Address>Demo Address</Address>
                    <City>Demo City</City>
                    <Area>Demo Area</Area>
                    <PostalCode>104 34</PostalCode>
                    <Country>Demo Country</Country>
                    <PhoneNumber1>210 8203230</PhoneNumber1>
                    <PhoneNumber2/>
                    <IssuedByEmployeeID>1</IssuedByEmployeeID>
                    <ShippingPurposeID>-1</ShippingPurposeID>
                    <DateIssued>9/3/2006</DateIssued>
                    <SerialNumber>0003</SerialNumber>
                    <ShippedFrom/>
                    <DestinationAddress/>
                    <AttentionOf/>
                    <Status/>
                    <ShipDateTime>9/3/2006</ShipDateTime>
                    <ArrivalDateTime/>
                    <ShipViaAgentName/>
                    <ShippingCost>0,00</ShippingCost>
                    <ShippingCostTaxRateID>-1</ShippingCostTaxRateID>
                    <ShippingCostTaxAmount/>
                    <TotalNetAmount>34,00</TotalNetAmount>
                    <TotalTaxAmount>6,46</TotalTaxAmount>
                    <TotalAmount>40,46</TotalAmount>
                    <Notes/>
                    <Temporary>False</Temporary>
                    <FiscalYearID>3</FiscalYearID>
                    <SQLTimestamp>00000000000FFEF6</SQLTimestamp>
```

continued on following page

Listing 12. continued

```
                            <ApplicationID>{51E5742F674C4E67A66A0403F0DE1F5426120
0614615}</ApplicationID>

                            <PaymentMethod>
                                    <Method>Cash</Method>
                            </PaymentMethod>
                            <Employee>
                                    <Code>0001</Code>
                                    <FirstName>Demo</FirstName>
                                    <LastName>SalesPerson</LastName>
                            </Employee>
                            <ShippingPurpose>
                                    <Purpose/>
                            </ShippingPurpose>
                            <TaxRate>
                                    <TaxRateCode/>
                                    <TaxRateName/>
                                    <TaxPercent>0,00</TaxPercent>
                            </TaxRate>
                            <TaxRateState>Regular</TaxRateState>
                            <InvoiceShippingSlipDetails>
                                    <InvoiceShippingSlipDetail>
                                            <InvoiceShippingSlipDetailID>97</
InvoiceShippingSlipDetailID>
                                            <InvoiceShippingSlipID>39</
InvoiceShippingSlipID>
                                            <ItemID>13</ItemID>
                                            <ItemDetailID>-1</ItemDetailID>
                                            <UnitMeasureID>26</UnitMeasureID>
                                            <UnitMeasureName>PCS</
UnitMeasureName>
                                            <UnitMeasureDecimalPlaces>0</
UnitMeasureDecimalPlaces>
                                            <TaxRateID>18</TaxRateID>
                                            <ItemUnitPrice>10,00</ItemUnitPrice>
                                            <ItemQuantity>1,00</ItemQuantity>
                                            <ItemDiscountPercent>0,00</
ItemDiscountPercent>
                                            <ItemAmountAfterDiscount/>
                                            <TaxAmount/>
                                            <TaxRate>
                                                    <TaxRateName>Φόρος 19%</
TaxRateName>
```

continued on following page

Listing 12. continued

```
                                        <TaxRateCode>0001</
TaxRateCode>

                                        <TaxPercent>19,00</TaxPercent>
                            </TaxRate>
                            <Item>

                                        <Code>0001</Code>
                                        <Name>Desktop Computer</Name>
                                        <DetailCode/>
                                        <DetailName/>
                                        <Description/>
                                        <RetailUnitPrice>60,00</
RetailUnitPrice>

                                        <WholeUnitPrice>0,00</
WholeUnitPrice>

                                        <Discontinued>False</
Discontinued>

                                        <Assembled>False</Assembled>
                                        <Serialised>False</Serialised>
                                        <MinimumQuantityRequired>0</
MinimumQuantityRequired>

                                        <ReorderQuantityLevel>0</
ReorderQuantityLevel>

                                        <SalesUnitMeasureID>26</
SalesUnitMeasureID>

                                        <SalesUnitMeasureName>PCS</
SalesUnitMeasureName>

                                        <PurchaseUnitMeasureID>26</
PurchaseUnitMeasureID>

                                        <PurchaseUnitMeasureName>PCS
</PurchaseUnitMeasureName>

                                        <StockUnitMeasureID>26</
StockUnitMeasureID>

                                        <StockUnitMeasureName>PCS</
StockUnitMeasureName>

                                        <SalesTaxRateID>18</
SalesTaxRateID>

                            <TaxRate>
                                        <TaxRateName>Φόρος
19%</TaxRateName>

                                        <TaxRateCode>0001</
TaxRateCode>

                                        <TaxPercent>19</
```

continued on following page

Listing 12. continued

```
TaxPercent>
                                          </TaxRate>
                              </Item>
                              <ItemQuantityReserved>0,00</
ItemQuantityReserved>
                              <CurrItemQuantityReserved>0,00</
CurrItemQuantityReserved>
                              <InvoiceShippingSlipDetailSources>
                                   <InvoiceShippingSlipDetailSource>

      <InvoiceShippingSlipDetailSourceID>5</InvoiceShippingSlipDetailSourceID>

      <InvoiceShippingSlipDetailID>97</InvoiceShippingSlipDetailID>
                                        <WarehouseOutputNoteID>-1</
WarehouseOutputNoteID>
                                        <OrderID>70</OrderID>
                                        <OrderCode>Σ. A / Αρ. 0015</
OrderCode>
                                        <OrderPrice>10,00</
OrderPrice>
                                        <ItemQuantity>1,00</
ItemQuantity>
                                        <MaxSourceItemQuantity/>
                                        <RelatedDocCode/>
                                   </InvoiceShippingSlipDetailSource>
                              </InvoiceShippingSlipDetailSources>
                         </InvoiceShippingSlipDetail>
                         <InvoiceShippingSlipDetail>
                              <InvoiceShippingSlipDetailID>98</
InvoiceShippingSlipDetailID>
                              <InvoiceShippingSlipID>39</
InvoiceShippingSlipID>
                              <ItemID>16</ItemID>
                              <ItemDetailID>-1</ItemDetailID>
                              <UnitMeasureID>26</UnitMeasureID>
                              <UnitMeasureName>PCS</
UnitMeasureName>
                              <UnitMeasureDecimalPlaces>0</
UnitMeasureDecimalPlaces>
                              <TaxRateID>18</TaxRateID>
                              <ItemUnitPrice>12,00</ItemUnitPrice>
                              <ItemQuantity>2,00</ItemQuantity>
```

continued on following page

Listing 12. continued

```
                                         <ItemDiscountPercent>0,00</
ItemDiscountPercent>

                                         <ItemAmountAfterDiscount/>
                                         <TaxAmount/>
                                         <TaxRate>
                                                  <TaxRateName>Φόρος 19%</
TaxRateName>

                                                  <TaxRateCode>0001</
TaxRateCode>

                                                  <TaxPercent>19,00</TaxPercent>
                                         </TaxRate>
                                         <Item>
                                                  <Code>0003</Code>
                                                  <Name>Hard Disk</Name>
                                                  <DetailCode/>
                                                  <DetailName/>
                                                  <Description/>
                                                  <RetailUnitPrice>0,00</
RetailUnitPrice>

                                                  <WholeUnitPrice>0,00</
WholeUnitPrice>

                                                  <Discontinued>False</
Discontinucd>

                                                  <Assembled>False</Assembled>
                                                  <Serialised>False</Serialised>
                                                  <MinimumQuantityRequired>0</
MinimumQuantityRequired>

                                                  <ReorderQuantityLevel>0</
ReorderQuantityLevel>

                                                  <SalesUnitMeasureID>26</
SalesUnitMeasureID>

                                                  <SalesUnitMeasureName>PCS</
SalesUnitMeasureName>

                                                  <PurchaseUnitMeasureID>26</
PurchaseUnitMeasureID>

                                                  <PurchaseUnitMeasureName>PCS
</PurchaseUnitMeasureName>

                                                  <StockUnitMeasureID>26</
StockUnitMeasureID>

                                                  <StockUnitMeasureName>PCS</
StockUnitMeasureName>

                                                  <SalesTaxRateID>18</
```

continued on following page

Listing 12. continued

```
                                        <SalesTaxRateID>18</
SalesTaxRateID>
                                        <TaxRate>
                                                <TaxRateName>Φόρος
19%</TaxRateName>
                                                <TaxRateCode>0001</
TaxRateCode>
                                                <TaxPercent>19</
TaxPercent>
                                        </TaxRate>
                                </Item>
                                <ItemQuantityReserved>0,00</
ItemQuantityReserved>
                                <CurrItemQuantityReserved>0,00</
CurrItemQuantityReserved>
                                <InvoiceShippingSlipDetailSources>
                                        <InvoiceShippingSlipDetailSource>

        <InvoiceShippingSlipDetailSourceID>6</InvoiceShippingSlipDetailSourceID>

        <InvoiceShippingSlipDetailID>98</InvoiceShippingSlipDetailID>
                                                <WarehouseOutputNoteID>-1</
WarehouseOutputNoteID>
                                                <OrderID>70</OrderID>
                                                <OrderCode>Σ. Α / Αρ. 0015</
OrderCode>
                                                <OrderPrice>12,00</
OrderPrice>
                                                <ItemQuantity>2,00</
ItemQuantity>
                                                <MaxSourceItemQuantity/>
                                                <RelatedDocCode/>
                                        </InvoiceShippingSlipDetailSource>
                                </InvoiceShippingSlipDetailSources>
                        </InvoiceShippingSlipDetail>
                </InvoiceShippingSlipDetails>
            </InvoiceShippingSlip>
        </SOAP-ENV:Body>
</SOAP-ENV:Envelope>
```

continued on following page

Clicking on this order will show the screen where the Salesperson will create the new Order (Figure 26).

The Salesperson fills in any comments he or she may have, and then clicks on the *Save & Send* button.

Now that the Order has been created, there is another pending job for the Salesperson; *Pending Invoice* (Figure 27).

Clicking on this pending job will show the interface where the Salesperson will create the corresponding Invoice (Figure 27).

After selecting the *Payment Method*, the Salesperson clicks on the *Save & Send* button, and the Invoice is saved (Figure 28). The Customer can then retrieve the corresponding Invoice by using the *Get Invoice* service. In the following interface, the Customer fills in the Quotation token and by clicking on the *Get Invoice* button he retrieves the Invoice of his Order (Figure 29).

The SOAP envelope returned by the *Get Invoice Service* is shown in Listing 12.

Chapter Summary

This chapter has put together the concepts, techniques, and methods discussed in Chapter VII by using the very important and ubiquitous business function of accounts receivable/accounts payable. Initially, we argued that this business area leads itself naturally to service-oriented thinking, because of its complex feedback type interrelationships with other systems both internal and external to the business. By analyzing the processes that take place within A/R-A/P, we identified three Web services that allow customers of the company to submit requests for quotations, accept quotations, or reject quotations. These Web services were derived in a top-down fashion by decomposing the higher level processes of A/R-A/P into networks of services. By applying principles of model-driven development, we systematically designed the data and processing elements of the Web services and we generated all the artifacts (WSDL, scripts, data schemas) necessary for deploying these services onto an execution platform. The unique characteristics of this platform is that it blends SOA and MDD principles and allows complete business systems to be modeled and realized in a service-oriented manner, ensuring continuity from the business to the software technology domains.

While in this chapter we demonstrated that the realization of business services in software is a viable proposition using today's technologies, there is still quite a distance to cover in this area. Chapter XI, the final chapter in this book, discusses what further steps must be taken and areas that must evolve before the complete realization of the service-oriented organization in software becomes a feasible proposition.

References

Checkland, P. (1981). *Systems thinking, systems practice*. New York: Wiley.

Colantoni, C. S., Manes, R. P., & Whinston, A. (1971). A unified approach to the theory of accounting and information systems. *The Accounting Review, 46*(1), 90-102.

Cushing, B. E., & Marshall, B. R. (1994). *Accounting information systems* (6th ed.) New York: Addison-Wesley.

Chapter XI

An Overview and Summary

An Overview of E-Services

This book has introduced a model-driven approach for identifying, designing, deploying, and managing business services in software. The concept of e-service is an extension of conventional business services, made possible thanks to the rapid explosion in popularity of the Internet and the World Wide Web (Rust & Kannan, 2003). The first generation of e-commerce was based largely on retailing commodity goods, such as books and CDs, and used mass media advertising to contact consumers. The premise of first generation e-commerce was that operational efficiencies (i.e., minimizing the need and therefore the expense to keep physical stores) would reduce the costs of selling. Unfortunately, selling commodities has low profit margins due to competition. An alternative is required, that allows companies to built sustainable competitive advantage, based on their capability to deliver more individualized and hence more profitable e-services.

The emerging e-service paradigm that we have been concerned with in this book is based on such principles. It uses two-way interactions to build customized service offerings, and exploits knowledge about the customer, to build strong customer relationships. Companies can use e-services to achieve profitability based on revenue expansion rather than cost reduction, with revenues driven by enhanced service and higher levels of customer satisfaction (Rust & Miu, 2006). Customized service offerings support high margins, by enabling a monopoly on the relevant information about the customer, obtained through better management of the customer relationship. Supermarkets, for example, employ loyalty cards and electronic purchase tracking to use service as a differentiator to ease price competition. Focused one-to-one promotion and marketing efforts based on information gathered using these cards, allow the supermarket chains to develop relationships with their customers. They provide value to customers through focused information-based marketing (e.g., targeted promotions and discounts), reduced search time, increased convenience, and a perception of control in their transactions. The added value of this service is, therefore, derived from information-based components rather than tangible products. In order to transform from sellers of physical products to providers of services, organizations need to be customer-centric. A one-time transaction becomes a longer term relationship, providing opportunities for focused selling of products/services that increase customers' value (Rust & Kannan, 2003).

Firms, therefore, must take full advantage of Internet-based e-service opportunities to establish long-term customer relationships and loyalty. New technologies such as wireless networking, broadband, smart cards, data warehousing, data mining, Web services, and software agents all contribute toward the effective accessibility and servicing of the correctly targeted customers while providing more choices, options, and, ultimately, power to customers. As the new technologies and possibilities shape customer expectations, organizations are under pressure to improve their business processes, to develop new markets and to improve their competitive positions using these technologies.

E-services are not, however, only about delivery medium (the Internet, in this case) they also require *content* and *infrastructure* for their consumption. Let us then examine the concepts of content and infrastructure more closely. The content of an e-service is the information, resources, capabilities, and capacity the consumer is prepared to pay for. Everything that can be digitized can effectively become content for an e-service. In this book we have already seen the limits of such digitization, as physical materials cannot be digitized, services have to deal with the alter ego of the physical world information. In today's economy, being restricted to information-based products is not normally a serious limitation. The developed world is increasingly dealing in mainly virtualized commodities (i.e., information-based ones), with the actual physical production of goods (manufacturing) gradually being shifted to the developing countries. Industries, even manufacturing ones, are becoming rapidly e-service-based. The gradual shift from physical products to pure e-service components has significant implications for building customer relationships and for exploring new service opportunities and markets, especially in the domain of network-based, digital, and information-based products.

The music recording industry, for example, has been forced to offer subscription-based music downloading services in response to competition from peer-to-peer (P2P) media sharing on the Internet, transforming their physical products (i.e., music CDs) to e-service offerings. In industries such as music, the e-services content is readily available, as, these days, music is recorded directly in digital format. For most organizations, making digital assets, capabilities, and resources available as e-services should not, in theory, at least, represent a serious technical problem. However, the third aspect of service delivery, *e-service infrastructure,* represents more of a challenge and merits a closer look: To consume an e-service, a consumer needs to tap into it using some software application. The simplest type of e-services, information services, can be consumed over the Web using a standard browser. Although this appears to be rather straightforward, it, in fact, has only become possible thanks to the joint effort of the international community to standardize on data definition formats (HTML) and transmission protocols (HTTP). However, only the simplest types of e-services can be delivered using this lowest common denominator technology (HTML/HTTP). Thus, the real obstacle for businesses with suitable content to provide as an e-service is the lack of standardized infrastructure to reach the maximum number of consumers. Incompatibilities between different (and competing) technologies for Web browsers, for example, means that companies need to develop and support several applications in parallel, to ensure complete coverage of the consumer market. The concept of a *service utility,* which allows consumers to access any e-service independently of the platform and technology on which it is being delivered, is still a challenge.

In this book, we saw that real-life business services involve a complex set of negotiations, agreements, and contracts between the involved parties. Complex e-services cannot be implemented using a simplistic *request-response* type of protocol; they typically require several steps of interaction between the two (or possibly more) involved parties. Thus, the infrastructure for delivering and consuming e-services has to be able to meet the requirements of the business reality and deal with asynchronous multiparty and multistep interactions. Service coordination and orchestration standards, such as BPEL (reviewed in Chapter IV), allow such synchronized multi party interactions.

Leaving aside the triad of e-service medium, content, and infrastructure, for the moment, let us revisit e-services from a business perspective. Companies typically will deploy e-services in the hope that they will turn into profitable operations. However, customers are prepared to pay for an e-service only if it provides them with a definitive clear benefit. Simply, as proven by several unsuccessful businesses on the Internet, customers are not prepared to pay for e-services that do not demonstratively, offer them something that they value. There is also the issue of competition. Unless a company offers a service that is unique in the whole wide world, there will typically be similar services provided by competitors. For a service to be chosen over a competing one, it must have a clear competitive advantage that can be in terms of price, features, or overall consumer experience.

So, e-services must not only offer something that a customer is prepared to pay for, but it must do so in a competitive manner. Take, for example, the case of early Internet-based information services. During the early days of the Internet, many companies believed that customers would be prepared to pay for simple information services like weather information or telephone directory enquiries. It was soon proved, though, that for a number of reasons, customers were not in fact prepared to pay. Also, very soon, for every paid-for information e-service, several other free offerings started to emerge. Today, with only a few exceptions of highly focused specialist information services, all e-services offering weather, news, directory searches and the like on the Web, are free. Companies have simply devised alternative business models for creating revenues from such e-services, by, for example, attracting advertising to the Web sites that offer these services.

Consumers however, although not usually prepared to pay for services that can be obtained for free or simply for the price of a newspaper, might be prepared to pay a premium for services that meet their exact needs and requirements and offer them a clearly identified benefit. People, for this matter, have of course always been prepared to pay for the services of a doctor or financial advisor. Provided that such services can be delivered equally effectively as e-services, there is no reason to doubt that they would continue to do so. Actually, accessing an e-service remotely has several advantages such as, for example, consumer convenience. E-services have the additional benefit that they can be consumed irrespective of physical proximity of provider and consumer. Their consumption can also be almost instantaneous, thanks to today's high-speed networking. Privacy and security concerns aside, few consumers would choose a service delivered physically (e.g., by post), to one that can be almost instantly consumed through the Internet, using a computer and a suitable application.

Consumers, therefore, are likely to embrace e-services provided that the latter, at least, match the capabilities of their conventional counterparts and, ideally, exceed them. And, when doing so, they will expect control in transactions, choice in service setting, efficiency, and effectiveness.

To recap, the delivery medium for e-services (Internet) is already here and most of the e-service content exists in a suitable format (that, of course, needs to be extracted from the various digital sources, transformed and suitably presented to match the requirements of the consumer). What remains is to deliver e-services that can match real-life expectations. Such e-services must be:

- *Customizable* to the exact needs of the consumer, while continuing to be profitable (i.e., to make financial sense to the provider). *Customizable* means that the service is delivered at the place, time, and format that suits the consumer.

- *Capable* of dealing with all alterations, exceptions, contract negotiations (i.e., conditions that one would expect to experience in the delivery of a physical service), in other words, be appropriately *intelligent.*

- *Interactive,* but, at the same time putting the consumer in control of the timing and process of interaction.

- Posing *minimal* consumer privacy and security risks during such interaction.

The ability to simultaneously customize market offerings for the masses on a one-to-one basis has, so far, been a futuristic vision. Next generation e-services are about to change that. E-services can be designed to be composed of building blocks, which can be atomic services or other composite services of finer granularity (see Chapter IV). This characteristic enables e-services to be readily customizable, which in turn allows for mass customization capabilities (Ritz, 2003). For example, an international travel service may bring together a variety of e-services from a number of different vendors, such as airline reservations, hotel reservations, translation, car rentals, and weather e-services, depending on the traveler's particular requirements. Similarly, a manufacturer may employ the assistance of an e-service that streamlines its employees' travel arrangements, another e-service that bills its customers, an e-service for procurement, and an e-service for enterprise resource planning (ERP).

A *personalized information service* is a service towards a customer comprising:

1. Filtering of information out of formerly gathered and qualified information regarding the customer's interests.
2. Presentation of this information, using a customer-defined time schedule and media appropriate with the customer's status and environment.

Electronic environments are ideally suited to gather information from customers—details of their transactions over the Internet or using smart cards, or preference information through surveys and inferences using data from other sources. Such information can be used to provide personalized and customized offerings. Focused, relevant offerings reduce overall costs for customers (because of lower search costs, risk costs, and transactions costs) and tie in the customers. For a supermarket chain, for example, it could be personalized promotions based on transaction history. Information-based service products and service delivery through personalization and customization technologies build customer relationships through superior value and higher switching costs, leading to higher customer retention. They also provide effective means to understand the customer's needs better.

In contrast to physical products, personalized e-services can be considered as a product with an enormous number of variations. For each user of the personalized service, there are a number of customization parameters such as content, delivery method and media, contract/agreement, and so on. Just multiplying these parameters with the total number of users can yield a huge number of personalized services. To realize customizable services, a configuration mechanism must be employed. The configuration mechanism of personalized information services configures service parameters that match the customer profile. For e-service personalization to be a feasible proposition, automated model-driven techniques for service generation, composition, and transformation, such as those reviewed in Chapter V, must be deployed.

Requirements for Future Generation E-Services

This section summarizes the consumer expectations from e-services, while the next one identifies the required technologies for meeting such expectations. From a strategic perspective, an e-service orientation calls for moving the emphasis from products and transactions to service and customer relationships. These need to be supported at the tactical level by personalization and customization, intelligence, self-service, privacy, and security risk management. Thus, in the concluding chapter of this book we look at what is needed to make e-services a more appealing proposition to the consumers than their physical counterparts. We have identified the following major requirements for e-services: customizability, intelligence, mobility, flexible interaction, and privacy and security risk management.

Interchangeable E-Services

E-services need to be interchangeable (Hoffman, 2003). This means that a service can be substituted for an equivalent one, even dynamically, as the consumer is about to access it. For example, a travel eservice may submit a customer's travel request to four or five different airline reservation e-services who compete (bid) for the customer's business. By providing a host of options, as opposed to forming a single, more static relationship, customers will have many more choices, and e-service providers will be much more able to provide customized solutions to customer requests. Due to the modularity of e-services, individual customer solutions can be easily customized.

Privacy and Security Management

Apart from benefits, e-service personalization and customization brings additional requirements for consumer privacy and security. Eradicating these risks is an e-service prerequisite for the acceptance of e-service by consumers. E-service orientation requires the design of systems and processes that minimize the degree of insecurity regarding electronic transactions. In an electronic environment, the consumer's need for control and protection of privacy is quite strong. This implies that organizations must protect the customer information they have from deliberate or unintentional unauthorized usage. Security and privacy concerns have a critical impact on the consumer's perceived control in online situations, which in turn determine the consumer's perceived e-service quality In the era of e-service, a firm effectively managing these concerns builds the trust of its customers and contributes to their lifetime value (Rust & Kannan, 2003). In Chapter VIII, we reviewed Web services technologies for security, encryption, and access management that can be employed to implement e-service security-management policies.

Self-Service Capabilities

Customers increasingly seek control of the timing and process of conducting transactions and interacting with businesses (Rust & Kannan, 2003). Many of the recent self-service offerings (such as 24/7 service, order status tracking, remote problem diagnosis, etc.) are geared toward providing customers the control they want. When self-service services are appropriately designed and implemented, customer satisfaction can be increased and customer defections reduced. Automated e-service capabilities allow access that is free from time and geographical restrictions, thus providing the perfect platform for self services

Services Anywhere (Mobile Services)

One of the most important features of next generation e-services will be *mobility.* One of the drawbacks of accessing a service through a conventional PC has been its lack of mobility. Today, and even more so in the future, e-services will be accessible from portable devices such as hand-held computers and mobile phones (Ellkara, 2003). Using a mobile e-service for passengers, for example, a traveler driving to the airport to catch a plane can be automatically rerouted, rescheduled for a later flight, and have the next day's appointments rebooked. If interlinked e-services based on global positioning system (GPS) identify a traffic jam on route to the airport, they can automatically reroute the traveler. These actions occur on behalf of the traveler, without her ever becoming aware of the impending traffic jam. The potential applications of mobile e-services are therefore limitless.

Enabling Technologies for E-Services

Figure 1 shows the evolution of technologies needed to support the next generation of e-services.

Service Grids

A grid is a geographically distributed computation platform composed of a set of heterogeneous machines that users can access via a single interface. A grid system is a decentralised network of computing resources that are not administrated centrally. Grids provide common resource-access technology and operational services across distributed virtual organizations composed of institutions or individuals that share resources. Although it originated in advanced science and engineering applications requiring high-volume computations, grid computing is now been promoted as a paradigm for coordinated resource sharing and problem solving in dynamic, multi-institutional, and virtual organizations in industry and business.

Grid and Web service standards have started to converge and overlap to a large extent (Globus Alliance, 2007). It is likely that, in the near future, the infrastructure for deployment and execution of Web services (as presented in Chapter VIII) will be grid based. With a grid infrastructure for e-services, consumers can experience dynamic and flexible services provided by grid nodes in a manner that is totally transparent to them. Thus, many of the typical activities of manually selecting service providers, composing services, and so on, will be eliminated under a grid approach.

Figure 1. Evolution of e-services

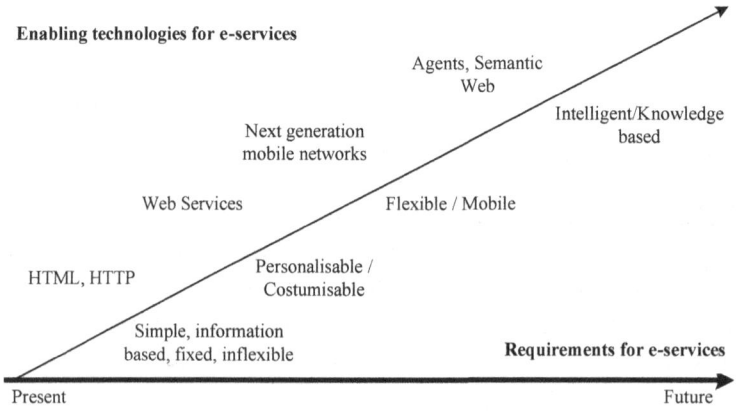

Knowledge-Based Services

The explosive growth of the Internet and the World Wide Web have accelerated the pace of change, and the move towards services that are based on a firm's intellectual assets/knowledge rather than on physical bricks-and-mortar assets. The challenge now for organizations is to use their business acumen, people capital, and computer technologies to create a culture that consistently identifies, assimilates, and exploits new knowledge in creating new e-services more efficiently and effectively than the competition. Thus, knowledge-based e-services allow organizations to capitalize on their knowledge assets. Intelligent organizations will derive their competitive edge not from ephemerally superior products, but from a deep understanding of a few highly developed knowledge-based *core competencies*. Successful service enterprises will derive sustainable advantage from knowledge-based e-services that leverage intellectual assets and increase value through increased technological sophistication, better knowledge bases, more creative customer responsiveness, and the management of intellectual capital that competitors cannot reproduce. To create and leverage knowledge-based core competencies for maximum focus and effectiveness, e-service providers need to redesign each value-creating activity as a knowledge-based e-service. Second, they need to determine whether or not they can deliver their service offerings better than anyone else in the world. The intangibility of an e-service dictates that knowledge assets will play a particularly relevant role in competitiveness. However, new attributes and measures are needed to capture the knowledge-based contents of service operations. Additionally, a better understanding of how intellectual capital is best leveraged, due to the adoption and use of advanced technologies, for delivering e-services is required. E-service technologies such as ontologies and agents are expected to provide the infrastructure for deploying knowledge-based services (Bryson, Martin, McIlraith, & Stein, 2002).

Intelligent Semantic Services

In Chapter VI, we argued that the current Web is a collection of human-readable pages written mainly in HTML that are virtually unintelligible to computer programs. While the Web emerged as a global repository of digitized information, this very information is, by and large, unavailable for automatic processing by computers. Two parallel efforts have emerged in recent years that could overcome this: the Semantic Web, which is providing tools for adding semantic meaning to Web content, and software agent technologies, delivering autonomous agents that produce and consume information, enabling automated business transactions. Ideally, these two efforts should support each other. The Semantic Web will help create a repository of computer-readable data, and agents will provide the tools for automatically using that data. E-services of the future will act as autonomous goal-directed agents that select other agents to interact with. The resulting e-services will use *ontologies* (see Chapter VI) as formal representations of different problem domains to automate the fulfillment of transactions (Heflin & Hendler, 2001). Enriching the Web services infrastructure with semantics will allow Web services to:

- Explicitly express and reason about business relations and rules.
- Represent and reason about the task a Web service performs.
- Understand the meaning of exchanged messages.
- Represent and reason about preconditions for using services and the effects of invoking them.
- Combine Web services to achieve more complex services.

The Semantic Web, therefore, has the potential to provide the Web services infra-structure with the information it needs, through formal languages and ontologies for reasoning about service descriptions, message content, business rules, and rela-tionships between ontologies. Current research efforts focus on the development of languages such as OWL-S (discussed in Chapter VI) that attempts to close the gap between the Semantic Web and Web services. As we saw in Chapter VI, OWL-S uses semantic annotations and ontologies to relate each Web service's description to a description of its operational domain. For example, an OWL-S description of a traffic-reporting service might specify the data it reports, and the cost of using the service. An agent client of such service might use that information to determine what kind of traffic data the service reports, how to contact it, and so on. Furthermore, OWL-S supports the use of WSDL (see Chapter III) to specify Web service interfaces, SOAP (see Chapter III) to describe the messaging layer, and some transport protocol to connect two Web services. Therefore, OWL-S enabled Web services use UDDI, WSDL, and SOAP to discover other services and interact with them, and they use OWL-S to integrate these interactions in their own problem solving.

OWL-S or similar ontologies can be published for client agents that can then send requests to and accept responses from the server agent and performs all the neces-sary translations between agent communication language messages (agent requests, responses) and SOAP messages (Web service calls, results), before and after calling the Web service, respectively. From the perspective of agents, Web services are simply programmatic entities that can be called upon to perform an advertised and typically single function. To consumers of Web services, agents can form a power-ful means of indirection, by making transparent the Web service for purposes of redirection, aggregation, integration, or administration. Agents can handle situations where a Web service may no longer be available for some reason, or the owner of the Web service wishes to temporarily redirect invocations to another Web service. Aggregation (see Chapter IV) allows several Web services to be composed into logically interconnected clusters providing abstractions of behavior that can be invoked through a single service interface. Service administration and automated service management (see Chapter VIII) will be handled by agents that will autonomously administer services without necessary intervention from a human user. Agent technology can also be used to personalize Web services. The goal is to allow human consumers to assign delegates (agents) that will programmatically interact with Web services, according to context when acting on behalf of a customer. To be able to do that, an agent must be able to discover services that are appropriate given a consumer's preferences and requirements. The delegate should also be able to adapt its behavior based on the dynamic characteristics of the Web services in a user's current physical and temporal context. Second, services must describe their abstract interfaces and protocol bindings so that agents can invoke them. Third, an agent should be able to carry out complex interactions (conversations) with multiple services while acting on behalf of a given consumer. This includes the monitoring of ongoing interactions so that the delegate can proactively follow alternatives should exceptions occur.

An Intelligent Web Services Scenario

A good way to sketch the capabilities of intelligent e-services of the future is by using the scenario of a business trip organizer e-service. The (human) user of the trip organizer e-service will allow the service to access her personal calendar that contains desired dates for the trip. The e-service will find dates that the user is free to travel and will schedule the return trip so as to avoid any conflicts with other commitments of the user. Finally, the e-service will deploy agents that will visit services on the Internet to book flight, car, and hotel. The trip organizer service will automatically synthesize service requirements (e.g., preferred mode of travel, type of accommodation, etc.) from data stored in the profile of its user. The service will negotiate with other discovered services quality of service contracts, to achieve the best matchmaking according to the user preferences. Scenarios like the above can only become feasible if ontologies (see Chapter VI) are deployed sufficiently in service environments, to resolve discrepancies and mismatches between the knowledge they are using. Ontology-based languages for describing Web services, such as those reviewed in Chapter VI, have enormous potential to support business on the Web.

Web Service Technologies as the Enabler of Next Generation E-Services

Until recently, the primary vehicle for delivering e-services has been Web languages protocols and applications such HTML, HTTP, Web servers, and browsers. E-service functionality is implemented using HTML, mainly for content, and scripting languages such as Java, Perl, Javascript, and others to implement the business logic behind the service. Today, Web services are being used primarily in the delivery of simple information e-services. This will gradually change, and as a ubiquitous technology, Web services will become the de facto approach for e-service implementation and deployment. Concerns regarding performance, security, use in mission critical situations, service levels, predictability, and cost will be overcome, as functionality added by the newer specifications provide more security and reliability features (see Chapter VIII) and tackle the important but complex issue of business process management (see Chapter IV). Service consumers want and need a framework that connects the Web services functionality and provides interoperability among the various functions. Web services therefore need an infrastructure that facilitates reliable communication, registries to locate services, repudiation services, guarantees of secure and private transactions, and so on.

The Future of Model-Driven Service Engineering

Throughout this book, we argued extensively that engineering of services must be based on models that depict fundamental properties of services, such as their producers and consumers, and their interrelationships such as service contracts. At the time of writing this book, there is still a significant conceptual gap between the business service itself and its IT realization, which is largely based on Web services technologies. Bridging this gap will require new tools and environments that allow business experts to specify the business services, which are then automatically transformed into executable computer-level services. Given the current investment in technologies for the Web and in enterprise platforms and technologies such as, for example, J2EE and .NET, it is unlikely that in the foreseeable future a new radical computer technology will emerge to replace existing ones, that is of sufficiently high level to allow the direct execution of business services models. Model-driven service engineering (i.e., the ability to derive executable services from business level ones), will remain an essential prerequisite for service engineering for the foreseeable future.

Some Final Thoughts

In this final chapter of the book, we argued that, in the contemporary business land-scape, quality and competitive prices are necessary, but no longer sufficient require-ments, for commercial success. In today's competitive marketplace, quick, flexible, customizable, and responsive e-services are increasingly becoming a standard and, hence, a pivotal capability. Determining how best to obtain a strategic advantage using e-services, is an increasing concern for modern businesses.

The new e-service paradigm takes advantage of the inherent nature of the online environment to feature information flows and computation as a means of learning more about customers and building long-term customer relationships. Its profit-ability model is based more on revenue expansion than on cost reduction, and those revenues come from expanding the service provision with new innovative services, rather than just automating the whole process. An e-service orientation is about taking advantage of the electronic environment and the advances in technologies, to stay competitive, agile, and customer- focused in a turbulent business landscape. The rapid technological changes and the emerging new forms of service have made it imperative that firms stay focused on all strategic and tactical facets of e-service (Rust & Kannan, 2003). Many novel ideas and technologies have the potential to revolutionize e-services, but it is very clear a technology focus alone cannot put a business on the path to success. The key to success remains the continued focus on customer attraction and retention, using value adding e-services (Rust & Kanna, 2003). Overall, e-services have much to offer in overcoming the obstacles traditional service approaches are faced with. Future opportunities for revenue lie in creating alternatives and additions to traditional service operations. Furthermore, businesses will need to broaden their focus and make their expectations from the automation of their processes clear. Automation must go beyond the objectives of reducing operat-ing costs and increasing profits to support the aim of offering truly innovative and captivating services that enhance the customer experience. Nevertheless, whatever the business objective behind the development of e-services one principle remains constant (i.e., that services need to be engineered in order to be effective) and that engineering requires automated, model-driven techniques.

To end this book with a final remark, e-service business models offer a number of strategic advantages to organizations, including customizability, mobility, flexibil-ity, interactivity, intelligence, and interchangeability. The ever-increasing demand for e-services can only be met by a methodical, model-driven approach to service engineering. Such an approach will allow the next generation of e-services to play a crucial role in forming the future business and consumer landscapes.

References

Bryson, J. J., Martin, D. L., McIlraith, S. A., & Stein, L. A. (2002). Toward behavioral intelligence in the Semantic Web. *IEEE Computer, 35*(11), 48-54.

Ellkara, N. (2003). A Web services strategy for mobile phones. Retrieved March 16, 2007, from http://Webservices.xml.com/pub/a/ws/2003/08/19/mobile.html

Globus Alliance. (2007). *Towards open grid services architecture*. Retrieved March 15, 2007, from http://www.globus.org/ogsa/

Heflin, J., & Hendler, J. (2001). A portrait of the Semantic Web in action. *IEEE Intelligent Systems, 16*(2), 54-59.

Hoffman, K. D. (2003). MARKETING + MIS = E-SERVICE. *Communications of the ACM, 46*(6), 53-58.

Johnston, S. K., & Brown, A. W. (2006, December 7). *A model-driven development approach to creating service-oriented solutions*. Paper presented to the Fourth International Conference on Service-Oriented Computing, Chicago.

Ritz, T. (2003). Production and distribution of personalized information services employing mass-customization. In *Proceedings of the MPC'03 Second Interdisciplinary World Congress on Mass Customization and Personalization*. Munich, Germany: Technical University Munich.

Rust, R. T., & Kannan, P. K. (2003). E-service: A new paradigm for business in the electronic environment. *Communications of the ACM, 46*(6), 36-42.

Rust, R. T., & Miu, C. (2006). What academic research tells us about service. *Communications of the ACM, 49*(7), 49-54.

About the Contributors

Bill Karakostas is a senior lecturer at the School of Informatics at the City University, London. Dr. Karakostas holds a BSc (Hons.) in computer engineering from the University of Patras, Greece, an MPhil and a PhD in software engineering from the Department of Computation at the University of Manchester Institute of Science and Technology (UMIST), England. He has a 16-plus years research track record in areas such as business engineering (process redesign, simulation, workflow management, ERP systems), and software engineering (requirements management, service and component-oriented development). He has been leading European Union funded research projects for over 15 years, and he has researched extensively in the areas of software engineering, IS modeling, and e-commerce technologies. He has published in excess of 100 research papers and is the co-author of a book on systems requirements engineering. Dr. Karakostas has acted as scientific advisor to several software houses in Greece and the UK. Dr Karakostas is a member of ACM an IEEE Computer Society.

Yannis Zorgios holds a PhD from the University of Manchester Institute of Science & Technology (UMIST), UK. In 1998, he joined CLMS (UK) LIMITED where he is the main architect and the product manager of the CLMS Enterprise Systems Management Server, a service-oriented platform that combines the latest research developments in systems engineering, model-driven development, and business process management. His research interests focus on the provision of contemporary learning management systems and ontological frameworks that support large, complex, and dynamic enterprise systems and empower the learning capability of individuals and organizations.

Graham Cox holds an MSc in economics research from UMIST, UK, and a BA (Hons.) in economics from University of Lancaster, UK. He is the general manager/angel financier of SoundTouch Ltd. He has developed a new acoustics-based technology to provide a leading-edge method for controlling touch-screen computers, subsequently sold to Tyco Electronics Inc in 2005. He is also the MD of Capital Connection Ltd., and a fundraiser and adviser for technology companies (early stage). He has held posts with Sun Life Group as advisor to the group board on fund management, economic, financial market, and regulatory issues. He ran McKenzie department during a period of reengineering, where he created and led Business Expansion Scheme unit. He has also served as business economist at the Confederation of British Industry and as international financial economist for the Reserve Bank of Australia, Bank of America, and the government of Saudi Arabia.

Index

A

A/R-A/P Services, modeling with IDEF0 and IDEF1X 323
A/R-A/P Services with CLMS Platform 338
A/R-A/P Transaction Cycle 320
A/R-A/P Transaction Cycle, importance of modeling 321
A/R Process, service identification 324
A/R processes 325
Accept envelope 292
access control list (ACL) 262
Account Payables 315
Account Receivables 315
Accounts payable (A/P) 321
Accounts receivables (A/R) 320
activity-oriented thinking 2
activity based costing and management 2
aggregate services 28
atomic process 166
atomic values 54
Authentication 256
Authentication Services 291
Authorization 256
Automatic Web Service Composition 164
Automatic Web Service Discovery 163
Automatic Web Service Invocation 164

B

Basic Security Profile (BSP) 259
BPEL (business process execution language) 101
BPEL Activities 105
BPEL Example 107
BPEL Specification 101
Business-to-business (B2B) integration 91
Business engineering 195
Business Modeling 129
business models of services 219
Business process automation 91
business process automation 88
business process collaboration 93
business process coordination, rationale 93
Business process engine 275
Business Processes Choreographies, automating 110
business process execution language for web services (BPEL4WS) 101
Business process integration 91
Business Process Management (BPM) 90
business process management system 91
Business Process Management Technologies and Standards 90
business process manager 91